Tourism
Principles and Practice

Tourism
Principles and Practice

Chris Cooper, John Fletcher,
David Gilbert and Stephen Wanhill

PITMAN
PUBLISHING

Pitman Publishing
128 Long Acre, London WC2E 9AN

A Division of Longman Group UK Limited

First published in 1993
Reprinted in 1993

British Library Cataloguing in Publication Data
A CIP catalogue record for this book can be obtained from
the British Library.

ISBN 0 273 60118 0

Typeset by PanTek Arts, Maidstone, Kent
Printed and bound in Great Britain by Clays Ltd, St Ives plc

The
publisher's
policy is to use
**paper manufactured
from sustainable forests**

CONTENTS

PREFACE

Each of the editors and contributors in this book has been closely involved in teaching tourism at the University of Surrey during the last few years. However, at both masters degree and undergraduate level we have been unable to recommend a tourism text which adequately covers the content of major areas of our course structure. Therefore, this book has been written to fulfil a specific need – a comprehensive text to support students and Faculty who are involved in the study of tourism at advanced level, not just in the UK, but also in other English-speaking countries throughout the world. In many respects this book closely follows the approach to the study of tourism which has been adopted at the University of Surrey which until now has not been available for a wider audience.

This book not only attempts to provide a way of thinking about tourism, but also aims to provide a set of underlying and guiding principles with which to approach the study of this exciting subject area. There are two ever present dangers associated with writing major textbooks, particularly texts on relatively new subject areas such as tourism where new developments in both theory and practice manifest on a regular basis. First, that texts and material rapidly become out of date; and second, that the links and relationships between the various elements of the subject are lost as they are separated out for teaching and learning purposes. We have focused as much as possible on underpinning the various concepts associated with tourism and we have adopted approaches which demonstrate the different linkages that are involved. We have purposely avoided specific examples which are only relevant to a particular time period. For the statistical sections of the book, we are fortunate to be writing in the early 1990s as this provides the opportunity to review pre-

vious decades up until and including 1990. These decades have been highly significant for both the activity of tourism itself, and also for the development of the subject area. Not the least of these developments has been the rapid growth of tourism as an activity, yet it is only relatively recently that it has been taken seriously as an area of study or as an industry. Recognition of the importance of tourism has led, naturally, to the need to adopt a professional approach towards its management – the world-wide growth of tourism courses in higher education from the mid-1980s onwards is partly a reflection of this. In this book we attempt to provide the basis for a higher level tourism course and in so doing, to communicate to future tourism professionals the underlying principles and concepts which will inform their work.

We have structured this book around four key elements of tourism – demand; the destination; the industry and government organisations; and marketing. In the introduction to the book we outline a way of thinking about tourism which will assist readers in locating the diverse subject approaches and examples found in tourism literature. In Part 1 of the book we examine tourism demand in detail. In this crucial though neglected area of tourism we outline the various concepts of demand, examine aspects of consumer behaviour and determinants of tourism demand, and consider the particular methods of demand measurement that are utilised in tourism. The section concludes with an analysis and commentary on world tourism flows and patterns of demand. Part 2 focuses on the key area of the tourist destination and includes a detailed review of tourism impacts, together with a state-of-the-art analysis of impact assessment, before going on to examine the planning and management process at the destination. The tourism industry and government organization provide the subject matter for Part 3 of the book. Here we outline the operating characteristics and issues for the key sectors of the tourism industry by focusing on the core business in each case. The tourism industry is one area where the sectors are separated out for teaching and learning purposes but where the commonality of operating characteristics and constraints across the industry require deliberation. We enlarge on the discussion of these features in the introduction to Part 3. Finally, in Part 4 we provide a detailed assessment and set of approaches for the marketing management of tourism. In the final chapter we draw together the other sections of the book and analyse the many trends and influences which will impinge upon tourism in the future.

At the end of each chapter a range of further reading is provided for those who wish to take the material one stage further. In addition, there are a number of tourism texts and journals available, a range which has expanded considerably since the mid-1980s and which now includes a number of encyclopedic tourism books and yearbooks. The yearbooks in particular often include useful commentaries on current statistical trends in tourism to complement the World Tourism Organization's volumes and summaries. The other group of publications worthy of separate mention are the Economist Intelligence Unit's special publications covering regions and themes in tourism.

We have grouped thematically the major texts and journals which were available at the time of writing at the end of this book. Of course, material relating to tourism is also found elsewhere – tourism is increasingly covered, for example, in regional geography texts, and tourism cases and examples are sometimes found in journals from other disciplines – economics, management and geography to name but a few. Computer-based literature searching greatly assists the accessing of this material, and there are two data bases which serve the tourism field: Leisure, Recreation and Tourism Abstracts; and Articles in Hospitality and Tourism.

In conclusion, we must thank the many people who have, wittingly or unwittingly, contributed to this book. The secretaries in the Department of Management Studies for Tourism and the Hotel Industries have been invaluable in their help, as has Mrs Cooper Senior; and last but not least we would like to thank our friends and colleagues who have contributed to this book, responding to deadlines with undoubted professionalism and to our pleading with characteristic indifference. Finally, Penelope Woolf at Pitman Publishing has been amazingly patient and skilful in her handling of this particularly unruly group of academics.

Chris Cooper, John Fletcher, David Gilbert and Stephen Wanhill
University of Surrey, January 1993

CONTRIBUTORS

Authors

Chris Cooper, B.Sc., Ph.D., is Senior Lecturer in Tourism in the Department of Management Studies for Tourism and Hotel Industries at the University of Surrey. Originally a geographer, he gained his Ph.D. in tourist geography from University College, London. He then worked in market planning for a major tour operator and retailer before returning to academic life. His research interests focus on tourism education and resort development.

John Fletcher, B.Sc., Ph.D., is Senior Lecturer in Tourism Development and Planning, Project Appraisal and Tourism Forecasting in the Department of Management Studies for Tourism and Hotel Industries at the University of Surrey. He is also Managing Director of the Surrey Research Group at the University and has undertaken research projects for the EC, WTO, USAID, and UNDP, working extensively in the Caribbean, South Pacific and Europe. He gained his first degree and Masters in Economics and his Ph.D. in Public Finance from the University College of North Wales in Bangor, and became Lecturer in Economics and then Director of the Institute of Economics at UCNW until 1985.

David Gilbert, B.A. (Hons.), M.A., Dip.M., Ph.D., is Marketing Lecturer and Course Tutor for the Diploma/M.Sc. course in Tourism Marketing at the University of Surrey. Alongside his academic duties, he has worked with several organisations and consultancies on project work. He also has over eight years' operational experience in tourism for the private sector, having worked as Product Manager and as Marketing Manager for Rank Leisure. He has organized and run courses in tourism and hospitality marketing in the UK, Cyprus, Mauritius, Portugal, Indonesia, Spain, Italy and Southern Ireland.

Stephen Wanhill is Professor of Tourism Research in the School of Consumer Studies, Tourism and Hospitality Management at the University of Wales, Cardiff.

Additional contributors

Dimitrios Buhalis is a research student at the Department of Management Studies for Tourism and Hotel Industries at the University of Surrey, Guildford.

Tim Knowles is Lecturer in Hospitality Management in the Department of Management Studies for Tourism and Hotel Industries at the University of Surrey, Guildford.

John Latham is Professor of Business Analysis in the Business Division at the Southampton Institute of Higher Education, Southampton.

Andrew Lockwood is Lecturer in Hospitality Management in the Department of Management Studies for Tourism and Hotel Industries at the University of Surrey, Guildford.

John Westlake is Senior Lecturer in Tourism at the Department of Management Studies for Tourism and Hotel Industries, University of Surrey, Guildford.

Acknowledgement of sources

Every effort has been made to trace and acknowledge ownership of copyright. The Publishers will be pleased to make suitable arrangements with any copyright holders whom it has not been possible to contact.

CHAPTER 1

An introduction to tourism

OVERVIEW

In this chapter we attempt to break some of the myths surrounding tourism and also to identify the problems inherent in studying the subject. In particular, it is important to recognize the variety and scope of tourism as an activity and to realize that the elements of tourism are interlinked, despite the fact that they have to be isolated for teaching and learning purposes. The chapter outlines a tourism system as a way of thinking and provides a framework of knowledge for students approaching the subject. It then considers the difficulties involved in attempting to define tourism and offers some ideas for approaching definitions. Finally, the chapter examines the options in terms of classifying tourists.

TOURISM MYTHS AND PROBLEMS

In a world of change, one constant over the last two decades has been the sustained growth of tourism as both an activity and an industry. By 1990 tourism was the world's third most important industry in terms of export earnings (behind oil and motor cars). Tourism has been remarkable in its resistance to adverse economic and political conditions, but growth is inevitably slowing as the market matures.

The combination of the youthfulness of the tourism industry – international mass tourism is at best only 25 years old – with the pace of growth in demand has given tourism a Cinderella-like existence. International organizations support tourism for its contribution to world peace, the benefits of mixing peoples and cultures, the eco-

nomic advantages which can ensue, and the fact that tourism is a relatively 'clean' industry. But as midnight strikes, tourism is uncloaked as a despoiler of destinations and a harbinger of adverse social change, and even the employment and monetary gains of tourism are seen to be illusory in many destinations.

Clearly, the glamorous image of tourism is becoming slightly tarnished, but in many respects general perceptions of tourism are misplaced. Tourism is surrounded by a number of myths which have contributed to the glamour, and these should be broken:

- Tourism in the world is dominantly domestic (people travelling in their own country) not international.
- Most tourism journeys in the world are by surface transport (mainly the car) not by air.
- Tourism is not purely for the purpose of leisure. It also includes business tourism, pilgrimages and tourism for health purposes.

In historical terms, much of tourism activity is a relatively new development, and only recently has it been considered worthy of serious business endeavour or academic study. However, the tourism industry is of sufficient economic importance and its impacts upon economies, environments and societies are significant enough for the subject of tourism to deserve serious consideration.

While tourism rightly constitutes a domain of study, at the moment it lacks the level of theoretical underpinning which would allow it to become a discipline. The popularity of tourism as a subject, and the recognition of its importance by governments, has accelerated its study, and tourism now has its own small academic community, some journals, a handful of professional societies and a growing number of textbooks. However, the youthfulness of tourism creates a number of problems:

- The subject area itself is problematic, bedevilled as it is by conceptual weakness and fuzziness. There is still no real agreement over definitions of tourism or just what comprises the tourism industry. This results in a basic lack of rigour and focus.

- Tourism encompasses a number of diverse industrial sectors and academic subjects, reinforcing the need for a disciplined approach, but also providing a source of confusion for students. It is therefore important to provide a framework within which these subject approaches and industries can be located.
- As if these problems were not sufficient, tourism also suffers from a particularly weak set of data sources – in terms of both comparability and quality.

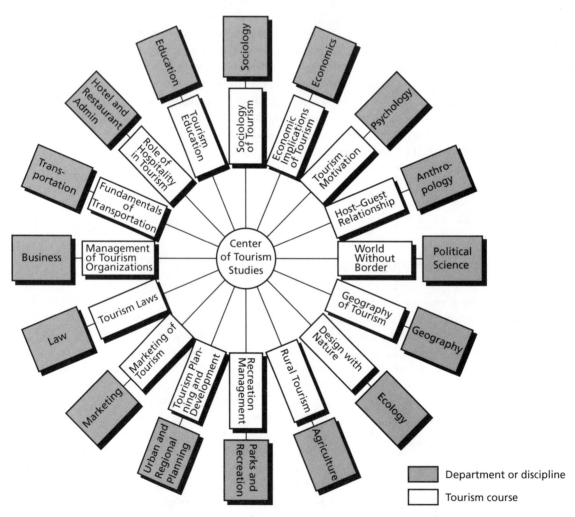

Source: Jafar Jafari, University of Wisconsin – Stout; McIntosh and Goeldner (1990).

Fig 1.1 Study of tourism choice of discipline and approach

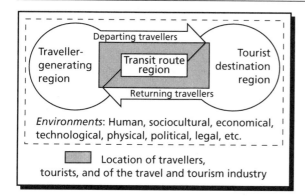

Source: Leiper (1990).

Fig 1.2 Basic tourism system

A TOURISM SYSTEM

In response to the problems identified above, we feel it is important at the outset to provide an organizing framework for the study of tourism. There are many ways to do this. Individual disciplines, for example, view the activity of tourism as an application of their own ideas and concepts, and an approach from geography, economics or another discipline could be adopted. An alternative is to take a multidisciplinary, or even an interdisciplinary, approach. Figure 1.1 shows one such attempt to integrate a variety of subjects and disciplines and to focus upon tourism.

However, in a book of this nature it is impossible to cover the complete range of approaches to tourism. Instead, as an organizing framework, we have adopted the model suggested by Leiper in 1979 and updated in 1990.

As Figure 1.2 shows, Leiper's model neatly takes into account many of the issues identified above by considering the activity of tourists, allowing industry sectors to be located, and providing the geographical element which is inherent in all travel. There are three basic elements of Leiper's model:

(1) *Tourists.* The tourist is the actor in this system. Tourism, after all, is a human experience, enjoyed, anticipated and remembered by many as a very important aspect of their lives. Defining the tourist and attempting to produce classifications of tourists forms the latter section of this chapter.

(2) *Geographical elements.* Leiper outlines three geographical elements in his model:

- Traveller-generating region.
- Tourist destination region.
- Transit route region.

The traveller-generating region represents the generating market for tourism, and in a sense provides the 'push' to stimulate and motivate travel. It is here that the tourist searches for information, makes the booking and makes the departure.

In many respects, the tourist destination region represents the 'sharp end' of tourism. At the destination, the full impact of tourism is felt and planning and management strategies are implemented. The destination is also the *raison d'être* for tourism. The 'pull' to visit destinations energizes the whole tourism system and creates demand for travel in the generating region. It is therefore at the destination 'where the most noticeable and dramatic consequences of the system occur' (Leiper, 1990, p. 23).

The transit route region represents not only the short period of travel to reach the destination, but also the intermediate places which may be visited en route: 'There is always an interval in a trip when the traveller feels they have left their home region but have not yet arrived . . . [where] they choose to visit' (Leiper, 1990, p. 22).

(3) *Tourism industry.* The third element of Leiper's model is the tourism industry, which we can think of as the range of businesses and organizations involved in delivering the tourism product. The model allows the location of the various industrial sectors to be identified. For example, travel agents and tour operators are predominantly found in the traveller-generating region, attractions and the hospitality industry are found in the destination region, while the transport industry is located in the transit route region.

Each of the elements of Leiper's tourism system interacts with the others, not only to deliver the tourism product, but also in terms of transactions and impacts of tourism and, of course, the differing contexts within which tourism occurs (see Figure 1.3). The fact that tourism is also an industry of contrasts is illustrated by examining two major elements of Leiper's model. Demand for tourism in the generating region is inherently volatile, seasonal and irrational. Yet this demand is satisfied by a destination region where supply is fragmented and inflexible – surely a recipe for the financial instability of tourism!

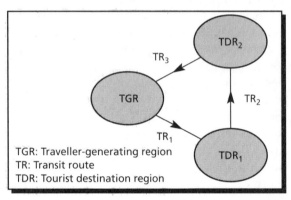

Source: Leiper (1990).

Fig 1.3 Geographical elements in a tourism system with two destinations

The major advantages of Leiper's model are its general applicability and simplicity, which provide a useful 'way of thinking' about tourism. But there are other advantages:

● It has the ability to incorporate interdisciplinary approaches to tourism because it is not rooted in any particular subject or discipline, but instead provides a framework within which disciplinary approaches can be located.
● It is possible to use the model at any scale or level of generalization – from a local resort to the international industry.
● Finally, the model demonstrates the highly important principle of tourism studies that all the elements of tourism are related and interact – in essence, we are studying a system of customers and suppliers who demand and supply the tourism product and services. Of course, in any textbook or course, the elements of tourism

have to be separated and examined individually, but in reality all are linked and the realization of the interrelationships provides a true understanding of tourism.

DEFINITIONS OF TOURISM

We can see from Leiper's model that tourism can be thought of as a whole range of individuals, businesses, organizations and places which combine in some way to deliver a travel experience. Tourism is a multidimensional, multifaceted activity, which touches many lives and many different economic activities. Not surprisingly, tourism has therefore proved difficult to define.

In some senses, this is a reflection of the complexity of tourism, but it is also indicative of its immaturity as a field of study. It is difficult to find an underpinning coherence of approach in defining tourism; instead, definitions have been created to cater for particular needs and situations. Yet, it is vital to attempt a definition of tourism not only to provide a sense of credibility and ownership for those involved, but also for the practical considerations of measurement and legislation.

For the purpose of this book, we can think of tourism as: 'the temporary movement to destinations outside the normal home and workplace, the activities undertaken during the stay and the facilities created to cater for the needs of tourists' (Mathieson and Wall, 1982, p. 1). While this is not a strict technical definition, it does convey the essential nature of tourism, i.e.:

● Tourism arises out of a movement of people to, and their stay in, various destinations.
● There are two elements in tourism – the journey to the destination and the stay (including activities) at the destination.
● The journey and stay take place outside the normal place of residence and work, so that tourism gives rise to activities which are distinct from the resident and working populations of the places through and in which they travel and stay.

- The movement to destinations is temporary and short term in character – the intention is to return home within a few days, weeks or months.
- Destinations are visited for purposes other than taking up permanent residence or employment.

Tourism definitions are unusual in that they are driven more by demand-side than by supply-side considerations. Some writers find this surprising: 'Defining tourism in terms of the motivations or other characteristics of travellers would be like trying to define the health-care professions by describing a sick person' (Smith, 1989, p. 33).

In part, attempts to define tourism have been led by the need to isolate tourism trips from other forms of travel for statistical purposes. These 'technical' definitions lay down minimum and maximum lengths of stay and strict 'purpose of visit categories'. Some countries also include a distance consideration, but this is not really practical (for example, a trip has to be over 100 miles to qualify as a tourist trip).

Supply-side definitions are less well developed. Leiper suggests one supply-side definition: 'The tourist industry consists of all those firms, organizations and facilities which are intended to serve the specific needs and wants of tourists' (1979, p. 400).

A major problem concerning supply-side definitions is the fact that a spectrum of tourism businesses exists, from those who are wholly serving tourists to those who also serve local residents and other markets. One approach to the problem is to classify businesses into two types:

- Tier 1: businesses which would not be able to survive without tourism.
- Tier 2: businesses which could survive without tourism, but in a diminished form (Figure 1.4).

This approach, taken from the 1985 Canadian National Task Force on Tourism Data, is consistent with other industrial sectors, and allows the size of the tourism industry to be gauged using standard industrial classifications.

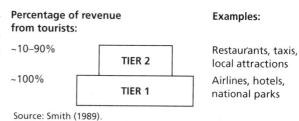

Source: Smith (1989).

Fig 1.4 Supply-side definition of the tourism industry

INTERRELATIONSHIPS AND CLASSIFICATIONS

Not only are the elements of tourism all inter-linked, but we can also see that tourism has close relationships with other activities and concepts. It is therefore a mistake to consider tourism in isolation from these other related activities.

For example, most tourism in the world is a leisure activity, and it is important to locate tourism in the spectrum of leisure activities. Defining leisure is, if anything, more problematic than defining tourism, but in essence leisure can be thought of as a combined measure of time and attitude of mind to create periods of time when other obligations are at a minimum. Recreation can be thought of as the pursuits engaged in during leisure time, and an activity spectrum can be identified from recreation around the home, at one end of the scale, through to tourism where an overnight stay is involved, at the other (see Figure 1.5). Excursions (which involve a trip away from home but do not involve an overnight stay) are a common recreational activity, but for tourism to occur, leisure time has to be blocked together to allow a stay away from home. Traditionally, these blocks of leisure time were taken as paid holiday entitlement, although in recent years innovations such as flexitime and three-day weekends have also facilitated tourism.

While all-embracing definitions of tourism and the tourist are desirable, in practice tourists represent a heterogeneous, not a homogeneous group, with different personalities, demographics and experiences. We can classify tourists in two basic ways which relate to the nature of their trip:

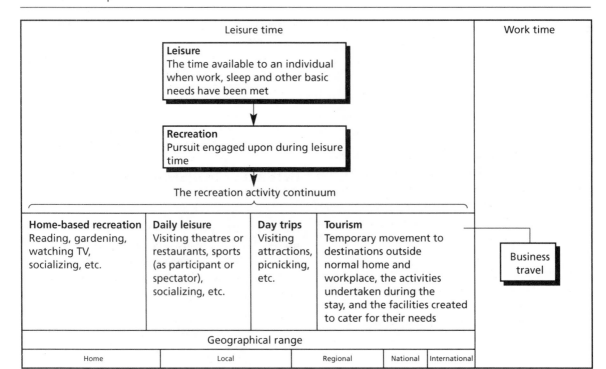

Source: Boniface and Cooper (1987).

Fig 1.5 Leisure, recreation and tourism

(1) A basic distinction can be made between domestic and international tourists, although this distinction is blurring in many parts of the world (for example, in the European Community). Domestic tourism refers to travel within the country of residence. There are rarely currency, language or visa implications, and domestic tourism is more difficult to measure than international tourism. As a consequence, domestic tourism has received little attention. In contrast, international tourism involves travel outside the country of residence and there may well be currency, language and visa implications.

(2) Tourists can also be classified by 'purpose of visit category'. Conventionally, three categories are used:

- Leisure and recreation – including holiday, sports and cultural tourism, and visiting friends and relatives (VFR).
- Other tourism purposes – including study and health tourism.

- Business and professional – including meetings, conferences, missions, incentive and business tourism.

These categories are useful not only for statistical purposes, but also for the marketing of tourism. Consider, for example, the flexibility of travel for each of the categories from the point of view of airline fare pricing and validity (see Figure 1.6).

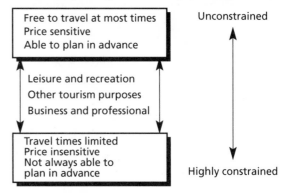

Fig 1.6 Airline pricing and purpose of visit categories

Table 1.1 Suggested socioeconomic characteristics for tourism analysis

Socioeconomic variable	Levels of measurement
1. Age	Collect by single years. It may be convenient to summarize by age cohorts.
2. Sex	Male/female. Age–sex cohorts may also be useful.
3. Education	Given the diversity of educational systems in North America, a basic four-part classification may be most useful: elementary, secondary, post-secondary non-university, and university. It may be useful in other circumstances to distinguish between completion of secondary or post-secondary programmes and partial work (drop-out before completion).
4. Occupational status	Categories can include employed full-time, employed part-time, retired (some reference to former occupation may be desired), homemaker, student, unemployed. If employed, refer the respondent to the next question, 'occupation'.
5. Occupation	This is best determined through an open-ended question. Responses can be summarized according to the *Occupation Classification Manual* or other comparable national statistical coding system such as the *Canadian Classification and Dictionary of Occupations*. These codes refer to the type of industry in which the traveller is employed.
6. Annual income	This is an especially sensitive subject; some of the concern over reporting income can be reduced by using income categories. The specific categories should be based on those used in the most recent national census. Household income is often the most relevant measure of income, although the respondent's income may be useful in special circumstances.

7. Family composition	This can be an especially important variable if the purpose of study includes some analysis of the effect of travel party composition on travel behaviour. One possible classification is:
	Single individual living alone
	Husband–wife family
	  No children under 18 years
	  No children at home or no children at all
	  Adult children living at home or other adult relatives
	With children under 18 years
	  With no other adult relatives
	  With other relatives
	Single-parent families
	  Male head
	  Female head
	All other families

8. Party composition	This is closely related to the previous variable for many travelling parties.
	Levels include:
	  One person alone
	  One family with children
	  Two families with children
	  Organized group
	  One couple
	  Two or more couples
	  Group of friends (unorganized group)
	  Other

Continued overleaf

Trip variable	Levels of measurement
1. Season or trip period	Calendar quarters: January to March April to June July to September October to December If the trip overlaps two or more quarters, the following convention is often used. For household surveys, use the quarter in which the trip ends. For exits or re-entry surveys, use the date of the survey. It is sometimes desirable to distinguish weekend trips from other trips.
2. Trip duration	Both days and nights are used as the unit of measurement. The number of nights is usually one less than the number of days; a three-day weekend lasts 'two nights'. The actual number of days or nights up to one week is often collected. Periods longer than one week are often measured as ranges, e.g. 8–15 days (or 7–13 nights).

3. Trip distance	This should be based, in part, on the threshold distance required for definition of a trip. Narrow ranges for lowest levels are desirable to permit aggregating or exclusion of data so that comparisons can be made between surveys using different distance thresholds. A possible classification would be:
	
	    25–49 miles
	    50–99 miles
	   100–499 miles
	   500–999 miles
	  1000–1499 miles
	  More than 1500 miles (2400 km)
	
	Metric conversion is usually necessary for international comparisons; however, international travel is normally not measured by distance.

4. Purpose of trip	Very simple classifications are used, such as business versus pleasure. This dichotomy is normally inadequate for analytical purposes and is too simplistic to represent the purposes of many trips. More precise classifications would include: Conventions or other business meetings Buying, selling, installation, or other business Recreation/vacation Touring/sightseeing Attending cultural/sporting events Participating in cultural/sporting events Visiting friends or relatives Other family or personal matters Shopping Study tour Health/rest Many trips involve more than one purpose, so it may be useful to specify 'primary' purpose.
5. Mode of transportation	Private automobile Rental automobile Bus/motor coach Train

	Scheduled airline
	Chartered airline
	Private aeroplane
	Boat/ship (additional categories for ferries, cruise ships, private boats may be added as necessary)
	Some trips involve multiple modes, such as a combination of scheduled airline and rental car. These combinations may be specified or a primary mode may be requested.
6. Expenditures	Transportation (broken out by mode, if desired)
	Accommodation (including camping fees, but not park entrance fees)
	Food and beverages (restaurant meals may be separated from food purchased at a store)
	Convention or registration fees
	Admission fees and other entertainment, including park admissions, licence fees for hunting and fishing
	Souvenirs
	Other purchase
7. Type of accommodation	Hotels and inns
	Motels and motor inns
	Resorts
	Campgrounds
	Hostels
	Commercial cottages
	Institutional camps
	Private cottages
	Bed and breakfast/tourist home
	Homes of friends or relatives
	Other
	Additional classifications could be based on size of accommodation, price, public versus private ownership, function (e.g. fishing camp; ski resort), type of location e.g. airport strip; downtown), availability of liquor, and so on.

Source: Tourism Research Planning Committee of the Federal–Provincial Conference on Tourism, 1975; Smith (1989).

There are many other ways to classify tourists (see, for example, Table 1.1). These range from their lifestyles and personalities, to their perception of risk and familiarity. However, one approach with increasing relevance to tourism in the late twentieth century is to classify tourists according to their level and type of interaction with the destination. Classifications of tourists which adopt this approach commonly place mass tourism at one extreme and some form of alternative, small-scale tourism at the other, with a variety of classes in-between. It is then argued that mass tourism has a major impact upon the destination because of the sheer scale of the industry and the nature of the consumer. On the other hand, small-scale, alternative types of tourism are said to have a much reduced impact upon the destination, not only because of the type of consumer involved, but also because they will shun the travel trade and stay in local *pensions* or with families. Unfortunately,

some commentators have oversimplified the complex relationship between the consumption and development of tourism resources. This is particularly true of the so-called 'alternative' tourism movement which is lauded by some as a solution to the ills of mass tourism. Indeed, the tenor of much of the writing about alternative tourism is that any alternative tourism scheme is good whilst all mass tourism is bad. There is, of course, a case for alternative tourism, but only as another form of tourism in the spectrum. It can never be an alternative to mass tourism, nor can it solve all the problems of tourism. (Archer and Cooper, forthcoming)

References and further reading

Archer, B.H., and Cooper, C. (forthcoming title) in Theobold, W. (ed.), *Critical Issues in Tourism*, Oxford: Heinemann.

Boniface, B., and Cooper, C. (1987) *The Geography of Travel and Tourism*, London: Heinemann.

Burkart, A., and Medlik, S. (1974) *Tourism: Past, Present and Future*, London: Heinemann.

Butler, R. (1990) 'Alternative tourism: pious hope or Trojan-Horse?', *Journal of Travel Research*, Winter, pp. 40–5.

Cooper, C. (1990) Editorial preface to Cooper, C. (ed.), *Progress in Tourism, Recreation and Hospitality Management*, Vol. 1, London: Belhaven.

Gilbert, D.C. (1990) 'Conceptual issues in the meaning of tourism, in Cooper, C. (ed.), *Progress in Tourism, Recreation and Hospitality Management*, Vol. 1, London: Belhaven.

Leiper, N. (1990) *Tourism Systems*, Department of Management Systems, Occasional Paper 2, Massey University, Auckland, New Zealand.

Mathieson, A., and Wall, G. (1982) *Tourism: Economic, Physical and Social Impacts*, London: Longman.

McIntosh, R.W., and Goeldner, C.R. (1990) *Tourism: Principles, Practices, Philosophies*, New York: Wiley.

Smith, S.L.J. (1988) 'Defining tourism: a supply side view', *Annals of Tourism Research*, vol. 15, no. 2, pp. 179–90.

Smith, S.L.J. (1989) *Tourism Analysis*, Harlow: Longman.

World Tourism Organization (1980) *Manila Declaration on World Tourism*, Madrid: World Tourism Organization.

World Tourism Organization (1982), *Acapulco Document*, Madrid: World Tourism Organization, June.

PART 1

Demand for tourism

CHAPTER 2

Introduction

In this part of the book we focus on the analysis of demand for tourism. This clearly relates to Leiper's traveller-generating region and is fundamental to the study and analysis of tourism. Yet in many texts and courses demand is given scant attention. For this reason we provide a comprehensive overview of tourism demand in the next five chapters.

We begin in Chapter 3 by defining demand and stressing the need to take into account not only those who consume tourism, but also those who wish to partake of travel but for some reason cannot. This raises the issue of barriers to travel and brings into focus the notion of 'social tourism', which attempts to remove these barriers for some groups in society. Of course, the relationship between variables such as price and income is important in this regard – tourism is a luxury activity and many people in the world cannot afford to take part. It is therefore important to consider the nature of demand schedules and elasticity, which characterize the relationship between the amount of tourism demanded and a particular variable.

In Chapters 4 and 5 we examine in some detail the nature of the variables which influence the consumption of tourism. There is some confusion here as to the level of aggregation to adopt – in much of the tourism literature the focus is upon variables such as gross domestic product and its impact upon travel in particular countries or regions. Another approach examines the role of such variables as mobility or personality at the level of the individual tourist. In these chapters we therefore provide an overview of both approaches. In Chapter 4 we focus on the main concepts and theories relating to the consumer's decision-making process as well as on the role of personality. In Chapter 5 we then provide a detailed examination of the 'parameters of possibility' for the individual in terms of the determinants of demand, before illustrating how these variables aggregate to provide the 'world-view' of tourism demand. Clearly, at this scale it is the world's affluent industrialized economies which can afford to consume tourism on a large scale.

Naturally, it would be impossible to examine these relationships and to gauge the scale of demand at the individual or world level without the ability to measure tourism demand. We see this as a critical area in the analysis and study of tourism, and it is an area which we cover in depth in Chapter 6. The measurement of tourism demand is a relatively recent activity, developed to meet the need not only for a more professional approach to the management of tourism, but also for countries to estimate the impact of tourism on their balance of payments. However, the very nature of tourism demand and the industry itself creates problems for measurement:

- First, there are issues relating to the activity of tourism itself. By definition, tourists are a mobile population, which means that it is difficult to 'catch' travellers. When questioning takes place after the event (often some time afterwards because of the short duration and infrequent nature of travel) problems of recall may be severe. At the same time the seasonal nature of tourism means that sampling has to be handled with care.
- Second, the tourism industry does not see measurement as a priority and is content to leave data collection to the public sector. Tourism is therefore an industry with a paucity of data.

Even where data do exist, they have to be treated with care. In Chapter 6 we provide an overview of these issues and outline examples of approaches to the measurement of tourism demand. The strengths and weaknesses of the techniques available are considered.

The final chapter in this part of the book takes advantage of the international statistics available on tourism demand and provides a detailed examination of the patterns of tourism around the world. These patterns are complex and range from the huge excursionist flows across borders to international long-haul tourism. The nature of measurement of tourism demand means that we have a clearer picture of international tourism than we do of domestic travel. Tourism demand generation is dominated by the affluent industrialized countries of the world, particularly Europe and the Americas. Emergent regions such as East Asia and the Pacific are, however, providing robust competition to these traditional areas and have become major players in the tourism scene in the 1990s.

In essence, then, we can identify some of the key issues relating to tourism demand:

- A number of official proclamations have affirmed every individual's right to demand tourism. In 1980 the Manila Declaration on World Tourism stated that the ultimate aim of tourism was 'the improvement of the quality of life and the creation of better living conditions for all peoples'. Yet, despite the fact that 450 million people travelled internationally in the early 1990s, the ability to demand international tourism remains an unobtainable luxury for the majority of the world's population.
- The difficulties inherent in measuring tourism demand underscore the need for caution in the interpretation of demand statistics and forecasts. This also raises the need for sharpening up tourism statistical series and the techniques used to measure and analyse tourism demand.
- The volatility of tourism demand creates major problems for tourism enterprises. Demand for tourism is easily influenced by irrational factors such as fashion; it is vulnerable to external events, such as the Gulf crisis of 1990–1; and it is seasonal in nature. This has to be set against the perishable nature of the tourism product and the high fixed-cost element of tourism supply. It is not surprising that this juxtaposition of volatile, unpredictable demand with fragmented and inflexible supply creates difficult trading conditions for many tourism enterprises.

This latter point raises the issue of the interrelationship between this first part of the book and the remaining parts. Demand for tourism is a result of the tourist's desire to travel to new places and to escape the routine of home. There is thus both a 'pull' and a 'push'. To an extent this part of the book examines the 'push' and the variables which determine whether the tourist has the resources to travel.

In Part 2 of the book we examine the 'pull' – the destination and its particular features – while in Part 3 we focus on the tourism industry, which makes the realization of demand possible. In Part 4 the central role of marketing is discussed. As we move into mature tourism markets, where growth is slowing and there may be greater capacity on offer than there is demand to fill it, successful tourism enterprises will increasingly utilize marketing to stimulate demand for their products. Tourism demand should not therefore be seen in isolation. The nature and scale of demand for tourism is inextricably linked to the other elements of the tourism system, and this has implications for the management of tourism.

CHAPTER 3

Concepts and definitions of demand for tourism

OVERVIEW

In Chapter 2 we saw that tourism represents a major contribution to the quality of life in the twentieth century. In this chapter we see that demand for tourism is made up not only of those who participate, but also of those who do not travel for some reason. We then outline a number of quantitative approaches to tourism demand. For example, travel propensity is a useful indicator of tourism participation as it gives the proportion of a population who actually engage in tourism. Travel frequency refers to the average number of trips taken by those participating in tourism, during a specified period. Demand schedules characterize the relationship between the amount of tourism demanded and a particular influence such as price. The relationship between this amount and a variable – such as price – is known as elasticity of demand. For tourism, this relationship is usually a negative one: the higher the price, the lower the demand.

THE DEMAND FOR TOURISM: DEFINITIONS

Definitions of demand vary according to the subject perspective of the author. For example, economists consider demand to be the schedule of the amount of any product or service which people are willing and able to buy at each specific price in a set of possible prices during a specified period of time. In contrast, psychologists view demand from the perspective of motivation and behaviour. Geographers, on the other hand, define tourist demand as 'the total number of persons who travel, or wish to travel, to use tourist facilities and services at places away from their places of work and residence' (Mathieson and Wall, 1982, p. 1).

Each approach is useful. The economic approach introduces the idea of elasticity – which describes the relationship between demand and price, or demand and other variables. The geographer's definition implies a wide range of influences, in addition to price, as determinants of demand, and includes not only those who actually participate in tourism, but also those who wish to, but for some reason do not. On the other hand, the psychologist scratches underneath the skin of the tourist to examine the interaction of personality, environment and demand for tourism.

The idea of some people having a demand for tourism but being unable to travel suggests that demand for tourism consists of a number of components. For our purposes, demand for tourism comprises three basic elements:

(1) *Effective* or *actual demand* is the actual number of participants in tourism, i.e. those who are actually travelling. This is the component of demand most commonly and easily measured, and the bulk of tourism statistics refer to effective demand.

(2) *Suppressed demand* is made up of that section of the population who do not travel for some reason.

Two elements of suppressed demand can be distinguished. First, *potential demand* refers to those who will travel at some future date if they experience a change in circumstances. For example, their purchasing power may increase, or they may receive more paid holiday entitlement, and they therefore have the potential to move into the effective demand category.

Deferred demand is a demand postponed because of a problem in the supply environment, such as a lack of capacity in accommodation, adverse weather conditions or perhaps terrorism activity. Again this implies that at some future date when the supply conditions are more favourable those in the deferred demand category will convert to effective demand.

(3) Finally, there will always be those who simply do not wish to travel, constituting a category of *no demand*.

We can also consider other ways in which demand for tourism may be viewed. For example, *substitution of demand* refers to the case when demand for one activity (say a self-catering holiday) is substituted by another (staying in serviced accommodation). This may be due to a shortage of supply in one activity and an excess of supply in another. A similar concept is *redirection of demand*, where the geographical location of demand is changed. Perhaps a trip to Spain is redirected to Greece because the flight or the accommodation in Spain was fully booked. Finally, the opening of new tourism supply – say, a resort, attraction or accommodation – will have the following effects:

- Redirect demand from similar facilities in the area.
- Substitute demand from other facilities.
- Generate new demand.

Economists refer to the first two of these as the 'displacement effect' – in other words, demand from other facilities is displaced to the new one and no extra demand is generated. This can be a problem in tourism and is an important consideration in appraising the worth of new tourism projects.

INDICATORS OF DEMAND

One of the most useful indicators of effective demand in any particular population is *travel propensity*. This measure simply considers the penetration of tourism trips in a population. There are two forms of travel propensity:

(1) *Net travel propensity* refers to the percentage of the population who take at least one tourism trip in a given period of time. In other words, it is a measure of the penetration of travel among 'individuals' in the population. The suppressed and no demand components will ensure that net travel propensity never approaches 100 per cent, and a figure of 70 or 80 per cent is likely to be the maximum for developed western economies.

(2) *Gross travel propensity* gives the total number of tourism trips taken as a percentage of the population. This is a measure of the penetration of 'trips', not individual travellers. Clearly then, as second and third holidays increase in importance, so gross travel propensity becomes more relevant. Gross travel propensity can exceed 100 per cent and often approaches 200 per cent in some western European countries, where those participating in tourism take more than one trip away from home.

Simply dividing gross travel propensity by net will give the *travel frequency*: in other words, the average number of trips taken by those participating in tourism during the period in question (see Case Study 3.1).

DEMAND SCHEDULES

In economic terms, a demand schedule refers to the quantities of a product that an individual wishes to purchase at different prices at a given point in time. Generally, the form of this relationship between price and quantity purchased is an inverse one, i.e. the higher the price of the product, the lower the demand; the lower the price, the greater the demand. This is shown in Figure 3.1.

CASE STUDY 3.1

Calculation of travel propensity and travel frequency

Out of a population of 10 million inhabitants:

3.0 million inhabitants
   take one trip of one
   might or more   i.e. $3 \times 1 = 3.0$m trips
1.5 million inhabitants
   take two trips of one
   night or more   i.e. $1.5 \times 2 = 3.0$m trips
0.4 million inhabitants
   take three trips of one
   night or more   i.e. $0.4 \times 3 = 1.2$m trips
0.2 million inhabitants
   take four trips of one
   night or more   i.e. $0.2 \times 4 = 0.8$m trips

5.1 million inhabitants
   take at least one
   trip   8.0m trips

Therefore:

Net travel propensity =

$$\frac{\text{Number of population taking at least one trip}}{\text{Total population}} \times 100 = \frac{5.1}{10} \times 100 = 51\%$$

Gross travel propensity =

$$\frac{\text{Number of total trips}}{\text{Total population}} \times 100 = \frac{8}{10} \times 100 = 80\%$$

Travel frequency =

$$\frac{\text{Gross travel propensity}}{\text{Net travel propensity}} = \frac{80\%}{51\%} = 1.57$$

A further refinement to the above calculations is to assess the capability of a country to generate trips. This involves three stages. First, the number of trips originating in the country is divided by the total number of trips taken in the world. This gives an index of the ability of each country to generate travellers. Second, the population of the country is divided by the total population of the world, thus ranking each country by relative importance in relation to world population. By dividing the result of the first stage by the result of the second the 'country potential generation index' (CPGI) is produced.

$$CPGI = \frac{\dfrac{N_e}{N_w}}{\dfrac{P_e}{P_w}}$$

where N_e = number of trips generated by country
N_w = number of trips generated in world
P_e = population of country
P_w = population of world

An index of 1.0 indicates an average generation capability. Countries with an index greater than unity are generating more tourists than expected by their population. Countries with an index below 1.0 generate fewer trips than average.

Source: Boniface and Cooper (1987), adapted from Burkart and Medlik (1975), pp. 53–60.

It is normal to characterize the demand curve *DD* in Figure 3.1 by an appropriate measure which expresses the responsiveness of quantity to changes in price. Such a measure is termed the *elasticity of demand* for product X with respect to its own price P_X. The own price elasticity of demand (*ei*) measures the ratio of the percentage change in quantity to the percentage change in price, i.e.

$$ei = \frac{\%\text{ change in quantity}}{\%\text{ change in price}}$$

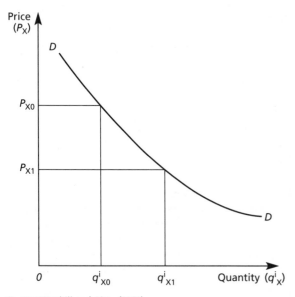

Source: Wanhill and Airey (1980).

Fig. 3.1 Individual's demand for product X

It is conventional to consider ei in its absolute or positive value. Thus, we refer to an own price elasticity of demand as 1.0, 2.0, 3.0, etc., and not –1.0, –2.0, or –3.0. The critical value of ei is 1.0. For goods which have an own price elasticity greater than one, demand is said to be elastic, since, for example, a 10 per cent change in price will produce more than a 10 per cent change in quantity. Products exhibiting this property are goods which are normally viewed as luxury items, e.g. holidays abroad, dining out and other tourism/leisure goods. When a good has an own price elasticity of demand of less than one it is classed as a necessity. For necessities, quantity adjustments respond sluggishly to price changes. Food is classed as a necessity.

So far we have examined individual consumer demand for a product only in terms of its own price, whereas in truth there are several other factors affecting a consumer's demand. These include prices of other goods, an individual's income, and social tastes and habits. Economists find that it is not practical to consider variations in all the components at one time, so they assume all components are constant except the one in question. In other words, when considering the effect of price on tourism demand it is assumed that changes in taste or an individual's budget are constant.

We can therefore see the effects of goods which are complementary to and substitutable for the good X in question. The effect of a change in the price of a substitute good is to cause a comparable change in the quantity of X demanded. For example, a fall in the price of holidays in one destination (say Spain) will cause a fall in demand for holidays in another destination (say Portugal). On the other hand, complementary goods are jointly consumed such that a rise in the price of one will cause a fall in demand for both.

Income or the consumer's budget is, perhaps, the most critical element in demand relationships: indeed, empirical demand functions reveal that income variations tend to dominate the explanation of demand changes, and this is particularly the case in tourism. For most goods, consumption rises with increases in income or spending power – these are referred to as 'normal' goods. For normal goods, elasticity takes positive values. However, there are some goods for which elasticity is negative – these are termed 'inferior' goods because as income rises consumption actually falls (this is unusual for tourism). The essential constraint on inferior goods is low income.

Until now we have examined the demand behaviour of individuals, whereas tourism is also concerned with the responses of the market to variations in the factors affecting demand. Since individual tourists make up the market, it is reasonable to suppose that market demand curves respond in a similar fashion to individual curves. Hence a first approach is to sum the individual demand schedules to arrive at the market schedule.

This is illustrated in Figure 3.2, which supposes that there are only two individuals in the market. The market demand schedule is derived from the horizontal summation of the two individual

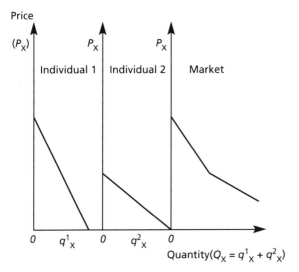

Source: Wanhill and Airey (1980).

Fig. 3.2 Derivation of a market demand curve

curves. We can see that the market curve has a distinct 'kink' where the two individual curves join. This arises because the market is assumed to consist of only two persons. As the number in the market increases, any kinks are ironed out and a more or less smooth curve results.

While it is acceptable to assume that all individuals demanding product X face similar prices, they certainly do not have similar incomes or budgets, or socioeconomic characteristics. The implication here is that to estimate a market demand curve for product X we require knowledge of the price of X, the price of substitutes for and complements to X, the income of each individual consumer and information on their particular socioeconomic circumstances. We will consider these variables in detail in Chapter 5.

References and further reading

Boniface, B., and Cooper, C. (1987) *The Geography of Travel and Tourism*, London: Heinemann.

Burkart, J., and Medlik, S. (eds) (1975) *The Management of Tourism*, London: Heinemann.

Johnson, P., and Thomas, B. (eds) (1992) *Choice and Demand in Tourism* , London: Mansell.

Lavery, P. (ed.) (1971) *Recreational Geography*, Newton Abbott: David and Charles.

Mathieson, A., and Wall, G. (1982) *Tourism: Economic, Physical and Social Impacts*, London: Longman.

Wanhill, S.R.C., and Airey, D.W. (1980) 'Demand for accommodation', in Kotas, R. (ed.), *Managerial Economics for Hotel Operation*, London: Surrey University Press.

CHAPTER 4

Consumer behaviour and tourism demand

OVERVIEW

In this chapter we provide an overview of the consumer decision-making process in tourism. This represents tourism demand at the personal level and complements the broader world-view provided in Chapter 5. We first consider the main concepts and theories relating to motivation, needs, roles and images, and review the major literature debates surrounding these concepts. We then go on to describe and provide a critical review of the major models of consumer behaviour in tourism.

Demand for tourism at the individual level can be treated as a consumption process which is influenced by a number of factors. These may be a combination of needs and desires, availability of time and money, or images, perceptions and attitudes. It is the aim of this chapter to explain how these factors influence individual behaviour in tourism and combine to shape an individual's demand for tourism.

THE INDIVIDUAL DECISION PROCESS

At the personal level it is clear that the factors influencing demand for tourism are closely linked to models of consumer behaviour in tourism. No two individuals are alike, and differences in attitudes, perceptions and motivation have an important influence on travel decisions. *Attitudes* depend on an individual's perception of the world. *Perceptions* are mental impressions of, say, a place or travel company and are determined by

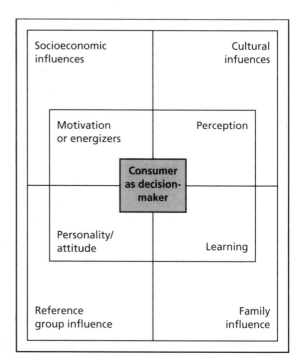

Fig 4.1 Consumer decision-making framework

many factors which include childhood, family and work experiences. However, attitudes and perceptions in themselves do not explain why people want to travel. The inner urges which initiate travel demand are called *travel motivators*.

We can view the tourism consumer decision process as involving four basic elements:

(1) *Energizers of demand.* These are the forces of motivation which lead a tourist to decide upon visiting an attraction or going on a holiday.

(2) *Filterers of demand.* Even though motivation may exist, demand is constrained or channelled

due to economic (e.g. discretionary income), sociological (reference groups, cultural values) or psychological factors (perception of risk, personality, attitudes).

(3) *Affecters*. The consumer will have developed ideas of a destination, product or organization from its promotion, development of image and information which is generally available (learning, attitudes, associations). These affecters will heighten or dampen the various energizers which lead to consumer action.

(4) *Roles*. The important role is that of the family member who is normally involved in the different tasks of the purchase process and the final resolving of decisions about when, where, and how the group will consume the tourism product (family influence, cultural influence).

MOTIVATION

The classic dictionary definition of motivation is derived from the word 'motivate' which is to cause (a person) to act in a certain way; or stimulate interest. There is also reference to the word 'motive' which is concerned with initiating movement or inducing a person to act.

Maslow's hierarchy model

It could be argued that, due to its simplicity, Maslow's needs hierarchy is probably the best-known theory of motivation. It is used in industrial, organizational and social science texts on a regular basis. The theory of motivation proposed by Maslow is in the form of a ranking, or hierarchy, of individual needs (see Figure 4.2).

The early humanistic values of Maslow seem to have led him to create a model where self-actualization is valued as the level to which 'man' should aspire. Maslow argued that, if none of the needs in the hierarchy were satisfied, then the lowest needs, the physiological ones, would dominate behaviour. If these were satisfied, however, they would no longer motivate and the individual would be motivated by the next level in the hierarchy.

LOWER 1. Physiological – hunger, thirst, rest, activity.

2. Safety – security, freedom from fear and anxiety.

3. Belonging and love – affection, giving and receiving love.

4. Esteem – self-esteem and esteem for others.

HIGHER 5. Self-actualization – personal self-fulfilment.

Fig 4.2 Maslow's hierarchy of needs

Maslow identified two motivational types of sequence mechanism in motivation. These can be greatly simplified as:

- Deficiency or tension-reducing motives.
- Inductive or arousal-seeking motives.

Maslow maintained that his theory of motivation can be applied to both work and non-work spheres of life. Maslow treated his need levels as universal and innate, yet of such instinctual weakness that they can be modified, accelerated or inhibited by the environment. He also stated that, while all the needs are innate, only those behaviours which satisfy physiological needs are unlearned.

While a great deal of tourism demand theory has been built upon Maslow's approach, it is not clear from his work why he selected five basic needs; why they are ranked as they are; how he could justify his model when he never carried out clinical observation or experiment; and why he never tried to expand the original set of motives. It is not that Maslow has been extended or distorted by tourism theorists, but simply that he has provided a convenient set of containers which can be relatively easily labelled. The notion that a comprehensive coverage of human needs can be organized into an understandable hierarchical framework is of obvious benefit for tourism theorists.

Within Maslow's model, human action is wired into predetermined, understandable and predictable aspects of action. This is very much in the behaviourist tradition of psychology, as opposed to the cognitivist approach which stresses the concepts of irrationality and unpredictability of behaviour. However, Maslow's theory does allow for 'man' to transcend the mere embodiment of biological needs, and this sets him apart from other species.

To some extent the popularity of Maslow's theory can be understood in moral terms. It suggests that, given the right circumstances, people will grow out of their concern for the materialistic aspects of life and become more interested in 'higher' things.

The study of motivation in tourism

The study of motivation has been derived from a range of disciplinary areas which have led to a diversity of approach. In tourism, Dann (1981) has pointed out that there are seven elements within motivation:

(1) *Travel as a response to what is lacking yet desired*. This approach suggests that tourists are motivated by the desire to experience phenomena which are different from those available in their home environment.

(2) *Destination pull in response to motivational push*. This analyses the motivation of the individual tourist in terms of the level of desire (push) and the pull of the destination or attraction.

(3) *Motivation as fantasy*. This is a subset of the first two factors and suggests that tourists travel in order to undertake behaviour which may not be culturally sanctioned in their home setting.

(4) *Motivation as classified purpose*. This is a broad category which invokes the main purposes of a trip as a motivator for travel. Purpose may include visiting friends and relatives, enjoying leisure activities, or study.

(5) *Motivational typologies*. This approach is internally divided into behavioural typologies

such as the motivator's 'sunlust' (search for a better set of amenities than are available at home) and 'wanderlust' (curiosity to experience the strange and unfamiliar) as proposed by Gray, and typologies which focus on dimensions of the tourist role.

(6) *Motivation and tourist experiences*. This approach is characterized by debate regarding the authenticity of tourist experiences and depends upon beliefs about types of tourist experience.

(7) *Motivation as auto-definition and meaning*. This suggests that the way in which tourists define their situations will provide a greater understanding of tourist motivation than simply observing their behaviour.

McIntosh and Goeldner (1986) utilize four categories of motivation:

(1) *Physical motivators*. These are related to refreshment of body and mind, health purposes, sport and pleasure. This group of motivators are seen to be linked to those activities which will reduce tension.

(2) *Cultural motivators*. These are identified by the desire to see and know more about other cultures, to find out about the natives of a country, their lifestyle, music, art, folklore, dance, etc.

(3) *Interpersonal motivators*. These include a desire to meet new people, visit friends or relatives, seek new and different experiences. Travel is an escape from routine relationships with friends or neighbours and the home environment, or it is used for spiritual reasons.

(4) *Status and prestige motivators*. These include a desire for the continuation of hobbies and education (i.e. personal development) and are also seen to be concerned with the desire for recognition and attention from others, in order to boost the personal ego.

Plog (1974) developed a theory within which the US population could be classified as a series of interrelated psychographic types. These types range from 'psychocentric', which is derived from the psyche where an individual centres his or her thoughts on the small problem areas of life, to 'allocentric' where the root 'allo' means varied in form.

The majority of the population were found to fall in the centre, in an area which Plog termed 'midcentric'. Plog also found that those who were at the lower end of income scales were more likely to be psychocentric types, whereas in the upper income band there was a higher likelihood of being allocentric. In a later study it was observed that middle-income groups exhibited only a small positive correlation with psychographic types. Moreover, there were a number of psychographic types who could not, through income constraint, choose the type of holiday they preferred even if they were motivated towards it.

Plog's research findings evolved from syndicated research for airline companies which were interested in converting non-flyers into flyers. His methodology was based upon in-depth interviews with non-flyers who had above-average incomes. On analysing the transcripts from the research, Plog found a common pattern among non-flyers that included the following:

- *Territory boundness* – the group was found not to be venturesome and members travelled very little within their lifetime.
- *Generalised anxieties* – they were insecure and uncertain within their daily lives.
- A *'sense of powerlessness'* – they felt they were not in control of their lives and they were pessimistic regarding their future.

Because of the common tendency for the above characteristics to appear in each non-flyer response, the term 'psychocentrism' was applied to the group.

While Plog's theory is a useful way of thinking about tourists, it is very difficult to apply. Tourists will travel with different motivations on different occasions. A second holiday or short-break weekend may be in a nearby psychocentric destination, whereas the main holiday may be in an allocentric destination.

Smith (1990) tested Plog's model, utilizing evidence from seven different countries. He concluded that his own results did not support Plog's original model of an association between personality types and destination preferences. Smith questioned the applicability of the model to countries other than the United States.

In answer to Smith, Plog (1990) questioned the validity of the variables of measurement and the sample frame used by Smith. He claimed that the research had fallen into unnecessary 'potholes'. He dismissed Smith's comparative study on the basis that it did not replicate adequately Plog's own methodology. Regardless of this defence, further controlled empirical studies will be required in order to ensure Plog's theory can be justified as a central pillar within tourism theory.

A summary of the concept of motivation

The dimensions of the concept of motivation in the context of travel are not easy to map out or comprehend. However, it would seem to include the following:

- Travel is initially need-related and this manifests itself in terms of a motivational or 'push', as the energizer of action.
- Motivation is grounded in sociological and psychological norms, attitudes, culture, perceptions and so on, leading to person-specific forms of motivation.
- The image of a destination created through 'induced' or 'organic' communication channels will influence motivation and subsequently affect the type of travel undertaken.

Although the literature on tourism motivation is still in an immature phase of development, it has been shown that motivation is an essential concept behind the different patterns of tourist demand. However, we should remember that, although motivation can be stimulated and activated in relation to a product, needs themselves cannot be created. They are dependent on the human element through the psychology and circumstances of the individual. Moreover, while some types of motivation may be innate in us all (curiosity, need for physical contact), other types are learnt (status, achievement) because they are judged as valuable or positive.

TOURIST ROLES

Tourists can be characterized into different typologies or roles, and these roles can be studied in relation to goal-oriented forms of behaviour or holiday choice activity. An understanding of tourist roles may therefore bring about a deeper understanding of the choice process of different consumer segments.

The majority of authors who have identified tourist roles have concentrated on the assessment of the social and environmental impact of tourism or the nature of the tourist experience. Any definition or interpretation of tourist roles, like those of motivation, varies according to the analytical framework used by the individual author.

The initial ideas of role developed from the work of sociological theorists such as Goffman (1959), who suggested that individuals behave differently in different situations in order to sustain impressions associated with those situations. As actors have different front and backstage performances, participants in any activity vary their behaviour according to the nature and context of that activity. Consequently, individual roles can be identified and managed according to social circumstances. Whereas tourists may vary considerably, a pattern of roles is seen to be constructed which can be studied. Theoretical studies focusing on the sociological aspects of tourism roles were developed in the 1970s through the work of Cohen, MacCannell and Smith.

The interaction of personality attributes such as attitude, perceptions and motivation allows different types of tourist role to be identified. One classification by Cohen (1974) is particularly useful. It is based on the theory that tourism combines the curiosity to seek out new experiences with the need for the security of familiar reminders of home. Cohen proposes a continuum of possible combinations of novelty and familiarity and, by breaking up the continuum into typical combinations of these two ingredients, produces a fourfold classification of tourists (Table 4.1).

Cohen described the first two roles as institutionalized and the latter types as non-institutionalized. He was interested in classifying groups in order to understand not demand as such, but the effects of institutionalized forms of tourism. These effects involved authenticity issues, standardization of destinations, festivals and the development of facilities. He also identified the impact of non-institutionalized forms of tourism upon the destination. This acted as a 'spearhead for mass tourism' as well as having a 'demonstration effect' on the lower socioeconomic groups of the host community.

Cohen's typology assists in formulating operational approaches to tourism research and forms a framework for management practice. Although it is not complete and cannot be applied to all tourists at all times, it does afford a way of organizing and understanding tourist activity.

Role and family influence

As the fundamental social unit, the family's influence on tourism demand is extremely important. The family often acts as the purchasing unit and may be supplying the needs of perhaps two or more generations. In addition, it socializes children to adopt particular forms of purchasing behaviour and acts as a wider reference group. Given the importance of family behaviour in the purchase of leisure products, we may want to question the preponderance of literature which treats consumer behaviour as an individual mode of action.

Lifestyle and lifecycle exert a great influence on buying behaviour. Each member of the family fulfils a special role within the group, acting as husband/father, wife/mother, son/brother or daughter/sister. Family decision making assigns roles to specific members of the family, and decisions may be shared or made by one person. In this way, the family acts as a composite buying unit with the different role patterns involved leading to particular forms of tourism product purchasing.

Table 4.1 Cohen's classification of tourists

The organized mass tourist
Low on adventurousness he/she is anxious to maintain his/her 'environmental bubble' on the trip. Typically purchasing a ready-made package tour off-the-shelf, he/she is guided through the destination having little contact with local culture or people.

Institutionalized tourism
Dealt with routinely by the tourism industry–tour operators, travel agents, hoteliers and transport operators.

The individual mass tourist
Similar to the above but more flexibility and scope for personal choice is built in. However, the tour is still organized by the tourism industry and the environmental bubble shields him/her from the real experience of the destination.

The explorer
The trip is organized independently and is looking to get off the beaten track. However, comfortable accommodation and reliable transport are sought and, while the environmental bubble is abandoned on occasion, it is there to step into if things get tough.

Non-institutionalized tourism
Individual travel, shunning contact with the tourism industry except where absolutely necessary.

The drifter
All connections with the tourism industry are spurned and the trip attempts to get as far from home and familiarity as possible. With no fixed itinerary, the drifter lives with the local people, paying his/her way and immersing him/herself in their culture.

Familiarity

Novelty

Source: Boniface and Cooper (1987), adapted from Cohen (1972).

The importance of image

An individual's awareness of the world is made up of experiences, learning, emotions and perceptions; or, more accurately, the cognitive evaluation of such experiences, learning, emotions and perceptions. Such awareness can be described as knowledge producing a specific image of the world. This image will obviously affect an individual's preference and motivation towards tourism, as it will provide a 'pull' effect resulting in different demand schedules.

Many definitions have been offered to describe the word 'image' in different fields. For example, the World Tourism Organization (1979) gives its definitions as follows:

- the artificial imitation of the apparent form of an object;
- form resemblance, identity (e.g. art and design);
- ideas, conceptions held individually or collectively of the destination.

The World Tourism Organization suggests that the tourist image is only one aspect of a country's general image, with the two being closely interrelated. Nobody is likely to visit a country for tourism if for some reason he or she dislikes its image. Conversely, a tourist discovery may lead to a knowledge of other economic, political or cultural aspects of that country. The WTO further adds that the presentation of a destination's image must allow for the fact that an image is not generally created from nothing, but involves the transformation of an existing image.

Tourist behaviour both of individuals and groups depends on their image of immediate situations and the world. The notion of image is closely related to behaviour and attitudes. Attitudes and behaviour become established on the basis of a person's derived image and are not easily changed unless this image is changed.

The holiday image

Mayo (1973) examined regional images and regional travel behaviour. Among other things he indicated that the image of a destination area is a critical factor when choosing a destination. He further concluded that, whether or not an image is in fact a true representation of what any given region has to offer, what is important is the image that exists in the mind of the vacationer.

The tourist may possess a variety of images in connection with travel: the image he or she has formed of the destination; of the term 'holiday' itself; of the mode of transport to be utilized; of the tour operator or travel agency; and of him or herself. For example, it is probable that the term 'holiday' evokes different images for different people. However, it is likely that similar images of a particular holiday experience are held by people within the same segment of society and who have experienced a similar lifestyle or education.

There are two levels of image. Viewed in terms of a country or destination, the 'organic' image is the sum of all the information that has not been deliberately directed by advertising or promotion of a country or destination. This information comes from geography books, history books, what other people have said about the area, newspapers and magazines. An imaginary picture is built up which is the result of all this information. The individual attempts to make sense of it by forming a pattern or a picture of what he or she imagines the area must be like.

The second level of image is the 'induced' image. This is formed by deliberate portrayal and promotion by various organizations involved with tourism. It is important to distinguish between these two levels since the induced image is controllable while the organic image is less easy to influence.

MODELS OF CONSUMER BEHAVIOUR IN TOURISM

Background

One approach to understanding tourism demand is to identify and evaluate the broader theories of consumer behaviour linked to purchasing behaviour. This is far from simplistic, for we are faced with a proliferation of research within a field of study which has displayed significant growth and diversity.

There have been three phases related to consumer behaviour theory. These are as follows:

- The early empiricist phase covered the years between 1930 and the late 1940s. It was dominated by empirical commercial research as industry attempted to identify the effects of distribution, advertising and promotion decisions.
- The motivational research phase of the 1950s placed a greater emphasis upon in-depth interviews, focus groups, thematic apperception tests and other projective techniques. There was a great deal of activity directed at uncovering 'real' motives for action which were perceived to lie in the deeper recesses of the consumer's mind.
- The formative phase from the 1960s provided the first general consumer behaviour textbook (Engel, Kollat and Blackwell, 1968), and other influential books (such as Howard and Sheth, 1969) followed soon after.

During the formative phase, models of behaviour proved useful as a means of organizing disparate knowledge of social action into a somewhat arbitrary yet plausible process of intervening psychological, social, economic and behavioural variables. These 'grand models' of consumer behaviour have been subsequently utilized or transformed by authors interested in the tourism choice process.

The models can be found to share several commonalities:

- They all exhibit consumer behaviour as a decision process. This is integral to the model.
- They provide a comprehensive model focusing mainly on the behaviour of the individual consumer.
- They share the belief that behaviour is rational and hence can, in principle, be explained.
- They view buying behaviour as purposive, with the consumer as an active seeker both of information stored internally and of information available in the external environment. Thus, the search and evaluation of information is a key component of the decision process.
- They believe that consumers limit the amount of information taken in, and move over time from general notions to more specific criteria and a preference for alternatives.
- All the 'grand models' include a notion of feedback: that is, outcomes from purchases will affect future purchases.

Wahab, Crampon and Rothfield

One of the first attempts to provide some understanding of tourism purchase behaviour is to be found in the work of Wahab, Crampon and Rothfield (1976). These authors presented the consumer as purposeful and conceptualized his or her buying behaviour in terms of the uniqueness of the buying decision:
- No tangible return on investment.
- Considerable expenditure in relation to earned income.
- Purchase is not spontaneous or capricious.
- Expenditure involves saving and preplanning.

They presented a model of the decision-making process based upon the preceding 'grand models' of consumer behaviour and having the stages shown in Figure 4.3.

Schmoll

Schmoll (1977) argued that creating a model of the travel decision process was not just a theoretical exercise, for its value could be found in its aid to travel decision making. His model was based on the Howard–Sheth (1969) and Nicosia (1966) models of consumer behaviour (Figure 4.4).

Schmoll's model is built upon motivations, desires, needs and expectations as personal and social determinants of travel behaviour. These are influenced by travel stimuli, the traveller's confidence, destination image, previous experience and cost and time constraints. The model has four fields, each of which exerts some influence over the final decision. According to Schmoll, 'The eventual decision (choice of a destination, travel time, type of accommodation, type of travel arrangements, etc.), is in fact the result of a distinct process involving several successive stages or fields' (1977).

- Field 1 *Travel stimuli.* These comprise external stimuli in the form of promotional communica-

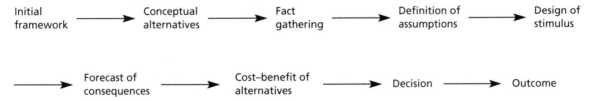

Fig 4.3 The Wahab, Crampon and Rothfield model of consumer behaviour

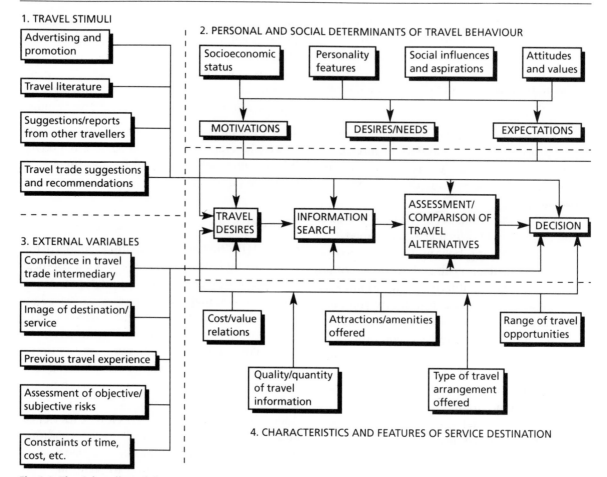

Fig 4.4 The Schmoll model

tion, personal and trade recommendations.

- Field 2 *Personal and social determinants.* These determine customer goals in the form of travel desires and expectations and the objective and subjective risks thought to be connected with travel.
- Field 3 *External variables.* These involve the prospective traveller's confidence in the service provider, destination image, learnt experience and cost and time constraints.
- Field 4 *Characteristics and features of the service destination.* These also have a bearing on the decision and its outcome.

This model (with the exception of some changes which incorporate the word 'travel' in the headings and the location of previous experience in field 3) has been borrowed directly from the 'grand models' already discussed. In Schmoll's model there is no feedback loop and no input to attitude and values. It is therefore difficult for us to regard the model as dynamic.

However, Schmoll does highlight many of the attributes of travel decision making which, while not unique in themselves, do influence tourism demand: for instance, the level of financial outlay, the destination image, the level of risk and uncertainty, the necessity to plan ahead, and the difficulty of acquiring complete information.

Schmoll, while highlighting some of the characteristics associated with the problem-solving aspects of travel, reiterates the determinants of cognitive decision-making processes. Within

Schmoll's work we are introduced to the importance of image, which plays a significant part in the demand process.

Mayo and Jarvis

Mayo and Jarvis have also borrowed from the grand theorists' models. They have taken the basic Howard–Sheth three-level decision-making approach where problem solving is seen as: extensive, limited or routinized.

Mayo and Jarvis follow the earlier theories by describing extensive decision making (destination purchase, for them) as being characterized by a perceived need for an information search phase and needing a longer decision-making period. The search for, and evaluation of, information is presented as a main component of the decision-making process whereby the consumer moves from general notions to more specific criteria and preferences for alternatives.

Mathieson and Wall

Mathieson and Wall offer a five-stage process of travel-buying behaviour (see Figure 4.5).

The framework offered by Mathieson and Wall (see Figure 4.6) is influenced by four interrelated factors:

- Tourist profile (age, education, income, attitudes, previous experience and motivations).
- Travel awareness (image of a destination's facilities and services, which is based upon the credibility of the source).
- Destination resources and characteristics (attractions and features of a destination).
- Trip features (distance, trip duration and perceived risk of the area visited).

In addition Mathieson and Wall recognize that a holiday is a service product with the characteristics of intangibility, perishability and heterogeneity, which in one way or another affect the consumer's decision making. However, apart from

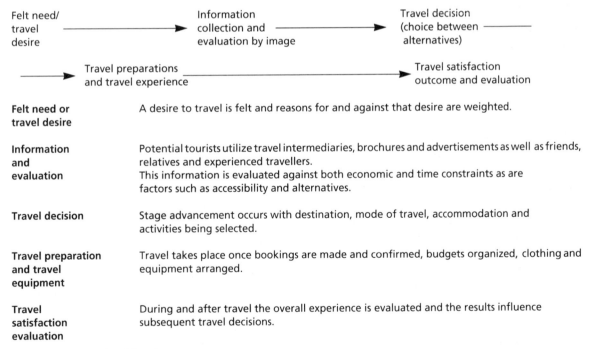

Felt need or travel desire	A desire to travel is felt and reasons for and against that desire are weighted.
Information and evaluation	Potential tourists utilize travel intermediaries, brochures and advertisements as well as friends, relatives and experienced travellers. This information is evaluated against both economic and time constraints as are factors such as accessibility and alternatives.
Travel decision	Stage advancement occurs with destination, mode of travel, accommodation and activities being selected.
Travel preparation and travel equipment	Travel takes place once bookings are made and confirmed, budgets organized, clothing and equipment arranged.
Travel satisfaction evaluation	During and after travel the overall experience is evaluated and the results influence subsequent travel decisions.

Source: Mathieson and Wall (1982).

Fig 4.5 Travel-buying behaviour

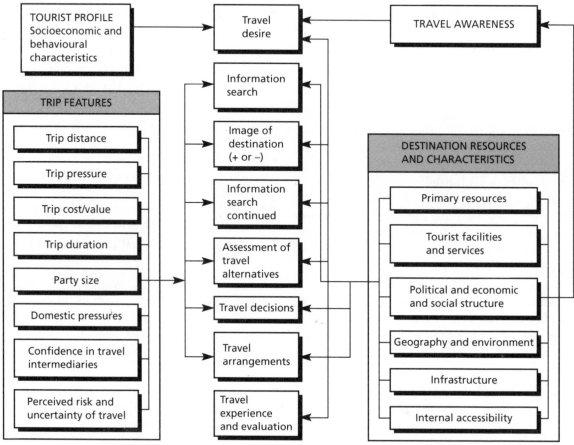

Source: Mathieson and Wall (1982).

Fig 4.6 The Mathieson and Wall model

pointing out that consumption and evaluation will occur simultaneously, the basis of their model relies on the previously reviewed grand models.

This is not to say that the Mathieson and Wall model reflects the depth of insight of these models; on the contrary, it only incorporates the idea of the consumer being purposive in actively seeking information and the importance of external factors. The model omits important aspects of perception, memory, personality and information processing, which are the basis of the traditional models. The model that Mathieson and Wall provide is based on a geographer's product-based perspective rather than that of a consumer behaviourist.

This chapter is based on Chapter 5 'An Examination of the Consumer Behaviour Process Related to Tourism', pp. 78–105, by D.C. Gilbert in *Progress in Tourism, Recreation and Hospitality Management*, Vol. 3, ed. Chris Cooper, Belhaven, London (1991).

References and further reading

Assael, H. (1987) *Consumer Behaviour and Marketing Action*, Boston, Mass.: Kent.

Boniface, B., and Cooper, C. (1987) *The Geography of Travel and Tourism*, London: Heinemann.

Cohen, E. (1972) 'Towards a sociology of international tourism', *Social Research*, vol. 39, no. 1, pp. 164–82.

Cohen, E. (1974) 'Who is a tourist? A conceptual clarification', *Sociological Review*, vol. 22, no. 4, pp. 527–55.

Cohen, E. (1984) 'The sociology of tourism: approaches, issues, findings', *Annual Review of Sociology*, pp. 373–92.

Dann, G.M.S. (1981) 'Tourist motivation: an appraisal', *Annals of Tourism Research*, vol. 8, no. 2, pp. 187–219.

Engel, J.F., Kollat, D.J., and Blackwell, R.D. (1968) *Consumer Behaviour*, New York: Holt Reinehart and Wilson.

Engel, J.F., Blackwell, R.D., and Miniard, P. (1986) *Consumer Behaviour*, New York: Dryden Press.

Gilbert, D.C. (1991) 'An examination of the consumer decision process related to tourism', in Cooper, C. (ed.), *Progress in Tourism, Recreation and Hospitality Management*, Vol. 3, London: Belhaven.

Goffman, E. (1959) *The Presentation of Self in Everyday Life*, Harlow: Pelican.

Goodall, B. (1991) 'Understanding holiday choice', in Cooper, C. (ed.), *Progress in Tourism ,Recreation and Hospitality Management*, vol. 3, London: Belhaven.

Gray, H.P. (1970) *International Travel–International Trade*, Lexington, Maine: Heath Lexington Books.

Holloway, J.C., and Plant R.V. (1988) *Marketing for Tourism*, London: Pitman Publishing.

Howard, J.A., and Sheth, J.N. (1969) *The Theory of Buyer Behaviour*, New York: Wiley.

Jenkins, R. (1978) 'Family vacation decision making', *Journal of Travel Research*, vol. 17, no. 4, pp. 2–7.

MacCannell, D. (1976) *The Tourist: A New Theory of the Leisure Class*, London: Macmillan.

Maslow, A.H. (1943) 'A theory of human motivation', *Psychological Review*, Vol. 50, pp. 370–96.

Maslow, A.H. (1954) *Motivation and Personality*, New York: Harper and Row.

Maslow, A.H. (1968) *Toward a Psychology of Being* (2nd edn), New York: Van Nostrand Reinhold.

Maslow, A.H. (1970) *Motivation and Personality* (2nd edn), New York: Harper and Row.

Mathieson, A., and Wall, G. (1982) *Tourism: Economic, Physical and Social Impacts*, London: Longman.

Mayo, E. (1973) 'Regional images and regional travel behaviour', *TTRA Conference Procedures*, Idaho, pp. 211–18.

Mayo, E., and Jarvis, L. (1981) *The Psychology of Leisure Travel*, Boston, Mass.: CBI Publishing Co.

McIntosh, R.W., and Goeldner, C.R. (1986) *Tourism Principles: Practices and Philosophies*, New York: Wiley.

Mill, R.C., and Morrison, A. (1985) *The Tourism System*, Englewood Cliffs, NJ: Prentice Hall.

Morrison, A. (1989) *Hospitality and Travel Marketing,* New York: Delmar.

Nicosia, F.M. (1966) *Consumer Decision Processes: Marketing and Advertising Implications*, Englewood Cliffs, NJ: Prentice Hall.

Pearce, P.L. (1982) *The Social Psychology of Tourist Behaviour*, Oxford: Pergamon.

Plog, S.C. (1974) 'Why destination areas rise and fall in popularity', *Cornell Hotel and Restaurant Quarterly*, vol. 14, no. 4, pp. 55–8.

Plog, S.C. (1990) 'A carpenter's tools: an answer to Stephen L.J. Smith's review of psychocentrism/allocentrism', *Journal of Travel Research*, vol. 28, no. 4, pp. 43–5.

Schmoll, G.A. (1977) *Tourism Promotion*, London: Tourism International Press.

Sheth, J. (1974) 'A theory of family buying decisions', in Sheth, J. (ed.), *Models of Buyer Behaviour*, New York: Harper and Row.

Smith, S.L.J. (1990) 'A test of Plog's allocentric/psychocentric model: evidence from seven nations', *Journal of Travel Research*, vol. 28, no. 4, pp. 40–3.

Smith, V. (1977) *Hosts and Guests*, Philadelphia, Pa.: University of Pennsylvania Press.

Wahab, S., Crampon, L.J., and Rothfield, L.M. (1976) *Tourism Marketing*, London: Tourism International Press.

Wells, W., and Gubar, G. (1966) 'Life cycle concepts in marketing research', *Journal of Marketing Research*, November, pp. 355–63.

World Tourism Organization (1979) *Tourist Images*, Madrid: World Tourism Organization.

CHAPTER 5

Determinants of tourism demand

OVERVIEW

In Chapter 4 we examined individual consumer behaviour and saw that, while an individual may be motivated to travel, the ability to do so will depend on a number of factors related to both the individual and the supply environment. These factors can be termed determinants of demand and represent the 'parameters of possibility' for the individual.

In this chapter we arrange the determinants of demand on two levels. On the world scale, those countries with a high level of economic development and a stable, urbanized population are major generators of tourism demand. The political regime of a country is also relevant here. On the individual scale, a certain level of discretionary income is required to allow participation in tourism, and this income, and indeed the type of participation, will be influenced by such factors as job type, lifecycle stage, mobility, level of educational attainment and personality. Even within the developed world, many are unable to participate in tourism for some reason. Demand for tourism is therefore concentrated not only in developed western economies, but also predominates among those with high discretionary incomes.

This chapter examines how participation in tourism differs between nations and also between individuals, and explains why, despite declarations to the contrary, tourism is an activity highly concentrated among the affluent, industrialized nations. For much of the rest of the world, and indeed many disadvantaged groups in industrialized nations, participation in tourism remains an unobtainable luxury.

DETERMINANTS OF TRAVEL PROPENSITY

In Chapter 3 we identified travel propensity as a useful measure of demand in a particular population. Broadly, travel propensity for a particular population will increase with characteristics such as:

- Income.
- Level of urbanization.
- Education levels.
- Mobility levels (such as car ownership).

However, it will decrease with characteristics such as:

- Large household size.
- Increasing age.

The relationship between travel propensity and the characteristics of a population is not straightforward. In particular, we must remember that the variables identified above are all related. A high travel propensity would be expected for a developed western economy with a high degree of urbanization, high incomes, small household sizes and high levels of mobility. Conversely, low travel propensities would be expected for rural societies with large family sizes and low incomes.

There are also a number of factors which will determine the propensity of a population to travel to particular destinations. These include economic distance, cultural distance and the relative cost of living at the destination. Economic distance relates to the time and cost of reaching a destination. Although the idea of 'friction of distance' (i.e. the cost of overcoming distance) can be used here, in practice distance alone is not the only consideration. For example, it is ironic that international destinations are often closer in economic distance terms than many domestic destinations. (It is easier, and often cheaper, for a traveller to reach the Spanish costas from London, than it is to reach the Scottish island of Skye).

Cultural distance refers to the difference in culture between the origin area and the destination. For more adventurous travellers this acts to attract rather than to deter a visit. Costs at a destination are not an absolute quantity, but have to be considered relative to the value of the traveller's own currency. This is graphically demonstrated by the ebb and flow of traffic across the Atlantic depending upon whether the dollar or the pound is the strongest currency. Also, perception of price is an important consideration – Switzerland is perceived by many as an expensive destination, but in fact prices have fallen in recent years *vis-à-vis* many European currencies.

The problem of scale

It is difficult to generalize about the determinants of travel propensity. There is, for example, a particular problem in terms of linking different levels of generalization. At one level we can consider the individual's consumer behaviour with reference to tourism and analyse the influences upon his or her behaviour. At another level we can consider the aggregate of these individual decisions in terms of the travel propensity of regions or countries.

In Chapter 4 we considered in detail individual personality influences. For the purpose of this chapter we have taken two further levels of generalization. First, we have taken a *personal view* of variations in travel propensity, which can be envisaged in such terms as lifestyle and lifecycle. Second, there are the influences that lie at the *national level* of generalization and comprise the world-view of travel propensity, including economic development, population characteristics and political regimes.

THE PERSONAL VIEW

Demand at the personal level

Once a decision has been taken to travel, the ability to undertake the trip and the nature of that trip will be influenced by a wide range of interrelated factors. These can be broadly divided into two groups:

- The first group of factors can be termed *lifestyle* and include income, employment, holiday entitlement, educational attainment and mobility.
- A second group can be termed *lifecycle*, where the age and domestic circumstances of an individual affect both the amount and type of tourism demanded.

Naturally, these factors are interrelated and complementary. In a western society, a high-status job is normally associated with an individual in middle age with a high income, above average holiday entitlement, education and mobility.

Lifestyle factors

(1) *Income and employment*. Income and employment are closely linked and exert important influences upon both the level and the nature of tourism demanded by an individual. Tourism is an expensive activity that demands a certain threshold of income before participation is possible. Gross income gives little indication of the money available to spend on tourism, nor does disposable income. Admittedly, it represents the money that actually reaches the public's hands to dispose of as they please, but demands on disposable income include essentials such as housing, food and clothing. The most useful measure of the ability to participate in tourism is discretionary income: that is, the income left over when tax, housing and the basics of life have been accounted for. Clearly, two households with the same gross incomes may have very different discretionary incomes.

The relationship between income and tourism is a complex one. For example, certain tourism activities are highly sensitive to income – additional holidays and expensive pursuits such as skiing holidays are a particular case in point. The relationship is also characterized by the fact that tourism demand is strongly affected at the extremes of the income spectrum, whereas in the middle of the spectrum it is much more difficult to discern a clear relationship. For example, a very low discretionary income markedly depresses travel propensity. As discretionary income rises, the ability to partake of tourism is associated with the purchase of leisure-oriented goods, until with a high discretionary income travel may reach a peak and then level off as the demands of a high-status job, and possibly frequent business trips, reduce the ability and desire to travel for pleasure.

A fundamental distinction is between those in employment and those unemployed. The impact of unemployment on tourism demand is obvious, but the nature of demand also changes with recession when employment uncertainty encourages later booking of trips, more domestic holidays and shorter lengths of stay, and switches demand away from commercial accommodation to VFR and therefore leads to lower spending levels.

The nature of employment not only influences travel propensity by determining income and holiday entitlement, but it also has an effect upon the type of holiday demanded, as the mechanism of peer- and reference-group pressure is felt.

(2) *Paid holiday entitlement.* The increase in leisure time experienced by most individuals since 1950 is well documented. However, the relationship between an individual's total time budget, leisure time and paid holiday entitlement is complex. A number of surveys suggest that, in a developed western economy, individuals have anything from 35 to 50 hours' free time at their disposal. Free time is greater for males, the young and single adults. Of this free time some two-thirds is spent around the home. However, to enable tourism, leisure time has to be blocked into two or more days to allow a stay away from home.

While this is obviously the case with paid holiday entitlement, patterns of leisure time have changed over the last 20 years to allow three-day weekends, flexitime and longer periods of absence for those in employment.

A variety of holiday arrangements now exist worldwide, with most nations having a number of one-day national holidays, as well as annual paid holiday entitlement by law or collective agreements. Individual levels of paid holiday entitlement would seem to be an obvious determinant of travel propensity, but in fact the relationship is not straightforward and, rather like the income variable, is clearer at the extremes. For example, low levels of entitlement do act as a real constraint upon the ability to travel, while a high entitlement encourages travel. This is due in part to the interrelationship between entitlement and factors such as job status, income and mobility. As levels of entitlement increase, the cost of tourism may mean that more of this entitlement will be spent at home.

Paid holiday entitlement tends to be more generous in developed economies and less so in the developing world. The pattern of entitlement is also responsible in part for the seasonality of tourism in some destinations simply because some of the entitlement has to be taken in the summer months. To an extent, this is historical and is rooted in the holiday patterns of manufacturing industries. It does, however, impact upon the nature of demand for tourism. In some countries, notably France, staggering of holiday entitlement has been attempted to alleviate seasonality.

(3) *Other lifestyle factors.* Level of educational attainment is an important determinant of travel propensity as education broadens horizons and stimulates the desire to travel. Also, the better educated the individual, the higher the awareness of travel opportunities and susceptibility to information, media, advertising and sales promotion.

Personal mobility also has an important influence on travel propensity, especially with regard to domestic holidays. The car is the dominant recreational tool for both international and domestic tourism. It provides door-to-door freedom, can carry tourism equipment (such as tents or boats) and has all-round vision for viewing. Ownership of a car stimulates travel for pleasure in all but recessionary times.

Race and gender are two critical determinants of tourism demand, but the relationships are not clearly understood. Most surveys of participation in tourism suggest that it is whites and males who have the highest levels of effective demand for tourism. However, changes in society will both alter and complicate this rather simplistic view.

Clearly, for the purposes of analysing each variable we have to separate them, but it must be remembered that they are all complementary and interrelated. Indeed, this interrelation is such that some writers have attempted to analyse tourism or leisure lifestyles by performing multivariate analysis on the determinants of tourism demand and then trying to group individuals into particular categories. To date these analyses have met

---

CASE STUDY 5.1

The VALS lifestyle categories

The 'values and lifestyles' segmentation of lifestyles has been commercially researched as a market segmentation technique in the USA. It was not designed for tourism, but does shed light on tourism behaviour. It attempts to combine demographic variables with people's needs, attitudes and wants. The lifestyle classification is as follows.

Need-driven groups

Here needs are greater than choice as the groups are poor or disadvantaged in some way. There are two lifestyle types:

(1) *Survivor lifestyle* – the most disadvantaged groups, who are removed from the mainstream of society.

(2) *Sustainer lifestyle* – a group who are struggling, but hopeful that circumstances will change.

Outer-directed groups

These groups are concerned with how they appear to others, so they live and behave according to other people's perceptions. There are three lifestyle types:

(1) *Belongers lifestyle* – a conservative, comfortable and conventional group.

(2) *Emulator lifestyle* – not so satisfied, status conscious, competitive, ambitious and often young.

(3) *Achiever lifestyle* – a successful, happy and hard-working group, middle-aged, prosperous, self-assured, the leaders of society.

Inner-directed groups

Lifestyle more to do with inner satisfaction than concern with other people's views. There are four lifestyle types:

(1) *I-am-me lifestyle* – very young, impulsive and confused, and fiercely individual.

(2) *Experiential lifestyle* – youthful, seeking experience, orientated to inner growth, artistic.

(3) *Societally conscious lifestyle* – a mission-orientated group, adopting say environmental concerns. They are mature and successful.

(4) *Self-directed lifestyle* – a group who see emotional rewards as important. They are not motivated by external views of them, or by materialistic rewards.

Combined outer- and inner-directed groups

Integrated lifestyle – this lifestyle group are mature, self-assured and aware.

For example, societally conscious groups will seek a holiday trip which offers value for money, is relaxing and provides good scenery, all within a 'safe' setting. The food and the people are more important than the accommodation. Increasingly, they will look for 'environmentally sound' destinations. On the other hand, achievers will show a different pattern of demand, typically flying to their destination, travelling on business and staying in hotels.

Source: Adapted from Shih (1986).

with limited success. Even where they have been commercially adopted as market segments, it is difficult to correlate them with other variables such as media habits (Case Study 5.1).

However, leisure or tourism lifestyles are considerations when viewing the important role of fashion and style in holiday choice. Tourism demand has always been susceptible to fashion and can be influenced perhaps more readily than demand for some other goods by marketing and promotional activity.

Lifecycle factors

The propensity to travel, and indeed the type of tourism experience demanded, is closely related to an individual's age. While the conventional measurement is chronological age, 'domestic age' better discriminates between types of tourist demand and levels of travel propensity. Domestic age refers to the stage in the lifecycle reached by an individual, and different stages are characterized by distinctive holiday demand and levels of travel propensity (Case Study 5.2).

CASE STUDY 5.2

Domestic age and tourism demand

Childhood

At this stage decisions are taken for the individual in terms of holiday taking, although, of course, children do have a significant influence upon the parents' decisions. By the age of 10 or 11 some children take organized holidays with school or youth groups. These are usually domestic, self-catering arrangements.

Adolescence/young adulthood

At this stage the preoccupation is for independence, socializing and a search for identity. Typically, holidays independent of parents begin at around 15 years, constrained by lack of finance but compensated by having few other commitments, no shortage of free time and a curiosity for new places and experiences. This group has a high propensity to travel, mainly on budget holidays using surface transport and self-catering accommodation. Here the priority is simply to 'get away' – the destination is unimportant.

Marriage

Marriage represents the first 'crisis' in terms of unscrambling the preoccupations, interests and activities of an individual. Preoccupations turn to establishment and lifetime investments. Before the arrival of children, young couples often have a high income and few other ties, giving them a high travel propensity, frequently overseas. The arrival of children represents the second 'crisis', which coupled with the responsibility of a home may mean that constraints of time and finance depress travel propensity. Holidays become more organizational than geographical, with domestic tourism, self-catering accommodation and visiting friends and relatives increasingly common.

Empty nest stage

As children grow up, reach the adolescence stage and begin to travel independently, constraints of time and finance are lifted from parents and their travel propensity increases. This is often a time for long-haul travel – the cruise market typically comprises this group.

Old age

The emergence of early retirement at 50 or 55 years is creating an active and mobile group in the population who will demand both domestic and international travel. In later retirement, lack of finance, infirmity and often the loss of a partner act to offset the increase in free time experienced by this group. Holidays become more hotel based and travel propensity decreases.

The distinctive pattern of demand found at each stage in the lifecycle comes about for a number of reasons. At each stage in the lifecycle individuals can be thought of as having the following:

- Preoccupations, which are the mental absorptions arising from motivations.
- Interests, which are feelings of what an individual would like to do, or represent the awareness of an idea or opportunity.
- Activities, which are the actions of an individual.

Each stage in the lifecycle is characterized by particular combinations of the three factors. For example, in adolescence the preoccupation is with socializing and finding independence, while in married adulthood the preoccupations are more with establishment and social institutions. As an individual progresses through life the combinations of the factors, and the nature of the factors themselves, change. At certain 'crisis' points the whole combination is 'unfrozen' and completely reformed. An example here would be having children. At this point in an individual's life previous constraints and influences on holiday taking are totally changed as holidays become more organizational and less geographical.

The lifecycle framework can also be linked to lifestyle variables to provide a multidimensional analysis. In married middle age, for example, holiday entitlement, income and mobility are often at a maximum, and this is reflected in the level of holiday taking (Figure 5.1).

The explanatory framework provided by the domestic lifecycle approach is a powerful one. It has implications for the supply of facilities and for the analysis of market needs of particular population groups (e.g. the large numbers of elderly people which some western countries will have by the end of the century), and has clearly been used as a basis for market segmentation by tour operators. However, the lifecycle as outlined in this chapter is only appropriate for developed western economies. Even here it is a generalization, so it does not consider one-parent families, divorcees, or other ethnic groups living within western economies.

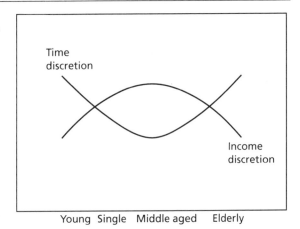

Fig 5.1 Traditional leisure paradox

THE WORLD-VIEW

When individual purchasing patterns and the influences upon them are aggregated to the national level, it is possible to gain a clearer view as to the influences upon global patterns of demand for tourism. These influences can be summarized as economic, demographic, political and technological.

Economic influences

A society's level of economic development is a major determinant of the magnitude of tourist demand because the economy influences so many critical, and interrelated, factors. One approach is to consider a simple division of world economies into the affluent 'north', where the countries are major generators and recipients of both international and domestic tourism, and the poorer 'south'. In the latter, some countries are becoming generators of international tourism, but mostly tourism is domestic, often supplemented by an inbound international flow of tourists. There have been a number of theories put forward to explain the process and sequence of economic development and one such theory (Rotow, 1959) shows that the economic development of nations can be divided into a number of stages, as outlined in Table 5.1.

Table 5.1 Economic development and tourism

Economic stage	Some characteristics	Examples
Traditional society Long-established land-owning aristocracy, traditional customs, majority employed in agriculture. Very low output per capita, impossible to improve without changing system. Poor health levels, high poverty levels.	*The undeveloped world* Economic and social conditions deny most forms of tourism except perhaps domestic VFR.	Much of Africa, parts of Southern Asia
Preconditions for take-off Innovation of ideas from outside the system. Leaders recognize the desirability of change.	*The developing world* From the take-off stage, economic and social conditions allow increasing amounts of domestic tourism (mainly visiting friends and relatives). International tourism is also possible in the drive to maturity. Inbound tourism is often encouraged as a foreign exhange earner.	South and Central America;[a] parts of the Middle East,[a] Asia and Africa
Take-off Leaders in favour of change gain power and alter production methods and economic structure. Manufacturing and services expand.		
Drive to maturity[b] Industrialization continues in all economic sectors with a switch from heavy manufacturing to sophisticated and diversified products.		Mexico; parts of South America
High mass consumption Economy now at full potential, producing large numbers of consumer goods and services. New emphasis on satisfying cultural needs.	*The developed world* Major generators of international and domestic tourism.	North America; Western Europe; Japan; Australia; New Zealand

Source: Boniface and Cooper (1987), adapted from Rotow W.W. (1959).

[a] Countries which are members of the Organization of Petroleum Exporting Countries (OPEC) are a notable exception in these regions; examples include Algeria, Libya, Nigeria, Kuwait, Saudi Arabia, Ecuador and Venezuela.

[b] Centrally planned economies merit a special classification, although most are at the drive to maturity stage; examples include China, Mongolia, North Korea and Vietnam

As a society moves towards the high mass consumption stage in Table 5.1, a number of important processes occur. The balance of employment changes from work in the primary sector (agriculture, fishing, forestry) to work in the secondary sector (manufacturing goods) and the tertiary sector (services such as tourism). As this process unfolds, an affluent society usually emerges and the percentage of the population who are economically active increases from less than a third in the developing world to half or more in the high mass consumption stage. With progression to the drive to maturity, discretionary incomes increase and create demand for consumer goods and leisure pursuits such as tourism.

Other developments are closely linked to the changing nature of employment. The population is healthier and has time for recreation and tourism (including paid holiday entitlement). Improving educational standards and media channels boost awareness of tourism opportunities, and transportation and mobility rise in line with these changes. Institutions respond to this increased demand by developing a range of leisure products and services. These developments occur in conjunction with each other until, at the high mass consumption stage, all the economic indicators encourage high levels of travel propensity. Clearly, tourism is a result of industrialization and, quite simply, the more highly developed an economy, the greater the levels of tourist demand.

As more countries reach the drive to maturity or high mass consumption stage, so the volume of trade and foreign investment increases and business travel develops. Business travel is sensitive to economic activity, and although it could be argued that increasingly sophisticated communication systems may render business travel unnecessary, there is no evidence of this to date. Indeed, the very development of global markets and the constant need for face-to-face contact should ensure a continuing demand for business travel.

Demographic influences

Levels of population growth and its development, distribution and density affect travel propensity. Population growth and development can be closely linked to the stages of economic growth outlined in Table 5.1 by considering the *demographic transition*, where population growth and development are seen in terms of four connected phases (Case Study 5.3).

CASE STUDY 5.3

The demographic transition and tourism

The high stationary phase

This corresponds to many undeveloped countries with high birth and death rates, keeping the population at a fluctuating but low level.

The early expanding phase

Here high birth rates continue, but there is a fall in death rates due to improved health, sanitation and social stability. This leads to a population expansion characterized by young, large families. Countries in this phase are often unable to provide for their growing populations and are gradually becoming poorer. Clearly, tourism is a luxury that cannot be afforded, although some nations are developing an inbound tourism industry to earn foreign exchange.

The late expanding phase

In this phase, a fall in the birth rate is rooted in the growth of an industrial society and birth control technology. Most developing countries fit into the early expanding and late expanding phases with a transition to the late expanding phase paralleling the drive to maturity.

The low stationary phase

This phase corresponds to the high mass consumption stage of economic development. Here, birth and death rates have stabilized to a low level.

Population density has a less important influence on travel propensity than has the distribution of population between urban and rural areas. Densely populated rural nations may have low travel propensities due to the level of economic development and the simple fact that the population is mainly dependent upon subsistence agriculture and has neither the time nor the income to devote to tourism. In contrast, densely populated urban areas normally indicate a developed economy with consumer purchasing power giving rise to high travel propensity and the urge to escape from the urban environment.

The distribution of population within a nation also affects patterns, rather than strictly levels, of tourist demand. Where population is concentrated into one part of the country, tourism demand is distorted. This asymmetrical distribution of population is well illustrated by the United States, where two-thirds of the population live in the eastern one-third of the country. The consequent east to west pattern of tourist focus (and permanent migrants) has placed pressure on the recreation and tourist resources of the western states.

Political influences

Politics affect travel propensities in a variety of ways. For example, the degree of government involvement in promoting and providing facilities for tourism depends upon the political complexion of the government. Governments which support the free market create an environment in which the tourism industries can flourish, rather than the administration being directly involved in tourism itself. Socialist administrations, on the other hand, encourage the involvement of the government in tourism and, through 'social tourism' often provide opportunities for the 'disadvantaged' to participate in tourism.

Governments in times of economic problems may control levels of propensity for travel overseas by limiting the amount of foreign currency that can be taken out of a country, or demanding a monetary bond to be left in the country while the resident is overseas. In 1983, for example, the French government placed a temporary currency restriction on French nationals travelling out of the country (a weak currency will also deter people from travelling abroad). Government restrictions on travel also include visa and passport controls as well as taxes on travel. Generally, however, these controls are not totally effective and, of course, they can be evaded.

We can also identify inadvertent political influences – for example, a government with an economy suffering high inflation may find that inbound travel is discouraged. In a more general sense, unstable political regimes (where civil disorder or war is prevalent) may forbid non-essential travel, and inbound tourism will be adversely affected.

Technological influences

There is no doubt that technology has been a major enabling factor in terms of converting suppressed demand into effective demand. This is particularly the case in terms of transport technology, where the development of the jet engine in the late 1950s gave aircraft both speed and range and stimulated the range of tourism products available in the international market to meet pent-up demand for international travel. Developments in aircraft technology have continued, but so have refinement and more widespread access to the motor car, and the development of computer reservation technology, which again is a critical enabling factor in terms of tourism demand.

Generally, technology acts to increase access to tourism by lowering the cost or by making the product more accessible. Examples here include developments in 'recreational technology', such as wind surfers, durable outdoor clothing, heli-skiing and heli-hiking, and off-road recreational vehicles.

SUPPRESSED DEMAND

Throughout this chapter the concern has been to identify factors which influence effective tourist demand. Yet tourism is still an unobtainable luxury for the majority of the world's population, not just in undeveloped and developing countries, but also for many in the developed world. There are a variety of reasons why people do not travel:

- Travel is expensive. A certain threshold of income is necessary before people can enter the market.
- Lack of time is a problem for some individuals who cannot allocate sufficient blocks of time to stay away from home. This may be for business or family reasons.
- Physical limitations (such as ill health) are a major reason for many people not travelling. In particular, heart disease and mental/physical handicap act as major constraints on travel.
- Family circumstances, such as for those who are single parents or who have to care for elderly relatives, may prevent travel.
- Government restrictions, such as currency controls and visas, may act as a real barrier to travel (both inbound and outbound) for some countries.
- Lack of interest/fear are real barriers for some individuals.

It is not uncommon for people to experience a combination of two or more of these barriers. For example, a one-parent family may find that lack of income and time will combine with family circumstances to prevent tourism travel. Obviously, it is just these groups who would most benefit from a holiday, and tourism planners are increasingly concerned to identify these barriers and devise programmes to encourage non-participants to travel. Perhaps the best-known example of this is the social tourism movement, which is concerned with facilitating the participation in travel of people with some form of handicap or disadvantage, and the measures used to encourage this participation.

References and further reading

Boniface, B., and Cooper, C. (1987) *The Geography of Travel and Tourism*, London: Heinemann.

Burkart, J., and Medlik, S. (1981) *Tourism: Past, Present and Future* , London: Heinemann.

Burton, R. (1991) *Travel Geography*, London: Pitman Publishing.

Chubb, M., and Chubb, H.R. (1981) *One Third of Our Time*, New York: Wiley.

Holloway, C. (1989) *The Business of Tourism*, London: Pitman Publishing.

Jefferson, A., and Lickorish, L. (1988) *Marketing Tourism*, Harlow: Longman.

McIntosh, R.W., and Goeldner, C.R. (1990) *Tourism: Principles, Practices, Philosophies*, New York: Wiley.

Mill, R.C., (1990) *Tourism: The International Business*, Englewood Cliffs, NJ: Prentice Hall.

Mill, R.C., and Morrison, A. (1985) *The Tourism System*, Englewood Cliffs, NJ: Prentice Hall.

Pearce, D. (1989) *Tourist Development*, Harlow: Longman.

Rapoport, R., and Rapoport, R.N. (1975) *Leisure and the Family Life Cycle*, London: Routledge Kegan Paul.

Rotow, W.W. (1959) *The Stages of Economic Growth*, Cambridge: Cambridge University Press.

Shih, D. (1986) 'VALS as a tool of tourism market research', *Journal of Travel Research*, Spring, pp. 2–11. *The Journal of Travel Research* is published by the Business Research Division, University of Colorado at Boulder, and the Travel and Tourism Research Association.

CHAPTER 6

Measuring the demand for tourism

OVERVIEW

The measurement of demand for tourism is a relatively recent activity. It is difficult to find estimates of international tourism demand relating to the period before the Second World War. Since then, however, measurement has gradually been taken more seriously, and statistics of international tourism demand between 1950 and 1990 are provided in Chapter 7.

The development of methods worldwide to provide reasonably reliable estimates of domestic tourism has been a relatively slow process due mainly to the fact that it is often given low priority, since there is no obvious or direct effect on a country's balance of payments. Also, since it involves no crossing of international boundaries, the monitoring of travel within a country is inherently more difficult.

In this chapter we initially describe and critically appraise the measurement of demand for both international and domestic tourism. We treat these separately for convenience, although it is recognized that international and domestic movements may be considered essentially the same activity. Certainly they have much in common. We consider why tourism demand is measured, what definitions are used and which statistics are normally compiled. We include a description of methods commonly used and an indication of their strengths and weaknesses.

Closely linked to the measurement of demand is the process of collecting market intelligence. In tourism, this often means using secondary data (for example, data produced by national or regional government bodies), combined with primary data through market surveys. In the latter part of this chapter we provide a practical guide to market research for the tourism industry, and in particular market surveys. The possible benefits of research to an organization are outlined. The various stages of research are also explained, from the agreement of research purpose and objectives, through research design, data collection and analysis, to the reporting of the research. We give emphasis to the importance of a manager making use of findings and feeding them into the decision-making process.

DEMAND FOR INTERNATIONAL TOURISM

Why measure international tourism?

National governments are generally extremely keen to monitor and attach measures to the movement of people into and out of their countries. This is for a variety of reasons, many of which have nothing whatsoever to do with tourism, such as security, health and immigration control. The measurement of tourism movement, however, has increasingly been seen as important because of its effects on a country's balance of payments.

The balance of payments is a country's financial accounts. There are movements of moneys into and out of these accounts. Any standard economics text will provide a detailed and proper explanation of the various components. An obvious way in which tourism impacts upon the balance of payments is through the spending of international tourists. We can identify two aspects here:

● Residents of country X, who travel abroad, spend money abroad. This has a negative effect on the balance of payments of country X (and positive effects on the balance of payments of countries visited). With regard to the movement of money, this can be thought of as an import as far as X is concerned. It is referred to as an invisible import, since there is no associated tangible good (such as a car or refrigerator).

- Residents of a foreign country, who are incoming tourists to country X, spend money in X. This has a positive effect on the balance of payments of X (and corresponding negative effects on the balance of payments of the country of origin of the tourist). As far as X is concerned, the direction of the spending is such that it is considered to be an invisible export.

The two components described above combine to form what is known as the *travel account* for a country. A positive travel account means that spending by incoming tourists exceeds spending abroad by outgoing tourists, and the combined effect will be of benefit to the balance of payments. Many commentators argue that any comparison of the two types of spending is unfair, since they reflect different activity.

The above analysis does not take into account fares paid to international passenger transport carriers and the various secondary effects of tourist spending. In Part 2 of this book we consider these impacts of tourism in detail.

We can see, then, that governments are keen to measure the movement of international tourism, but particularly incoming tourism because of its economic benefits. There are, however, a number of other important reasons. Official records can be built up and trends in movements can be monitored over a period of time. This means, for example, that the effectiveness of the marketing arm of government can be monitored, or that any particular promotional campaign which attempts to attract visitors from a particular country can be assessed. In general, information about the origins of visitors, their trip and attitudes can be used for a variety of purposes in marketing or planning. This is true also for tourism organiza-

tions at regional and local levels, provided that data collected at international level are able to be disaggregated and still reliable.

Some commercial organizations, although a minority, can and do make use of international tourism statistics. An incoming tour operator, for example, needs to be aware of current trends in order that programmes can be adjusted accordingly. Similarly, international and national hotel chains monitor changes in demand as part of their intelligence activity.

Some definitions

In collecting any information on the movement of travellers, it is essential to decide who is to be included. Everyone would agree that a family on holiday should count in the figures, but what about a businessperson, or the crew of a passenger liner, or even a member of the armed forces on duty in a foreign land? See Figure 6.1 for the answers! We can identify a number of principles which should govern the formation of a terminology:

- Definitions should be unambiguous and easy to understand.
- Definitions should normally be consistent with established usage of the words concerned.
- Definitions should, as far as is reasonably possible, facilitate measurement.

We have a major difficulty concerning the word 'tourism' itself. The normal and everyday use of the word relates to pleasure travel, but it would certainly exclude business travel. This is unfortunately not in line with what has become accepted as standard in the tourism literature. It is standard practice to include, as tourists, not only people who travel for pleasure, but also those who travel for the purposes of business, visiting friends and relatives, or even shopping. The reasons concern the use that is made of tourism statistics. After all, passenger transport carriers would wish for such a broad range of travellers to be included; a large number of hoteliers are interested in business travel because of the business it generates for them, and so on.

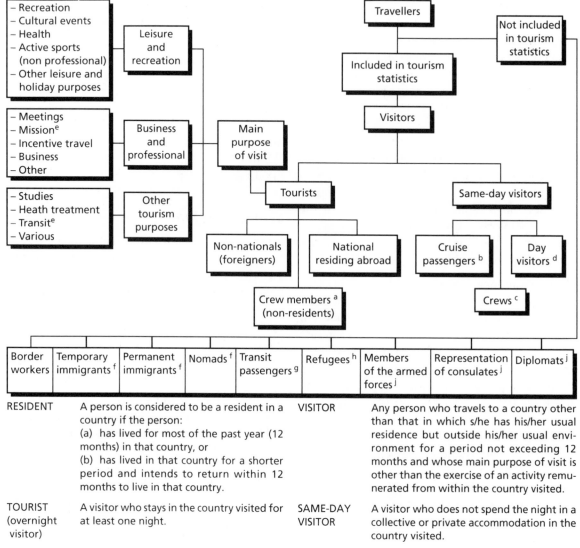

RESIDENT A person is considered to be a resident in a country if the person:
(a) has lived for most of the past year (12 months) in that country, or
(b) has lived in that country for a shorter period and intends to return within 12 months to live in that country.

TOURIST (overnight visitor) A visitor who stays in the country visited for at least one night.

VISITOR Any person who travels to a country other than that in which s/he has his/her usual residence but outside his/her usual environment for a period not exceeding 12 months and whose main purpose of visit is other than the exercise of an activity remunerated from within the country visited.

SAME-DAY VISITOR A visitor who does not spend the night in a collective or private accommodation in the country visited.

Notes:

a Foreign air or ship crews docked or in lay over and who use the accommodation establishments of the country visited.

b Persons who arrive in a country aboard cruise ships (as defined by the International Maritime Organization, 1965) and who spend the night aboard ship even when disembarking for one or more day visits.

c Crews who are not residents of the country visited and who stay in the country for the day.

d Visitors who arrive and leave the same day for leisure and recreation, business and professional or other tourism purposes including transit day visitors *en route* to or from their destination countries.

e Overnight visitors *en route* from their destination countries.

f As defined by the United Nations in the *Recommendations on Statistics of International Migration*, 1980.

g Who do not leave the transit area of the airport or the port, including transfer between airports or ports.

h As defined by the United Nations High Commissioner for Refugees, 1967.

j When they travel from their country of origin to the duty station and vice versa (including household servants and dependants accompanying or joining them).

Source: World Tourism Organization

Fig 6.1 Classification of international visitors

The definitions we give here are those which have become accepted. Figure 6.1 shows the breakdown of all travellers who cross international frontiers into those who are to be included in tourism statistics (to be called 'visitors') and those who are not. The decision as to whom to include is based on the purpose of visit. Visitors are divided according to whether or not there is an overnight stay in the country: if there is, then the visitor is deemed to be a tourist; otherwise he or she is a same-day visitor (previously called an 'excursionist'). In summary, for the purposes of classifying international travellers:

- A visitor is a traveller who is included in tourism statistics, based on his or her purpose of visit, which includes holidays, visiting friends and relatives, and business. A fuller list is shown in Figure 6.1.
- A tourist is a visitor who spends at least one night in the country visited.
- A same-day visitor is a visitor who does not spend the night in a collective or private accommodation in the country visited. So, for example, those returning to ship or train to sleep are considered as same-day visitors.

What is measured?

The measurement of demand normally includes statistics of volume, value and profiles, as we describe in some detail below. In addition, during the collection of such data from visitors, questions are also often asked which relate to visitor opinions and attitudes.

Volume statistics

The total number of international tourist arrivals to a country and the total number of international tourist departures from that country are key measures of demand. It can be seen that such measures are actually of trips. They are not counts of individuals since, for example, a businessperson who makes 20 visits to a country will be counted 20 times. However, the numbers of trips and of individuals are related by the following equation:

$$\text{Number of trips} = \text{Number of individuals} \times \text{Average number of trips taken per individual}$$

Estimates for any two of the variables in this equation will therefore provide an estimate for the third. The equation is general in the sense that it can be applied to any group of tourists. For example, the number of trips made in total by Japanese tourists to Ruritania in the year 2000 will be equal to the product of the number of individuals involved and the average number of trips they make to Ruritania.

A serious weakness in using international tourism arrivals, as far as most tourism suppliers are concerned, is that the length of stay is not taken into account. The length of stay is important for accommodation establishments, beach managers, retail outlets and so on, although not, of course, for passenger termini. A better measure of volume for many purposes is therefore total tourist nights. This also acts as a measure of likely impact on a tourist destination. It can be defined as follows:

$$\text{Total tourist nights} = \text{Number of tourist trips} \times \text{Average length of stay (nights stayed)}$$

Value (expenditure) statistics

Total visitor expenditure is a simple measure of the economic value of foreign visitors to a country. It normally includes spending within a host country, and excludes fare payments made to international passenger carriers for travel into and out of that country. Similarly, the expenditure of outgoing tourists while abroad is a measure of the economic cost to a country due to its nationals travelling abroad. International tourism expenditure can typically be classified under the headings of accommodation, food and drink, entertainment, shopping and travel within the host country. For the purposes of comparison between countries, value statistics are often converted to US dollars.

Visitor profile statistics

Profile statistics are made up of statistics relating to the visitor and those relating to the visit. Typically, information collected contains the following details:

The visitor	The visit
● age	● origin and destination
● sex	● mode of transport
● group type	● purpose of visit
(e.g. alone, family)	● time of visit
● nationality or	● length of stay
country of residence	● accommodation used
● occupation	● activities engaged in
● income	● places visited
	● tour or independently
	organized

Methods used

Statistics relating to international tourism are normally estimates rather than exact values. We cover the reasons for this in Chapter 7, but they mainly centre on the fact that monitoring and measuring what are at times complex movements of people is not easy and is subject to error. We can most easily understand this when contemplating how to obtain detailed profile or expenditure information about tourists. Even the controls at international boundaries and currency controls do not normally work to provide accurate information.

Volume statistics are often obtained using counting procedures at entry and exit points to a country, or (for inbound tourism) sometimes through the use of registration forms at accommodation establishments. They can be supplemented by summaries of records kept by international passenger carriers, and by surveys of households, such as a national travel survey which will elicit information on foreign (outgoing) as well as domestic tourism. Research at tourist destinations also provides some information on the movement of international visitors to a country.

Procedures used at entry and exit points have normally been determined on the basis of administrative control and other reasons not specifically related to tourism. Tourism statistics are thus a by-product of the process rather than its main aim. Nevertheless, there are many countries that do make counts and collect information at frontiers for tourism-related purposes. Clearly, islands such as the UK or the West Indies have an advantage in this respect, since there are likely to be fewer entry/exit points anyway. A major problem with counting using accommodation establishments alone is that they give only partial coverage. No estimates would be possible for those staying with friends or relatives, for example.

CASE STUDY 6.1

The UK International Passenger Survey (IPS)

The UK has one single survey, the International Passenger Survey, which measures both incoming and outgoing tourism flows. It started in 1961 and then covered major routes only. It now covers all ports of entry/exit.

The survey is based on a stratified sample of passengers entering and leaving the country, sampling being carried out separately for air and sea. Grossing-up procedures are used to provide estimates, e.g. of numbers of visitors from the USA, or total spend by visitors from Japan. Statistics resulting from the IPS are published quarterly in Business Monitor MQ6.

The aims of the IPS can be summarized as follows:

● To collect data for the UK balance of payments travel account, which acts to compare expenditure by overseas visitors to the UK with expenditure overseas by visitors from the UK.
● To provide detailed information on foreign visitors to the UK, and on outgoing visitors travelling abroad.
● To provide data on international migration.
● To provide information on routes used by passengers as an aid to aviation and shipping authorities.

Expenditure statistics are notoriously difficult to collect. We can derive them using foreign currency estimates from banks, or from suppliers of tourism services and facilities. These methods are cumbersome and not normally satisfactory. Increasingly, therefore, information is collected directly from the tourists themselves, through sample surveys of foreign tourists as they leave the country, and from nationals as they return from a foreign trip.

Systems for tourism statistics

There is in the early 1990s a need for a common framework worldwide which encompasses definitions, methodology and the presentation of information. Such a framework would need to allow for national differences where appropriate. A recent significant move was made to develop European Community tourism statistics, initially through a two-year programme starting in 1991, which aimed to create national and international statistical systems capable of satisfying the demand for information from a wide range of public- and private-sector bodies. The Statistical Office of the European Communities (EURO-STAT) is responsible for much of this development, working closely with the WTO and OECD.

DEMAND FOR DOMESTIC TOURISM

Why measure domestic tourism?

Worldwide, relatively few people enjoy the opportunity to travel to and within countries other than their own. By far the most common form of travel is that by residents of a country within that country. International travel, although given high priority by segments of the populations of industrialized nations, is still very much a minority activity. As a very rough guide, we estimate that expenditure worldwide on domestic tourism may be worth up to ten times that on international tourism.

The WTO reported in 1984 that 'there are relatively few countries that collect domestic travel and tourism statistics', and the situation has not changed significantly since then. Much more information is available on international tourism. Why is this?

First of all, international travel involves, by definition, the crossing of a frontier. It is therefore easier to observe and monitor. Domestic tourism involves movement internally and is therefore more difficult to research. Countries which make use solely of registration forms at hotels miss out all aspects of domestic tourism which involve staying at supplementary accommodation establishments or with friends and relatives. Many countries do not even try to measure domestic demand because it is considered unimportant due to the nature of their own domestic tourism. For example, in many developing countries very little domestic movement involves staying in serviced accommodation, and so it does not compete with demand from international visitors. The benefits of collecting information always have to be set against its costs, particularly in a developing country where resources may be severely limited.

On the other hand, within the major international tourism-receiving countries of North America and western Europe, domestic demand and international demand often compete with and complement each other. We can see this clearly in hotel lobbies, on beaches, in restaurants, at attractions and so on. In countries such as the USA, Canada and the UK, therefore, the measurement of domestic tourism is important.

Use is made of domestic tourism statistics in a variety of ways:

● To measure the contribution of tourism to the overall economy. Although it is impossible to assess accurately, estimates can be produced which measure the effect of tourism on a country's gross domestic product.
● For promotion and marketing policies. Many countries promote themselves strongly as destinations to their own residents – in this sense, they compete with foreign destinations for their own tourists' spending.

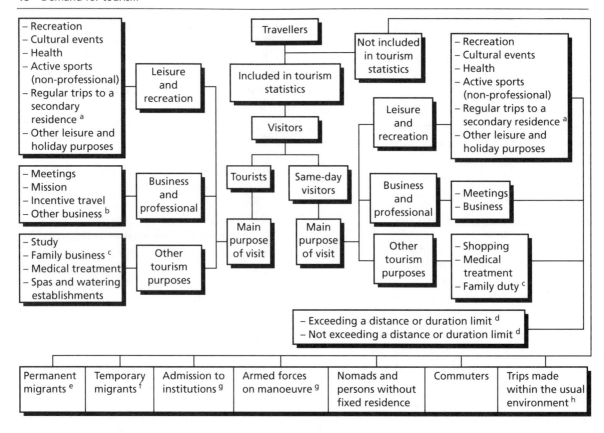

RESIDENT — A person is considered to be a resident in a place if the person:
(a) has lived for most of the past year (12 months) in that place, or
(b) has lived in that country for a shorter period and intends to return within 12 months to live in that place.

VISITOR — Any person residing in a country, who travels to a place within the country, outside his/her usual environment for a period not exceeding twelve months and whose main purpose of visit is other than the exercise of an activity remunerated from within the place visited.

TOURIST (overnight visitor) — A visitor who stays in the place visited for at least one night.

SAME-DAY VISITOR — A visitor who does not spend the night in a collective or private accommodation in the place visited.

Notes:
a   Weekly trips to the place of second residence (whether owned, inhabited free of charge or rented) should be classified separately under leisure and recreation.
b   Persons undertaking frequent trips within the country, e.g. crew members, drivers, tourist guides, salespeople, itinerant sellers, inspectors, artists, sportspeople, etc.
c   Attending funerals, visiting sick relatives, etc.
d   Minimum distance and duration of minimum absence and duration of journey may be required for a person to qualify as a same-day visitor.

e   For a period of more than 6 months, or the minimum time necessary to establish a new residence, including dependants.
f   For a period of less than 12 months with the purpose of exercising an activity remunerated from within the place of destination, including dependants.
g   Admission to a hospital, prison and other institutions.
h   Trips of a routine character, part of a regular business schedule or frequent visits to a place for whatever reason.

Source: World Tourism Organization

Fig 6.2 Classification of internal visitors

- To assist area development policies. This can involve attempting to ensure a high quality of environment in the main tourism areas, as well as developing other areas to relieve congestion.
- To aid social policies. A statistical knowledge of the holiday-taking habits of nationals is required, for example, for providing aid to the underprivileged, perhaps in the form of subsidies to socially orientated sites.

In addition to the above, local and regional tourism organizations and individual businesses make use of domestic tourism statistics as an aid to decision making.

Some definitions

Definitions do vary country by country. When detailed accuracy is important it is advisable to check against the original source. Figure 6.2 gives definitions and classifications of internal (domestic) visitors as recommended by the WTO.

What is measured?

The measurement of domestic tourism demand covers similar areas to that of international demand: volume, value and visitor profile statis-

---

CASE STUDY 6.2

The United Kingdom Tourism Survey (UKTS)

Background

Prior to 1989 the four UK national tourist boards obtained estimates of domestic tourism volume and value from other surveys. The UKTS came about, following reviews of statistical needs by and among the boards, as a result of a requirement for better data: better in the sense of being compatible over the UK as a whole, of covering aspects of tourism not covered by the earlier surveys, and of deriving from larger, and hence more statistically robust, samples.

Objectives

The first objective of the UKTS is to provide measurements of tourism by residents of the United Kingdom, in terms of both volume (trips taken, nights spent away from home) and value (expenditure on those trips and nights). Its second aim is to collect details of the trips taken and of the people taking them. These objectives extend to the following:

- Tourism by residents of any age.
- Tourism for any purpose.
- Tourism in the sense of trips away from home which last for one night or more up to a maximum of 60 nights.

- Tourism to any country of the world, using any accommodation type.

Method

Each month interviews are conducted face-to-face in the homes of a fresh representative sample of UK adults aged 15 or over. The sample used is carefully constructed, and leads to named persons for interview. Up to four recalls are made at different times and on different days of the week: no substitutes are used in the sample. By this method, approximately 80 000 interviews are conducted each year in the course of fieldwork.

The questionnaire asks, each calendar month, about trips taken away from home which began in the month prior to interview, and the month before that. The two-month memory period is adopted to obtain the most cost-effective use of the interviews, while minimizing the risk of poor reporting due to failing memory.

Publication of findings

Findings are published annually.

Source: Adapted from *The UK Tourist Statistics*, published jointly by the English Tourist Board, Northern Ireland Tourist Board, Scottish Tourist Board and Wales Tourist Board.

tics. These can be presented for the country as a whole, but they are often more useful if they can be broken down to provide reliable information for specific destination areas. It is common for individual destinations to conduct their own research, and to complement their findings with the general data of a national study.

Methods used

Statistics of domestic tourism are just like those of international tourism in that they are estimates, normally representing informed guesses and subject to different levels of error. Although some countries base them on returns from accommodation establishments, this does not provide proper coverage. It is increasingly common to collect information from the visitors themselves. This is normally done through sample surveys and can take different forms, as follows.

Household surveys

Household surveys are based on a knowledge of the resident population, and provide a balanced view of domestic tourism for pleasure or business purposes. A structured sample of households is constructed and interviewers are employed to collect information using a questionnaire. Questions normally relate to past behaviour, covering trips already made, although studies of intentions are sometimes undertaken. Domestic tourism surveys, national travel surveys and holiday travel surveys (the latter excluding business travel) can all be based on household surveys. They also provide, as a matter of course, information on foreign travel by residents and information on those who do not travel.

Enroute surveys

Enroute surveys are surveys of travellers during the course of their journey. Strategic points are selected to stop or approach people, who are then either interviewed or given a questionnaire or other documentation to complete in their own time for return by post. A major problem with this type of work is that the representativeness of the sample can be in doubt because of incomplete knowledge of traffic movement within a country. There is evidence (see Hurst, 1987) that response rates are optimized by selecting respondents at propitious points in their trip and collecting information *in situ*.

Destination surveys

Surveys are often conducted at popular tourist destinations or in areas where there are high levels of tourist activity. They typically take the form of personal interviews by teams of interviewers. The information provided leads to estimates of the volume and value of tourism to the destination, of profiles of visitors and of their visits. Questions are also asked to elicit opinions about the destination and associated attitudes. It is difficult in this type of work to ensure that the sample of visitors is representative, though efforts are made to ensure a spread across appropriate days and weeks, and that interviews are conducted at a wide range of sites.

Surveys of suppliers

Surveys of the suppliers of tourism services are sometimes undertaken in order to gain information on occupancy rates, visitor numbers, etc. Accommodation occupancy surveys are in fact common worldwide. In North America, airlines have been required through the Civil Aeronautics Board (in the USA) and the Canadian Transport Commission to produce origin and destination data.

RESEARCHING TOURISM MARKETS

The value of research

Many managers and organizations in the tourism industry attach great value to research, using it to place themselves in a strong competitive position.

Sound market intelligence is gained from a variety of formal and informal methods, and bridges the gap between the provider of the product or service and the consumer. Decisions such as those concerning product development and marketing activity can be based on research findings. Moreover, research can be used to highlight specific problems, and even to demonstrate a caring attitude to customers.

We can see that marketing intelligence and marketing research in tourism can therefore:

- Provide information for decision making.
- Keep an organization in touch with its market.
- Identify new markets.
- Monitor the performance of certain aspects of a business.
- Draw attention to specific problems.
- Monitor consumer reaction to a service or facility.
- Reduce waste.
- Demonstrate a caring attitude to the consumer.

However, research is viewed with suspicion by others. It may be seen as an unnecessary cost, taking up valuable resources which could be used in a better way. There may just not be the time for it, given the high level of pressure under which many people work. Others may see research as an essentially academic activity with no real value for the business. In any case, some organizations are able to 'feed off' the research conducted and published by others with greater market share, or to make use of the findings and advice of national and regional tourist offices.

The potential benefits of research vary considerably by type of organization and by size. Major airlines and international hotel chains, for example, collect and analyse data as an aid to making decisions. Individual hotels and attractions often conduct surveys of guests and visitors to gain profile information, opinions and satisfaction ratings. A small restaurant owner or retailer is unlikely to engage in formal research. All businesses monitor sales, however, and all good managers have an instinct for changes in the market place.

The research process

There is no standard way of approaching research. However, it is instructive to model the research process using the flow diagram shown in Figure 6.3, bearing in mind that the stages shown often overlap in time rather than following the precise sequence implied. Some organizations generate research through a planning or marketing department which is able to identify research needs. The reporting of the outcomes can then be fed back into the department concerned for action, and an information base built up. Most organizations, however, generate *ad hoc* projects if and when the need arises.

Research can be undertaken 'in house' by an organization using its own resources, or an external agency may be employed. In either case, the same principles apply and the process is essentially the same. There are numerous reputable organizations – such as advertising agencies, market research agencies, consultants and academic institutions – that offer their services, and which either specialize in research or are experienced in research as part of their activity. A common practice when commissioning research is for the sponsor to issue a detailed brief. Following discussions, external agencies usually submit research proposals, often in competition, the successful one gaining a contract to undertake the research.

The principles we cover in the rest of this chapter are valid not only for research within the tourism industry, but also for students of tourism in a more academic setting. Research projects at all levels of study will benefit from the structure imposed by Figure 6.3.

Agreeing the purpose and setting the objectives

Research based on a clear picture of its purpose is likely to lead to findings which will be of benefit. The overall purpose should be agreed by the major parties concerned. This is particularly important for the many public-sector projects in tourism which have to satisfy or are steered by representatives from a wide range of interested organizations.

Identify the need for research

Agree on research purpose

Establish research objectives

Develop a research design

Implement the chosen approach

Analyse the data

Report the findings

Use the research!

Source: Cooper and Latham (1987)

Fig. 6.3 The research process

The purpose is satisfied through the attainment of the research objectives set. The objectives should always be formally stated, and again agreed. This not only avoids later misunderstanding, but also gives a focus to the research. It is possible later to match findings with the objectives set in order to assess the success of the research.

Research design

A research design is a detailed description or plan;

it can be used to guide the implementation of the research. The most significant decision involved in design concerns the approach to be taken. For example:

- What reliance is to be placed on secondary sources?
- Should a sample survey or group discussions be used?
- Which survey technique – personal interviews, telephone interviews or postal survey?

Primary or secondary data?

Secondary data are those which have already been collected, possibly by some other individual or organization and for some other purpose. In any country the most prolific source is government. Although its data are normally too general in nature to be of practical benefit, they often provide good background information. The same applies to data provided by other national and local bodies such as tourist offices. Before engaging in what may prove to be expensive primary data collection (i.e. of your own), it is worth a researcher identifying and assessing possible sources of information which could supplement primary data or even remove the need for it. There is no point in collecting information that already exists in an accessible form.

CASE STUDY 6.3

Research objectives from a survey of educational visits to the National Maritime Museum

The objectives of the survey were as follows:

- To elicit the profile of educational groups visiting the museum in terms of age, geographical location, sector of school, and size of school group.
- To elicit the profile of visits by educational groups in terms of the number of visits made, whether schools were on a day trip or staying in London, any publicity or event prompting the visit, and the mode of travel.

- A final objective related to the schools' use and opinions of the museum as an educational resource. The survey aimed to discover the level of use of the educational service and also to obtain schools' opinions of the service and the museum, and to identify areas in which the service might be improved.

Source: Cooper and Latham (1987) (unpublished study).

In particular, a tourism enterprise's own records are particularly valuable. Data can be taken from sales invoices, booking forms, general accounts, operating data, internal reports and so on. Many organizations have built up databases over a period of time, and these can form the basis of research data.

Nevertheless, there are times when it is necessary to collect primary data, even though it is normal to supplement this with secondary data.

Methods of collecting primary data

In tourism, the most common method by far is the sample survey, either of visitors themselves or of businesses. The three main types of survey are personal interview, telephone interview and postal survey. The choice as to which to use depends on the nature of the research concerned, and takes account of the advantages and disadvantages of each method.

Visitor surveys at attractions are often based on personal interviews using questionnaires at or near exit points. Telephone interviewing has become increasingly popular. It can be used in its own right or as part of an overall strategy. For example, an occupancy survey may involve contact by telephone, followed by a personal visit and the delivery of self-administered questionnaires. Postal questionnaires are often used when the manager does not have direct access to the user, or as a follow-up when a holiday is sold, using customer addresses. It is also possible to hand out questionnaires for self-completion: for example, on a return holiday flight or return coach journey. There is also scope in tourism for the use of observation methods – in monitoring the popularity of displays or exhibits, or the movement of visitors at open-air sites – but this does not seem to be particularly well developed.

In a detailed study of attitudes or perceptions, it is likely that a qualitative approach will be taken

---

CASE STUDY 6.4

Comparing data collection procedures

Personal interview

Advantages:
- Initial interest can be aroused.
- Complex questioning is possible.
- Visual aids and showcards can be used
- Flexible.
- Shows a caring attitude.
- Visitors are usually happy to co-operate.

Disadvantages:
- Time consuming.
- Administratively difficult.
- Costly.

Telephone interview

Advantages:
- Close supervision and control is possible.
- Access is easy and call-backs are possible.
- Response rates are usually good.
- Many interviews are possible in a given time period.

Disadvantages:
- Visual aids and complex tasks are not possible.
- Only verbal communication is possible.
- Interview is short (people hang up).

Postal surveys

Advantages:
- Low cost.
- No intermediary, so answers are reliable.
- Superior for sensitive questions (confidentiality must be stressed).

Disadvantages:
- Many variables are not controlled, due to absence of interviewer.
- Mailing list is needed.
- Response rates are low.
- Bias due to non-response.
- Detailed or long questionnaires reduce response.

Source: Adapted from Cooper and Latham (1990).

in order to achieve greater insight and understanding. This might involve in-depth interviews or discussions with individuals, say with successful managers to analyse their decision-making processes. It can also involve the formation of discussion groups of between six and ten people, led by an experienced discussant. In this case the interaction between people can stimulate and encourage ideas, or draw out factors such as those which affect holiday choice.

Designing questionnaires

Questionnaires are by far the most common type of form used for primary data collection in tourism. They are difficult to construct, though much easier to criticize, and it is certainly sensible for a researcher to pass round his or her attempts to colleagues for suggested changes. Final versions are usually very different from early drafts. It is important to bear in mind the objectives of the research when constructing a questionnaire, as they give focus to it. The temptation to include questions not relevant to the study, but for interest's sake, should normally be resisted. Their inclusion can lead to a respondent tiring or losing interest, and can put at risk answers to more important questions.

The steps involved in the design of a questionnaire are as follows:

(1) Plan what to measure, based on the objectives of the research.
(2) Formulate the questions.
(3) Decide on the layout and order of questions.
(4) Pilot test the questionnaire.
(5) Correct problems that arise and retest if necessary.

Here are some general guidelines for constructing or assessing the likely effectiveness of a questionnaire:

- Questions should follow a logical order; the questionnaire should flow.
- There should be a simple introduction and early questions should be straightforward.

- Language used should be appropriate to the respondent.
- Questions should be unambiguous.
- Avoid bias within a question, i.e. a question which suggests that a particular answer is acceptable.
- Do not tax the memory of the respondent.
- Instructions on the form (to the interviewer or, in the case of self-completion, the respondent) should be highlighted.
- The questionnaire should be as short as possible.
- The form should be attractive, well laid out and easy to follow.

Sampling

Normally research in tourism seeks to gain information on a large number of people (or sometimes businesses). The term 'population', or 'universe', is used to describe all those under consideration. Examples of populations are all holiday makers at a resort, all businesspeople using hotels in a city, all users of a leisure complex, or all visitors to an attraction.

For populations which are relatively small – say, the 17 coach operators who use a particular stop – it is possible to undertake a census. However, populations are usually large and it is not practical or cost-effective to contact every single member. Instead a sample survey is undertaken. The way in which a sample is constructed is a key element in the research process, since the sample must mirror the population from which it is taken. Then findings based on the sample will be valid for the population as a whole. The technicalities of sampling and the validity of making inferences about populations are complex, and are covered in texts on statistics and research methods.

There are a variety of sampling methods in use. The most common is what might be considered a 'loose' approach, where interviewers are given target numbers of interviews to achieve and are asked to contact a representative spread of people by age and gender. This almost certainly leads to a biased sample. At attractions and passenger termini, it is possible to take the selection of respondent away from the interviewer through the use of 'tighter' procedures such as systematic sampling (say, every twentieth person to pass an exit point).

It is difficult to construct with confidence a representative sample of visitors at a tourist destination such as a resort, or within large recreation areas. This is because visitors are scattered over large areas and their movement is complex. It is normal to take account of the time of year (sample more heavily in the peak months) and to conduct interviews in places that tourists are likely to frequent (attractions, accommodation establishments, shopping centres, places of interest for destinations, popular sites for recreation areas).

Data analysis

Data from questionnaire returns or other data sheets can be input into computer files for analysis. The use of an appropriate software package speeds up the process and assures accuracy within the analysis. The scope of analysis is also increased because the relationships between variables can be examined in depth.

The first stage is often merely establishing counts or frequencies of response. These are often best expressed as percentages. Thus, 40 per cent of visitors are in family groups, 80 per cent arrive by car and so on. This is followed by the 'cross-tabulation' of variables, in which responses to one question are matched with responses to another. An example of output from this form of analysis is: 30 per cent of holiday visitors to the hotel were dissatisfied with the leisure facilities, compared to only 5 per cent of business visitors.

The use of counts and cross-tabulations is sufficient for the majority of studies. More detailed forms of analysis make use of higher-level statistics, and are common in project work undertaken by students registered for higher degrees.

The reporting of research

An essential part of the research process is the final report. This is often accompanied by a formal presentation of findings. The level, method and timing of the reporting should be discussed and agreed at an early stage.

Research results may well confirm what the manager already believed, and thus provide him

---

CASE STUDY 6.5

Towards effective reports: pointers on writing research reports

Presentation

- Reports should be actionable.
- Findings and recommendations should be linked to objectives set.
- There should be a clear summary of findings and recommendations – it is normal for these to appear at the beginning.
- Language should be appropriate and clearly expressed. The main body of the report should be able to be understood by a non-technical manager. Appendices of technical detail should be included if relevant.

Source: Cooper and Latham (1990).

Content

- Background information may be included.
- Research methodology should be included.
- Copies of forms (e.g. blank questionnaire) and letters used in the research should be included, normally as appendices.
- Details of analysis and tables should be clear and easy to understand.
- Diagrams may be used in addition to or instead of tables in order to enhance interpretation.
- Information should be full and complete.
- Appendices should be used for technical or other information that would otherwise detract from the reading of the report.

or her with hard evidence to make a case to others. They can also lead to some surprises and to changes which were not anticipated.

It is a waste of resources to commission research and then not consider the findings. Provided that the research purpose is clear from the beginning and that the objectives set were appropriate to it, the relevance to decision making should be clear. The research report then represents an objective view, relevant to the needs of the organization.

References and further reading

Aaker, D.A., and Day, G.S. (1986) *Marketing Research*, New York: Wiley.

Allard, L. (1989) 'Statistical measurement in tourism', in Witt, S., and Moutinho, L. (eds), *Tourism Marketing and Management Handbook*, London: Prentice Hall.

Baille, J.G. (1985) 'The evolution of Canadian international travel documentation', *Annals of Tourism Research*, vol. 12, no. 4, pp. 563–79.

Begg, D., Fischer, S., and Dornbusch, R. (1991) *Economics*, New York: McGraw-Hill.

British Tourist Authority/English Tourist Board (quarterly) *Tourist Intelligence Quarterly*, London: BTA/ETB.

Churchill, G.A., Jr. (1991) *Marketing Research: Methodological Foundations*, Chicago, Ill.: Dryden Press.

Cooper, C., and Latham, J. (1990) 'A layman's guide to market research for the tourist industry', in *Insights*, London: English Tourist Board.

Easterby-Smith, M., Thorpe, R., and Lowe, A. (1991) *Management Research*, London: Sage.

Gordon, W., and Langmaid, R. (1988) *Qualitative Market Research: A Practitioner's and Buyer's Guide*, Aldershot, UK/Brookfield, USA: Gower.

Hurst, F. (1987) 'Enroute surveys', in Ritchie, J.R.B., and Goeldner, C.R. (eds), *Travel, Tourism and Hospitality Research*: New York: Wiley.

Latham, J. (1989) 'The statistical measurement of tourism', in Cooper, C. (ed.), *Progress in Tourism, Recreation and Hospitality Management*, Vol. 1, London: Belhaven.

McIntosh, R.W., and Goeldner, C.R. (1986) *Tourism: Principles, Practices, Philosophies*, New York: Wiley.

Middleton, V.T.C. (1988) *Marketing in Travel and Tourism*, Oxford: Heinemann.

Organization for Economic Co-operation and Development (annual) *Tourism Policy and International Tourism in OECD Member Countries*, Paris: OECD.

Parasuraman, A. (1991) *Marketing Research*, New York: Addison-Wesley.

Ritchie, J.R.B., and Goeldner, C.R. (eds) (1987) *Travel, Tourism and Hospitality Research*: New York: Wiley.

World Tourism Organization (annual) *Yearbook of Tourism Statistics*, Madrid: WTO.

World Tourism Organization (1984) *Domestic Tourism Statistics*, Madrid: WTO.

CHAPTER 7

Patterns of demand

OVERVIEW

We have already seen that demand for the tourism product is complex, ranging from the family day-trip to a nearby resort to the intercontinental flight of a business traveller. Patterns of demand are therefore difficult to establish. The level of monitoring of domestic travel is highly variable and it is not possible to provide detailed coverage of it.

This chapter concentrates on patterns of demand for international tourism, and provides an historical account with statistical focus of the rapid build-up of international tourism since the Second World War and up to 1990. We show that rates of growth have not been constant, but have tended to decrease with time, and that growth has not been spread evenly across all parts of the world. Over the 40-year period, we can see that tourism globally has shown itself to be resilient against major forces that act against travel – individual destinations are not, of course, immune in the same way. Demand is heavily concentrated in western Europe and North America. However, we can note the emergence of many countries in the East Asia and Pacific region as receivers and generators of international tourism.

We then go on to discuss the analysis of patterns of demand over time. Although this is intended to be an introduction to what is a complex and highly technical subject, it does provide a practical guide to the interpretation of time-series demand data. The points we cover are equally applicable to a wide range of tourism demand, from that for a specific facility, hotel or attraction to that for a country or region. Consideration is given to simple trend analysis, seasonality and other factors influencing demand patterns. Finally, we provide a worked example to illustrate a standard method of deseasonalizing demand data in order to establish the trend and seasonal indexes.

USING TOURISM STATISTICS

Some words of caution

According to the World Tourism Organization, international tourist arrivals in 1990 numbered 455 million. It is not so much the size of this figure that is so impressive, but the fact that anybody should know its value or be able to work it out. In Chapter 6 we detailed methods for measuring tourism demand and it is important to bear them in mind when interpreting the results.

Collecting tourism statistics is time consuming and complex. In some countries it is taken very seriously, to the extent that attempts are made to assess the size of potential errors. It is then possible not merely to provide a point estimate (that is, a single value) of, say, tourist numbers, but to give lower and upper bounds within which the true value is thought to lie. Some countries review their data collection procedures with a view to minimizing errors subject to an acceptable cost. However, not all countries attach the same importance to tourism statistics in general, and to certain measures in particular. For example, the expenditure of incoming tourists normally has high priority attached to it, because of its positive contribution to the balance of payments. On the other hand, the number and spending of tourists who are visiting friends and relatives may be underestimated in countries in which measurement is through serviced accommodation establishments.

It is not surprising, then, that the interpretation of tourism data is fraught with danger. Key points to bear in mind are the following:

- Tourism statistics are normally estimates, often derived from sample surveys. As such, they are liable to various forms of error, many of which are impossible to quantify.
- For measurements which result from sample surveys, in general the smaller the sample size, the greater is the likely error.
- Even though the sample size for data relating to a region or country may give rise to acceptable levels of error, analysis of a subset of the data pertaining to a smaller area or region may not be feasible due to the much reduced sample size.
- Sample size is not everything! The true random sampling of tourists who are, by their very nature, on the move is not normally possible. A sample has to be formally and carefully constructed.
- Where methodology in collecting data changes (even when it is for the better), it is dangerous to compare results.
- There are serious problems involved in attempting either to compare or to combine figures collected by different countries.

The final point arises because there is not only considerable variation in the methods employed by different countries, but also variation in the measures adopted. A notable example is that some countries count tourist arrivals (at least one night spent in the country visited), whereas others prefer to count visitor arrivals (this includes excursionists, i.e. those who do not stay overnight).

Interpreting tourism statistics

What, then, are we to make of the fact that we are told that international tourist arrivals in 1990 worldwide numbered 455 million? This total is certainly arrived at by grossing up figures submitted to the WTO by governments or national bodies throughout the world. Each component

value is subject to different levels of error, arising from different methodologies. It is clear, therefore, that the quoted figure is an estimate, and it is difficult to say how accurate it might be.

The points made above apply more generally than to total international tourist arrivals worldwide. They apply equally to many other situations in which data relating to tourists are collected: at resorts, attractions, passenger termini and so on. However, exact values are not normally what is important and, bearing in mind the shortcomings, we can see that tourism statistics often represent the best estimates available and also provide a guide as to true magnitudes. As a result, they have the following benefits:

- They often provide valuable trend data, where information is produced over a number of time periods.
- They contribute towards a database which may influence decision making, particularly in the areas of marketing, and planning and development.
- They enable the effects of decisions or changes to be monitored.
- They enable current data to be viewed in context.
- They provide a means of making forecasts.

PATTERNS OF DEMAND

An historical view

Since the Second World War, there has been rapid growth worldwide in international tourism (see Tables 7.1 and 7.2, and Figure 7.1). Increasing proportions of the populations of the industrialized nations were in possession of both the time (in the form of paid leave from employment) and the money (due to increased disposable incomes) to engage in international travel. Supply to meet this increased demand for leisure tourism in particular was developed mainly in the form of the standard, mass package tour. This was made possible by the arrival of the jet aircraft in 1958, and by

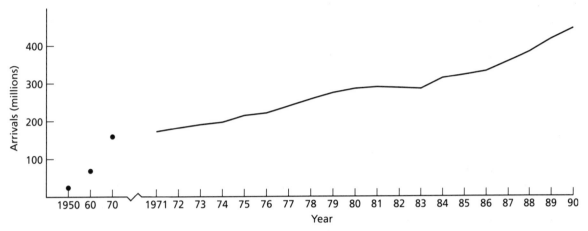

Source: WTO.

Fig 7.1 International travel arrivals, 1950–90

cheap oil. Further, international travel has been boosted by a substantial increase in business travel.

Table 7.1 International tourism trends: arrivals and receipts worldwide, 1950–90

	Arrivals (thousands)	Receipts [a] (US$ million)
1950	25 282	2 100
1960	69 296	6 867
1970	159 690	17 900
1980	284 841	102 372
1981	288 848	104 309
1982	286 780	98 634
1983	284 173	98 395
1984	312 434	109 832
1985	321 240	116 158
1986	330 746	140 019
1987	356 640	171 319
1988	381 824	197 692
1989	415 376	211 366
1990	454 800	255 000
1991	448 500[b]	260 700[b]

[a] Excludes international fare receipts.

[b] Estimate.

Source: World Tourism Organization.

Table 7.2 Rates of growth of international tourism, 1950–90

	Average annual percentage increase	
	Arrivals	Receipts
1950–1960	10.6	12.6
1960–1970	8.7	10.0
1970–1980	6.0	19.1
1980–1990	4.5	9.5
1980–1985	2.5	2.6
1985–1990	6.7	17.0

Note: The average percentage increase is calculated as the constant annual percentage increase which would result in the overall change over the specified period.

Over this period, international tourism has shown itself on a worldwide scale to be robust and resilient against factors such as terrorism and political unrest in many parts of the world, worldwide economic recession and fluctuating exchange rates. Generally, at times of economic growth, demand for travel has increased; on the other hand, at times of recession demand has either remained constant or soon recovered. This global experience of almost uninterrupted growth is not, however, equally shared by all destinations.

For example, tourists tend to stay well clear of any destination that they rightly or wrongly perceive to be unsafe – this has clearly affected tourism to the Middle East and North Africa. Other destinations might suffer because they are just no longer fashionable.

Industrialized and developing countries have become all too aware of the potential of incoming tourism as an invisible export to support the current account of their balance of payments. By 1990 tourism accounted for up to 10 per cent of world trade in goods and services, and could be considered to be one of the world's top three industries, along with oil and motor vehicles. Every day, well over one million people were taking an international trip.

The 1980s: a decade of change

As the market has matured, the average annual growth rate has tended to decrease (Table 7.2). During the period up to 1980, international arrivals doubled every 10 years or so. In contrast, the 1980s experienced a slowing of average annual growth rates to a little over 4 per cent, although growth in the latter half of the decade was in fact more in line with that of the previous two decades.

We can explain this unevenness of tourism demand in the 1980s by a number of major factors and events. The decade opened with economic recession which acted to dampen international travel, and volume did not really recover until 1984. The years 1984 and 1985 were in fact record years with European destinations doing particularly well. However, 1986 witnessed the Chernobyl disaster, terrorist activity, the Libyan bombing incident and the weakening of the US dollar against other major currencies. As a result, international travel was severely affected. The effect was not so much in terms of total numbers, which were up on the previous year anyway, but in terms of tourism flows and changes in the types of trip taken. Many destinations suffered badly, whereas others gained. The second half of the decade saw a return to some sort of normality, both in terms of growth rates and in terms of types of trip taken.

CASE STUDY 7.1

The early 1980s: the effects of recession

CAUSE

● Worldwide economic recession.

EFFECTS

● Falling disposable incomes and increased cost of travel depressed markets.
● Average length of stay fell.
● Cheaper forms of accommodation were used.
● Consumers switched to cheaper or nearer foreign trips, or to domestic trips.

CASE STUDY 7.2

1986: a year of disruption in international travel

CAUSES

- Chernobyl disaster.
- Terrorist activity.
- Fall in value of US dollar.

EFFECTS

- Shift in choice of destination by many Americans away from Europe and North Africa, in favour of countries in the Pacific and within North America itself.
- International tourist arrivals to Africa and the Middle East were down significantly on the previous year.

CASE STUDY 7.3

The early 1990s: the effects of the Gulf War

CAUSE

- The Gulf War.

EFFECTS

Short term
- Initially, virtual cessation of travel to the Gulf and nearby countries.
- Uncertainty for international tourism.
- Gulf War aggravated effects of a recession that was being felt anyway.
- In 1991 international tourist arrivals fell for the first time in a decade (according to provisional estimates).
- Cancellations increased dramatically, occupancies were down (particularly in higher-grade hotels), and tour operators and travel agents specializing in leisure travel were badly affected.

Long term
???

International tourist arrivals grew at an average rate of 4.5 per cent during the 1980s, made up of 2.5 per cent in the first half and 6.7 per cent in the second. These figures could be regarded as reflecting average growth worldwide and therefore conceal considerable variation in performance by region, continent, country or even different destinations within the same country. Some countries (such as Turkey, Hong Kong, Australia, Thailand, China and Portugal) successfully encouraged rapid growth; others experienced either no growth (Ireland) or decreases (Sri Lanka and Lebanon) in visitor numbers.

The 1990s opened with the Gulf War and further economic recession, leading to great uncertainty for international tourism. In the short term, the build-up to the Gulf War, the war itself and the aftermath led initially to the virtual cessation of travel to the Gulf, eastern Mediterranean and North Africa. It also depressed international tourism further afield. The economic recession experienced by the majority of industrialized countries (which would have been severe anyway) was aggravated by it. The lessons of earlier years were that international tourism would recover and develop with new products, destinations and generating markets.

Regional shares of international tourism

Table 7.3 shows over the 40-year period 1950 to 1990 the changes in the share of international tourism worldwide of the different regions. Regional shares have to be viewed in the context of a greatly changing total, and so even a constant share represents substantial growth.

Europe and, to a lesser extent, the Americas have for some time dominated the international travel scene in terms of numbers of arrivals and receipts. More specifically, it is western Europe and North America that have given rise to a high level of geographical concentration of movement. In 1990 western Europe accounted for just over half of all international tourist arrivals, with the European Community alone hosting 40 per cent of the total.

Table 7.3 Regional share of international tourism, 1950–90

	1950 (%)	1960 (%)	1970 (%)	1980 (%)	1990 (%)
(a) Share of arrivals					
Europe	66.5	72.5	70.5	68.4	63.5
Americas	29.6	24.1	23.0	18.9	18.8
East Asia/Pacific	0.8	1.0	3.0	7.0	11.4
Africa	2.1	1.1	1.5	2.5	3.4
Middle East	0.9	1.0	1.4	2.4	2.1
South Asia	0.2	0.3	0.6	0.8	0.7
(b) Share of receipts					
Europe	41.3	56.8	62.0	59.3	54.4
Americas	50.5	35.7	26.8	24.9	26.1
East Asia/Pacific	1.4	2.8	6.2	7.3	14.4
Africa	4.2	2.6	2.2	2.7	1.9
Middle East	2.3	1.5	2.3	4.3	2.5
South Asia	0.3	0.5	0.6	1.5	0.8

Note: Columns do not necessarily add to 100 per cent due to rounding.

We can identify a number of factors which explain the leading position held by Europe:

- Large segments of the populations receive relatively high incomes, resulting in high levels of disposable income.
- Paid leave from work is normal in western European countries.
- High proportions of the populations of, for example, Germany, France and the UK attach very high priority to the annual foreign holiday and are reluctant to let it go even in times of recession.
- There is a wealth of both man-made and natural attractions.
- Demand for foreign travel is satisfied by a large tourist industry and the necessary infrastructure.
- International travel need not involve great distances, due to the number of relatively small countries.

A number of these factors are equally applicable to North America. However, the sheer size of the USA and Canada mean that the majority of their populations prefer to take domestic trips. Nevertheless there are substantial numbers of North Americans who do engage in foreign travel each year, and not merely within their own continent but also on long-haul trips.

The shares of Europe and the Americas have fluctuated somewhat over the years, with some evidence of a decline in terms of both numbers of arrivals and receipts. The clearest trend, though, has been the emergence of countries of the East Asia and Pacific (EAP) region as both receivers and generators of international tourism. The EAP share of arrivals worldwide was only 1 per cent in 1960 but grew to 3 per cent in 1970, 7 per cent in 1980 and 11 per cent in 1990. The increasing share is of an expanding market. This represents remarkable growth in a highly competitive environment. Examples of countries in EAP which have been part of this success are Hong Kong, Singapore, Thailand, Australia, Korea and Indonesia.

We can see that the shares of international tourism of Africa, the Middle East and South Asia have throughout the period 1950 to 1990 been small, though with a high level of fluctuation. As regions, they are not able to compete with Europe, the Americas and EAP in terms of either generating or receiving large numbers of international tourists. The reasons for this are mainly economic. Destination countries within these regions can compete for specific markets from the major generating countries. Many, however, have been vulnerable to the effects of unrest and war, not necessarily in their own countries but near enough for them to be perceived as dangerous places to visit. In general, their incoming international tourism has suffered when business conditions have been depressed in the traditional tourism-generating countries.

Statistics for international travel in each of the regions individually are given in Tables 7.5 to 7.10.

The tables also give lists of the major destination countries in each region, as well as major generating markets.

Table 7.4 Regional summary statistics of international tourism, 1990

	Arrivals (millions)	Average annual growth 1980–90 (%)	Receipts (current US$ bn)	Average annual growth 1980–90 (%)
Africa	15.2	8.0	4.8	5.9
Americas	83.4	4.5	66.5	10.1
EAP	50.8	9.8	36.7	17.2
Europe	281.4	3.7	138.5	8.6
Middle East	9.5	3.2	6.3	3.8
South Asia	3.2	3.4	2.0	2.4
World	443.5	4.5	254.8	9.5

Notes:
1. EAP = East Asia and Pacific.
2. The average annual growth is calculated as the constant annual percentage increase which would result in the overall change over the specified period.

Table 7.5 International tourism in Africa

International tourist arrivals, 1990	15.2 million
International tourism receipts, 1990	US$4.8 billion
Receipts as a percentage of exports, 1989	8.9%
Receipts as a percentage of services, 1989	41.3%

Major destination countries in Africa	*Major generating markets for Africa*
Tunisia	France
Morocco	Germany
Algeria	UK
S. Africa	Italy
Botswana	USA
Kenya	Spain
Zimbabwe	Switzerland
Swaziland	Netherlands

Source: World Tourism Organization.

Table 7.6 International tourism in the Americas

International tourist arrivals, 1990	83.4 million
International tourism receipts, 1990	US$66.4 billion
Receipts as a percentage of exports, 1989	9.2%
Receipts as a percentage of services, 1989	18.8%

Major destination countries in the Americas		*Major generating markets for the Americas*	
USA	Puerto Rico	USA	UK
Canada	Dominican Rep.	Canada	Germany
Mexico	Bahamas	Mexico	France
Argentina	Brazil	Japan	Scandinavia

Source: World Tourism Organization.

Table 7.7 International tourism in East Asia and the Pacific

International tourist arrivals, 1990	50.8 million
International tourism receipts, 1990	US$36.7 billion
Receipts as a percentage of exports, 1989	4.8%
Receipts as a percentage of services, 1989	15.1%

Major destination countries in East Asia and the Pacific		*Major generating markets for East Asia and the Pacific*	
China	Malaysia	Japan	UK
Hong Kong	Japan	USA	Germany
Thailand	Korea	Korea	Thailand
Singapore	Australia	Australia	New Zealand

Source: World Tourism Organization.

Table 7.8 International tourism in Europe

International tourist arrivals, 1990	281.4 million
International tourism receipts, 1990	US$138.5 billion
Receipts as a percentage of exports, 1989	6.7%
Receipts as a percentage of services, 1989	15.1%

Major destination countries in Europe		*Major generating markets for Europe*	
France	Austria	Germany	Netherlands
Spain	UK	UK	France
Italy	Germany	Italy	Scandinavia
Hungary	Switzerland	USA	Belgium

Source: World Tourism Organization.

Table 7.9 International tourism in Middle East

International tourist arrivals, 1990	9.5 million
International tourism receipts, 1990	US$6.3 billion
Receipts as a percentage of exports, 1989	9.6%
Receipts as a percentage of services, 1989	21.8%

Major destination countries in the Middle East	*Major generating markets for the Middle East*
Jordan	Egypt
Egypt	Jordan
Israel	USA
Saudi Arabia	Germany
Iraq	UK
United Arab Emirates	France
Syria	Turkey
Bahrain	Italy

Note: The above lists are based on provisional estimates of international tourist arrivals in 1990: that is, the year prior to the Gulf War.

Source: World Tourism Organization.

Table 7.10 International tourism in South Asia

International tourist arrivals, 1990	3.2 million
International tourism receipts, 1990	US$2.0 billion
Receipts as a percentage of exports, 1989	5.1%
Receipts as a percentage of services, 1989	21.8%

Major destination countries in South Asia	*Major generating markets for South Asia*
India	UK
Pakistan	India
Sri Lanka	USA
Nepal	Germany
Maldives	France
Bangladesh	Japan
Iran	Italy

Source: World Tourism Organization.

International tourism flows

Table 7.11 provides a guide to international tourism flows worldwide. It is in effect a numerical and practical summary of the complex movement of travellers. Although it would be possible to construct something similar for a large number of key countries, it would then be difficult to gain the same level of insight and understanding. The table shows movement between regions, and thus provides measures of intercontinental travel. However, it also shows international movement within regions, and thus provides measures of international travel within continents. Naturally, this latter type of movement far outstrips intercontinental travel.

If we take the two largest figures in Table 7.11, it is clear that the vast majority of international travel worldwide takes place either within Europe (for example, the British to France or Germans to Spain) or within the Americas (for example, travel between the USA and Canada). This is then followed by travel within EAP (for example, from Japan to Thailand). The major intercontinental travel, by far, occurs between the Americas and

Europe, and in particular between North America and western Europe. This results not merely from a desire of substantial segments of the main populations to engage in such travel. The other major influencing factor is the readily available provision of flights across the Atlantic, and at prices that large segments of the populations can afford.

The other major flows exhibited by the table are those from Europe to EAP, the Middle East and Africa; within Africa and within the Middle East; from the Americas to EAP; and from EAP to the Americas and Europe.

Tourism destination countries

The major destination countries for international tourism are listed in Table 7.12. At the top of this list are countries of western Europe and North America, for reasons already described in this chapter. Had the table been extended, the relatively recent and dramatic emergence of the East Asia and Pacific region would have been apparent through Singapore, Thailand, Malaysia, Korea, Australia and Indonesia.

Table 7.11 Flows of international tourism, 1990 (millions)

	Inbound to:					
	Africa	Americas	EAP	Europe	Middle East	South Asia
Outbound from:						
Africa	5.9	0.2	*	0.8	1.3	*
Americas	0.6	58.9	4.6	18.8	0.7	0.3
EAP	0.2	5.8	22.3	5.7	0.2	0.4
Europe	5.6	11.0	6.2	240.2	5.8	1.2
Middle East	0.6	0.4	0.1	0.7	4.0	0.2
South Asia	*	0.3	0.9	0.2	0.6	1.0

Notes:

*less than 0.1 million.

1. EAP=East Asia and the Pacific.

2. The table shows international tourism flows across regions of the world. Thus, for example, the number of international arrivals from the Americas to countries of Europe in 1990 was 18.8 million.

3. It also shows international flows within regions. For example, the number of international tourist arrivals to countries of Africa from (other) African countries in 1990 was 5.9 million.

Source: Adapted from World Tourism Organization data.

Table 7.12 The top 20 destination countries for international tourism, based on numbers of international tourist arrivals in 1990

	Country	Tourist arrivals (million)	Rank 1980	Average annual growth rate 1980–90 (%)
1	France	50.0	1	5.2
2	USA	39.8	3	5.9
3	Spain	34.3	2	3.9
4	Italy	26.7	4	1.9
5	Hungary	20.5	9	8.1
6	Austria	19.0	5	3.2
7	UK	18.0	7	3.8
8	Germany	17.0	8	4.4
9	Canada	15.3	6	1.7
10	Switzerland	13.0	10	3.9
11	China	10.5[a]	13	6.3
12	Greece	8.9	18	6.3
13	Czechoslovakia	8.1[a]	17	4.8
14	Portugal	8.0	21	11.5
15	Yugoslavia	7.9	12	2.1
16	USSR	7.2	15	2.6
17	Mexico	6.4	19	4.4
18	Hong Kong	5.9	27	13.0
19	Netherlands	5.8	20	7.6
20	Turkey	5.4	43	19.3

Notes:

[a]Preliminary estimate.
The top five destinations as measured by international tourism receipts in rank order are the USA, France, Italy, Spain and the UK.

Source: World Tourism Organization.

More general points to note are as follows:

- Traditional destinations tend to dominate any list of top tourist receivers, with some inroads being made by emerging destinations.
- There are a large number of countries in the world with over one million international tourist arrivals (in 1990 there were about 50), and a significant number with over five million (23 in 1990).
- The ordering of top tourism destinations by receipts would not be the same as that by arrivals. This is because of different patterns of spending at different destinations. The world's top international tourism earners in 1990 were the USA, France, Italy, Spain and the UK.

Generators of international tourism

The major generating countries of international tourism, based on expenditure, are listed in Table 7.13. The list is dominated by countries of western Europe and North America, with the notable exception of Japan. Japan has in recent years developed a policy of strong encouragement of foreign travel, mainly to help offset an embarrassing positive balance of payments. There is much commonality between lists of top destinations and receiving countries. It tends in fact to be

Table 7.13 The top 20 generating countries of international tourism, based on international tourism expenditures in 1990

	Country	Tourism expenditure (US$bn)	Rank 1980	Average annual growth rate 1980–90 (%)
1	USA	38.7	2	14.1
2	Germany	30.1	1	3.9
3	Japan	24.9	6	18.4
4	UK	19.8	3	11.1
5	Italy	13.8	13	21.9
6	France	13.5	4	8.4
7	Canada	8.4	9	10.4
8	Netherlands	7.4	5	4.7
9	Austria	6.3	10	8.2
10	Switzerland	6.0	11	9.9
11	Sweden	6.0	12	10.4
12	Belgium	5.7	8	5.6
13	Mexico[a]	5.4	7	2.6
14	Spain	4.3	18	13.2
15	Australia	4.1	15	8.9
16	Denmark	3.7	16	9.1
17	Norway	3.4	17	10.0
18	Korea, Rep. of	3.2	28	24.6
19	Finland	2.8	22	17.7
20	Singapore	1.4	29	15.9

Note:

[a]For Mexico, data are not strictly comparable due to change in methodology as from 1982.

Source: World Tourism Organization.

CASE STUDY 7.4

Characteristics of generating markets

A specific country's market normally has the following features:

- It includes at least one of the four top generators of international tourism worldwide – Germany, the USA, Japan and the UK.
- It includes neighbouring states, since the distance and cost involved are relatively small.
- It includes countries further afield if, as is the case between the USA and western Europe, air travel is available and at a cost within the reach of large segments of the population.

- It depends on the size of the population of generating states and their propensity to travel.
- It depends on ease of movement across borders.
- It depends on the real and perceived price of trips to the destination.
- It depends on the attractiveness of the destination.
- It depends on the social, cultural and historic links between countries.
- It depends on marketing activity and an appropriate supply in terms of transport, accommodation, etc.

---

the major industrialized nations that engage heavily in international tourism, and between which are the major tourism flows.

The major generators of international tourism are regarded worldwide as key markets to attract, and thereby to boost (often ailing) balances of payments through invisible exports. Accounting for almost half of all international tourism spending in the world in 1990, the top four generators – the USA, Germany, Japan and the UK – are important markets worldwide, and not solely in their own backyards.

ANALYSING PATTERNS OF DEMAND OVER TIME

Trends

An analysis of tourism demand in the long term requires an examination of trends. This involves consideration of various qualitative aspects of demand and supply, including the following:

- Fashion: destinations, or even countries, may become more or less fashionable with tourists over time.
- The quality of the product: this may change with time due, for example, to overcrowding or to increased or lack of investment.

There are numerous quantitative approaches to analysing patterns of demand, ranging from the simplistic to the highly technical. At the complex end of the spectrum is econometric modelling, using multiple regression. A mathematical relationship is sought which establishes demand as a function of influencing variables (such as income of populations in the generating markets, price of the tourism product, and time). However, for most managers who work within tourism such an approach is neither possible nor beneficial. It is far more important to be able to undertake relatively simple analyses in order to interpret demand data, and to highlight trends and clear changes in trends.

A recommended first step in the search for a trend within demand data is to sketch or draw a graph showing demand over time. It may be possible to describe the movement simply. The four diagrams in Figure 7.2 provide simple illustrations of patterns of demand over a period of time. The continuous lines drawn are suggested models which 'fit' the given demand values and which may then be used to describe the demand and, if required, to project future demand by extrapolation.

The process of formally fitting a line or curve to data to produce a model of demand is called *trend curve analysis*. In many cases, this can be done

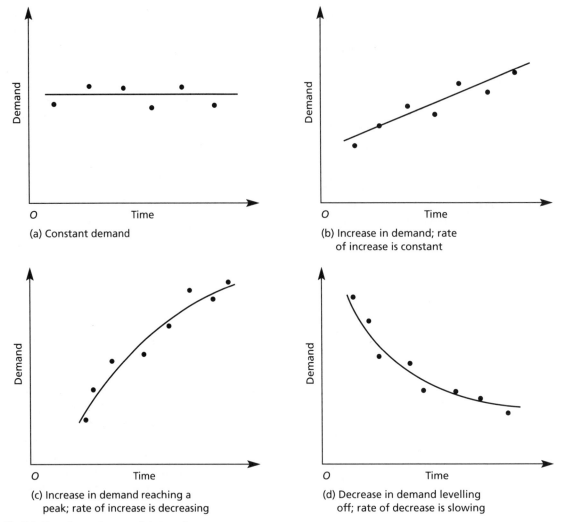

Fig 7.2 Regular patterns of demand

'by eye', without employing statistical methods. Should the importance of the analysis require a more formal and rigorous approach, then standard regression analysis can be employed to find a curve of best fit. Software packages, such as spreadsheets or statistics, will perform what were once tiresome calculations, and even inexpensive electronic calculators often have the facility to produce regression output. In this way, and using transformations of variables, a wide range of demand patterns can be analysed.

Seasonality

We know that, within most patterns of demand in tourism, there are regular fluctuations due solely to the time of year. This phenomenon is called *seasonality*. It is often the result of changes in climate over the calendar year. Thus a destination which is essentially attractive because of its beaches and hot summers is likely to have a highly seasonal demand. The same applies to demand for holidays at a ski resort which has snow for only part of the year. There are, however, other influencing factors, such as the timing of school and work holidays, or regular special events held at a destination.

As tourism is a service industry, it is not possible merely to stockpile the product – a hotel room which is unsold on a particular night, an unsold seat on a flight, or an unsold theatre ticket all have an economic value of zero. Seasonality of demand therefore causes major problems for the tourist industry. It can result in only seasonal employment for employees, and the underuse or even closing down of facilities at certain times of the year. It can also result in an overstretching by some destinations and businesses at times of peak activity, to compensate for low demand off-season. This leads to overcrowding, overbookings and high prices, and ultimately to customer dissatisfaction and a worsening reputation.

Responses vary to seasonality and the need to reduce it. Typically, they involve attempts to create or shift demand to the shoulder or trough months, either through setting price differentials or through the introduction or enhancement of all-year facilities. Marketing may be targeted at groups which have the time and resources to travel at any time of the year, notably the elderly. Two examples of successful responses are the following:

● While Michigan was once viewed primarily as a summer destination, the development and promotion of winter sports in resort areas, foliage tours, and superb salmon fishing in the autumn and spring have created new markets for these off-season periods (McIntosh and Goeldner, 1986).

● In the late 1980s, a number of Center Parcs were opened in northern Europe. These are holiday villages set in woodland which offer all-weather facilities, such as a large indoor water complex and various sporting and leisure pursuits. Demand for short breaks is high throughout the year.

Figure 7.3 illustrates a pattern of demand which is seasonal. In this particular example, there is seen to be an upward general trend, with much seasonal variation about this trend. When attaching quantitative measures to the influence of seasonality, we need to distinguish between additive and multiplicative effects:

● *Additive seasonality* refers to the addition of demand at certain times of the year to the trend. For example, in August there may be an extra 100 000 visitors, and in February 75 000 fewer, both purely because of the time of year.

● *Multiplicative seasonality* refers to the proportional increase or decrease of the trend at certain times of the year. For example, August may be double the trend, whereas February is 40 per cent of the trend, both purely because of the time of year.

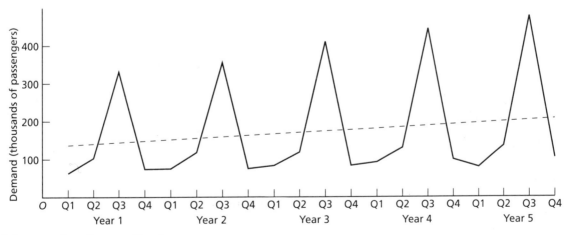

Note: – – – – shows the upward trend.

Fig. 7.3 A pattern of seasonal demand (artificial)

Additive seasonality implies that, with an increasing trend, the difference between actual demand and the trend value remains constant for any particular month. On the other hand, multiplicative seasonality would imply that the difference (the extra demand due to the seasonal effect) would increase in proportion. In practice, most seasonal demand data in tourism are multiplicative.

The analysis of seasonal demand is through the standard decomposition of a time series. Demand D in a particular month is written as the product

$$D = T \times S \times R$$

where T is the trend value for that month, S is the seasonal index for that month, and R is a random or unpredictable element. Here it has been assumed that seasonality is multiplicative. A worked example is given at the end of this chapter which illustrates the construction of this form of model, and shows how forecasts can then be derived for future demand.

Other calendar effects

In an analysis of monthly demand data, note is often taken of the number of days in the month. Even with identical daily demand in January and February, one would expect their monthly demand figures to differ by about 10 per cent.

There can be substantially different levels of demand for the tourism product on different days of the same week, depending on the precise business or activity involved. Hotels often experience differences in room bookings at weekends compared to weekdays. This is particularly the case where a hotel is able to fill with businesspeople during the week at high rates, and achieves at best only reasonable occupancy at weekends through special offers. Sundays are often 'dead' nights for large, city-centre hotels. Attractions or recreation sites often attract more visitors at weekends than on weekdays.

Certain destinations receive tourists on certain days of a month as determined by passenger transport schedules. This can affect tourism businesses, and needs to be taken into account when comparing sales in the same month of successive years – there may, for example, be four Saturdays in August one year, and five the next.

Our normal calendar can also affect the way demand data are analysed. This is particularly the case for Easter, which occurs in different weeks of successive years. It can be in March or April. Thus comparing monthly figures year on year for these two months can be misleading, particularly if Easter is a period of high demand. Other national holidays may cause problems for the business analyst, since demand is affected considerably. The comparison of a week's business with that of the corresponding week of the previous year should take account of the dates of bank holidays and so on.

Cycles

Like any business activity, tourism is subject to and part of general economic cycles. Also regular events such as festivals, games or exhibitions cause cycles in tourism movement.

Irregularity

In the latter part of this chapter we have described the main components of tourism demand which can be identified, and which can be isolated if required. Aspects of demand introduced here can be developed into formal and often complex models. However, it has to be recognized that even the most complete analysis of a pattern of tourism demand provides a model which will vary from the true demand by some degree. All series contain elements of the irregular, random or unpredictable. These can take the form of sudden price changes, epidemics, floods, unseasonal weather or even wars.

Forecasting

A major use of the analysis of demand is to provide estimates of future values.

Worked example

Table 7.14 shows the (artificial) quarterly demand for trips on the Smithson ferry over a five-year period. It is required to construct a model for this demand, and hence to produce forecasts for the following year.

Table 7.14 Demand (thousands of passengers)

Year	Quarter			
	Q1	Q2	Q3	Q4
1	63	103	331	74
2	75	118	355	75
3	83	118	410	83
4	92	130	444	99
5	79	135	477	103

Even a cursory glance at the data shows us that demand is highly seasonal. Quarter 3 is the peak season of the year. By considering any of the four quarters over the five-year period, there is clear evidence of upward movement, so at this stage it is expected that the analysis will identify an increasing trend. It can be noted that demand in year 5, quarter 1, is not in line with the previous values for the same quarter, and hence is unusual.

The aim is to construct a multiplicative model for the demand D of the form described earlier: that is,

$$D = T \times S \times R$$

where T is the trend value for that quarter, S is the seasonal index for that quarter, and R is the random or unpredictable element.

The first stage is to compute a four-quarter moving average. For each four consecutive values in the series, their average is calculated and is set against the middle of that time period. For example, take the four consecutive values starting with year 4, quarter 2; these values are 130, 444, 99, 79. Their average is 188 and this is set against the middle of the time period in Table 7.15. Note that, since the four values taken cover all quarters of the year, their average is 'deseasonalized'.

Table 7.15 Demand (thousands of passengers)

Year	Quarter			
	Q1	Q2	Q3	Q4
1 Original series	63	103	331	74
4-quarter m.a.		142.75	145.75	149.5
Centred m.a.			144	148
2 Original series	75	118	355	75
4-quarter m.a.	155.5	155.75	157.75	157.75
Centred m.a.	153	156	157	158
3 Original series	83	118	410	83
4-quarter m.a.	171.5	173.5	175.75	178.75
Centred m.a.	165	173	175	177
4 Original series	92	130	444	99
4-quarter m.a.	187.25	191.25	188	189.25
Centred m.a.	183	189	190	189
5 Original series	79	135	477	103
4-quarter m.a.	197.5	198.5		
Centred m.a.	194	198		

Note: m.a. = moving average.

The four-quarter moving averages are now centred as shown, so as to correspond with the given quarterly time periods. For example, the first two four-quarter moving averages 142.75 and 145.75 are averaged to give 144 (to the nearest whole number). In this way, each consecutive pair is converted to a centred moving average.

A table showing seasonal indexes can now be produced. The centred moving averages, having been constructed using all seasons of the year, are divided (one by one) by the demand figures of Table 7.14 to produce a seasonality factor for each period of time. The answers are normally multiplied by 100 to give a percentage. So, for example, using Tables 7.14 and 7.15, the seasonality factor for year 1, quarter 3, is equal to:

$$(331/144) \times 100 = 230\%$$

Table 7.16 Seasonal index of demand

Year	Quarter			
	Q1	Q2	Q3	Q4
1			230	50
2	49	76	226	47
3	50	68	234	47
4	50	69	234	52
5	41	68		
Average (seasonal index)	48	70	231	49

The average of the seasonal factors for each quarter is calculated and shown at the foot of Table 7.16. These four values are the seasonal indexes of demand.

Using standard simple regression analysis based on the centred moving averages of Table 7.15, trend values can be calculated for any time period. The regression line in fact has the equation:

$$\text{Trend} = 133.3 + 3.67 \times t$$

where t = time, starting with the value 1 at year 1, quarter 1; the value 2 at year 1, quarter 2, and so on. Figure 7.4 shows the original data together with this trend line.

Incidentally, regression output gives a correlation coefficient of 0.99, indicating an excellent straight-line fit to the centred moving averages. Substituting $t = 1, 2 \ldots 20$ into the equation for the regression line, and taking trend values to the nearest whole number, the results are as shown in Table 7.17.

Table 7.17 Trend (thousands of passengers)

Year	Quarter			
	Q1	Q2	Q3	Q4
1	137	140	144	148
2	152	155	159	163
3	166	170	174	177
4	181	185	188	192
5	196	199	203	207

Since the original demand data are to be modelled by the product $T \times S \times R$, dividing the values by the corresponding trend value of Table 7.17, and then by the appropriate seasonal index from the base of Table 7.16, produces for each period of time the random element R. For example, for year 1, quarter 1, it is calculated as

$$(63/48\%)/137 = 95.8$$

Table 7.18 represents a complete table of values of R, given to the nearest whole number.

Table 7.18 Residual index of demand (%)

Year	Quarter			
	Q1	Q2	Q3	Q4
1	96	105	100	102
2	103	109	97	94
3	104	99	102	96
4	106	100	102	105
5	84	97	102	102

These values represent the extent to which demand is made up of the trend identified, combined with the seasonal index. Where the value of R is close to 100 per cent, the random or unpredictable element is negligible in its effect. Only in the case of year 5, quarter 1, is there a sizeable effect on demand due to R. Demand in this quarter could not have been predicted (by this model) because of some random event, which would in practice probably be known.

In order to use the model of demand established to forecast future demand, it is simply a matter of forming for any particular future time period the product of the trend value for that period (found using the regression-line equation), and the appropriate seasonal index from the base of Table 7.16. Some results are shown in Table 7.19. This method is only suitable for short-term forecasting.

Table 7.19 Forecasts of demand for year 6

Year 6	Quarter			
	Q1	Q2	Q3	Q4
Trend (000s)	210	214	218	221
Seasonal index (%)	48	70	231	49
Forecast (000s)	101	150	504	108

Taking into account that passenger numbers throughout have been in thousands, the forecasts of demand for year 6 are as follows:

Quarter 1	101 000
2	150 000
3	504 000
4	108 000

References and further reading

Allcock, J.B. (1989) 'Seasonality', in Witt, S.F., and Moutinho, L. (eds), *Tourism Marketing and Management Handbook*, Hemel Hempstead: Prentice Hall.

Archer, B.H. (1989a) 'Trends in international tourism', in Witt, S.F., and Moutinho, L. (eds), *Tourism Marketing and Management Handbook*, Hemel Hempstead: Prentice Hall.

Archer, B.H. (1989b) 'Demand forecasting and estimation', in Ritchie, J.R.B., and Goeldner, C.R. (eds), *Travel, Tourism and Hospitality Research*, New York: Wiley.

Boniface, B., and Cooper, C. (1987) *The Geography of Travel and Tourism*, London: Heinemann.

Goeldner, C.R. (1991) '1990: a year of transition', *Journal of Travel Research*, vol. 29, no. 4, pp. 47–50.

Latham, J. (1991) 'Statistical trends in tourism, up to 1989', in Cooper, C. (ed.). *Progress in Tourism, Recreation and Hospitality Management*, Vol. 3, London: Belhaven.

Latham, J. (1992) 'International tourism statistics', in Cooper, C. (ed.), *Progress in Tourism, Recreation and Hospitality Management*, Vol. 4, London: Belhaven.

McIntosh, R.W., and Goeldner, C.R. (1986) *Tourism : Principles, Practices and Philosophies*, New York: Wiley.

Organization for Economic Co-operation and Development (annual) *Tourism Policy and International Tourism in OECD Member Countries*, Paris: OECD.

Owen, F., and Jones, R. (1990) *Statistics*, London: Pitman.

Shackleford, P. (1987) 'Global tourism trends', *Tourism Management*, vol. 18, no. 2, pp. 98–101.

Witt, S.F., and Martin, C.A. (1989) 'Demand forecasting in tourism and recreation', in Cooper, C. (ed.), *Progress in Tourism, Recreation and Hospitality Management*, Vol. 1, London: Belhaven.

Witt, S.F., Brooke, M.Z., and Buckley, P.J. (1991) *The Management of International Tourism*, London: Unwin Hyman.

World Tourism Organization (quarterly) *Travel and Tourism Barometer*, Madrid: WTO.

World Tourism Organization (1991) *Impact of the Gulf Crisis on International Tourism (Special Report)*, Madrid: WTO.

World Tourism Organization (1992) *Tourism Trends Worldwide 1950–1991*, Madrid: WTO.

PART 2

The tourist destination

CHAPTER 8

Introduction

Returning to Leiper's (1990) tourism system (see p.3, Chapter 1), the destination region is perhaps one of the most important elements. The destination represents the *raison d'être* for tourism; it is the reason for travelling, and the attractions at the destination generate the visit. At the same time, because of the inseparable nature of tourism consumption – it is consumed where it is produced – the destination comes under considerable pressure from high levels of demand focused both in time and at specific sites. In many cases the destination itself, again because of the nature of tourism, is a valued, vulnerable and/or unique resource at risk from alteration by tourist pressure. Clearly, as tourism demand has risen many more places have succumbed to this threat.

The careful professional management and planning of the destination is therefore critical if tourism is to conserve its destinations and to be perceived as an 'acceptable' industry in a world which is now sensitive to environmental issues. In this part of the book we examine these issues in detail, drawing on international examples and providing both a way of thinking about the destination and consideration of 'state of the art' planning, management and impact measurement techniques.

We begin by providing an overview of the patterns and characteristics of the supply of tourism. A major problem in the tourism literature is that, while there are many case studies of tourism destinations, there are few writers who attempt to generalize and draw out the common characteristics of tourism supply. Yet, as Chapter 9 shows, there are a number of common characteristics and approaches which can be used to generalize. First, all destinations are made up of an amalgam of facilities, attractions and transportation. Until all the elements are in place the tourism service cannot be performed, and in addition there needs to be a consistency of quality across the elements. For purpose-built destinations this is relatively easy to plan, but for most destinations it is difficult to co-ordinate the offerings made by a mosaic of enterprises and other providers.

Destinations are also perishable, not only in the sense that they can be altered by tourist pressure, but also, as for all services, because if they are not consumed they are lost – they cannot be stored. However, we must not forget the tourist in our consideration of the destination. Destinations are cultural appraisals. If the visitor does not feel that a place is worthy of visit then it will disappear from the tourist map. For many destinations this is less of a problem as tourism is not the primary economic activity anyway. In fact tourism commonly has to be 'fitted in' with other uses and is often resented as a land use.

Of course, destinations are not static – they change and evolve as new markets and new providers enter and leave. The idea of a tourist area lifecycle can therefore be applied to destinations as a framework for considering the interaction between demand and supply and also as a way of thinking about the longer-term implications of tourism development. It is the longer-term perspective that is embodied in the idea of 'sustainable' tourism development. The concept of sustainable development demands a long-term view to ensure that tourism consumption does not exceed the ability of the host destination to provide for it. Sustainability also raises the issue of carrying capacity – the ability of the destination to take use without deteriorating. None of these concepts is new. In geography and resource management they have been utilized for many years. The fact that tourism has belatedly discovered these approaches is to be welcomed, although it is unfortunate that the quality of some of the writing and analysis surrounding these issues, and the consequent call for alternative forms of tourism, is superficial.

A major issue in relation to the destination is the impact of tourism. In Chapters 10 and 11 we provide an in-depth examination of the nature of these impacts and their measurement. In the past, economic impact assessment has dominated. This is not only because the impacts are more easily measured and the data are available, but also because the sponsors of the research felt that the findings would be optimistic – which indeed they were, showing the positive benefits of tourism spending and employment. However, in recent years these benefits have been increasingly questioned when set against the negative impacts of tourism upon the host community and environment. Unfortunately, techniques of impact assessment in these areas are nowhere near as well developed as they are for economic impact assessment. This is partly due to the complexity of measuring social and environmental impacts. Not only is it difficult to take into account the full range of impacts on, say, an ecosystem, but also the data relating to the position before tourism intervened are often lacking. Moreover, it is sometimes difficult to determine the true extent of tourism's involvement in, for example, social change when set in the context of other variables, such as the mass media. However, in many cases tourism can become a scapegoat. As we demonstrate in Chapters 10 and 11, the impact of tourism is a complex issue, influenced by the type of tourism involved, the nature of the destination and the level of planning and management.

Clearly, effective planning and management of tourism is essential at the destination. In Chapter 12 we present an overview of the tourism planning and management process at the destination. Planning and management are essential to maintain the integrity of the destination, to ensure that the destination's unique attributes are protected and to prevent the ubiquitous 'tourism landscapes' of sunset strips. The process of tourism planning is now well established, yet there are many barriers to its effective implementation. These include the nature of the industry, which often resents planning; the expense of planning; and poorly formulated plans. In Chapter 12 we provide a detailed analysis of why plans fail, since this contributes to the poor reputation of tourism at some destinations associated with the negative impact of unrestrained development.

Some general issues and trends relating to the destination therefore emerge from this part of the book:

- The notions of sustainable development and carrying capacity will become central to the management of destinations in the 1990s.
- The measurement of tourism's environmental and sociocultural impacts is not yet as developed as that of its economic impacts. However, this situation is slowly being addressed.
- New, more robust types of destination are being developed which will take pressure from the more fragile and unique places in the world.
- Planning and management of destinations will become more acceptable and professional in the 1990s.
- Tourism development will no longer be able to abandon resorts which have gone into decline, but strategies will need to be devised to rejuvenate such destinations. After all, mass international tourism is a young industry and this problem is only now emerging.

As with the other elements of tourism, the destination cannot be divorced from demand, marketing or the industry. Demand for tourism very often shapes the nature of development at a destination, while the cohesion and professionalism of the industry, and in particular the transportation system and the public sector, can make or break a destination. The marketing activities of public-sector agencies such as convention and visitor bureaus are well known, but increasingly the issues surrounding the marketing of tourist destinations are being debated as the implications for the host culture are found to be considerable. Finally, the co-ordination of the promotional theme with the actual experience at the destination is becoming important.

CHAPTER 9

Patterns and characteristics of the supply of tourism

OVERVIEW

Without the richness and variety of tourism environments around the world we would not have the same quality of tourist experience. In this chapter we introduce the characteristics of tourism supply and outline the key issues involved. You will see that, in order to understand the supply of tourism, consideration has to be given to the differing environmental, social and economic contexts around the world within which tourism destinations are located. Tourism supply represents an amalgam, or mix, of attractions and support facilities which demonstrate a number of common features. These include the fact that destinations are cultural appraisals; they are perishable because tourism is consumed where it is produced; destinations involve multiple use of tourism with other uses; and to be successful the components of the amalgam need to be of equivalent quality.

It is important for the destination to deliver a quality experience and product, and in this regard, careful planning and management is essential to ensure a tourism industry based on sustainable principles. We contend that central to the issue of sustainability is the concept of carrying capacity. We also introduce the idea of a destination evolving over time and continuing to do so, in order to provide a future range of destinations where technology, authenticity and professionalism will dominate.

THE DESTINATION AS A FOCUS FOR TOURISM

The supply of tourism demonstrates a complex pattern across the world because it is located in diverse environments and in differing economic and social contexts. The supply of tourism is also continually expanding as the 'pleasure periphery' reaches ever more distant and remote locations.

The tourist destination, however defined geographically, provides a convenient focus for the examination of the tourist movement and its impact and significance. Indeed, the destination brings together all aspects of tourism – demand, transportation, supply and marketing – in a useful framework. It represents the third element of Leiper's tourism system, but in many respects the most important one because destinations, and their images, attract tourists, motivate the visit and therefore energize the whole tourism system. We can therefore see that the destination is where the most significant and dramatic elements of tourism occur and where the inbound tourism industry is located: that is, where the attractions and all the other support facilities needed by the visitor are found.

As the demand for tourism has increased, pressure from the growing number of visitors – often concentrated into a short season – has degraded some destinations. In response, planning and management strategies have been implemented in the busier destinations; indeed, planning and management are the key to making existing tourist destinations and resources more effective in meeting demand. In this respect, the operation of major tourist destinations is increasingly co-ordinated by a 'destination marketing/management oranization' (dmo) or 'convention and visitor bureau' (cvb).

We can think of a destination as 'the focus of facilities and services designed to meet the needs of the tourist'. Most destinations comprise a core of the following components, which can be characterized as the four As:

- Attractions.
- Access (local transport, transport terminals).
- Amenities (accommodation, food and beverage outlets, entertainment, retailing and other services).
- Ancillary services, in the form of local organizations (dmo, cvb).

Of course, each of these components has to be in place before tourism can be supported – accommodation alone, for example, will rarely suffice (except perhaps in the case of major luxury hotels such as the Savoy or the Ritz). The mix of facilities and services at a destination is therefore known as an *amalgam* – the complete mix has to be present for it to work and the tourism experience to be delivered.

This amalgamation of the components of a destination comes together in many different ways, and in many different cultural, economic and environmental contexts to create the range of destinations available. These include coastal resorts, mountain resorts, historic towns and cities, festivals and events, single purpose-built destinations – such as Euro-Disneyland – and conference/meeting complexes for business travellers.

COMMON FEATURES OF TOURIST DESTINATIONS

We believe, however, that the diversity of tourist destinations can be clarified by identifying their common features. These include the following:

- Destinations are cultural appraisals.
- They are inseparable: that is, tourism is produced where it is consumed.

- They are used not just by tourists but also by many other groups.
- The various elements of the destination have to be complementary.

Cultural appraisals

Visitors have to consider a destination to be attractive and worth the investment of time and money to visit. Because of this we can think of destinations as cultural appraisals. For example, Victorian tourists visited English abattoirs and the sewers of Paris as they felt that they were worthy of a visit. In the nineteenth century, too, the perception of mountains changed from fearsome places to attractive landscapes, which then became popular tourist destinations. An example of this idea from the 1990s is the British nuclear fuel reprocessing plant at Sellafield, which has become a popular visitor attraction.

These examples show that, as tastes and fashion change, so they are reflected in the tourist destinations which we patronize. This means that, while new opportunities are always available, there is also a constant threat to established destinations, which may go out of fashion. It is therefore vital to maintain the difference between the destination and the home environment through good design and management, and therefore to avoid the development of 'uniform tourism landscapes'.

Inseparability

Tourism is consumed where it is produced – visitors have to be physically present at the destination to experience tourism. Because tourism, by its very nature, is attracted to the unique and the fragile parts of the world, destinations are vulnerable to tourist pressure and may suffer alteration. This is exacerbated by the fact that visitor pressure is often concentrated seasonally in time and at specific popular locations.

Like all services, the destination is perishable in the sense that, if it is not used, it is lost – the availability of beds, restaurant seats and attraction tickets cannot be stored in the off-season for sale in the peak. Seasonality is a major problem for many destinations, prejudicing profitability and rendering them inefficient in terms of the use of the capital assets of the destination. This is because most elements of a destination have a high ratio of fixed to variable costs and therefore, for a highly seasonal destination, the peak (of, say, three or four months) has to make the majority contribution to fixed costs, which are chargeable for 12 months of the year. For example, for many tourist destinations anything up to 80 per cent of total costs are in physical plant, and construction involves long lead times. Of course, destinations with a year-round season (such as the Caribbean) have a considerable advantage in this respect. There is therefore an imperative to ensure that market volume and characteristics are accurately forecast before construction begins.

Multiple use

Destination amenities serve residents and workers throughout the year, but at some, or all, times of the year, there are temporary users of these amenities – day visitors or tourists – who are away from their normal place of residence and work. The multiple use of destinations means that it is possible to classify enterprises according to whether they depend upon tourism only, residents only, or a mix of the two. In fact, only the purpose-built destinations (such as theme parks) are in existence purely to serve the tourist. Most destinations share tourism with other uses; indeed, tourism is often the most recent and least respected user. For example, tourism at the coast is shared with other uses such as power generation and fishing, while tourism in the countryside is shared with nature conservation, agriculture and forestry (Case Study 9.1). Tourism may

---

CASE STUDY 9.1

Integrating tourism uses in upland areas

In many upland areas of Britain, tourism and excursionism are a major source of income. However, the traditional use of the uplands – livestock rearing – has suffered at the hands of both deliberate and accidental interference with farming operations by visitors. This is a serious problem in upland areas for two reasons.

- Upland farmers are at the economic and physical margin and cannot afford the time and expense to repair damage.
- Access to upland areas is usually unrestricted as the land is unfenced.

Particular problems have arisen which have threatened the livelihood of upland farmers. These include the following:

- Accidental worrying of livestock by dogs, resulting in abortion.
- Damage to walls and fences, allowing mixing of stock.
- Trespass and damage to crops in the valleys as visitors gain access to climb higher ground.

- Inconsiderate parking in gateways, preventing the farmer's access.

Although in themselves these problems sound trivial, they have led to open antagonism between farmers and visitors in the past.

To combat this problem an upland management service has been established in some areas which uses the following solutions:

- Instant cash handouts to allow farmers to make physical repairs to walls, fences, etc.
- Redirection of footpaths away from sensitive areas (such as during lambing) or valuable crops.
- Interpretation to educate the visitor about the farming regime.
- Clear-way marking of paths to ensure that visitors do not trespass accidentally or have to cross walls, etc. at the wrong point.

The scheme has been highly successful in allowing tourism to 'fit in' with the more traditional uses of upland areas.

Source: Countryside Commission (1974).

CASE STUDY 9.2

Tourism – a strategy? The Royal Borough of Windsor and Maidenhead

We have a problem

Windsor Castle is a major tourist location attracting several million visitors per year and this has a considerable impact on the town and its residents. Whilst there are advantages and benefits to be obtained from such a buoyant activity the presence of tourism in Windsor has a generally undesirable effect. However, having accepted that the tourists will not disappear, the Council has considered the possibility of a new approach with the following key objectives:

1. The reduction of the adverse effects of tourism on the town and local inhabitants.
2. Improvement of facilities for local residents and visitors.
3. Involvement of the Council in the management and control of the tourist industry in Windsor.
4. Environmental improvements to key areas of the town.
5. Benefits to the local economy by increasing tourist expenditure in Windsor and Eton.

Just what is the problem?

The problem is basically the pattern of tourism in Windsor. This in general involves a short stay which combines the disadvantages of frequent vehicle movements and limited patronage of the shops and other facilities in the town.

Why should the Council be involved in a strategy for management of tourism?

Recognising that tourists will come to Windsor in any case, it is considered that the pattern of tourism should be influenced with a view to overcoming the difficulties previously identified. This can best be achieved under the auspices of the Council which can provide better reception facilities, influence routes of access to the town, encourage the promotion of Windsor and Eton as tourism venues in their own right, encourage local enterprise to give value for money and attractive packages and at the same time provide benefits for the local residents.

Is it all necessary?

A soundly based tourist industry can assure a good economic future for the town and could have special benefit for Eton, helping to keep its businesses viable and to prevent the decline which threatens due to their nature and location.

At present the residents and ratepayers of Windsor suffer the effects of tourism and at the same time must pay for the services provided to deal with them. Indeed, the services are inadequate and more money will be needed. These proposals would mean that money expended would benefit both resident and visitor, providing much needed facilities for Windsor.

The emergence of the Council as a major influence on the Tourist industry will take time, as will the proposed land developments. Whilst the aims may take several years to achieve, the adoption of the strategy will, it is considered, have immediate results and produce a response from the industry.

Can it work?

Yes – with the co-operation of all parties.

Source: The Royal Borough of Windsor and Maidenhead.

---

become a source of conflict in such shared destinations, with open antagonism displayed between tourists and other users.

Solutions to this problem involve the careful integration of tourism activities in a variety of ways:

- Phasing tourism uses in time.
- Zoning tourism uses in space.
- Management schemes to reduce tension and conflict by intervening in problem situations.
- Community-driven tourism planning to ensure

that tourism develops in harmony with community wishes.

- Publicity campaigns to local residents (see Case Study 9.2).
- Information campaigns targeted at the tourist.

Complementarity

The very fact that the destination is an amalgam has a number of implications which are also common across all destinations. In particular, it is important that the quality of each component of the destination and the delivery of the tourism service at these components is reasonably uniform – a poor restaurant or hotel bedroom can detract from an otherwise satisfactory vacation. This complementarity of destination components is difficult to control by destination managers given the fragmented nature of enterprises in tourism. Integration of enterprises by larger organizations (tour operators owning hotels and transport carriers) is one means of such control, but for public-sector tourist boards the problem is a critical one.

COMPONENTS OF THE DESTINATION AMALGAM

Before introducing the components of a destination and demonstrating their place in the destination amalgam, we must make the major distinction between attractions and support services. Attractions generate the visit to a destination, while the other support services and facilities are also essential for tourism at the destination, but would not exist without attractions. This is because demand for their products is derived from those tourists drawn to the area by attractions. For example, it is unusual for a hotel to be the main reason for visiting a destination, and yet if the hotel were not there as a support service, tourism could not take place at that destination.

A particular focus of these components is the *resort*, which we can define as a place which attracts large numbers of tourists and which tourism endows with special characteristics, so that revenue produced by tourism plays an important role in its existence.

Attractions

As we have just observed, it is the attractions of a destination – whether they be man-made features, natural features or events – that provide the initial motivation to visit. Traditionally, attractions have been a neglected sector of the tourist industry due to their variety and fragmented ownership pattern. However, a welcome future development will be increased professionalism in the management of attractions. This will include a closer match between the market and supply of attractions through the adoption of marketing philosophy; better training for attractions' personnel; greater involvement of technology in the development of a wide range of exciting new types of attraction; and renewed focus upon and professional management of 'mega-events', which are emerging as an important subset of attractions. Alongside this more enlightened management approach, the attractions industry is forming professional bodies and seeking representation in wider tourist industry circles.

Amenities

A range of amenities, support facilities and services are required by a tourist at a destination. We can characterize this sector as having a low level of concentration of ownership. Indeed, these enterprises are often operated by small businesses, which is at once an advantage and a problem. It is an advantage because it means that tourist expenditure flows quickly into the local economy, but it is a problem because small businesses are fragmented and lack a coherent lobby. Often, too, they lack the investment capability to upgrade and the management/marketing expertise which will be demanded by the tourism market place in the 1990s.

The provision of amenities demonstrates the multisectoral nature of tourism supply and the interdependence of the various sectors. For example, the supply of many facilities and services at a resort depends on the number of bed spaces available – that is, the number of tourists who will visit. For example, provision of around 1000 beds will support up to six basic retail outlets, while 4000 beds will support specialist outlets such as hairdressers. Similar ratios can be calculated for restaurants, car parking, entertainment, swimming pools, etc.

Accommodation, food and beverage

The accommodation/food and beverage sector of the destination not only provides physical shelter and sustenance, but also creates the general feeling of welcome and a lasting impression of the local cuisine and produce.

Traditionally dominated by small businesses, the accommodation sector usually offers a mix of type of establishment, and it is important for destinations to adapt and change this mix to meet market aspirations. In some resorts, for example, there is a movement towards flexible forms of accommodation, such as apartments and time-share, and away from more traditional serviced forms. Accommodation can be both commercial (hotels, self-catering apartments, etc.) or in the private informal sector (second homes, caravans, etc.), which is a large, though neglected part of the accommodation industry.

Retailing and other services

There is an increasing range of facilities and services available to a tourist as the size of destinations increases. These include retailing, security services and other functions, such as hairdressing, banks, exchange bureaux and insurance. These services tend to locate close to the main attractions of a destination – in some destinations a clear 'recreational business district' is discernible.

Access

Clearly the development and maintenance of efficient transport links to the generating markets are essential for the success of destinations. Indeed, there are examples of destinations where transport has made, or broken, the tourist industry. The distance of the West Country of England and the Highlands of Scotland from generating markets renders them vulnerable in recession as they are primarily domestic destinations accessed by long car journeys. In contrast, Spain and Mexico are ideally situated to take advantage of international tourism from Europe and North America respectively. In international terms, developing countries have particular problems attracting a share of the market because they are generally distant from the generating markets.

Catchment areas will also vary for destinations according to their 'drawing power'. Tightly drawn geographical catchments will characterize smaller resorts without a particular attraction. For example, the Isle of Man is a domestic British resort catering mainly for markets in northern England and southern Scotland. However, major destinations, such as the theme parks of Orlando, or the Taj Mahal, can draw upon an international catchment.

We can therefore see that physical and market access to the destination are important, but so is the provision of services such as car rental and local transport, in order to service excursion circuits and provide transfers to accommodation at the destination. An increasingly imaginative approach to transportation at the destination adds to the quality of the tourist experience, and there are many examples of innovative transport provision in this respect, which include the following:

- Scenic drives.
- Park and ride schemes.
- Shuttle buses for walkers.
- Cycle ways.
- Explorer buses.

Ancillary services

Most major destinations provide ancillary services to both the consumer and the industry through a local tourist board. These services include marketing, development and co-ordination activities. The organization may be in the public sector, may be a public/private sector co-operative or, in some cases, may exist totally within the private sector. Such organizations are often linked to regional and national tourist boards and provide the framework within which tourism operates at the destination.

The main services normally provided by the local organization are as follows:

- Promotion of the destination.
- Co-ordination and control of development.
- Provision of an information/reservation service to the trade and the public.
- Advice to and co-ordination of local businesses.
- Provision of certain facilities (catering, sports, etc.).
- Provision of destination leadership.

INFRASTRUCTURE AND SUPERSTRUCTURE

We can consider infrastructure and superstructure as an alternative way of looking at the components of a destination.

Infrastructure represents all forms of construction above or below ground needed by an inhabited area, with extensive communication with the outside world as a basis for tourism activity in the area. Adequate infrastructure is essential for destination areas and is mainly in the form of transportation (road, railway, airport, car parks), utilities (electricity, water, communications) and other services (health care and security). It is normally shared by residents and visitors alike. There are examples where lack of adequate infrastructure prevents growth of tourism (such as restricted water supplies on the Kenyan Mombassa coast). Infrastructure does not normally generate income and is treated as a public investment in most tourist developments. Seasonality is a major problem for infrastructural development and most construction is planned to meet a percentage of peak load rather than peak.

Whereas infrastructure tends to be provided by the public sector, superstructure is normally a private-sector activity, as it is the profit-generating element of the destination. It includes accommodation, built attractions and retailing and other services. We should remember, however, that in many countries the public sector is active in providing financial incentives (grants, loans, tax holidays) for private-sector tourism investment.

Although the norm is for the public sector to provide infrastructure as a prerequisite for private-sector development of the superstructure, in many cases combinations of public- and private-sector finance are used to develop destinations.

SUSTAINABLE TOURISM DEVELOPMENT

Clearly the components of the tourist destination can be effective only if careful planning and management deliver a sustainable tourism product. However, it is only in recent years that the negative effects of tourism on destinations have been set more fully against the tangible economic gains. Add to this the rise of environmentalism and 'green' consciousness in the mid to late 1980s, and the stage has been set for a reassessment of the role and value of tourism to destinations.

In particular, this reassessment has discovered the concept of sustainable development. The Brundtland Report (World Commission on Environment and Development, 1987) defines sustainability simply as 'meeting the needs of the present without compromising the ability of future generations to meet their own needs'. For tourist destinations, this concept will be the guiding principle for the 1990s.

There are a number of forces which promote sustainable tourism:

- Consumer pressure: for example, in the form of vacation decisions being taken on the basis of environmental considerations.
- Public authority planning guidelines: not simply in the case of regulating development, but also in the form of encouraging good environmental practice (e.g. polluter-pays policies).
- Movements towards environmental impact assessment and environmental auditing: major tourist developments such as the Channel Tunnel are subject to impact assessment, and tourism companies (such as Disney) carry out environmental audits of their operation.

There are also other, primarily economic, forces resisting the adoption of sustainable tourism. In particular, these include the following:

- The economic imperative of the tourist industry and developers, which may put return on investment and profit before longer-term considerations.
- Some developing countries where the need for foreign exchange and employment is felt to outweigh environmental considerations.

We can see that the concept of sustainability demands a long-term view of tourism and ensures that consumption of tourism does not exceed the ability of a host destination to provide for future tourists. In other words, it represents a trade-off between present and future needs. In the past, sustainability has been a low priority compared with the short-term drive for profitability and growth, but with pressure growing for a more responsible tourism industry, it is difficult to see how such short-term views on consumption can continue long into the 1990s. Indeed, destination 'regulations' are being developed in some areas, and already the bandwagon for sustainable development and responsible consumption is rolling (see Case Study 9.3).

Perhaps the central issue for us here is the gradual shift from short-term to longer-term thinking and planning at the destination. It is no longer acceptable for the industry to exploit and 'use up' destinations and then move on, as has happened, for example, in some coastal areas of Spain.

CASE STUDY 9.3
Principles for sustainable tourism

• The environment has an intrinsic value which outweighs its value as a tourism asset. Its enjoyment by future generations and its long-term survival must not be prejudiced by short-term considerations. • Tourism should be recognized as a positive activity with the potential to benefit the community and the place as well as the visitor. • The relationship between tourism and the environment must be managed so that the environment is sustainable in the long term. Tourism must not be allowed to damage the resource, prejudice its future enjoyment or bring unacceptable impacts.	• Tourism activities and developments should respect the scale, nature and character of the place in which they are sited. • In any location, harmony must be sought between the needs of the visitor, the place and the host community. • In a dynamic world, some change is inevitable and change can often be beneficial. Adaptation to change, however, should not be at the expense of any of these principles. • The tourism industry, local authorities and environmental agencies all have a duty to respect the above principles and to work together to achieve their practical realization. Source: English Tourist Board (1991).

Carrying capacity

At the heart of the concept of sustainability is the idea of carrying capacity.

Simply, the carrying capacity of a site, resort, or even a region refers to its ability to take tourism use without deteriorating. In other words, capacity intervenes in the relationship between the tourist and tourist resource, or destination. The concept of carrying capacity, like sustainability, has its roots in resource management, but it is particularly important now in a situation where finite destination resources are under growing pressure from users (see Case Study 9. 4).

Mathieson and Wall (1982, p. 21) define carrying capacity as 'the maximum number of people who can use a site without an unacceptable alteration in the physical environment and without an unacceptable decline in the quality of experience gained by visitors'.

The main problem with carrying capacity is that the concept is easy to grasp but very difficult to put into practice because carrying capacity is a management decision. Managers of the tourist destination – as well as the tourists themselves – decide what is 'unacceptable' and when the 'quality of experience' has declined. Indeed, any destination can be managed to a high or low

---

CASE STUDY 9.4

Psychological carrying capacity: The Boundary Waters Canoe Area, USA

A number of studies have examined the idea of different tourists having differing capacity 'thresholds', basically by attempting to zone a destination into differing 'activity complexes' to match more closely the needs of users and therefore reduce impacts. One of the best examples is the zoning of the Boundary Waters Canoe Area (BWCA) on the US/Canadian border.

The BWCA is an area of forest, lakes and streams, formally designated as semi-wilderness because some logging and motorized use is permitted. The main use of wilderness areas in North America is for high-quality recreation.

In the early 1960s, Lucas (1964) surveyed users of the BWCA to establish their perceptions of wilderness in general and the BWCA in particular. Different perceptions were elicited between canoeists and those using motorized boats.

- Canoeists viewed the true wilderness area to be relatively small, and their standards in defining wilderness were demanding, particularly in terms of tolerance of other users, such as motorboats.
- Motorboat users viewed the wilderness area as very much larger than the canoeists, and tolerated roads and high levels of recreational use.

The implications of these differing perceptions of the same destination are outlined by Lucas:

> The differences [in perception] between these wilderness [users] may provide a key to increasing the capacity of the area in order to provide high-quality recreation. The highest priority use by established policy is wilderness canoeing. The canoeists' wilderness is easily destroyed by heavy use, especially [motor]boat use. The [motor] boaters value wilderness much less highly and fishing more highly, accept heavy use, and are usually in their wilderness before they reach the areas used by the canoeists, or the canoeists' wilderness. It would seem that the canoeists' satisfaction could be raised, or kept high as visitors increase, without reducing the motorboaters' satisfaction by concentrating new access points, campgrounds, and resort or cabin site leases, and managing the fishing intensively in the band of forests and lakes away from the Boundary Waters Canoe Area but inside the wilderness for most boaters. (p. 410)

In other words, by accepting the differing views of wilderness and zoning an area for canoeists and one for motorboats, the integrity of supply is maintained and both groups of users are satisfied.

Source: Lucas (1964).

CASE STUDY 9.5

Types of carrying capacity

Physical

This relates to the amount of suitable land available for facilities, and also includes the finite capacity of the facilities (such as car-parking spaces, covers in restaurants, or bed spaces in accommodation). It is the most straightforward of all capacity measures, and can be used for planning and management control (by, say, limiting car-parking spaces at sensitive sites).

Psychological

The psychological (or perceptual) capacity of a site is exceeded when a visitor's experience is significantly impaired. Of course, some people are 'crowd tolerant' and enjoy busy places, while others shun them. Psychological capacity is therefore a very individual concept and difficult to influence by management and planning, although landscaping can be used to reduce the impression of crowding.

Biological

The biological capacity of a site is exceeded when environmental damage or disturbance is unacceptable. This can relate to both flora and fauna, although more work has examined the capacity thresholds of vegetation (for example, at picnic sites, along paths, or in dune eco-systems) to take use than has looked at the tolerance of animals or birds to tourism. It is also important to consider the total ecosystem (such as the Norfolk Broads) rather than individual elements.

Social

The concept of social carrying capacity is derived from ideas of community-based tourism planning and sustainability. It attempts to define levels of development which are acceptable to the host community residents and businesses.

---

capacity, a level which is determined as much by management as by the innate characteristics of the resource, culture and so on.

DESTINATION EVOLUTION

There is no doubt that the evolution of tourism has been closely linked to the evolution of destinations – and, in particular, resorts. The evolution of resorts has been driven by transport developments. Most are now touring centres rather than destinations in their own right, and in response touring circuits and clusters of attractions have developed. At the same time markets also develop and change, and resorts have had to respond to this in terms of their tourist facilities and services. A more formalized representation of these ideas is expressed by the tourist area lifecycle (TALC). This states that destinations go through a cycle of evolution similar to the lifecycle of a product

(where sales grow as the product evolves through the stages of launch, development, maturity and decline). Simply, numbers of visitors replace sales of a product. Some writers suggest three stages of this TALC – discovery, local response and initiative, and 'institutionalization' – but a more detailed framework is helpful (see Figure 9.1 and Case Study 9.6).

Obviously, the shape of the TALC curve will vary, but for each destination it will be dependent upon factors such as the rate of development, access, government policy, market trends and competing destinations – each of which can delay or accelerate progress through the various stages. Indeed, development can be arrested at any stage in the cycle, and only tourist developments promising considerable financial returns will mature to experience all stages of the cycle. In turn, the length of each stage, and of the cycle itself, is variable. At one extreme, instant resorts such as Cancun (Mexico) or time-share developments

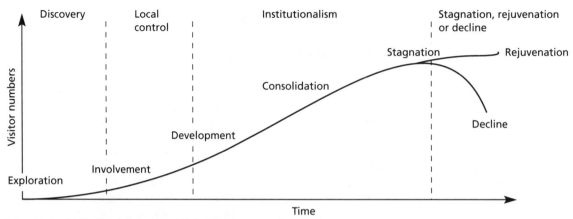

Source: Butler (1980). (Reprinted with permission from Pergamon Press Ltd.)

Fig 9.1 Hypothetical tourist area lifecycle

move almost immediately to growth; at the other extreme, well-established resorts such as Scarborough (England) have taken three centuries to move from exploration to rejuvenation.

We can see that one particular benefit of the tourist area lifecycle is as a framework for understanding how destinations and their markets evolve. The shape of the curve varies depending upon supply-side factors such as investment, capacity constraints, tourist impacts and planning responses. Indeed, it could be argued that an understanding of the cycle aids the development of community-based and sustainable tourism strategies at the involvement stage. To implement such approaches in later stages may be inappropriate. In other words, tourist destinations are dynamic, with changing provision of facilities and access matched by an evolving market in both quantitative and qualitative terms, as successive waves of different numbers and types of tourists with distinctive preferences, motivations and desires populate the resort at each stage of the lifecycle.

It is as a conceptual framework that the TALC is best utilized, although other writers have suggested that it can be used to guide strategic planning at destinations, or as a forecasting tool. There are significant problems with these approaches:

- The difficulty of identifying stages and turning points.

- The difficulty of obtaining long runs of visitor arrivals data from which to assemble the curve.
- The danger of planners responding to (possibly false) warning signs, which may be influenced anyway by management intervention.
- The danger of a tailor-made strategy for each stage.
- The level of aggregation is open to many interpretations. After all, there will be a lifecycle for a hotel, a resort and a region – as well as differing curves for each market segment.

The TALC has many critics, in part drawn by its very simplicity and apparent deterministic approach. Some argue that, far from being an independent guide for decisions, the TALC is determined by the strategic decisions of management and is heavily dependent on external influences. However, as a framework within which to view the development of destinations, albeit with hindsight, and as a way of thinking about the interrelationship of destination and market evolution, it provides many useful insights.

FUTURE DEVELOPMENTS

The tourist destination of the future will be influenced by a variety of factors, but technology and the demands of the new tourist will be dominant.

CASE STUDY 9.6

The tourist area lifecycle

Exploration

Small numbers of adventurous visitors are attracted by the unspoilt natural beauty or culture at the destination. Numbers are small due to poor access and facilities. At this stage, the attraction of the destination is that it is as yet unchanged by tourism and contact with local people will be high. Parts of Latin America and the Canadian Arctic are examples here.

Involvement

By this stage, local initiatives to provide for visitors and later to promote the destination have begun. This results in increased and regular numbers of visitors. A tourist season and market area emerges, and pressure may be placed on the public sector to provide infrastructure. The smaller, less-developed Pacific and Caribbean islands are examples of this stage.

Development

Large numbers of visitors are now arriving, at peak periods perhaps equalling or exceeding the number of local inhabitants. The control of tourism passes out of local hands, and external companies emerge to provide up-to-date facilities which may alter the appearance of the destination. In this very success lies the roots of failure, however. With increasing numbers and popularity the destination may suffer problems of overuse and deterioration of facilities. Regional and national planning and control become necessary, in part to ameliorate problems but also to market to the international tourist-generating areas as visitors become more dependent upon travel arrangements booked through the trade. Parts of Mexico and the north African coast exemplify this stage.

Consolidation

The rate of increase of visitors has now declined, although total numbers are still increasing and exceed permanent residents. The destination is now fully fledged with all the major franchises and chains represented, and there is an identifiable recreational business district (RBD). Many Caribbean and northern Mediterranean destinations are examples here.

Stagnation

Peak numbers have by now been reached and the destination is no longer fashionable. It relies on repeat visits and business use of its extensive facilities, and major efforts are needed to maintain the number of visits. The destination may have environmental, social and economic problems. The Costa Brava typifies this stage.

Decline

By this stage, visitors have been lost to newer resorts and the destination has become dependent on a smaller geographical catchment for day-trips and weekend visits. Property turnover is high and tourist facilities such as accommodation are converted into other uses. Alternatively, the authorities may recognize this stage and decide to 'rejuvenate'.

Rejuvenation

This involves deciding on new uses, new markets and new distribution channels, and thus repositioning the destination. Changing the attraction such as by introducing a casino (as at Schveningen in the Netherlands and Atlantic City in the USA is a common response. Similarly, some destinations capitalize on previously unused natural resources, such as winter sports, to extend the season and attract a new market. These facility developments often reflect joint public/private-sector ventures to seek new markets and invest in the destination in order to reach a cycle/recycle pattern.

Source: Adapted from Butler (1980) and Cooper (1989).

Technology permeates destination development in many ways – from hotel communication systems and ensuring energy efficiency, through computer reservation systems (CRS), which allow closer matching of demand with supply, to computer-generated imagery and the use of virtual reality at attractions. Add to this a consumer of tourism who is discerning, experienced and probably computer literate, and the stage is set for a range of new tourist destinations to be developed, and for the more effective management of existing destinations. There is no doubt that these new destinations will need to be better planned and managed, and show more concern for their environment and host community, than did their earlier counterparts.

Middleton (1988) observes two opposing tendencies in destination development for the future.

First, there is the development of purpose-built, enclosed and closely controlled environments or 'enclaves' (such as large-scale theme parks) and self-contained resorts where the emphasis is on escape from everyday life to immersion in a safe, high-quality fantasy environment.

This development will be accelerated by CRSs which, combined with a more knowledgeable tourist market, will see the emergence of a growing number of independent travellers and a changing role for intermediaries – travel agents and tour operators – in the tourism distribution chain. Suppliers will attune their products more closely to the desires of their customers in enclaves which will be promoted as a 'market-orientated' alternative to the real, and increasingly fragile, 'resource-based', non-reproducible attractions of natural, historic or cultural destinations.

Second, Middleton observes a trend towards 'authentic' or 'sensitive' travel experiences, where management inputs are minimal and the tourist – or traveller – controls the experience, shunning contact with the travel trade and enjoying unsullied authentic contact with landscapes and/or cultures.

In fact, the trend towards authentic travel experiences is potentially more damaging than enclave tourism (where contacts with local cultures and environments are controlled and routinized). Destinations are responding to this threat in a variety of ways. Resource-based destinations are adopting sophisticated planning, management and interpretive techniques to provide both a welcome and a rich experience for the tourist, while at the same time ensuring protection of the resource itself. It is felt that, once tourists understand why a destination is significant, they will want to protect it. Good planning and management of the destination lies at the root of providing the consumer of the 1990s with a high-quality experience, and it may be that tourists will have to accept increasingly restricted viewing times at popular sites and even replicas of the real thing.

Throughout all of these developments the enhanced professionalism of management and planning at destinations will become evident as the tourism industry collectively attempts to deliver a quality experience at the destination, while at the same time protecting the integrity of the resource itself.

References and further reading

Ashworth, G. (1984) *Recreation and Tourism*, London: Bell and Hyman.

Boniface, B., and Cooper, C. (1987) *The Geography of Travel and Tourism*, London: Heinemann.

Burkart, A., and Medlik, S. (1981) *Tourism: Past, Present and Future*, London: Heinemann.

Burton, R. (1991) *Travel Geography*, London: Pitman Publishing.

Butler, R.W. (1980) 'The concept of a tourist area cycle of evolution', *Canadian Geographer*, Vol. 24, pp. 5–12, Oxford: Pergamon Press Ltd.

Chubb, M., and Chubb, H.R. (1981) *One Third of Our Time*, New York: Wiley.

Coppock, J.T., and Duffield, D.B. (1975) *Recreation and the Countryside*, London: Macmillan.

Countryside Commission (1974) *Upland Management Experiment*, Cheltenham: Countryside Commission.

English Tourist Board (1991) *Tourism and the Environment: Maintaining the Balance*, London: ETB.

Goodall, B. (1992) 'Environmental auditing for tourism', in Cooper, C. (ed.), *Progress in Tourism Recreation and Hospitality Management*, London: Belhaven.

Hewison, R. (1987) *The Heritage Industry*, London: Methuen.

Inskeep, E. (1991) *Tourism Planning*, New York: Van Nostrand Reinhold.

Leiper, N. (1979) 'The framework of tourism', *Annals of Tourism Research*, vol. 6, no. 4, pp. 390–407.

Lucas, R.C. (1964) 'Wilderness perception and use: the example of the Boundary Waters Canoe Area', *Natural Resources Journal*, January, pp. 394–411.

McIntosh, R.W., and Goeldner, C.R. (1990) *Tourism: Principles, Practices and Philosophies*, New York: Wiley.

Mathieson, A., and Wall, G. (1982) *Tourism: Economic, Physical and Social Impacts*, Harlow: Longman.

Medlik, S. (ed.) (1991) *Managing Tourism*, Oxford: Heinemann.

Mercer, I. (1980) *In Pursuit of Leisure*, Melbourne: Sorret.

Middleton, V.T.C. (1988) *Marketing in Travel and Tourism*, Oxford: Butterworth-Heinemann.

Mill, R., and Morrison, A. (1985) *The Tourism System*, Englewood Cliffs, NJ: Prentice Hall.

Murphy, P.E. (1985) *Tourism: A Community Approach*, London: Methuen.

Patmore, J.A. (1972) *Land and Leisure*, Harmondsworth: Penguin.

Patmore, J.A. (1983) *Recreation and Resources*, Oxford: Blackwell.

Pearce, D. (1987) *Tourism Today*, London: Longman.

Pearce, D. (1989) *Tourist Development*, London: Longman.

Pearce, D. (1992) *Tourism Organisations*, London: Longman.

Pigram, J. (1983) *Outdoor Recreation and Resource Management*, New York: Croom Helm.

Poon, A. (1989) 'Competitive strategies for a new tourism', in Cooper, C. (ed.), *Progress in Tourism Recreation and Hospitality Management*, London: Belhaven.

Seekings, J. (1989) 'Components of tourism', in Witt, S., and Moutinho, L. (eds), *Tourism Marketing and Management Handbook*, Hemel Hempstead: Prentice Hall.

Smith, S.L.J. (1983) *Recreation Geography*, London: Longman.

Smith, S.L.J. (1988) 'Defining tourism: A supply side view', *Annals of Tourism Research*, vol. 15, no. 2, pp. 179–90.

Smith, V.L. (1992) *Tourism Alternatives*, Philadelphia, Pa.: University of Pennsylvania Press.

Turner, L., and Ash, J. (1975) *The Golden Hordes: International Tourism and the Pleasure Periphery*, London: Constable.

World Commission on Environment and Development (1987) *Our Common Future*, Brundtland Report, New York: Oxford University Press.

CHAPTER 10

Carrying capacity and the sociocultural and environmental impacts of tourism

OVERVIEW

Any form of industrial development will bring with it impacts upon the social and physical environment in which it takes place. In view of the fact that tourists have to visit the place of production in order to consume the output, tourism is clearly responsible for such impacts. The literature on the social and environmental impacts of tourism is often biased, painting highly negative pictures. In this chapter we examine the central concept of carrying capacity and the issues surrounding its determination. We then consider the ways in which tourism impacts upon the host community and the host environment from both positive and negative viewpoints.

IMPACT ANALYSIS

A number of researchers have attempted to bring the different approaches made to the study of tourism's impact on the destination into a unified framework for analysis. Unfortunately, much of the work done on impact analysis has been descriptive in nature and, as such, does not provide a framework for analysis. To examine the impact of tourism in an objective manner it is necessary to move away from concepts such as 'water pollution', 'traffic congestion' and 'beach overcrowding' which all carry value judgements with them.

The impact of tourism on any destination will be determined by a wide variety of factors:

- The volume of tourist arrivals.
- The structure of the host economy.
- The types of tourism activity.
- The difference in sociocultural characteristics between the hosts and the tourists.
- The fragility of the local environment.

We believe that it is better to examine how tourism affects each relevant factor (whether it be social, physical, cultural or economic) and only then to move on to the value judgement of just how much change on each parameter may be considered as acceptable to the host community.

There are a wide variety of issues to be discussed under the heading of impact analysis. However, diverse as these issues may be, they are often interrelated. In this chapter, all types of impact are brought together in order to examine the concept of 'carrying capacity'. As tourism development in a destination takes place, the magnitude of impacts, and whether or not they are primarily positive or negative in nature, will change. Every destination will be subject to a carrying capacity: that is, a level of tourism activity that can be sustained into the long term without creating serious or irreversible changes to the destination. If the carrying capacity is exceeded, the destination will find that the negative impacts rapidly increase while the positive impacts diminish.

CARRYING CAPACITY

The fact that tourism activity has an impact on the social, cultural, environmental and economic character of a destination, together with the belief that these impacts grow in magnitude as the volume of tourist arrivals increases, suggests that there may be some threshold level of visitor presence beyond which the impact becomes unacceptable or intolerable. Such threshold limits are best referred to as 'saturation limits' rather than 'carrying capacity' since the latter carries with it some notion of sustainability.

Carrying capacity, for the purpose of this chapter, is defined as that level of tourist presence which creates impacts on the host community, environment and economy that are acceptable to both tourists and hosts, and sustainable over future time periods. Note that tourist presence is used rather than tourist numbers. This is because it is necessary to adjust the absolute number of visitors to take account of a number of factors:

● The length of stay.
● The characteristics of the tourists/hosts.
● The geographical concentration of visitors.
● The degree of seasonality.

It is important to measure tourism presence in some unambiguous manner. This could be done in terms of tourism 'units', where the number of visitor arrivals is weighted according to the above factors in order to provide a standardized unit. However, there are difficulties in incorporating day visitors with those visitors who stay overnight. The former are likely to have a different impact *per hour of stay* than their staying visitor counterparts, largely because of the different sense of time budgeting and expenditure patterns.

Such a definition of carrying capacity fits in well with tourism development plans because these plans often attempt to impose some constraint on the ultimate level of development to prevent damaging impacts on the environment and society. However, even the expression of carrying capacity given above is fraught with difficulties because it implies that the carrying capacity is some absolute limit. In practice, exposure to stimuli brings with it acceptability, and it is likely that carrying capacity, particularly from the social and cultural point of view, will increase over time as tourist presence becomes more expected and accepted.

Furthermore, given that tourism is associated with impacts on society, culture, environment and the economy, the carrying capacity threshold is likely to occur in one of these areas first rather than in all of them at once. Thus, a destination may find that tourism activity brings pressure to, say, the local ecosystem before it creates any serious threats to, say, the social structure, culture or the economy. This means that the carrying capacity for this particular destination is determined by environmental considerations and that the other factors may be running below capacity level.

In order to examine the carrying capacity it is necessary to delineate the areas of study. Figure 10.1 provides a schematic framework for the determination of carrying capacity. The determination

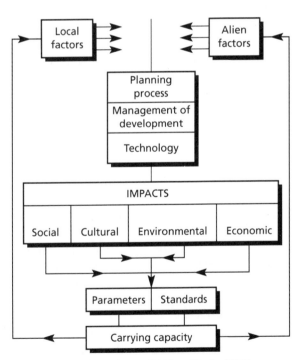

Source: Adapted from Atherton (1991) and Shelby (1984).

Fig 10.1 Carrying capacity

of carrying capacity can be shown as a function of a variety of factors which, following planning and regulation, generate an impact on the destination. However, the carrying capacity feeds back both to hosts and to visitors (alien factors), and over time this influences the impact and, consequently, the carrying capacity. The concept of carrying capacity is a dynamic rather than a static concept.

Local factors

Social structure

The social structure of, say, London or New York is much more able to absorb and tolerate the presence of tourists than, say, the extended family structure which exists in Western Samoa in the South Pacific.

Culture

The cultural characteristics of the destination play an important role in determining impact. The more unusual the cultural background, the more attractive a destination may become, but the more likely it is to be affected by the presence of tourists. The result may be either a destruction of local culture or, more likely, the commercialization of cultural features and traditions, such as dances, costumes and the arts and crafts.

Environment

The environment *will* be changed by the presence of tourists. The environment can be either natural or man-made, generally the latter is (or can be made) far more resilient to tourism impact than the former. Environmental change is inevitable – to take an extreme example, the moon has, to date, received only a few visitors, yet its landscape has been irrevocably altered by that presence. The more sensitively an environment is balanced, the greater is the danger of irreversible environmental damage.

Economic structure

The economic structure will determine the benefits and costs associated with tourism activity. In general, the more developed and industrialized the economy, the more robust it will be. Such economies are able to secure the maximum benefits from tourism while incurring the minimum costs.

Political structure

The political structure often (but not always) reflects the ideals and beliefs of the host community, and can actively encourage tourism development or hinder it.

Resources

The availability of local resources (labour, capital, land, etc.) will have a major influence on the acceptability and desirability of tourism development, and even on the form that development takes. Where local resources are scarce, competition for them will be high and the opportunity cost of using these resources for tourism will also be high. The local infrastructure is also part of the local resource base. If tourism development means that the infrastructure will be overutilized then this will generate resentment against tourism and bring the hosts and tourists into conflict. On the positive side, tourism development may result in improved infrastructure, which will be available to hosts as well as tourists and thereby will enhance the quality of life for the local residents.

Alien factors

Tourist characteristics (social)

The characteristics of the tourists are an important factor in determining the social and cultural impact of tourism on the host community. For instance, visitors who belong to the 'mass tourism' group are likely to have a much greater social and cultural impact than those who belong to the explorer and adventurer category. The former demand western amenities and do not adapt to the local norms and customs, whereas the latter derive enjoyment and satisfaction from taking part in them. In general, the greater the difference between the local and the visitor's social and cultural background, the greater the impact and consequent change. Tourist characteristics also include visitor expenditure patterns, mode of transport, party structure and size, age, educational background, income and purpose of visit. All of these factors will influence the nature and magnitude of the impact on the host community.

Type of tourist activity

The types of tourist activity will be closely linked to the characteristics of the tourists who take part in them. However, the presence of certain activities, such as gambling, can bring social impacts which are far greater in magnitude than those associated with the same groups of tourists undertaking different activities. Gambling can bring with it increased risks to the host community in terms of exposure to prostitution, drugs and crime.

It should not be forgotten that tourist presence, together with the effects of tourist presence on local factors, will influence the satisfaction rates of visitors. Thus, carrying capacity relates not only to how much tourist presence the destination can cope with at a sustainable level, but also to how much tourist presence and local factor change the visitor is prepared to tolerate.

Planning, management and technology

Planning is concerned with the organization of factors in order to manipulate future events. The management of tourism is the process by which plans are put into practice. Changes in technology will have a direct effect on the difficulty associated with the planning and management tasks. Given the interaction of the local and alien factors

within the host environment, the planning and management process should aim to secure the maximum positive benefits (as dictated by the planning objectives) while incurring the minimum costs.

Impacts

The local and alien factors, manipulated by planning and the management of tourism development, will result in impacts on the social structure, culture, environment and economic structure.

Parameters

The parameters refer to the various changes which take place to the local factors as a result of different levels of tourist presence. They are factual in the sense that they are devoid of value judgements and simply relate tourist presence to changes in social, cultural, environmental and economic factors.

Standards

The standards refer to the value judgements imposed by the hosts and the visitors in terms of how much change is acceptable without damaging the sustainability of tourism.

Carrying capacity

The carrying capacity is the dependent variable. Note that it is a variable and not a fixed value of tourist presence. Over time exposure to tourist presence and changing local factors are likely to influence how much change the host community and visitors are prepared to accept.

It is the feedback over time, between carrying capacity and the local and alien factors, which will be responsible for increasing/decreasing the magnitude of acceptable tourist presence (carrying capacity). If the carrying capacity is exceeded with respect to any of the impact areas, the tourism development process will be hindered and irreversible damage may be experienced. The damage may be concerned with social, environmental or economic aspects, but the end result will be the same – the tourists will experience a reduction in visitor satisfaction (because of the resentment that will grow from the impact) and the destination will decline.

THE SOCIOCULTURAL IMPACT OF TOURISM

There are a variety of ways in which we can look at tourism and socioeconomic development. The development of the tourist product is inextricably linked to the contribution that tourism development can make to general economic development. The development of the tourism product will to some extent be determined by the type of tourism activity, which will, in turn, be partly determined by the socioeconomic characteristics of the tourists. Similarly, the economic and sociological impact of tourism on the host population will be partly determined by the type of tourism product.

The impact brought about by the interaction of hosts and tourists is a well-documented phenomenon, and the findings of Smith (1989) in her book on the anthropology of tourism have rapidly gained acceptance in the academic world. As already stated, any form of economic development will carry with it implications for the social structure and cultural aspects of the population. Even domestic tourism, where hosts and tourists are generally from the same sociocultural background, results in social and cultural change as a result of this host/tourist contact.

The tourism development process

A typical development scenario, considering the tourism product as it grows from infancy to maturity, looks something like this:

- A few tourists 'discover' an area or destination.
- In response to this discovery, local entrepreneurs provide new facilities or special facilities

to accommodate the growing number of visitors and, more importantly, to attract more.

- The public sector provides new or improved infrastructure to cater for the inflow of visitors.
- Finally, institutionalized or mass tourism is developed, which is commonly resort based and sold as a package. It is based upon large-volume production in order to exploit economies of scale in marketing, accommodation and transport, such as high payload factors for aircraft.

Many regional development plans have attempted to short-cut the evolution of tourist destinations by aiming for the final stage of mass tourism straight away, but few developing regions or countries can make this leap without first securing outside capital and expertise.

Unfortunately, there is no single coherent body of knowledge or theory which comprehensively explains tourism development. Evidence, such as it is, is rather piecemeal and comes from a number of case studies. Furthermore, the situation is compounded by the fact that different disciplines approach the subject matter in different ways, and although many aspects of the studies overlap, it is difficult to tie the different conclusions together into a single body of thought.

The different approaches may be categorized under the following headings:

- Psychological.
- Sociological.
- Socioeconomic.

The psychological basis of development

In Chapter 4 we introduced Stanley Plog's (1977) approach to a typology of tourists. Plog devised this classification in terms of psychographic analysis, and in this way attempted to explain why resort destinations appear to follow a pattern which causes them to rise through development and then to decline. He saw a continuum of market segments with two diametrically opposed groups at either pole (see Figure 10.2).

Plog's theory suggests that the tourist segments can be divided into allocentrics, near allocentrics,

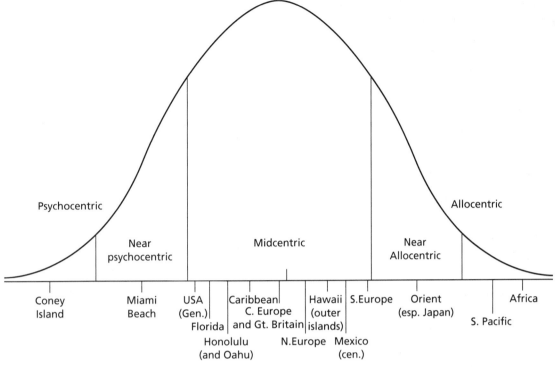

Source: Plog (1977)

Fig 10.2 Psychographic positions of destinations

midcentrics, near psychocentrics and psychocentrics. The allocentrics seek culture and environmental differences from their norm, belong to high income groups, are adventurous and require very little in the way of tourist plant. The psychocentrics, on the other hand, seek familiar surroundings, belong to lower income groups, are unadventurous and require a high level of tourist plant.

As the resort develops in order to attract the bulk of the tourist market, which in Plog's terminology is the midcentric group, so it alienates the trendsetters (the allocentrics) who then look for a new destination to 'discover'.

Resorts which have a strong competitive advantage, in terms of climate, location or top-quality tourist plant, such as Disneyland, may continue to hold on to the midcentric market. However, most resorts tend to lose favour (perhaps because tourists begin to regard them as being too commercialized) and from there on in they move down

to the psychocentric market by offering lower rates, more comprehensive packaging and more scheduling of activities – 'the no surprises vacation'.

Plog's theory is not immutable – it is not inevitable that resort destinations will end up with the psychocentric market. It may have been true in the past, but once decision-makers realize that limited tourism development is an attractive means of growth, they may develop tourism plants that are compatible with the environment and the indigenous characteristics of a region, and target them at the 'desired' market segments.

The sociological basis of development

The typology of tourists and development

Typology is a method of sociological investigation which seeks, in this instance, to classify tourists according to a particular phenomenon, usually motivations or behaviour. Two examples of typology which have implications for the development of the tourism product are as follows:

- Package tourist – usually demand western amenities, are associated with rapid growth rates and often lead to the restructuring of the local economy.
- Independent tourists – usually fit in better with the local environment, are associated with relatively slow growth rates and often lead to local ownership.

Tourism as a social phenomenon

Several factors of the modern world can be identified as the seeds from which international tourism has grown as an inescapable social phenomenon:

- Population growth.
- Increasing urbanization and the numerous pressures of urban life, creating the desire to escape.
- Growth in communications and information technology, creating awareness and stimulating interest.
- Changes in mobility and accessibility, brought about largely by the growth of air transport and private motor car ownership.

Frequency of types of tourist and their adaptations to local norms		
Types of tourist	Number of tourists	Adaptations to local norms
Explorer	Very limited	Accepts fully
Elite	Rarely seen	Adapts fully
Off–beat	Uncommon but seen	Adapts well
Unusual	Occasional	Adapts somewhat
Incipient mass	Steady flow	Seeks western amenities
Mass	Continuous flow	Expects western amenities
Charter	Massive arrivals	Demands western amenities

Source: Smith (1989).

Fig 10.3 Typology of tourism

- Increased leisure time and longer periods of vacation, together with rising real incomes in the wake of economic growth.
- Increase in world trade for business tourism.

The socioeconomic basis of development

There are a number of factors that will influence the attitude of people towards tourism at both domestic and international levels. These include the following:

- *Age.* It is unlikely that most elderly people will decide to take up a trekking or mountaineering vacation, or choose a resort because of its nightclubs.
- *Education.* There is a tendency to associate the more adventurous and independent vacations with the more educated portion of the population.
- *Income levels.* Income levels have an obvious influence on the decision of people to travel, the location to which they travel and often the mode of transport.
- *Socioeconomic background.* The previous experiences of people will play an important role in determining the type of holiday they will consume in future time periods. For instance, children from the higher socioeconomic groups, who are accustomed to frequent trips abroad, are likely to continue this pattern throughout adulthood.

In addition to the socioeconomic characteristics of the tourists, the tourism development process, together with its implications, should be examined. This approach encompasses the psychological basis for tourism development, the sociological basis for tourism development and the socioeconomic basis for tourism development.

In general, there is a *direct* sociocultural impact which results from the contact between hosts and tourists. De Kadt (1979) suggests that there are three broad categories of such contact:

- When the tourists buy goods and services from the hosts;

- When the hosts and tourists share a facility (beach, transport, restaurant, etc.).
- When tourists and hosts meet for cultural exchange.

The first two of these types of contact are associated with the majority of the negative aspects of social contact, whereas the last type of contact is primarily positive in nature. By comparing these three areas of contact with Smith's (1989) typology of tourists, it is evident that the explorer/adventurer tourist is most likely to take part in the latter, positive type of interaction and the mass tourist with the former type of contact. This means that the negative types of interaction are by far the most common and the positive type of contact is relatively rare.

The 'demonstration effect' is also an aspect of direct sociocultural impact. Tourists influence the behaviour of hosts by example. This is an area where tourism development is at a distinct disadvantage when compared with other forms of economic development. Tourism cannot be exported to consumers outside the national boundary – the consumers must visit the destination to enjoy the tourism product, and in so doing they act as a stimulus to social change.

Of course, tourists do not have to come into direct contact with hosts for there to be a social impact. New employment opportunities created by the increase in activity will bring about social change. Additionally, new forms of communications, transport and infrastructure provided for tourism development will also add to the process. These may be considered to be *indirect* sociocultural effects and are evident with many types of economic development, not just tourism. However, the diversity of industries involved in the production of the tourism product makes this type of sociocultural impact more likely.

Finally, increases in income levels and the spread of the monetized sector will alter consumption patterns. Such changes, if they include consumer durables such as television and radio, will expose the host population to a greater range of wants and speed up the process of social change. These effects may be seen as *induced* sociocultural effects. This latter type of sociocultural impact will also be evident irrespective of the type of economic development, and is not uniquely attributable to tourism development.

The magnitude of the direct sociocultural impact associated with tourism development will also be determined by the extent of the difference in sociocultural characteristics between hosts and guests. Inskeep (1991) suggests that these differences include the following:

- Basic value and logic systems.
- Religious beliefs.
- Traditions.
- Customs.
- Lifestyles.
- Behavioural patterns.
- Dress codes.
- Sense of time budgeting.
- Attitudes towards strangers.

Compounding the issue, the tourists' cultures when abroad (it is likely that the tourists will represent several different cultures) are different from the tourists' cultures at home. In other words, tourists often take on different values and so on when they are on vacation than when they are in their normal environment.

The sociocultural impact can be either positive or negative. As we have seen, one of the rare but positive aspects is the exchange of cultural information. But tourism can help to stimulate interest in, and conserve aspects of, the host's cultural heritage. This is a significant positive sociocultural impact which includes the preservation of ancient monuments, historic buildings and sites, traditional arts and crafts and customs. If tourists appreciate the cultural heritage of a destination, it can stimulate the hosts' pride in their heritage and foster local crafts, traditions and customs.

The negative sociocultural impacts are sometimes the result of direct contact and the demonstration effect, but can also be generated if tourism development is not managed properly and potential economic benefits are not realized. For instance, foreign employment in tourism-related jobs and foreign investment in tourism projects both add to the resentment of tourism activity. The exclusion of hosts from certain tourist facilities (such as private beaches, casinos and transport services) will further increase the pressure of resentment and may create conflict between hosts and tourists.

As with any form of development, the new income-earning opportunities created are unlikely to be evenly distributed, and the creation of new jobs with higher than average wage levels may create social pressures between the hosts who occupy those posts and their families and peers. A major problem can also occur because of a real (and sometimes apparent) difference in wealth between the tourists and their hosts. It is often true that the international tourist is wealthier than the average host with whom he or she comes into contact, but this difference may be compounded by the fact that tourists exhibit spending patterns and behaviour that is not their norm, simply because they are away on holiday. The hosts may not appreciate that the tourist spends the majority of his or her life working and living under conditions of stress – all that the host sees is a tourist who is free spending and high living, and who spends the day lounging on the beach and the night painting the town red!

When attempting to measure the level of irritation generated by tourist–host contact, Doxey (1976) drew up the following index:

(1) *The Level of Euphoria* – the initial thrill and enthusiasm that comes along with tourism development means that the tourist is made welcome.

(2) *The Level of Apathy* – once tourism development is under way and expansion has taken place, the tourist is taken for granted and is now seen as a source of profit taking; contact is now on a more formal basis.

(3) *The Level of Irritation* – as the industry approaches saturation point, the hosts can no longer cope with the number of tourists without additional facilities.

(4) *The Level of Antagonism* – the tourist is now seen as the bringer of all ills, hosts are antagonistic towards tourists, and tourists are regarded as being there to be exploited.

(5) *The Final Level* – during the above process of development the hosts have forgotten that all they once regarded as being special was exactly what attracted the tourist, but in the rush to develop tourism circumstances have changed.

As we have seen, the level and extent of social impact will be determined by a number of factors, but exceeding the capacity constraints of the destination is clearly a major determinant.

THE ENVIRONMENTAL IMPACT OF TOURISM

The environment, whether it is natural or man-made, is the most fundamental ingredient of the tourism product. However, as soon as tourism activity takes place, the environment is inevitably changed or modified either to facilitate tourism or during the tourism process. Environmental preservation and improvement motives are now at the forefront of many development decisions, and such considerations are treated with much greater respect than they were during the first half of this century.

A brief survey of the literature shows that relatively little research has been undertaken in analysing tourism's impact on the environment. The empirical studies which have taken place have been very specific – such as the impact of tourism on the wildlife of Africa, on the pollution of water in the Mediterranean, or on particular coastal areas and mountains. The diverse areas studied and the wide range of tourism activities involved make it difficult to bring these findings together in order to assemble a comprehensive framework within which to work.

In order to study the physical impact of tourism it is necessary to establish the following:

● The physical impacts created by tourism activity as opposed to other activities.

● What conditions were like before tourism activity took place, in order to derive a baseline from which comparisons can be made.

- An inventory of flora and fauna, together with an unambiguous index of tolerance levels to the types of impact created by different sorts of tourism activity.
- What indirect and induced levels of environmental impact are associated with tourism activity.

The environmental impacts associated with tourism development can also be considered in terms of their direct, indirect and induced effects. The impacts can be positive or negative. It is not possible to develop tourism without incurring environmental impacts, but it is possible, with correct planning, to manage tourism development in order to minimize the negative impacts while encouraging the positive impacts.

The direct environmental impacts of tourism include the following positive effects:

- The preservation/restoration of historic buildings and sites.
- The creation of national parks and wildlife parks.
- The protection of reefs and beaches.
- The maintenance of forests.

It should be remembered, however, that such conservation and preservation may rate highly from the point of view of researchers, or even tourists, but if they are not considered to be important from the hosts' point of view it is questionable whether they can be considered to be positive environmental impacts. African game parks, for example, limit the grazing lands of nomadic tribes and certainly constrain food production capability.

On the negative side, tourism may have direct environmental impacts on the quality of water and air, and on noise levels. Sewage disposal into water will add to pollution problems, as will the use of powered boats on inland waterways and sheltered seas. Increased usage of the internal combustion engine for tourist transport, and oil burning to provide the power for a hotel's air conditioning and refrigeration units, add to the diminution of air quality, and noise levels may be dramatically increased in urban areas through discos and nightclubs, and by increased road, rail and air traffic.

Physical deterioration of both natural and man-made environments can have serious consequences. Hunting and fishing have obvious impacts on the wildlife environment; sand dunes can be damaged and eroded by overuse; vegetation can be destroyed by walkers; camp fires may destroy forests; ancient monuments may be worn away or disfigured and damaged by graffiti; and the improper disposal of litter can detract from the aesthetic quality of the environment and harm wildlife. These are just a few examples of direct negative environmental impacts.

The building of high-rise hotels on beach frontages is an environmental impact of tourism that achieves headline status. This kind of obvious environmental rape is now less common than it was during the rapid growth periods of the 1960s and 1970s. In a number of countries, particularly island economies, land availability is often high on the awareness ratings of planners. They have sometimes introduced regulations to restrict beach front developments to a height no greater than that of the palm trees (as in Mauritius), or to restrict development to a certain distance back from the beach (as in some parts of India).

In the same way that the economic impacts associated with tourism development can be direct and indirect, the same is true of environmental impacts. If tourism activity requires the production of output from a diverse range of industries, including those that do not supply tourist goods and services directly, then the environmental impact associated with the output and production processes of those industries should also be included. Thus, if tourism increases and this causes hotels to increase their purchases from the building and construction industry, then the environmental damage created by that increased building and construction must also be included – so too must the effects of the quarries that supply the builders and the transport system that facilitates it.

Environmental impact assessment (EIA)

There are no generally accepted models for environmental impact assessment. In many environmentally sensitive tourism destinations, there are few legislative acts and even fewer agencies empowered to safeguard the environment with respect to tourism development (as in the South Pacific – see Case Study 10.1). However, the absence of legislation to support environmental planning should not deter tourism planners from undertaking their own environmental impact assessment on proposed developments. Environmental protection is so much easier and less costly than environmental correction, and such remedial action is not always possible.

In some areas, attempts have been made to construct tourism/environment balance sheets to assess the net effect of tourism development with respect to the environment. One such approach for Scotland concluded that tourism is an important sector of the Scottish economy and that, although there are widespread environmental impacts associated with tourism activity, these could only be regarded as serious in a few specific locations. With careful management it was considered that these problems could be overcome (Case Study 10.2). The Department of Employment set up a task force to examine the relationship between tourism and the environment in England (1991) and its report supported the major views expressed by the Scottish Tourism Co-ordinating Group.

EIA: the process

It is important to identify environmental impacts associated with tourism development at an early stage:

- It is easier to avoid environmental damage by either modifying or rejecting developments than it is to rectify environmental damage once a project has been implemented.
- Projects which rely heavily upon areas of outstanding beauty may become non-viable if such developments degrade the environment.

There are a variety of methods which may be used for EIA, including checklists and network systems, but generally EIA is a process which enables researchers to predict the environmental consequence associated with any proposed development project. To draw up a checklist of environmental impacts it is necessary to establish what potential impacts can occur as a result of tourism activity (see Case Study 10.3).

Once the potential impacts have been considered, a checklist consisting of the fundamental elements at risk can be assembled. This checklist can then be used to form the basis of an evaluation matrix, which will assess the impact of proposed developments on each of the fundamental elements according to whether the development will have no impact, minor impacts, moderate impacts, or major impacts.

EIA will examine the following:

- Environmental auditing procedures.
- Limitations to natural resources.
- Environmental problems and conflicts which may affect project viability.

CASE STUDY 10.1

Environmental protection in the South Pacific

Papua New Guinea is the only member of the Tourism Council for the South Pacific (TCSP) that currently has legislation covering environmental impact assessment (The Environmental Planning Act, 1978). This statute allows the minister to require potential developers to produce an environmental impact statement when any development project associated with foreseeable major environmental impacts is proposed. However, even in Papua New Guinea the legislation has not been as effective as its proponents would have wished because the requirement to produce an environmental impact statement is at the discretion of the minister and is not compulsory; nor is there any requirement for approval of the environmental plan prior to project implementation.

CASE STUDY 10.2

Scottish Tourism Co-ordinating Group environmental balance sheet for Scotland, 1992

This report found that the specific beneficial effects of tourism activity on the physical environment included the following:

- Environmental improvement schemes to create more attractive areas for visitors, including urban regeneration, reclamation projects and conservation schemes.
- The adaptation and restoration of redundant buildings for tourist and visitor use.
- Increased provision of recreation and sporting facilities for use by both locals and visitors.
- The restoration of historic buildings and ancient sites.
- Improved infrastructure, including roads, car parks, footpaths and transport services.
- The generation and encouragement of sympathetic design and an appreciation of environmental quality in the development process.

There were a number of environmental costs associated with tourism development:

- Volume pressure – deterioration of footpaths, disturbance to wildlife, damage to vegetation, damage to areas of wilderness and the loss of peace and quiet.

- Traffic pressure – generally incurred at specific locations and including traffic bottlenecks, parking problems, slow-moving vehicles (caravans) on main routes and the pollution caused by increased traffic.
- Visual pressure – some tourism facilities detract from the aesthetic quality because of poor siting, bad design or inadequate screening. Examples of such facilities include caravan sites and ski centres.
- Waste pressure – the increased number of visitors to Scotland has resulted in increasing untidiness and danger to wildlife through inadequate or thoughtless disposal of litter.
- User conflict pressure – wherever there are scarce natural resources there will be user conflict. For example, the growing interest in activities such as bird watching, walking, climbing and photography quickly result in pressure on the facilities available and detract from user satisfaction. More obviously, there is the conflict which exists between the competing uses of resources, such as when jet-skiing and power boating use water also used by anglers or general water-based recreation.

- Possible detrimental effects to people, flora and fauna, soil, water, air, peace and quiet, landscapes, and cultural sites, etc. that are either within the proposed project area or will be affected by it.

Figure 10.4 sets out a typical process which an environmental impact assessment might adopt. A proposed development is put forward by a developer and this is initially assessed, bearing in mind the destination's environmental policy. Following this initial evaluation the proposal moves forward to site selection and undergoes a preliminary environmental impact assessment. This assessment is compared with the environmental policy to investigate potential conflicts. Once the preliminary assessment has been completed a pre-feasibility study is undertaken, followed by a more detailed environmental impact assessment. Again the results of the impact assessment are compared with the environmental policy and, if no serious conflicts arise, the proposal can move forward to a full feasibility study. Modifications can then be introduced to minimize the environmental impact and bring the project in line with policy.

CASE STUDY 10.3

Green's checklist of the environmental impacts caused by tourism

The Natural Environment

A Changes in floral and faunal species composition
(1) Disruption of breeding habits.
(2) Killing of animals through hunting.
(3) Killing of animals in order to supply goods for the souvenir trade.
(4) Inward or outward migration of animals.
(5) Destruction of vegetation through the gathering of wood or plants.
(6) Change in extent and/or nature of vegetation cover through clearance or planting to accommodate tourism facilities.
(7) Creation of a wildlife reserve/sanctuary.

B Pollution
(1) Water pollution through discharges of sewage, and spillage of oil/petrol.
(2) Air pollution from vehicle emissions.
(3) Noise pollution from tourist transportation and activities.

C Erosion
(1) Compaction of soils, causing increased surface run-off and erosion.
(2) Change in risk of occurrence of land slips/slides.
(3) Change in risk of avalanche occurrence.
(4) Damage to geological features (e.g. tors, caves).
(5) Damage to river banks.

D Natural resources
(1) Depletion of ground and surface water supplies.
(2) Depletion of fossil fuels to generate energy for tourist activity.
(3) Change in risk of occurrence of fire.

E Visual impact
(1) Facilities (e.g. buildings, chairlifts, car parks).
(2) Litter.

The built environment

A Urban environment
(1) Land taken out of primary production.
(2) Change of hydrological patterns.

B Visual impact
(1) Growth of the built-up area.
(2) New architectural styles.
(3) People and belongings.

C Infrastructure
(1) Overload of infrastructure (roads, railways, car parking, electricity grid, communications systems, waste disposal, water supply).
(2) Provision of new infrastructure.
(3) Environmental management to adapt areas for tourist use (e.g. sea walls, land reclamation).

D Urban form
(1) Changes in residential, retail or industrial land uses (move from houses to hotels/boarding houses).
(2) Changes to the urban fabric (e.g. roads, pavements).
(3) Emergence of contrasts between urban areas developed for the tourist population and those for the host population.

E Restoration
(1) Reuse of disused buildings.
(2) Restoration and preservation of historic buildings and sites.
(3) Restoration of derelict buildings as second homes.

F Competition
(1) Possible decline of tourist attractions or regions because of the opening of other attractions or a change in tourist habits and preferences.

Source: Green et al. (1990).

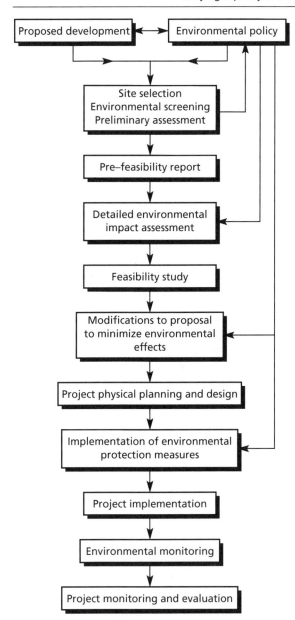

Fig 10.4 The environmental impact assessment process

The physical planning and design of the project can then take place, together with the introduction of measures designed to protect the environment in line with environmental policy. At this stage, the project can be implemented and the project's development can then be monitored in terms of its future environmental impact.

References and further reading

Atherton, T.C. (1991) 'Regulation of tourism destination planning, development and management, including a critique of the systems and practice in Australia', (unpublished)MSc dissertation, University of Surrey.

Burnett, G.W., and Conover, R. (1989) 'The Efficacy of Africa's national parks: an evaluation of Julius Nyrere's Arusha Manifesto of 1961', *Society and Natural Resources*', vol. 2, pp. 251–60.

Cohen, E. (1978) 'The impact of tourism on the physical environment', *Annals of Tourism Research*, vol. 5, no. 2, pp 215–37.

de Kadt, E. (ed.) (1979) *Tourism: Passport to Development?*, New York: Oxford University Press.

Doxey, G.V. (1976) 'When enough's enough: the natives are restless in Old Niagara', *Heritage Canada*, vol. 2, no. 2, pp. 26–7.

Getz, D. (1986) 'Models in tourism planning', *Tourism Management*, vol. 7, no. 1, pp. 21–32.

Green, D.H., Hunter, C.J. and Moore, B.(1990) 'Applications of the Delphi Technique in Tourism', *Annals of Tourism Research*, vol. 17, pp 270–9.

Inskeep, E. (1991) *Tourism Planning: An Integrated and Sustainable Development Approach*, New York: Van Nostrand Reinhold.

Jafari, J. (1987) 'Tourism models: the sociocultural aspects', *Tourism Management*, vol. 8, no. 2, pp. 151–9.

Mathieson, A., and Wall, G. (1982) *Tourism: Economic, Physical and Social Impacts*, Harlow: Longman.

Murphy, P.E. (1985) *Tourism: A Community Approach*, New York: Methuen.

Plog, S.C. (1977) 'Why destination areas rise and fall in popularity,' in Kelly, E.M. (ed.), *Domestic and International Tourism*, Insitute of Certified Travel Agents, Wellesley: Mass.

Shelby *et al* (1984) 'A conceptual framework for carrying capacity determination', *Leisure Sciences*, vol. 6, no. 4, pp. 433–51.

Smith, V.L. (1989) *Hosts and Guests: The Anthropology of Tourism*, 2nd edn, Philadelphia, Pa.: University of Pennsylvania Press.

CHAPTER 11

The economic impact of tourism

OVERVIEW

In this chapter we present both the positive and negative economic impacts of tourism. In the same way that the literature tends to exaggerate the negative impact of tourism upon host societies and environments, so is the positive impact of tourism upon economies often oversold. An integral part of this chapter is the critical assessment of the methods of measuring economic impact – particularly through multiplier analysis. We show that all of the multiplier models we describe provide information which is valuable to policy-makers and planners, and that within its known limitations multiplier analysis is a powerful and valuable tool for analysing the impact of tourism.

TOURISM AND THE SERVICE ECONOMY

In spite of the many altruistic and well-meaning reasons sometimes put forward to support the case for tourism development (such as those in the Manilla Declaration (World Tourism Organization, 1980)), it is the economic advantages that provide the main driving force for tourism development. Tourist expenditure is as 'real' as any other form of consumption, and international tourist expenditure can be seen as an invisible export from the host country, whereas domestic tourism can be seen as an 'export' between the local regions and, perhaps, an import substitute for the national economy. The former is easier to measure than the latter because it involves custom/immigration procedures and currency exchange, which is measured by central banks and

often included in national accounts. Domestic tourist expenditure can only be accurately estimated by undertaking visitor expenditure surveys which are time consuming and costly.

During the past few decades many economies have experienced growth in their service sectors, even when the more traditional agricultural and manufacturing sectors have been subject to stagnation or decline. Tourism is a service-based industry and, as such, has been partly responsible for this service-sector growth. In developing countries, the service sector is responsible for around 40 per cent of gross domestic product (GDP), while in developed or industrialized economies it is responsible for more than 65 per cent of GDP.

In spite of its economic importance, however, the service sector has been sadly neglected in myopic economic textbooks that have continued to concentrate on the more traditional manufacturing industries. The dearth of material on service-based industries in the major textbooks can, in part be explained (if not excused) by the lack of readily available and comparable statistics for service-based sectors. But in general it is tradition rather than pragmatism that has dictated the content of such books. Nevertheless, the latter half of the 1980s saw a growing interest in the operation and performance of service industries, and it was observed, that because of the strength of intersectoral linkages, the service sector generally performs a more important function in the process of development than that suggested by the service sector's contribution to a country's GDP.

Tourism as a major element of the service economy has for some time been applauded for its sustained and rapid growth. However, not even its most ardent supporters would have forecast just how well it has been able to stand up to the pressures of global economic recession. In spite of the fact that the world has staggered from recession to recession over the past decade with little respite, and that even the mighty giants of world industry, such as IBM, have been forced to rationalize their operations, tourism activity has not only been able to maintain its presence, but in many areas has continued to grow.

Although the purpose of this chapter is to examine the economic impact of tourism, it is useful to consider the economic significance of tourism to a number of countries, most notably the prime generators and/or recipients of international tourists. The economic significance of tourism is determined not only by the level of tourism activity that is taking place, but also by the type and nature of the economy being considered. For instance, the economic significance of tourism activity to a developing country may well be measured in terms of its ability to generate an inflow of foreign exchange or provide a means for creating greater price flexibility in its export industries. In a developed or industrialized economy, on the other hand, the researcher may be looking for its ability to assist diversification

and combat regional imbalances.

The significance of tourism may be assessed in terms of the proportion of total global visitors attributable to individual countries, for here one can assess the relative importance of single countries in determining world travel. On the other hand, the significance of tourism may be examined with respect to the importance of tourist activity to the economy of each destination. This chapter examines both aspects in order to establish how some countries are extremely important as tourist generators and how other countries are dependent upon such tourism activity.

TOURISM-GENERATING/RECEIVING COUNTRIES

The selection of countries for inclusion in tables of top generating and top recipient countries is at best difficult and at worst arbitrary. However, the seven countries shown in Tables 11.1 and 11.2 (France, Germany, Italy, Spain, the UK and the USA) have been included because they are among the top five tourist-generating countries and/or the top five countries with respect to tourism receipts.

Table 11.1 Principal tourist generating countries, 1985–90

Country	Expenditure (in US$bn)					
	1985	*1986*	*1987*	*1988*	*1989*	*1990*
West Germany	12.8	18.0	23.3	25.0	23.7	30.1
United States	25.1	26.7	30.0	33.1	33.5	38.7
United Kingdom	6.4	8.9	11.9	14.6	15.1	19.8
Japan	4.8	7.2	10.8	18.7	22.5	24.9
France	4.6	6.5	8.5	9.7	10.3	13.5
Top 5 countries	53.7	67.4	84.5	101.1	105.2	126.9
Rest of world	40.8	57.5	71.4	85.1	93.2	114.0
World total	94.5	124.9	156.0	186.2	198.4	241.0
Top 5 as % of world total	56.8	53.9	54.1	54.3	53.0	52.6

Source: Derived from figures published by World Tourism Organization, (1988, 1992).

Table 11.1 shows the principal tourist-generating countries, with respect to their level of tourist expenditure, over the time period from 1985 to 1990. It can be seen that, over the six years covered by the table, the proportion of the world's total tourist expenditure attributable to the top five generating countries fluctuated slightly with a gradual erosion of their share of the market in the last two years. Some countries, like Japan, increased their tourist expenditure over this period by a factor of more than five, whereas others barely doubled the total value of tourist expenditure for which they were responsible.

Table 11.2 shows the top five countries in terms of tourism receipts. With the exceptions of 1988 and 1989, when there was a slight dip in the proportion of total global tourist receipts attributable to them, the significance of the top five countries steadily increased from just over 41 per cent in 1983 to almost 45 per cent in 1990. The USA has improved its position as top recipient by increasing its receipts fourfold over the eight-year period; and whereas in 1983 the USA was responsible for 11.7 per cent of the world total, in 1990 this figure had risen to 15.9 per cent.

It is clear from Tables 11.1 and 11.2 that there is a high degree of correlation between the top tourist-generating countries and the top tourist expenditure recipients: that is, tourism does not appear to perform a great role as a global redistributor of income in the same way that it is claimed to do for regional redistribution. This is particularly true if the relationship between developed and developing countries is considered. It is the developed and industrialized countries that number among both the top generators of tourist expenditure and the top recipients.

The division between the performance of developed and developing countries is of additional significance when it is considered that, on average through the latter half of the 1980s, the developed countries were responsible for 70 per cent of all world exports and received over 72 per cent of all tourism receipts. This contrasts with the developing countries which were responsible for 20 per cent of all world exports and received only 25 per cent of all tourist receipts, the outstanding exports and tourism receipts being accounted for by the non-market economies of that decade.

Table 11.2 Principal destinations in terms of tourism receipts, 1983–90

Country	Tourism Receipts (US$bn)							
	1983	*1984*	*1985*	*1986*	*1987*	*1988*	*1989*	*1990*
United States	11.4	11.4	11.7	20.4	23.5	28.9	34.5	40.6
Spain	6.8	7.7	8.2	12.1	14.8	16.7	16.2	18.6
Italy	9.0	8.6	8.4	9.9	12.2	12.4	12.0	19.7
France	7.2	7.6	7.9	9.7	12.0	13.8	16.2	20.2
United Kingdom	6.1	6.1	7.1	8.2	10.2	11.0	11.2	15.0
Top 5 countries	40.5	41.4	43.3	60.3	72.7	82.8	90.1	114.1
Rest of world	58.0	61.1	64.8	77.3	94.1	114.9	121.3	140.7
World total	98.5	102.5	108.1	137.6	166.8	197.7	211.4	254.8
Top 5 as % of world total	41.1	40.4	40.1	43.8	43.6	41.9	42.6	44.8

Source: Derived from figures published by World Tourism Organization (1988, 1992).

DEPENDENCE UPON TOURISM

Table 11.3 provides another way of examining the economic significance of tourism for countries by looking at dependence on tourism receipts relative to total export earnings and GDP. It can be seen that, among these economies, tourism receipts as a percentage of total export earnings range from the relatively unimportant 1.1 per cent for Japan to the quite dependent 22 per cent experienced by Spain. Confirming this is the percentage of GDP attributable to tourism receipts, which shows that only 0.2 per cent of Japan's GDP is attributable to tourist receipts as compared to 4 per cent for Spain.

Table 11.4 shows travel account receipts as a percentage of gross domestic product and also travel account expenditure as a percentage of both private final consumption and the import of goods and services. Comparison of travel account expenditure and private final consumption is a useful indicator of how significant tourism is as an element of final demand. In Turkey, for instance, travel account expenditure is equivalent to only 0.8 per cent of private final consumption, whereas in Austria the corresponding figure is almost 9 per cent. This shows that international tourism is more significant as an element of consumption in Austria than it is in many other countries. Also of note is the fact that major recipients of tourist expenditure, such as Spain (1.4 per cent) and France (1.7 per cent), do not show the same propensity to spend overseas as the rest of their European neighbours (average 3.1 per cent).

In the same way that international tourism receipts may be seen as an export of services, travel account expenditure may be regarded as being equivalent to an import of services from other countries. Table 11.4 shows the proportion of goods and services imported attributable to travel account expenditure. With only a few exceptions, the proportion of imports attributable to travel account expenditure is higher than the proportion of private final consumption attributable to the same source. Some 11 per cent of all Icelandic imports are accounted for by travel account expenditure and almost the same figure is recorded by Austria (10.7 per cent), whereas the figure for Turkey is less than 2 per cent.

Two major problems which exist when making international comparisons of tourism expenditure and receipts are that the data are generally expressed in current prices and that they are standardized in US dollars. This form of presentation means that (a) it does not take into account the effects of inflation and (b) movements in the value

Table 11.3 Tourism receipts expressed as a percentage of total export earnings and gross domestic product, 1990

Country	Tourism receipts (US$mn) (1)	Export earnings (US$mn) (2)	(1) as a % of (2)	GDP US$bn (3)	(1) as a % of (3)
Spain	18 426.1	83 930	21.9	459 400	4.0
Italy	19 741.7	229 090	8.6	923 600	2.1
France	20 184.8	269 410	7.5	983 500	2.0
UK	13 828.3	239 560	5.8	902 500	1.5
USA	30 253.0	528 400	17.4	5 392 200	0.06
Germany	10 683.1	476 020	2.2	1 156 600	0.9
Japan	6				

of the dollar exchange rate (which have been both frequent and dramatic over the past decade) will manifest as changes in the local value of tourist receipts and expenditure. In an attempt to circumvent some of these problems, Figure 11.1 shows an index of tourism receipts in real prices from 1983 to 1990, using 1982 as the base year (1982 = 100).

Table 11.4 Travel account receipts as a percentage of GDP, and travel account expenditure as a percentage of private final consumption and imports of goods and services, selected countries, 1990

Country	As a percentage of:		
	As a percentage of GDP (%)	Private final consumption (%)	Imports (%)
Austria	8.5	8.9	10.7
Belgium/ Luxembourg	1.9	4.6	2.7
Denmark	2.5	5.4	6.8
Finland	0.9	3.8	6.9
France	1.7	1.7	3.6
Germany	0.7	3.7	6.6
Greece	3.9	2.3	5.0
Iceland	2.2	7.2	11.0
Ireland	3.4	4.9	3.9
Italy	1.8	2.0	5.3
Netherlands	1.3	4.5	4.5
Norway	1.4	6.7	7.8
Portugal	6.0	2.3	3.0
Spain	3.8	1.4	3.9
Sweden	1.3	5.1	7.2
Switzerland	3.8	5.6	7.0
Turkey	3.0	0.8	1.8
United Kingdom	1.4	2.9	4.4
Europe	**1.9**	**3.1**	**5.2**
Canada	1.1	3.2	6.3
United States	0.8	1.1	5.4
North America	**0.8**	**1.2**	**5.5**
Australia	1.2	2.4	6.3
New Zealand	2.5	5.0	9.0
Japan	0.1	1.5	6.2
Australia–Japan	**0.3**	**1.6**	**6.3**

Source: OECD (1992).

The diagram shows a contrast of events for countries such as Japan and Spain. In the former, real tourism receipts have increased consistently and rapidly since 1986. However, in Spain real tourism receipts peaked in 1988 and have fallen quite dramatically since then. Other countries, such as Germany, have maintained the real value of their tourism receipts over the period, whereas France and the UK have managed to achieve some real gain despite some marked fluctuations throughout the period. The USA began the period poorly with a slight decline being recorded between 1983 and 1985. However, since that time there have been sustained and increasing rates of growth and the USA started the 1990s with a strong growth rate.

Table 11.5 takes the analysis one step further and examines the relationship between tourism receipts and expenditures in order to establish the net effect of travel on selected regions of the world. For the period 1988 to 1990, Europe was in the healthy position of having a positive balance on its travel account. This does, of course, disguise the fact that within Europe some countries performed well in this respect while others did not. The travel trade surplus in Europe increased from US$4.1 billion to US$6 billion over this time period.

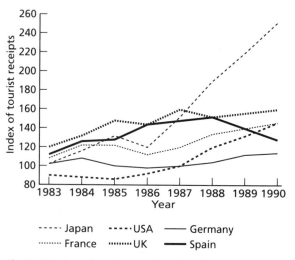

Fig 11.1 Index of tourist receipts in real prices (1992 = 100)

In contrast to this the Australia–Japan region of the world experienced an ever-widening travel trade gap with the deficit increasing from US$15 billion in 1988 to US$20.7 billion in 1990. The increasing deficit in the Australia–Japan region is largely a result of increased expenditure combined with relatively stagnant receipts. The North America region, although suffering from a travel trade deficit over this period, was able to reduce the size of this deficit from US$4.6 billion in 1988 to US$2.3 billion in 1990.

Table 11.5 Tourism balance sheet for Europe, North America and Australia–Japan, 1988–90

	US$bn		
	1988	1989	1990
Europe			
Receipts	100.2	102.7	128.7
Expenditure	96.1	96.8	122.7
Balance	4.1	5.9	6.0
North America			
Receipts	33.8	39.4	44.5
Expenditure	38.4	41.6	46.8
Balance	−4.6	−2.2	−2.3
Australia–Japan			
Receipts	7.7	7.7	8.8
Expenditure	22.7	27.3	29.5
Balance	−15.0	−19.6	−20.7

Note: Minus sign indicates deficit. Due to rounding of figures, balances are not always equal to difference between receipts and expenditure.
Source: OECD (1992).

EMPLOYMENT IN THE TOURISM INDUSTRY

Tourism involves a wide variety of industrial sectors, and this makes it particularly difficult to derive estimates concerning the number of employees associated with tourism. Furthermore, the nature of employment in the tourism industry

together with the diverse range of linkages between tourism sectors and other sectors of the economy also compound the problem of attempting to make realistic estimates concerning the magnitude of the industry.

Table 11.6 Employment in the tourism industry, selected countries, 1988

Country	Workforce in tourism industry	Percentage of inter-national tourism	Interna-tional tourism workforce
UK	2 049 000	26.2	537 453
Spain	1 452 600	66.6	967 432
Italy	1 065 000	30.5	324 825
France	870 800	30.6	266 465
Germany	797 000	13.7	109 189

Source: Derived from figures published by International Labour Organization, HRS/1983/1, and World Tourism Organization (1988).

Table 11.6 shows the numbers employed in the tourism industry in selected countries, together with an estimate of the proportion of the workforce that is employed by international tourism activity. A few European countries have been selected in order to demonstrate the direct employment opportunities created by tourism activity. The results shown in Table 11.6 should be seen as indicative rather than precise because (a) tourism is not recognized as an industry in the Standard Industrial Classification (SIC), and thus there are wide variations in the estimates of the total number employed in the industry, and (b) the estimation of the proportion of employees supported by international tourism activity is a crude one, taking the percentage of total tourism activity that is attributable to international tourism and using this figure as a ratio to derive the proportion of the workforce related to international tourism. In a more precise estimate it would be necessary (a) to have better employment statistics in general and (b) to take into account the fact that international tourism activity is more likely to be associated with a higher labour content than domestic tourism activity.

Table 11.7 shows the number of people employed in the hotel and restaurant industries in selected countries together with a breakdown of the workforce by sex.

Table 11.7 Employment in hotels and restaurants, selected countries, 1990

Country	No. employed	% male	% female
Austria	126 034	38.7	61.3
Belgium	93 376	46.7	53.3
Finland	75 000	24.0	76.0
Germany	692 700	43.2	56.8
Netherlands	71 400	55.2	44.8
Sweden	98 000	37.8	62.2
United Kingdom	603 700	40.1	59.9
Canada	768 000	41.7	58.2
Australia	94 000	39.4	60.6

THE GENERATION OF ECONOMIC IMPACTS BY TOURIST SPENDING

Tourists spend their money on a wide variety of goods and services. They purchase accommodation, food and beverage, transport, communications, entertainment services, goods from retail outlets and tour/travel services, to name just a few. This money may be seen as an injection of demand into the host economy: that is, demand which would otherwise not be present. However, the value of tourist expenditure represents only a partial picture of the economic impact. The full assessment of economic impact must take into account other aspects, including the following:

- Indirect and induced effects;
- Leakages of expenditure out of the local economy;
- Displacement and opportunity costs.

Direct, indirect and induced economic effects

Tourist expenditure has a 'cascading' effect throughout the host economy. It begins with tourists spending money in 'front-line' tourist establishments, such as hotels, restaurants and taxis, and then permeates throughout the rest of the economy. It can be examined by assessing the impact at three different levels – the direct, indirect and induced levels.

The direct level of impact is the value of tourist expenditure *less* the value of imports necessary to supply those 'front-line' goods and services. Thus, the direct impact is likely to be less than the value of tourist expenditure except in the rare case where a local economy can provide all of the tourist's wants from its own production sectors.

The establishments which directly receive the tourist expenditure also need to purchase goods and services from other sectors within the local economy. For example, hotels will purchase the services of builders, accountants, banks, food and beverage suppliers, electricity and water, etc. Furthermore, the suppliers to these 'front-line' establishments will also need to purchase goods and services from other establishments within the local economy, and so the process continues. The generation of economic activity brought about by these subsequent rounds of expenditure is known as the indirect effect. The indirect effect will not involve all of the moneys spent by tourists during the direct effect, since some of that money will leak out of circulation through imports, savings and taxation.

Finally, during the direct and indirect rounds of expenditure, income will accrue to local residents in the form of wages, salaries, distributed profit, rent and interest. This addition to local income will, in part, be respent in the local economy on goods and services, and this will generate yet further rounds of economic activity.

It is only when all three levels of impact (direct *plus* indirect *plus* induced) are estimated that the full positive economic impact of tourism expenditure is fully assessed. However, there can be negative aspects to the economic impact of tourist expenditure.

Negative economic impacts

The production of tourist goods and services requires the commitment of resources which could otherwise be used for alternative purposes. For instance, the development of a tourism resort may involve the migration of labour from rural to urban areas, which brings with it economic implications for both the rural and the urban areas – the former losing a productive unit of labour and the latter likely to experience additional infrastructure pressure for health, education and other public services. If labour is not in abundance then meeting the tourists' demands may involve the transfer of labour from one industry (such as agriculture or fishing) to tourism industries, involving an opportunity cost which is often ignored in the estimation of tourism's economic impact. Furthermore, if there is a shortage of skilled labour then there may be a need to import labour from other countries. This will result in additional economic leakages as income earned from this imported labour may, in part, be repatriated.

Similarly, the use of capital resources (which are often a scarce resource) in the development of tourism-related establishments precludes their use for other forms of economic development. To gain a true picture of the economic impact of tourism it is therefore necessary to take into account the *opportunity costs* of using scarce resources for tourism development as opposed to alternative uses.

Where tourism development substitutes one form of expenditure and economic activity for another, this is known as the *displacement effect*. The displacement effect should be taken into account when the economic impact of tourism is being estimated. Displacement can take place when tourism development is undertaken at the expense of another industry, and is generally referred to as the opportunity cost of the devel-

opment. However, it is more commonly referred to when a new tourism project is seen to take away custom from an existing facility. For instance, if a destination finds that its all-inclusive hotels are running at high occupancy levels and returning a reasonable yield on the investment, the construction of an additional all-inclusive hotel may simply reduce the occupancy levels of the existing establishments, and the destination may find that its overall tourism activity has not increased by as much as the new business from the development. This is displacement.

THE MEASUREMENT OF ECONOMIC IMPACT

The measurement of the economic impact of tourism is far more complicated than simply calculating the level of tourist expenditure. Indeed, estimates of the economic impact of tourism based on tourist expenditure or receipts can be not only inaccurate, but also very misleading. Before examining how the economic impact is measured, it is necessary to look at the different aspects of the economy that are affected by tourism expenditure.

To begin with, a difference can be drawn between the economic impact associated with tourist expenditure and that associated with the development of tourism. The former refers to the ongoing effects of, and changes in, tourist expenditure, whereas the latter is concerned with the impact of the construction and finance of tourism-related facilities. A comprehensive review of project appraisal methods is provided in Curry and Weiss (1992). The difference between these two aspects of impact is important because they require different methodological approaches. The calculation of the economic impact of tourist expenditure is achieved by using multiplier analysis, and the estimation of the economic impact of tourism development projects is achieved by resorting to project appraisal techniques such as cost–benefit analysis.

Measuring the economic impact of tourist expenditure

At a national level the World Tourism Organization publishes annual tourist statistics for countries throughout the world. These statistics include figures relating to tourist expenditure and tourist receipts. It would not be correct to assume that the tourist receipts figures reflect the economic impact of tourist expenditure on any particular economy. They relate to how much tourists spend in the destination and take no account of how much of that sum leaks straight out of the economy (paying for imported goods and services to satisfy tourist needs), or how much additional impact is experienced through the 'knock-on' effects of this tourist spending.

At a sub-national level the availability of tourist expenditure data is far more sparse. Some countries, such as the United Kingdom, undertake visitor expenditure surveys (such as the International Passenger Survey (IPS) and the United Kingdom Tourist Survey (UKTS)) which allow expenditure estimates to be made at the regional level. It is often necessary to undertake specific tourist expenditure surveys to establish the tourist spend in particular areas.

In order to translate tourist expenditure data into economic impact information the appropriate multiplier values have to be calculated. The *multiplier* is one of the most quoted economic concepts in the study of tourism. Multiplier values may be used for a variety of purposes and are often used as the basis for public-sector decision making.

The multiplier concept

The concept of the multiplier is based upon the recognition that sales for one firm require purchases from other firms within the local economy: that is, the industrial sectors of an economy are interdependent. This means that firms not only purchase primary inputs such as labour, imports, etc., but also purchase intermediate goods and services produced by other establishments within the local economy. Therefore, a change in the level of final demand for one sector's output will affect not only the industry that produces the final good/service, but also other sectors that supply goods/services to that sector, and the sectors that act as suppliers to those sectors as well.

Because firms in the local economy are dependent upon other firms for their supplies, any change in tourist expenditure will bring about a change in the economy's level of production, household income, employment, government revenue and foreign exchange flows (where applicable). These changes may be greater than, equal to, or less than the value of the change in tourist expenditure that brought them about. The term *tourist multiplier* refers to the ratio of two changes – the change in one of the key economic variables such as output (income, employment or government revenue) to the change in tourist expenditure.

Therefore, there will be some value by which the initial change in tourist expenditure must be multiplied in order to estimate the total change in output – this is known as the *output multiplier*. In the same way, there will be a value that, when multiplied by the change in tourist expenditure, will estimate the total change in household income – this is known as the *income multiplier*. The reason why the initial change in tourist spending must be subject to a multiplier effect can be seen from Figure 11.2.

Figure 11.2 shows that the tourist expenditure goes, initially, to the front-line tourist establishments which provide the tourists with their goods and services. This money will be respent by the firms which receive it. A proportion of the money will leak directly out of the economy in the form of imports. These imports may be in the form of food and beverage that the tourist eats but that are not provided locally, or in respect of services provided to the establishment by individuals or firms located outside the economy being analysed. The money paid to persons outside the economy cannot have any further role in generating economic activity within the local economy, and thus the value of tourist expenditure that actually circulates in the local economy is immediately reduced. The remaining sum of money will be

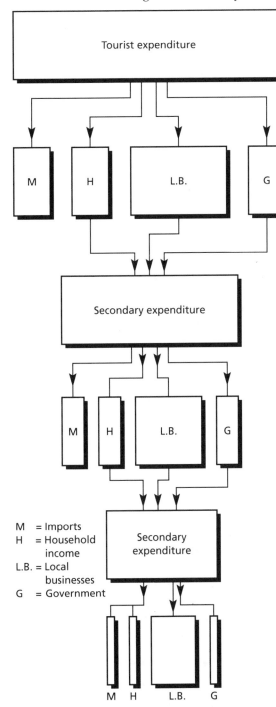

M   = Imports
H   = Household income
L.B. = Local businesses
G   = Government

Fig 11.2 The multiplier process

used to purchase locally produced goods and services, labour and entrepreneurial skills (wages, salaries and profits) and to meet government taxes, licences and fees. These are all direct effects.

We can see from Figure 11.2 that money will flow from the tourism-related establishments to other local businesses. This money will also be respent, some of it leaking out as imports, some of it leaking out of circulation as savings and some going to the government. The remainder will be spent on labour and entrepreneurial skills and purchases from other businesses for goods and services. The businesses which receive money in payment for their goods/services will also make purchases locally, import goods and services and pay government taxes. These are indirect effects.

It can be seen that, during each round of expenditure, some proportion of money accrues to local residents in the form of income (wages, salaries and profits). Some of this money will be saved (by either households or businesses) and will cease to circulate in the economy: that is, there will be a leakage. The income which accrues to local households and is not saved will be respent. Some of it will leak out of the system as imports and some of it will go to the government as tax. The remainder will be respent as household consumption. This spending of income accrued as a result of the initial tourist expenditure will generate further rounds of economic activity. This is the induced effect.

The value of any tourism multiplier is meaningless unless it is qualified by both the methodology used to estimate it, and the type of multiplier involved.

Types of multipliers

There are a number of multipliers in regular use and each type has its own specific function. However, misleading conclusions can be derived if they are misused or misinterpreted. This issue will be discussed later in the chapter. The major types of multiplier are as follows.

A transactions (or sales) multiplier

This measures the amount of additional business revenue created in an economy as a result of an increase in tourist expenditure. Similar to this in concept is the output multiplier.

An output multiplier

This measures the amount of additional output generated in an economy as a result of an increase in tourist expenditure. The principal distinction between these two multipliers is that the output multiplier is concerned with changes in the actual levels of production and not with the volume and value of sales. Not all sales will be related to current production (some sales may have been made from inventories and some productive output may not be sold within the time-frame of the model and may, therefore, result in an increase in inventories). For this reason, the value of an output multiplier may well be larger or smaller than the value of the corresponding transactions multiplier.

An income multiplier

This measures the additional income (wages and salaries, rent, interest and distributed profits) created in the economy as a result of an increase in tourist expenditure. Such income can be measured either as *national income* (*regional* in the case of domestic tourism) or as *disposable income*: that is, the income which is actually available to households either to spend or to save. However, as mentioned earlier, the income which accrues to non-nationals who have been 'imported' into the area should be extracted because the incomes which they receive cannot be considered to be benefits to the area. On the other hand, the secondary economic effects created by the respending of non-nationals' incomes within the area must be included within the calculations.

An employment multiplier

This is a measurement of *either* the total amount of employment generated by an additional unit of tourist expenditure *or* the ratio of the total employment generated by this same expenditure to the direct employment alone. Employment multipliers provide a useful source of information about the secondary effects of tourism, but their measurement involves more heroic assumptions than in the case of other multipliers, and care is needed in their interpretation.

A government revenue multiplier

This measures the impact on government revenue, from all sources, associated with an increase of tourist expenditure. This multiplier may be expressed in gross terms – that is, the gross increase in government revenue as a result of an increase in tourist spending – or in net terms, when the increase in government revenue is reduced by the increase in government expenditures associated with the increase in tourist activity.

Since the different types of multiplier are calculated using the same database, they are closely interrelated. However, the concepts involved in each of the above multipliers are very different, as are the magnitudes of each of the different multipliers calculated for the same economy. Some examples of these multiplier values are shown later in the chapter. Given the number of different multiplier concepts that are available, it is not surprising to find that there has been some confusion over their interpretation. This confusion has been compounded by the fact that there are also a variety of methods that may be used to calculate each of the multipliers.

Methodological approaches

Four major techniques have been employed to measure the value of the tourist multiplier.

CASE STUDY 11.1

Multiplier analysis using base theory

One early and interesting application of the technique by R.R. Nathan Associates (1966) was used to calculate the short-run employment effects created by tourism expenditure in each of 375 counties and independent cities of Appalachia. The final model used took the form:

$$\frac{E_r}{E_{rx2}} = \frac{1}{1 - E_{rc}/E_r}$$

(11.1.1)

where E_r is total local employment, E_{rc} is local employment servicing local consumer demand and E_{rx2} is the direct change in employment created by a change in tourism expenditure.

Nathan Associates developed the multiplier model further, to measure long-term effects, by incorporating investment acitivity. This model took the form:

$$\frac{E_r}{E_{rx2}} = \frac{1 + i_2}{1 - E_{rc}/E_r}$$

(11.1.2)

where i_2 is a statistically estimated parameter (the value of which lies between 0 and 1) which relates the change in investment to the change in tourism activity.

This model is far too simplistic to be accurate in calculating tourism multiplier values.

Base Theory Models

The basic assumption underlying base theory models is that there exists a stable relationship between each of the export sectors and the local sectors of an economy, so that changes in the level of tourist expenditure will create predictable and measurable changes in the level of activity in local sectors. An example of this approach is given in Case Study 11.1. Base theory multipliers are normally oversimplified formulations and are now rarely used.

Alternative and more detailed and accurate methods of measuring the long-term multiplier will now be described.

Keynesian Multiplier Models

These multipliers are designed to measure the income created in an economy by an additional unit of tourist expenditure. The simplest formulation of the multiplier (k) is shown in equation 11.1 below

$$k = \frac{1}{1 - c + m}$$

(11.1)

where 1 is the additional unit of tourism expenditure and leakages are the proportion of this expenditure which goes into savings $(1 - c)$ and imports (m).

i.e.

$$k = \frac{1}{\text{leakages}}$$

The development of this model into a long-run formulation, which takes investment into account, is shown in equation 11.2.

$$k = \frac{1}{1 - c + m - i}$$

(11.2)

where i is the marginal propensity to invest.

Similarly, the effects of respending money accruing to the public sector can be built into the model, and this is shown in equation 11.3.

$$k = \frac{1}{1 - c + m - i - g}$$

(11.3)

where g is the marginal propensity of the public sector to spend.

A typical Keynesian short-run multiplier model is shown in equation 11.4. The derivation of this model is given in Archer (1976).

$$k = \frac{1 - L}{1 - c(1 - t_i)(1 - t_d - b) + m}$$

(11.4)

where,

L = the first round leakages out of the economy
t_i = the marginal rate of indirect taxation
t_d = the marginal rate of taxation and other deductions
b = the marginal rate of transfer payments.

The difference in the value of the multiplier created by applying exactly the same data to the short-run models shown in equations 11.1 and 11.4 highlights the dangers of relying on a model whose structure is too simplistic. For example, if we let

L = 0.5
c = 0.9
m = 0.7
t_i = 0.16
t_d = 0.2 and
b = 0.2

and calculate the income multipliers first using the model shown in equation 11.1 and then again, using the more developed model shown in equation 11.4, the results are:

$$\frac{1}{1-c+m} = \frac{1}{1-0.9+0.7} = 1.25$$

and

$$\frac{1-L}{1-c(1-t_i)(1-t_d-b)+m}$$

$$= \frac{1-0.5}{1-0.9(1-0.16)(1-0.2-0.2)+0.7} = 0.4012$$

The two multiplier values derived from the same database are very different and would result in very different policy implications. However, even the more developed model shown in equation 11.4 is far too simplistic and is unable to measure variations in the form and magnitude of sectoral linkages and leakages out of the destination's economy during each round of transactions. Even the most complex and comprehensive Keynesian models developed for some studies are unable to provide the level of detail that is required for policy making and planning. One practical solution is to use *ad hoc* models.

Ad hoc Models

These models, although similar in principle to the Keynesian approach discussed above, are constructed specifically for each particular study. The simplest form of *ad hoc* model, using matrix algebra, is shown in equation 11.5.

$$A \times \frac{1}{1-BC} \tag{11.5}$$

where

A = the proportion of additional tourist expenditure remaining in the economy after first round leakages, i.e. A equals the $(1-L)$ expression in the Keynesian model;
B = the propensity of local people to consume in the local economy;
C = the proportion of expenditure by local people that accrues as income in the local economy.

The *ad hoc* model shown in equation 11.5 is too simplistic for serious application, but more advanced models have been developed and used widely to calculate tourist multipliers to estimate the effect of tourist expenditure on income, public-sector revenue, employment and imports. One such model, developed by Archer and Owen (1971), is shown as equation 11.6 below.

$$\sum_{j=1}^{N} \sum_{i=1}^{n} Q_j K_{ij} V_i \quad \frac{1}{1-c\sum_{i=1}^{n} X_i Z_i V_i} \tag{11.6}$$

where

j = each category of tourist, $j = 1$ to N;
i = each type of business establishment, $i = 1$ to n;
Q_j = the proportion of total tourist expenditure spent by the jth type of tourist;
K_{ij} = the proportion of expenditure by the jth type of tourist in the ith category of business;
V_i = the direct and indirect income generated by unit of expenditure by the ith type of business;
X_i = the pattern of consumption, i.e. the proportion of total consumer expenditure by the residents of the area in the ith type of business;

Z_i = the proportion of X_i which takes place within the study area; and

c = the marginal propensity to consume.

In order to trace the flow of expenditure through successive rounds, separate equations are estimated for a range of V_i values. Examples of these are provided in the literature (see, for example, Archer and Owen (1971)).

Multiplier studies using *ad hoc* models are commonly used and examples can be found in the USA, UK, South Pacific islands, Caribbean and elsewhere. More recent models have achieved even greater levels of disaggregation, even down to the levels of individual establishments.

Although models of this type can produce a large quantity of detailed and accurate information

SALES TO		INTERMEDIATE DEMAND Productive sectors					FINAL DEMAND Final demand sectors				TOTAL OUTPUT
PURCHASES FROM		Industry 1	2	3	4	. . . . m	H	I	G	E	
Productive sectors	Industry 1	X_{11}	X_{12}	X_{13}	X_{14}	. . . . X_{1m}	C_1	I_1	G_1	E_1	X_1
	Industry 2	X_{21}	X_{22}	X_{23}	X_{24}	. . . . X_{2m}	C_2	I_2	G_2	E_2	X_2
	Industry 3	X_{31}	X_{32}	X_{33}	X_{34}	. . . . X_{3m}	C_3	I_3	G_3	E_3	X_3
	Industry 4	X_{41}	X_{42}	X_{43}	X_{44}	. . . . X_{4m}	C_4	I_4	G_4	E_4	X_4
	. . .	.	.	.	.	. . . . .	.	.	.	.	.
	. . .	.	.	.	.	. . . . .	.	.	.	.	.
	Industry m	X_{m1}	X_{m2}	X_{m3}	X_{m4}	. . . . X_{mm}	C_m	I_m	G_m	E_m	X_m
Primary inputs	Wages and salaries	W_1	W_2	W_3	W_4	. . . . W_m	W_C	W_I	W_G	W_E	W
	Profits/ dividends	P_1	P_2	P_3	P_4	. . . . P_m	P_C	P_I	P_G	P_E	P
	Taxes	T_1	T_2	T_3	T_4	. . . . T_m	T_C	T_I	T_G	T_E	T
	Imports	M_1	M_2	M_3	M_4	. . . . M_m	M_C	M_I	M_G	M_E	M
Total inputs		X_1	X_2	X_3	X_4	. . . . X_m	C	I	G	E	X

where:
X = Output
C = Consumption (households)
I = Investment (private)
G = Government expenditure

E = Exports
M = Imports
W = Wages and salaries
P = Profits and dividends
I = Taxes

Final demand sectors:
H = Household consumption sector
I = Investment expenditure sector
G = Government expenditure sector
E = Exports sectors

Fig 11.3 Basic input–output transactions table

for policy-making and planning purposes, they are unable to provide the wealth of data yielded by the final methodological approach to be discussed: input–output analysis.

Input-output analysis

The input–output model approach, unlike the alternative methods discussed above, presents a general equilibrium approach to studying economic impacts, rather than the partial equilibrium approach used in Keynesian and *ad hoc* models.

Input–output analysis begins with the construction of a table, similar to a table of national/regional accounts, which shows the economy of the destination in matrix form. Each sector of the economy is shown in each column as a purchaser of goods and services from other sectors in the economy, and in each row as a seller of output to each of the other sectors. The structure of an input–output table is shown in Figure 11.3. The table may be subdivided into three major quadrants. First, the inter-industry matrix, located in the top left-hand quadrant, details the sales and purchases which take place between the various sectors of the economy (e.g. $X_{11}, X_{12}, X_{13},$ etc. are the sales of sector 1 to all other sectors within the economy, whereas $X_{11}, X_{21}, X_{31}, X_{41},$ etc. represent the purchases of sector 1 from all other sectors within the economy). Second, the bottom left-hand quadrant shows each sector's purchases of primary inputs (such as payments to labour (W), profits (P), taxes (T) and imported goods and services (M)). Third, the right-hand quadrant shows the sales made by each sector to each source of final demand.

The simplest formulation is shown in equations 11.7 and 11.8, where, for ease of explanation, all forms of final demand are represented by a column vector ($\mathbf{Y}$).

$$\mathbf{X} = A\mathbf{X} + \mathbf{Y} \qquad (11.7)$$
$$\mathbf{X} - A\mathbf{X} = \mathbf{Y}$$
$$(I - A)\mathbf{X} = \mathbf{Y}$$
$$\mathbf{X} = (I - A)^{-1}\,\mathbf{Y}$$
and $\quad \Delta\mathbf{X} = (I - A)^{-1}\Delta\mathbf{Y} \qquad (11.8)$

where

$\mathbf{X}$ = a vector of the total sales of each sector of the economy, i.e. $[X_1 + X_2 + X_3 + X_4]$;

A = a matrix of the inter-industrial transactions within the economy;

$\mathbf{Y}$ = a vector of final demand sales; and

I = an identity matrix (equivalent to 1 in simple algebra).

A change in the level of final demand ($\Delta\mathbf{Y}$) will create an increase in the level of activity within the economy, which manifests itself as changes in the output and sales of each sector. Further sub-models are required to calculate the effects on business revenue, public-sector revenue, employment and incomes. The model shown in equation 11.8 is still too simplistic for practical application and must be developed further.

For instance, in the simplified model discussed above the imports of the economy are shown as a single row vector. However, the robust and flexible framework of input–output models allows the researcher to incorporate a matrix of import functions in order to draw distinctions between competitive and non-competitive imports. This is an extremely useful distinction because competitive imports are, by their very nature, far less predictable than non-competitive imports.

Incorporating an import function matrix which examines the trade-off between domestic production and competitive imports results in equation 11.8 being revised as follows:

$$\Delta\mathbf{X} = (I - K^*A)^{-1}\,\Delta\mathbf{Y} \qquad (11.9)$$

where,

K^* = a matrix where the diagonal values reflect the level of competitive imports associated with each sector, which, when applied to the A matrix, reduces the domestic component of output by the required amount.

In this manner, changes in primary inputs (P) created by a change in tourist expenditure (T) will be given by

$$\Delta P = B(I - K^*A)^{-1}\Delta T \qquad (11.10)$$

where,

B = an $m \times n$ matrix of primary inputs.

Furthermore, the input–output model can be developed in order to provide information with respect to changes in employment levels brought about by changes in tourism expenditure. Let ΔL represent the change in employment and E be an $m \times n$ matrix of employment coefficients. The model will now take the form shown in equation 11.11.

$$\Delta L = E(I - K^*A)^{-1}\Delta T \qquad (11.11)$$

In general, the input–output model can be as comprehensive as data, time and resources allow. Notwithstanding the fact that input–output analysis has been subject to criticism because of its general approach and the aggregation of firms into 'whole industries', the sectors of the model can be disaggregated to achieve the highest level of detail.

Weaknesses and limitations of multiplier models

Each of the multiplier model approaches outlined above contains several inherent problems which must be overcome for practical applications.

Data deficiencies

Secondary data (both published and unpublished) are rarely adequate to meet the requirements of the more demanding and advanced models. This means that researchers need to spend considerable time, effort and money collecting data for multiplier purposes.

Other data difficulties arise out of the nature of tourism itself as a multiproduct industry directly affecting a large number of sectors in an economy. Tourist expenditure is spread across several sectors of an economy, and accurate surveys of visitor expenditure are required in order to obtain an acceptable breakdown of this expenditure into its various components, such as accommodation, meals, beverages, transportation, shopping, etc.

Furthermore, problems often arise when attempting to integrate this visitor expenditure into the categories disaggregated in the input–output table. Rarely are pre-existing input–output tables produced in a form sufficiently disaggregated to accept the detailed data derived from visitor expenditure surveys. In such cases, either the tourist expenditure data have to be compressed to fit the sectors already identified in the input–output table, with a consequent loss in the accuracy of the results, or else much time and effort has to be expended on disaggregating the existing input–output table.

If, however, an input–output (or alternative) model is constructed especially for the study, the matrix can be arranged in a form which fits the tourist expenditure pattern and the data can be fed directly into the model.

Restrictive assumptions and operational limitations

Many of the weaknesses of multiplier analysis arise out of the restrictive assumptions that are made during the construction of the model. However, research is progressively removing the worst of these assumptions.

Supply constraints

These can inhibit the ability of an economy to supply the quantity and quality of goods and services required to provide for an increase in tourism expenditure. If capacity is inadequate to meet the additional demand, and if insufficient factors of production, especially labour, are available, then additional tourism expenditure creates inflation and additional goods and services may have to be imported. Thus the size of the multiplier, if measured by an appropriate model, will fall.

Most multiplier models are static in nature but can be made dynamic. Static models assume the following:

- That production and consumption functions are linear and that the inter-sectoral expenditure patterns are stable.
- That all sectors are able to meet any additional demands for their output.
- That relative prices remain constant.

The first of these assumptions – linear production and consumption functions and stable inter-sectoral expenditure patterns – assumes that any additional tourism expenditure which occurs will generate the same impact on the economy as an equivalent amount of previous tourism expenditure. Thus, any additional production in the economy is assumed to require purchases of inputs in the same proportions and from the same sources as previously. Similarly, any consequential increase in consumer demand is assumed to have exactly the same effect upon the economy as previous consumer expenditure. With respect to the stability of the production functions, tourism, being a labour-intensive personal service, tends to be associated with fairly stable production functions. Thus, the use of average technical coefficients and the assumption of linear homogeneity in production tends not to be a serious drawback when using input–output analysis to study service-based economies.

Dynamic models have been constructed to remove some of these constraints, but the increase in data requirements tends to be prohibitive.

Multiplier values – some examples

The magnitude of multiplier values will vary under different circumstances because its size is dependent upon the nature of an area's economy and upon the extent to which the various sectors of the economy are linked in their trading patterns.

A large number of tourism multiplier studies have been carried out over the past two decades. Table 11.8 shows the value of tourism output multipliers ranging from 1.16 in a regional economy within the UK, to 3.198 for the national economy of Turkey. The range of output multipliers of states within the USA spans from 1.58 in Sullivan

County, Pennsylvania, to 2.17 in Door County, Wisconsin, and examples in the UK include the City of Edinburgh at 1.51 and a value of 1.16 for Gwynedd, North Wales.

Table 11.8 Tourism output multipliers for selected destinations

Country or region	Tourism output multiplier
Turkey	2.339–3.198
Door County, Wisconsin, USA	2.17
Clinton County, Pennsylvania, USA	1.98
Grand County, Colorado, USA	1.94
Walworth County, Wisconsin, USA	1.87
Sullivan County, Pennsylvania, USA	1.58
Edinburgh, Scotland, UK	1.51
Barbados	1.41
Gwynedd County, Wales, UK	1.16

Source: Compiled by the author from published articles and unpublished reports to governments.

For policy-making and planning purposes, income multipliers are the most useful because they provide information about national income rather than merely business output or turnover.

Table 11.9 shows multiplier values for a number of countries. Although the income multiplier values are listed in order of magnitude, care must be taken when comparing multiplier values between countries. First, the analyses were undertaken over different time periods and, even though multiplier values are not subject to drastic changes even over two decades, they do tend to increase as economies develop and improve their sectoral linkages. Second, and more important, not all of the multipliers shown in these tables have been calculated using the same methodology, and this can make a significant difference to the value. For instance, input–output models, because they are based upon a general equilibrium approach, tend to yield significantly higher multiplier values than *ad hoc* models and, depending upon the level of comprehensiveness and detail achieved in the *ad hoc* models, this difference may be as high as 30 per cent.

Table 11.9 Tourism income multipliers for selected destinations

Country or region	Income multiplier
United Kingdom	1.73
Republic of Ireland	1.72
Sri Lanka	1.59
Jamaica	1.27
Egypt	1.23
Dominican Republic	1.20
Cyprus	1.14
Northern Ireland	1.10
Bermuda	1.09
Fiji	1.07
Seychelles	1.03
Malta	1.00
Mauritius	0.97
Antigua	0.88
Missouri State, USA	0.88
Hong Kong	0.87
Philippines	0.82
The Bahamas	0.79
Walworth County, USA	0.78
Malta	0.68
Gibraltar	0.66
Western Samoa	0.66
Cayman Islands	0.65
Iceland	0.64
Barbados	0.60
Grand County, USA	0.60
British Virgin Islands	0.58
Door County, USA	0.55
Solomon Islands	0.52
Republic of Palau	0.51
Victoria Metropolitan Area, Canada	0.50
Sullivan County, USA	0.44
City of Carlisle, UK	0.40
Edinburgh, Scotland, UK	0.35
East Anglia, UK	0.34

Source: Compiled by the author from published articles and unpublished reports to governments.

It is also noticeable from Table 11.9 that the size of the income multiplier values tends to be correlated with the size of the economy. In general, the larger the economy, the higher will be the multiplier value, although there will obviously be some exceptions to this. The reason for this correlation is that larger economies tend to have a more devel-

oped economic structure, which means that they have stronger inter-sectoral linkages and lower propensities to import in order to meet the demands of tourists and the tourist industry.

Table 11.10 The impact of $1000 tourist expenditure on Fiji's balance of payments

		$'s
Tourist expenditure (+)		1000.0
Import requirements (−)		
Direct	120.8	
Indirect	115.3	236.1
Net effect on balance of payments		763.9
Induced imports (−)	326.3	326.3
Net impact after induced effects		437.6

Note: Impact figures include F$53.0 repatriated income.
Source: Tourism Council for the South Pacific (1992).

In addition to calculating the levels of output, income, employment and government revenue generated by additional units of tourist expenditure, multiplier analysis provides valuable information concerning its impact on a country's net foreign exchange flows. Table 11.10 provides an example of the type of information that can be derived from such analysis. Using the national economy of Fiji as an example, Table 11.10 shows that, for each additional $1000 of tourist expenditure, $120.8 immediately leaks out of the economy as imports necessary to meet the tourists' demand. A further $115.3 then leaks out of the economy as imports required throughout the Fiji economy in order to support this additional level of tourist activity, leaving a net inflow of foreign exchange equivalent to $763.9. Therefore, for each additional $1000 of tourist expenditure Fiji's foreign exchange account benefits by $763.9.

However, the resulting increase in income levels in Fiji will generate further imports as a portion of this additional income is respent. Some of this respending of income will be on goods and services that are produced by firms and individuals located outside Fiji's national boundaries, resulting in an increase in imports of $326.3, leaving a net inflow of foreign exchange of $437.6.

Great care must be exercised in the interpretation of employment multipliers. The data used for their measurement and the assumptions underlying the model constructions are more heroic than for other types of multiplier. There are two major problems:

- In the majority of studies, employment is assumed to have a linear relationship with either income or output, whereas the available evidence suggests that this relationship is non-linear.
- Multiplier models assume that employment in each sector is at full capacity, so that meeting any increase in demand will require additional employment. In practice, this is unlikely to be true and increases (or decreases) in the level of tourist expenditure will not generate a corresponding increase (or decrease) in the number of people employed.

In consequence, tourism employment multipliers should be interpreted only as an *indication* of the number of full-time job opportunities created by changes in tourist expenditure. Whether or not these job opportunities will materialize depends upon a number of factors, most notably the extent to which the existing labour force in each sector is fully utilized, and the degree to which labour is able to transfer between different occupations and between different sectors of the economy.

Table 11.11 Tourism employment multipliers for selected destinations

Country or region	Employment multiplier
Bermuda	0.000044
Jamaica	0.000128
Malta	0.000159
Fiji	0.000079
Edinburgh, Scotland, UK	0.000037

Table 11.11 shows the employment multipliers for several countries and regions. We can see that

these employment multipliers are of a different magnitude from those relating to either output or income. This reflects the need for considerably larger amounts of tourist spending to generate one new full-time equivalent job opportunity.

Unlike the income and output multipliers, it is not possible to compare employment multipliers between different destinations when they are presented in this form. This is because the above figures show the number of full-time equivalent job opportunities created by one unit of tourist expenditure where that unit is expressed in the local currency. Thus, differences in the unit value of local currencies will provide employment multipliers of different magnitudes. A more sensible way of making international comparisons of employment multipliers is to express them as a ratio of total employment generated to direct employment. Examples of this latter type of employment multiplier are shown in Table 11.12.

Table 11.12 Standardized employment multipliers for selected destinations

Country	Employment multiplier
Jamaica	4.61
Mauritius	3.76
Bermuda	3.02
Gibraltar	2.62
Solomon Islands	2.58
Malta	1.99
Western Samoa	1.96
Republic of Palau	1.67

Table 11.12 shows that in Jamaica, for every new full-time employee directly employed as a result of an increase in tourist expenditure, a further 4.61 full-time equivalent job opportunities are created throughout the Jamaican economy. Again, we can see that the more developed the tourism economy, the larger the employment multiplier. Comparison between Tables 11.11 and 11.12 shows that Malta, which records the highest multiplier value when expressed per unit of tourist expenditure,

Table 11.13 Tourist income multiplier[2], tourist density and tourism dependence, selected island economies[1]

Country	Income multiplier	Tourism receipts (US$m)	GNP (US$m)	Tourist density[3] (tourist/ population)	Tourism dependence[4] (receipts/ GNP)
Sri Lanka	1.59	75	6 448	0.02	1.2
Jamaica	1.27	407	2 090	0.35	19.5
Dominica	1.20	9*	90*	0.56	10.0
Cyprus	1.14	497	2 821	2.22	17.6
Bermuda	1.09	357*	1 030*	7.11	34.7
Seychelles	1.03	40**	146	1.55	27.4
Malta	1.00	149*	1 190*	2.46	12.5
Mauritius	0.96	89	1 188	0.27	7.5
Antigua	0.88	114	195	2.59	58.5
Hong Kong	0.87	2 211	36 664	7.02	6.0
Philippines	0.82	647	30 800	0.02	2.1
Bahamas	0.78	870*	1 670*	6.17	52.1
Fiji	1.07	169	1 190	0.37	14.2
Western Samoa	0.66	7*	110*	0.29	6.4

Notes:
1 The data other than the multipliers relate to the year 1986, except where marked * for 1985 or ** for 1984.
2 The tourist income multipliers were not all calculated by the same techniques, nor do they all relate to the same year.
3 Tourist density would be better measured in terms of tourist-nights divided by resident population. Unfortunately, the source data were insufficient to use this method.
4 Tourism dependence is measured here as tourist receipts divided by GNP (and is expressed as a percentage). It should be remembered, however, that GNP includes net tourist receipts – that is, receipts minus expenditure – and the values in the final column of this table should be used only as a measure of dependence upon tourism. They do not indicate tourism's contribution to GNP.
('Tourist' means 'international tourist'.)

does not rank as highly when expressed in the ratio form. This is because of the differences in real value of the local currency per unit.

Finally, Table 11.13 shows a variety of indicators that may be used as the basis for decision making, including tourist income multipliers, receipts, tourist density (as measured by the ratio of arrivals to the host population) and tourism economic dependence (as measured by the contribution of tourism, at the direct level, to GNP). The range of tourist density values and tourism dependence ratios is large. For instance, Bermuda has the highest tourist density factor with a ratio of 7.11, whereas Antigua shows the greatest dependence given that tourism receipts accounted for over 58 per cent of GNP.

The policy implications of multiplier analysis

Tourism multipliers measure the present economic performance of the tourism industry and the short-run economic effects of a change in the level or pattern of tourism expenditure. They are particularly suitable for studying the impact of tourist expenditure on business turnover, incomes, employment, public-sector revenue and the balance of payments.

In the 1970s some economists argued strongly in favour of rejecting multiplier analysis as an appropriate technique for studying impact, on the grounds that these models yield 'no useful guideline to policy-makers as regards the merits of tourism compared with alternatives' (Bryden,

1973, p. 217). Yet a number of writers have shown that this is precisely the type of information which multiplier analysis can provide in a short-term context. For example, Diamond (1976) used an input–output model of the Turkish economy to measure sectoral output multipliers (for tourism and other sectors) in relation to four policy objectives which reflected Turkish planning priorities. His work demonstrated that multiplier analysis deals effectively with problems associated with short-term resource allocation.

However, resource allocation is not the primary use of multiplier analysis. The technique is most frequently used to examine short-run economic impacts where policy objectives other than the efficiency of resource allocation are considered important. A detailed input–output model, for example, yields valuable information about the structure of an economy, the degree to which sectors within the economy are dependent upon each other, the existence of possible supply constraints and the relative capital and labour intensities of each sector.

Detailed multiplier models are suitable for the following tasks:

- Analyzing the national or regional effects of public- or private-sector investment in tourism projects.
- Simulating the economic impact, sector by sector, of any proposed tourism developments.
- Examining the relative magnitudes of the impacts made by different types of tourism and by tourism compared with other sectors of the economy.

For instance, a tourism input–output study of Jamaica (Fletcher, 1985) examined the economic impact of tourism expenditure by purpose of visit, winter or summer visit, first and repeat visit in order to determine which tourists generated the highest level of income, employment and government revenue per unit of expenditure. This type of information can be used to target future marketing in order to maximize the benefits derived from tourism activity.

References and further reading

Archer, B.H. (1976) 'The anatomy of a multiplier', *Regional Studies*, vol. 10, pp. 71–7.

Archer, B.H. (1982) 'The value of multipliers and their policy implications', *Tourism Management*, vol. 3, no. 2. pp. 236–41.

Archer, B.H. (1985) 'Tourism in Mauritius: an economic impact study with marketing implications', *Tourism Management*, vol. 6, no. 1, pp. 50–4.

Archer, B.H. (1986) 'The secondary economic effects of tourism in developing countries', in *Planning for Tourism and Tourism in Developing Countries*, London: PTRC.

Archer, B.H. (1989a) 'Tourism and island economies', in Cooper, C. (ed.), *Progress in Tourism, Recreation and Hospitality Management*, London: Belhaven, vol. 1.

Archer, B.H. (1989b) *The Bermudian Economy: An Impact Study*, Ministry of Finance, Government of Bermuda.

Archer, B.H., and Fletcher, J.E. (1989) 'The tourist multiplier', *Teoros*, vol. 7, no. 3, pp. 6–9.

Archer, B.H., and Fletcher, J.E. (1990) *Multiplier Analysis*, Les Cahiers du Tourisme, Series C, No. 130, April.

Archer, B.H., and Owen, C. (1971) 'Towards a tourist regional multiplier', *Regional Studies*, vol. 5, pp. 289–94.

Bryden, J.M. (1973) *Tourism and Development: A Case Study in the Commonwealth Caribbean*, Cambridge: Cambridge University Press.

Curry, S. and Weiss, J. (1993) *Project Analysis in Developing Countries*, Basingstoke: Macmillan Press Limited.

Diamond, J. (1976) 'Tourism and development policy: a quantitative appraisal', *Bulletin of Economic Research*, vol. 28, no. 1, pp. 36–50.

Fletcher, J.E. (1985), (unpublished) *The Economic Impact of International Tourism on the National Economy of Jamaica*, report to Government of Jamaica, USAID/UNDP/WTO.

Fletcher, J.E. (1989) 'Input–output analysis and tourism impact studies', *Annals of Tourism Research*, vol. 16, no. 4, pp. 541–56.

Fletcher, J.E., and Archer, B.H. (1990) 'The development and application of multiplier analysis', in Cooper, C. (ed.), *Progress in Tourism, Recreation and Hospitality Management*, London: Belhaven, vol. 3.

Fletcher, J.E., and Snee, H.R. (1985) 'The service industries and input–output analysis', *Service Industries Review*, vol. 2, no. 1, pp. 51–79.

Kottke, M. (1988) 'Estimating tourism impacts', *Annals of Tourism Research*, vol. 15, no. 1, pp. 122–33.

Leontief, W. (1966) *Input–Output Economics*, New York: Oxford University Press.

Milne, S.S. (1987) 'Differential multipliers', *Annals of Tourism Research*, vol. 14, no. 4, pp. 499–515.

Nathan, R.R., and Associates (1966) *Recreation as an Industry*, a report prepared for the Appalachian Regional Commission, Washington, DC.

O'Connor, E., and Henry, E.W. (1975) *Input–Output Analysis and its Applications*, Griffin's Statistical Monographs, No. 36, London: Charles Griffin & Co.

OECD (1992) *National Accounts*, Paris: OECD.

Sinclair, M.T., and Sutcliffe, C.M.S. (1978) 'The first round of the Keynesian income multiplier', *Scottish Journal of Political Economy*, vol. 25, no. 2, pp. 177–86.

Sinclair, M.T., and Sutcliffe, C.M.S. (1982) 'Keynesian income multipliers with first and second round effects: an application to tourist expenditure', *Oxford Bulletin of Economics and Statistics*, vol. 44, no. 4, pp. 321–38.

TCSP (1992) *The Economic Impact of International Tourism on the National Economy of Fiji*, a report published by the Tourism Council for the South Pacific, Suva, Fiji.

Wanhill, S.R.C. (1988) 'Tourism multipliers under capacity constraints', *Service Industries Journal*, vol. 8, no. 1, pp. 136–42.

World Tourism Organization (1980) *Manila Declaration on World Tourism*, Madrid: WTO.

World Tourism Organization (1980) *Tourism and Employment: Enhancing the Status of Tourism Professions*, Madrid: WTO.

World Tourism Organization (1988) *Yearbook of Tourism Statistics*, Madrid: WTO.

World Tourism Organization (1992) *Yearbook of Tourism Statistics*, Madrid: WTO.

CHAPTER 12

Tourism and development planning

OVERVIEW

Any form of economic development requires careful planning if it is to be successful in achieving the implicit or explicit objectives which underlie that development. In this chapter we show that tourism development, because it is a multisector activity and because it brings with it environmental, social and economic impacts, requires considerable planning if it is to be successful and sustainable.

We also state that the development of tourism will not be optimal if it is left entirely in the hands of private-sector entrepreneurs, for they are primarily motivated by the profit and loss accounts. But on the other hand, if tourism development is dominated by the public sector then it is unlikely to be developed at the optimal rate from the economic point of view. We therefore point out in this chapter that tourism development planning requires careful co-operation and co-ordination of both the public and private sectors.

We show that the emphasis of tourism development planning has moved away from the rigid 'grand design' master plan in favour of more flexible and reactive development plans. This change in approach is, in no small way, due to the recognition that development is not a finite concept. Development is infinite and takes place in an ever-changing environment. Therefore development plans should attempt to facilitate the desired objectives while taking into account the changing factors which influence both the objectives and the means of achieving them.

INTEGRATED PLANNING AND DEVELOPMENT

If tourism is to be incorporated into a country's development plan, it must itself be organized and developed according to a plan constructed on sound foundations. These foundations should take account of the co-ordination of the tourism sector, and supply and demand for the tourism product. The process of development planning involves a wide cross-section of participants who may bring with them goals which are conflicting as well as incompatible perceptions about the industry and the development process itself. Before looking at the process of tourism development planning, it is worth considering why tourism should be selected as a development option.

Unique product characteristics

Few products can compete with the wide variety of activities included under the tourism heading. The tourism product is often considered to be unique to the individual tourist, as each tourist 'adds' his or her own characteristics to the product. It is generally consumed as a 'package' within the geographical boundaries of the producing destination and affects most sectors of the economy.

Fast earner of foreign exchange

Tourism is widely recognized to be one of the fastest earners of foreign exchange and one of the most effective redistribution factors in international development.

Labour intensive

Tourism, in common with most personal service industries, is labour intensive. For developing countries with surplus labour, tourism is an attractive proposition. For industrialized countries, tourism provides an effective means of generating employment opportunities in regions where there is little industrial development. In general, when the labour/capital ratio is moving strongly against labour in most production industries, the importance of tourism's labour-absorbing qualities cannot be overlooked.

However, this view should be tempered by the characteristics of the labour force associated with tourism-related establishments. The employment profile of large hotels, for example, tends to yield a relatively flat occupational pyramid, such as that shown in Figure 12.1.

This means that middle and senior management posts are relatively scarce compared with low-skill employees. Such an occupational pyramid results in a lack of career development and, consequently, a lack of staff motivation. Moreover, there is also a predominance of women and young people among those employed in tourism-related establishments. This brings with it implications for both the segment of the labour market that is faced with such employment opportunities and the likely wage rates that are associated with them.

Attempts have been made to increase the height of the occupational pyramid by, for example, the introduction of departments and layers of middle-

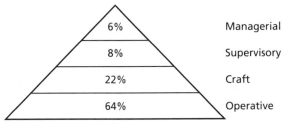

Source: Progress in Tourism, Recreation and Hospitality Management, ed. Chris Cooper, Belhaven, London (1991). Reproduced with permission.

Fig 12.1 Typical hotel employment structure

management posts in the more luxury hotels. This, it was hoped, would provide a much needed impetus to career prospects and motivation. However, more recently, the world recession has seen a reversal of this trend and 'delayering', and the career development prospects in large hotels are not significantly better than those exhibited two decades ago.

On the job training

The development of travel and hospitality skills in the local labour market will not make large demands on educational resources. The pattern of employment in the accommodation sector is heavily weighted towards those with only a rudimentary education. This is an aspect of tourism employment that has been known for more than a decade, as Table 12.1 demonstrates.

Table 12.1 Level of training in tourism

Level	Accommodation (%)	Supplementary activities (%)
University	1	3
Other higher education	4	5
Secondary		
Higher	30	45
Lower	34	40
No qualifications	31	7

Source: World Tourism Organization (1980).

This educational profile has both a positive and a negative implication for tourism as a development option. On the positive side, it means that the labour force for tourism development can be mobilized relatively quickly. The training can be undertaken on the job, which means that units of labour can be brought in quickly from either the unemployed or, as is often the case in developing countries, from agriculture and fishing industries.

On the negative side, the lack of educational

qualifications found in tourism-related businesses means that the development of tourism does not necessarily result in a more educated labour force – one of the factors perceived to be an important ingredient in the economic development process.

Protectionism

The very nature of tourism as an export industry means that foreign countries do not see it as a serious threat to the level of employment in their own countries. Thus, tourism tends to escape the danger of being singled out for protectionism or trade retaliation, except as part of a general macroeconomic policy which restricts foreign exchange allowances to correct balance of payment problems. Having said that, it is often the existence of foreign exchange restrictions in many of the developing regions of the world that explains the relatively slow rates of growth in interregional tourism (as, for example, in South-East Asia).

Multitude of industries

Tourism is a composite industry product which has strong linkages with many sectors of the economy. It is the strength of these linkages which determines the value of the output, income and employment multipliers associated with tourist expenditure.

Pricing flexibility

Many developing countries are dependent upon the world market prices in primary agriculture produce for their foreign exchange receipts: that is, the prices of, say, cocoa, sugar and rice are determined in world commodity markets and are not within the control of the individual producing country. Tourism provides a source of foreign exchange which is subject to some degree of control by the host country. However, tourism is also highly price competitive.

Price competitive

The bulk of the tourism market, which is resort tourism, is extremely price sensitive and, consequently, internationally competitive. This fact is adequately demonstrated by the effects of currency fluctuations on the number of international arrivals and the volume of tourist expenditure. Although most mass tourism destinations claim a high degree of product differentiation, a brief examination of the major tour operators' brochures, selling sun, sand and sea products, will show that the major battleground is not hotels, the quality of beaches or the sea, but the price of the package. Price competition is a fundamental feature of the budget tourism market for both destinations and operators.

Seasonality

A striking feature of tourism in many countries is the way in which the level of activity fluctuates throughout the year. This is not a characteristic unique to tourism – agriculture is also an industry used to seasonal fluctuations in activity – but the majority of industries are not subject to the degree of seasonality experienced by tourism establishments. The seasonality of tourism is reflected in: employment (casual/seasonal staff); investment (low annual returns on capital); and pricing policies (discounted off-season prices).

From an economics point of view, any business subject to seasonal fluctuations in demand for its output is faced with a dilemma. If it purchases sufficient resources to meet the peak load demand, it will have to carry spare productive capacity for the remainder of the year. If it gauges its resources according to the average level of demand, it will spend part of the year carrying spare capacity and will be unable to meet the peak load demand level. Alternatively, it can take on variable resources (staff) to meet the peak load demand and then shed these variable factors during the off-season. Although attractive from the point of view of the profit and loss account, this widely practised

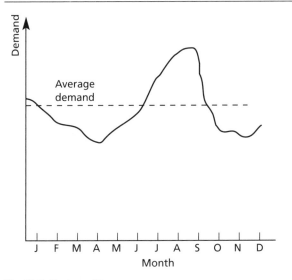

Fig 12.2 Seasonality

option does nothing to improve employer/ employee relations. Also there is an inherent waste in taking on staff each year on a temporary basis, investing in human resources (by training) and then losing that investment at the end of the main season.

In order to offset some of the costs associated with seasonality, many hotels and operators offer holidays for off-season periods with heavily discounted prices. By offering lower prices it is possible to induce visitors to a destination at a time when they would otherwise not visit. However, there are limits to such discounting.

First, the revenue that establishments receive during the off-season must *at least* cover the variable costs of production. If this is the case then, by opening in the off-season, they will be able to maintain their staff and perhaps make some contribution to their fixed costs.

Second, the discounting of off-season packages should not be so great as to damage the desirability of the main season product.

High operating leverage/fixed costs

Many of the tourism-related industries are subject to high levels of fixed costs: that is, there is a large

capital element that must be committed before any output is produced. In industries subject to this type of cost structure, the volume of sales becomes the all-important factor. This aspect is shown in Figure 12.3.

In Figure 12.3 the vertical axis measures revenue and costs, whilst the horizontal axis depicts the quantity of output produced during the time period under consideration. The cost curve C_1 relates to the cost function of a non-tourism industry, while C_2 relates to the cost function of a typical tourism-related industry. We can see that both industries are subject to the same variable cost structures (that is why the two cost functions run parallel to each other), but the tourism-related industry is subject to a higher fixed cost element. The end result is that the break-even point[1] for the tourism-related industry (BEP_2) is much higher than that for the non-tourism industry. Thus, the volume of output becomes all-important for high fixed cost industries.

We can therefore see that there are a number of factors related to the tourism industry which make it an attractive development option, but some of

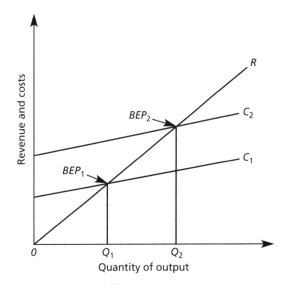

Fig 12.3 Fixed cost effects

[1] Break-even point refers to that level of revenue and output which will just cover the costs involved in producing the output.

those factors may make it less attractive if they are not controlled or alleviated by proper planning.

THE TOURISM DEVELOPMENT PLANNING PROCESS

The concept of planning is concerned with organizing some future events in order to achieve pre-specified objectives. Integrated planning and development is a form of comprehensive planning. Comprehensive because it integrates all forms of planning – economic, physical, social and cultural. We can subdivide the planning process into eight major aspects:

(1) Study preparation.
(2) Determination of objectives.
(3) Surveys.
(4) Analysis.
(5) Policy and plan formulation.
(6) Recommendations.
(7) Implementation.
(8) Monitoring and reformulation.

Study preparation

The study preparation is really concerned with the recognition by the planning authorities (normally the government) and the resident population that tourism is a desirable development option, together with some awareness of the constraints within which it must develop.

Determination of objectives

In order to design a development plan successfully, it is necessary to have a clear understanding of the objectives which are to be achieved by the development of tourism. Some major objectives, commonly found in tourism development plans, are set out below.

- To develop a tourism sector which, in all respects and at all levels, is of high quality, though not necessarily of high cost.

- To encourage the use of tourism for both cultural and economic exchange.
- To distribute the economic benefits of tourism, both direct and indirect, as widely and to as many of the host community as feasible.
- To preserve cultural and natural resources as part of tourism development, and to facilitate this through architectural and landscape design which reflects local traditions.
- To appeal to a broad cross-section of international (and domestic) tourists through policies and programmes of site and facility development.
- To maximize foreign exchange earnings to ensure a sound balance of payments.
- To attract high-spending 'up-market' tourists.
- To increase employment opportunities.
- To aid peripheral regions by raising incomes and employment, thus slowing down or halting emigration.

It is important that the objectives set out in the development plan are clear, unambiguous, non-conflicting and achievable. We can see from the above list of objectives that they are often not specific in nature, and thus it can be difficult to assess whether or not the objectives have indeed been achieved. Also, some of the objectives may be conflicting, particularly those relating to the type of tourist to be attracted and the desired impact.

Surveys

This is the data collection section, where information is gathered from both primary and secondary sources. The data requirements for development planning are quite comprehensive and include the following:

- Tourist characteristics/travel patterns.
- Tourist attractions.
- Accommodation facilities.
- Other tourist facilities.
- Land availability and use.
- Economic structure.
- Environment.

- Sociocultural characteristics.
- Investment and available capital.
- Public- and private-sector organizations.
- Relevant legislation and regulation.

All of the above factors are considered with respect to their existing states and to their projected states within the development plan's time scale.

Analysis

Once the objectives have been formulated, the analytical framework chosen will determine the precise set of data to be collected. Once collected, the data are analysed by considering a wide range of issues. The major issues to be considered generally fall into one of four subject areas:

- Asset evaluation.
- Market analysis.
- Development planning.
- Impact analysis.

Asset evaluation

This area of analysis examines the existing and potential assets, the ways in which they can be developed and the likely constraints on that development. The asset evaluation should also include an appraisal of the infrastructure to establish whether or not further investment is required.

Market analysis

Market analysis attempts to determine whether or not the proposed developments are appropriate, the markets that are likely to be attracted by these developments and the price level or tariff structure that should be adopted. The market analysis must also incorporate a study of developments in competitive markets and/or in competitive modes of transport.

Development planning

A major issue to be studied under this heading is the time phasing of the development plan in order to ensure implementation. The possible sources of funding of the development are examined, and the appropriate level of foreign funding (if any) is calculated. Issues such as the number of foreign employees, the marketing strategy to be adopted, investment incentives, organizational structures and training programmes are all undertaken during the analysis section.

Impact analysis

Impact analysis should be all-embracing, covering issues such as the likely effects that the development will have on the host community and the environment, the economic implications in terms of key indicators (employment, income, government revenue and foreign exchange flows) and the likely economic rate of return. Analysis should also examine the risks involved and the sensitivity of the results to changing assumptions.

The analyses set out above are of both a quantitative and a qualitative nature, and most of these issues must be faced before a move can be made towards formulating policy recommendations.

Policy and plan formulation

The results from the analyses of the survey data are unlikely to yield a single solution, and instead will tend to yield a number of possibilities for development strategies. The process from here is one of formulating draft plans on the basis of each policy option derived from the analyses. The alternative plans are then evaluated in terms of their potential economic, physical and sociocultural costs and benefits, together with any likely problem areas which may result from the implementation of the plan. The plan which achieves the most objectives while not exposing the destination to potentially serious problems is selected and then drawn up in full.

Recommendations

The plan which has been selected on the basis of the analyses, having now been completed in detail, is submitted to the authorities by the research team, together with recommendations concerning the optimum methods of developing tourism in the destination and achieving the plan's objectives. It is more than likely that the research team will present the authorities with a selection of recommendations which all fulfil the requirements of the selected plan. It is at this stage that feedback between the authorities and the development plan team is essential, in order to focus attention on issues where attention is needed and to play down areas where it is not. During these discussions the final development plan is formulated.

Implementation

The methods of implementing the development plan will have been considered throughout most stages of its construction. Thus, by the time that the implementation stage is reached, all the necessary legislation and regulation controls will have been brought into effect.

Monitoring and reformation

Once the development plan has been implemented, it must be closely monitored in order to detect any deviations which may occur from the projected path of development. Any deviations, and there are likely to be some, must be analysed in order to assess how they will affect the development plan and its objectives. Once this secondary analysis has been completed, the research team can report back to the authorities with recommendations as to how the plan and its policy recommendations should be modified in order to stay on target.

THE DEVELOPMENT PLAN TEAM

The development plan team will need considerable expertise and experience in the formulation of such plans. In general, the team will consist of four groups of specialists, falling into the broad

categories of technical services, marketing specialists, planners and economists. In more detail, the likely spread of specialist skills includes the following:

- Market analysts.
- Physical planners.
- Economists.
- Infrastructure engineers.
- Transport engineers.
- Draughtsmen and designers.
- Legal experts.

PHASES OF THE DEVELOPMENT PLAN

The plan will be constructed over a period of time and this time can be broken down into five distinct phases:
(1) Identification and inventory of the existing situation.
(2) Forecasts for the future.
(3) Plan formulation.
(4) Specific project development.
(5) Implementation.

Identification and inventory of the existing situation

This phase includes the following:

- Characteristics and structure of current consumer demand.
- Study of consumer choice.
- Current land use, land tenure and land use control.
- Existing natural and man-made attractions.
- Accommodation facilities.
- Tourist services facilities.
- Infrastructure facilities and their capacities.
- Transport facilities and their capacities.
- Graphic presentation of physical inventory.

The above data will be used to establish the adequacy of existing structures and facilities, the classification and cost organization of existing facilities (together with an index of standards currently achieved), and the economic impact of present tourism activity. This then leads on to the second phase.

Forecasts for the future

This phase will include forecasts of future demand and likely tourist movements and needs. These will be complemented by an analysis of the implications of these forecasts for future production levels of each relevant service and good, together with the infrastructural requirements. Anticipated standards of service will be examined, and the economic forecasts of local repercussions will be estimated.

Plan formulation

The formulation of the plan will include proposed programmes of market organization and promotion, comprehensive land use and control planning, detailed infrastructural plans and the economic evaluation associated with the proposed development plan. Again it is likely to include a graphic presentation of land use and infrastructure.

Specific project development

This phase will include an analysis of specific policies and projects for marketing, and for tourism management. Selections of alternative layouts relating to specific projects will be drawn up by the physical planners, and alternative solutions to infrastructural development problems will be provided by planners and architects. Costs of the alternative projects and infrastructural schemes will be assessed along with the economic analysis of the various possible investment projects. Once the specific projects have been selected from the various alternatives, these will again be subject to graphic presentations.

Implementation

The implementation programme will be set into motion with construction and supervision, technical and managerial assistance in tourism devel-

opment projects, financial analysis and the commencement of the recommended infrastructure investment programme.

TOURISM DEVELOPMENT PLAN FAILURE

A large number of tourism development plans are unsuccessful. Given the fact that such plans operate in an environment which is constantly changing because of forces acting outside the control of the authorities, often outside the geographical area of the destination, perhaps this is not surprising. However, many plans fail as a result of the development plans themselves. Discussions about this latter type of failure can be broken down into two categories:

- Failure at the design stage.
- Failure at the implementation stage.

Design stage plan failure

Many tourism development plans fail because, at the design stage, they follow no more than the basic formulation of tourism development. Consider the basic tourism development plan in Figure 12.4.

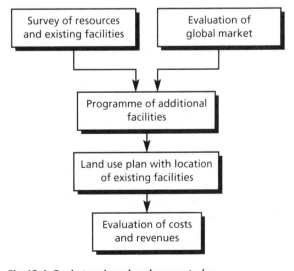

Fig 12.4 Basic tourism development plan

A plan of this structure will provide a general framework for state and municipal/local investments and will help to guide and evaluate the proposals of private developers. However, this type of plan structure lacks the analytical detail necessary for a successful plan. Quite often this absence of analytical components is a reflection of the planning bodies which carry out the construction of the plan – bodies lacking in planning expertise and experience.

More importantly, the plan does not give a clear statement with respect to its objectives – objectives must be achievable, unambiguous and non-conflicting.

The development plan takes no consideration of the impact of tourism on the host community, the environment and the economy.

The projects are only evaluated on a financial basis (profit and loss accounts) and take no account of social costs and benefits.

Too much emphasis is placed upon physical development. In other words, this is supply-led tourism development without proper consideration of returns to capital investments and effects on the market.

The plan structure fails to make adequate market assessment. The global approach of examining tourist flows from the tourist-generating countries and projecting forward to future time periods, under the assumption that all destinations will receive their fair share, fails to address the fundamental issue: *why do people want to come to this particular destination?* Unless this issue is addressed, future projections can be wildly off target.

Taking the above points into account, the basic development plan structure can be modified as in Figure 12.5.

Implementation stage plan failure

Problems encountered at the implementation stage are largely, but not exclusively, concerned with miscalculations regarding the use of land and the control of land usage. Tourism is, after all, an activity largely involved in real estate devel-

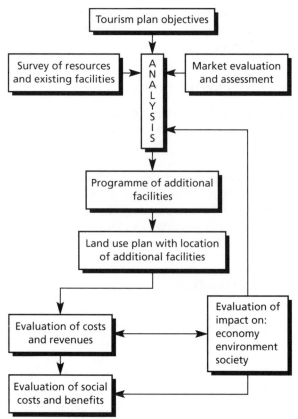

Fig 12.5 Modified basic development plan

opment. The types of land difficulty encountered during the implementation stage include the following:

- Those who actually undertake the development are sometimes more concerned with real estate speculation than with the operation of tourist facilities. Thus, the motivation for development (particularly when incentives are on offer) may be more to do with capital gain than the tourism product. Such speculative development can lead to poorly designed facilities which are inefficient to operate, or to facilities sited in poor locations.

- Development often takes place on the basis of a high debt/equity ratio, using land values as security for the loans. This may lead to financial failure when property sales and operating profits do not materialize.

- The planning authorities often underestimate the difficulties that can be encountered when attempting to control the use of land. The only certain way of controlling land usage is by ownership.
- Failure to introduce the required planning legislation in time to implement the development plan, or the lack of ability to enforce such legislation.
- If the specific sites earmarked for development are 'leaked' prior to the implementation of the development plan, land speculation and price inflation may follow. This will alter the economic evaluations and may turn a viable project into a certain failure.

Other problems may also be encountered:

- Failure to co-ordinate intermediaries in the travel trade, private-sector development and public-sector provision. Such a lack of co-ordination can: result in supply bottlenecks, affecting most aspects of the tourism product; reduce the economic benefits associated with the tourism activity; adversely affect visitor satisfaction; and consequently cause the plan to miss its targets.
- Poor communications and infrastructure.
- Inadequate machinery to deal with public opposition and representations concerning the proposed development. A lack of such a mechanism can slow the development process down considerably and can result in plan failure.

DEVELOPMENT PLANNING LAYERS

Tourism development planning can take place at international, national and subnational levels.

International tourism planning

At the international level, organizations such as the European Community, the Organization for Economic Co-operation and Development (OECD), the Caribbean Tourism Organization (CTO) and the Tourism Council for the South Pacific (TCSP) all undertake, albeit limited, forms of tourism planning. This level of planning is often weak in structure and lacks enforcement. It is generally provided in a guideline form in order to assist the member states.

National tourism planning

National tourism planning encapsulates the tourism development plans for a country as a whole, but often includes specific objectives for particular subnational regions or types of area within the national boundary. The plans manifest themselves in a variety of forms, including the following:

- Tourism policy.
- Marketing strategies.
- Taxation structure.
- Incentive/grant schemes.
- Legislation (e.g. employment, investment, repatriation of profits).
- Infrastructure developments.
- External and internal transport systems and organizations.
- Education/training and manpower programmes.

Regional/local tourism planning

Regional and local tourism planning deals with specific issues which affect a sub-national area. They tend to be much more detailed and specific than their national counterpart and can vary quite significantly from sub-national area to area. For instance, there may be areas where tourism development is to be encouraged and others where specific types of tourism activity are actively discouraged. Such plans may relate to a state within a country, to a county, a city or even a local resort area.

However, there are constraints on how different regional plans can be from other regional plans or from the national plan. Certainly they should not detract from the overall aims and objectives of the national plan or those of another region. Ideally, the sub-national plans should work in harmony with the national plan as far as local conditions will allow.

References and further reading

Inskeep, E. (1991) *Tourism Planning: an Integrated and Sustainable Development Approach*, New York: Van Nostrand Reinhold.

Lawson, F., and Baud-Bovy, M. (1977) *Tourism and Recreation: A Handbook of Physical Planning*, Boston: CBI.

Lea, J. (1988) *Tourism and Development in the Third World*, New York: Routledge, Chapman and Hall.

Pearce, D. (1989) *Tourism: A Community Approach* (2nd ed.), Harlow: Longman.

Williams, A.M., and Shaw, G. (1990) *Tourism and Economic Development: Western European Experience* (2nd ed.), London: Pinter Publishers.

World Tourism Organization (1980).

PART 3

The tourism industry and government organizations

CHAPTER 13

Introduction

Many texts and courses in tourism provide an extensive description of the tourism industry, the organizations involved and something of their operating environment. There is no doubt that for many of you reading this book the tourism industry will provide employment. We have therefore written this section of the book from an analytical point of view to give insights into the operating characteristics, trends and issues in the industry. We do not attempt a description, but rather try to unravel the workings of the industry and its practices.

From the point of view of Leiper's tourism system (see p. 3, Chapter 1), the industry represents a key element. He defines the industry as 'the range of businesses and organizations involved in delivering the tourism product'. From the point of view of this section of the book we have focused upon government organizations, attractions, accommodation, transport and intermediaries. While these do not represent the complete range of enterprises in the tourism industry, we believe that by focusing upon these sectors we can fully demonstrate the operation of the tourism industry.

In Chapter 14 we examine in detail the role of government intervention in tourism. We accept that tourism involves a public/private-sector partnership, but argue that the nature of the tourism industry does require a clear public-sector involvement. Not only are many core tourist attractions public goods (landscapes, the cultural and built heritage), but also many activities – research, planning and management, regulation – can only effectively be achieved by the public sector. In part this reflects the lack of concentration in the industry, but it is also a recognition of the resource allocation issues which

tourism raises. Clearly, in the case of resource allocation only the public sector has the overview and impartiality to act. However, in many parts of the world, the public sector is withdrawing from tourism and private-sector organizations are being encouraged to step in. We believe this demonstrates a fundamental lack of understanding of the nature of tourism and the issues involved.

In Chapter 15 we provide an operational analysis of the accommodation industry. Accommodation is a support industry to tourism, surviving on the demand derived from tourist attractions. In the following chapter we examine the critical role of the transport industry in bringing together the tourist and the destination. Whilst it is important to consider the relative roles of different transport modes and consumer choice we also examine the increasing environmental pressures upon operators as tourists begin to make modal choice on that basis. The other key element of transportation for tourism is the controversial role of public sector regulation – a role which has decreased in North America and will do so in Europe. Closely linked to transportation are the intermediaries (Chapter 17) – tour operators and travel agents who, by packaging up the tourist product and making it available to consumers actually are 'making markets'. Tourism is unusual in its almost exclusive use of intermediaries in the distribution chain and we examine the nature of the distribution process, the power struggles within them and the operating features – and risks of intermediaries. Finally, in Chapter 18, attractions are considered. Attractions are central to tourism yet receive very patchy and undisciplined coverage in the literature. We address this problem and provide an approach to attractions to aid your understanding of their varied features and operation.

Overall, the different sectors of the tourism industry demonstrate many characteristics and trends in common. These include:

- The low level of concentration in the industry. Domination by small businesses is offset by the market prominence of the few large corporations in the industry.
- The high ratio of fixed costs to variable costs. This has considerable implications for the operation of the industry and for its financial stability.
- The high level of customer contact, which demands high standards of training.
- The general lack of expertise in marketing, and of human resource management among small businesses.
- The importance of location vis-à-vis access to markets.
- The perishable nature of the product, which demands investment in computer reservation and yield management systems.
- The lack of loyalty in the distribution chain.
- Seasonal and irrational demand patterns, which involve enterprises in promotional and pricing strategies to combat them.
- A belated adoption of environmental auditing and EIA techniques.
- The increasing degree of both vertical and horizontal integration in the industry.
- The fragmentation of the industry which, allied to its geographical dispersion, acts to discourage the formation of industry associations.
- The traditional outlook of the industry, like many services, and, some would argue, its

under management. This means that it is vulnerable to ideas and takeovers from other industrial sectors.

- The increasing professionalism of the industry.

While it is important to understand the operation of the industry and the trends which shape industry practices, it is equally important to understand the linkages and relationships which exist among the various parts of the tourism industry. Take, for example, a Mediterranean inclusive tour. The assembly of the tour, its distribution, and the delivery of the service to the customer involve just about every sector of the industry, but the relationships are revealing. The providers of accommodation to the tourist may well be operating on very tight costs due to financial pressure from the tour operator, which is attempting to offer the tour at a low price in order to achieve a target load factor. Yet the travel agent which racks the operator's brochure may be placing pressure on the operator for higher commission levels as the sales of that particular operator's products increase. In turn, the operator may have 'locked in' the agent to its own CRS. All of this may fly in the face of the relevant national tourism organization's policy to market its country to up-market tourists in order to increase the financial yield per visitor.

At the end of the day it is the demand generated by the tour operator which will determine a proportion of the destination's market. In other words each sector of the industry is involved in a power play based on differing objectives and its own particular role in the service delivery process. In the next five chapters we outline the key elements of the tourism industry so as to provide a greater understanding of their core business and their operating practices.

CHAPTER 14

Government organizations

OVERVIEW

Governments are involved with tourist organizations at both the international and the national level. In the latter case, they are normally the instigators for the establishment of a national tourist office, while in the former instance, they are partners along with other member states in such bodies as the World Tourism Organization, the European Travel Commission, and the Pacific Asia Travel Association. All these bodies can contribute to the formation of a country's tourism policy.

In this chapter we look at the overall policy framework and consider the experience of the United Kingdom to illustrate the changes that occur in policy and the very many organizations that express an interest in tourism at the national level. As national tourist offices are commonly the executive agency for government policy, their administrative structure and functions are considered in some detail. In the last part of the chapter we examine intervention by the public sector in tourism. Particular consideration is given to the variety of instruments governments have at their disposal to manage the direction of tourism development in the interests of the host community.

PUBLIC POLICY FRAMEWORK

We already know that, worldwide, the significance of tourism as a mechanism for economic development has meant that it is an investment opportunity that few governments can afford to ignore. Since the tourist industry does not control all those factors which make up the attractiveness of a destination, and since the impact on the host population can be considerable, it is necessary that the options concerning the development of tourism should be considered at the highest level of government and the appropriate public administrative framework be put in place. As a rule, the greater the importance of tourism to a country's economy, the greater is the involvement of the public sector, to the point of having a government ministry with sole responsibility for tourism.

Beyond this, governments are involved in supporting a variety of multinational agencies. The official flag carrier for international tourism is the World Tourism Organization (WTO) (see Case Study 14.1). Elsewhere there are a number of other international bodies whose activities impinge upon tourism: these include the World Bank, the United Nations, the International Air Transport Association (IATA), the International Civil Aviation Organization (ICAO) and the Organization for Economic Cooperation and Development (OECD).

At a lower level, there are a variety of regional bodies such as the Organization of American

---

CASE STUDY 14.1

The World Tourism Organization (WTO)

The WTO is an operative rather than a deliberative body. Its functions include helping members to maximize the benefits from tourism, identifying markets, assisting in tourism planning as an executing agency of the United Nations Development Programme (UNDP) (until the mid-1990s), providing statistical information, advising on the harmonization of policies and practices, sponsoring education and training, and identifying funding sources.

States (OAS), the Pacific Asia Travel Association (PATA) and the European Travel Commission (ETC) (see Case Study 14.2). Most of their efforts are devoted to promotion and marketing, though they do provide technical assistance. Funds for developing the tourist infrastructure in low-income countries may be obtained from regional development banks such as the Asian Development Bank in Manila, which was rejuvenated by a large influx of Japanese money.

CASE STUDY 14.2

The European Travel Commission (ETC)

The European Travel Commission was established as a non-profit-making body by the national tourism organizations (NTOs) of European states in 1948; it has 21 member countries. The objectives of the Commission are as follows:

- To foster international tourism co-operation in Europe.
- To exchange information on tourism development projects and marketing techniques.
- To undertake/commission appropriate travel research.
- To promote tourism in and to Europe, particularly from North America and Japan.

The work of the ETC is supported by the European Commission, which sees tourism as an industry of great economic and social significance within the Community.

Taking a European perspective, officially tourism in the European Commission comes under Directorate General XXIII, but the regional development work of Directorate General XVI also involves tourism projects as a means of overcoming regional disparities. Commercial funding of tourism projects is obtainable from the European Investment Bank. The role of the European Community in tourism is seen as one of simplification, harmonization and easing restrictions on

trade. Specifically, strategy is developed around the following objectives:

- Improving the quality of European tourism services.
- Stimulating the demand for European tourism outside common borders.
- Improving the business environment in which tourist enterprises operate.

It is important then, in developing its strategy for tourism, that the European Commission does not duplicate the work of other organizations. Ultimately, tourism policy will, to a large degree, be the responsibility of member states, but the provision of research and statistics, facilitation in terms of easing frontier formalities and improving transport infrastructure, together with general image promotion in association with the ETC, appear to be the most favoured policies for the European Commission.

All the 23 western European countries (as opposed to the old Eastern bloc) have national tourism organizations (NTOs): some are part of government as in France or Spain, while others are established independently of government but are supported by central grants and other income-generating activities, as in the UK. The United States Travel and Tourism Administration (USTTA) is supported by the federal government, but the major responsibility for tourism marketing and development rests with the individual states. All NTOs normally have a statutory obligation to promote tourism in favour of the private tourist industry in the home country. For example, the USTTA is required to undertake the following:

- Stimulate travel to the USA.
- Co-operate with local, state and foreign governments.
- Reduce barriers to travel.
- Encourage low-cost tours and visitor services.
- Collect and exchange tourism statistics.

The USTTA represents the USA at the World Tourism Organization.

The United Kingdom experience

Local government can trace its involvement in UK tourism back to the eighteenth century and the development of spa towns. However, central government did not support tourism until 1929 when £5000 was granted annually by the Department of Overseas Trade to the Travel Association of Great Britain (formerly the 'Come to Britain' movement). Thereafter, the promotion of tourism to and within the country – with the exception of the Northern Ireland Tourist Board (NITB), which was established by statute in 1948 – was left in private hands until the passing of the Development of Tourism Act in 1969. This Act, which is the substantive legislation that still applies in the early 1990s, was in three parts:

- Establishment of the British Tourist Authority (BTA), English Tourist Board (ETB), Scottish Tourist Board (STB) and Wales Tourist Board (WTB), and their powers. This part also included an assistance scheme (known as Section 4) for particular tourist projects.
- Provision of a hotel development grants scheme (which ceased in 1973).
- Enabling legislation for the compulsory registration of accommodation.

The NITB was not covered by the Act, since it was already established and was responsible to the then Northern Ireland Parliament at Stormont. Many years on, the outcome of the Act for Britain is the structure shown in Figure 14.1, whereby the BTA and ETB report to the Department of National Heritage and other boards to their respective offices of state. As the BTA has the major responsibility of marketing in Britain, links are maintained between the BTA and all other boards and their respective reporting authorities.

The vast scope of the tourist industry means that the statutory tourist board framework in the UK can only be regarded as the core of public-sector involvement in tourism. The Departments of Trade and Industry, Transport, Environment, Education and Science, Health and Social Secu-

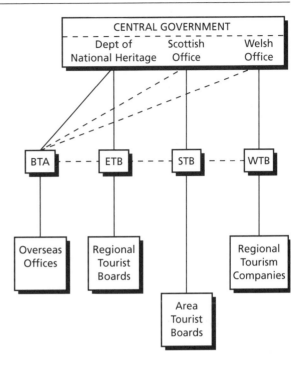

Fig 14.1 Statutory tourist board framework in Britain

rity, together with the Ministry of Agriculture, Fisheries and Food, and the Home Office all undertake activities which can impinge upon tourism. These may vary from road construction, the management of historic sites and the development of water-based recreation on reservoirs and canals, through to urban cultural provision, tourism education, liquor licensing and the provision of holidays for the socially disadvantaged.

Furthermore, besides the departments of state, appointed government agencies and the local authorities which have the planning powers to implement tourism programmes on the ground, there are a whole host of national non-governmental organizations which have an interest in tourism. The latter include such bodies as the Automobile Association and the Royal Automobile Club, the National Trust, the Council for Nature, the Council for Small Industries in Rural Areas, the National Angling Council, the Civic Trust, the Cyclists' Touring Club and the National Farmers'

Union to name but a few. In this respect it may easily be seen that the need for co-ordination and working together is paramount because there are a myriad ways in which duplication and conflicts of interest may arise. The tourist boards are faced with the daunting task of liaising with all these groups, at a national as well as at a local level.

The 1969 Act was instigated by the recognition of tourism as an important earner of foreign exchange after the devaluation of 1967. Over the years since the Act's inception, the economic policy emphasis for tourism has shifted back and forth. In the mid-1970s greater emphasis was given to regional policy by pushing marketing and development expenditures towards the economically deprived areas in order to establish tourism growth points. There is nothing wrong with the idea of growth points, but it was somewhat unrealistic to assume that tourism potential would be coincident with areas of high unemployment.

During the early 1980s priority was given to employment, and the regional restrictions on Section 4 project assistance were lifted. Tourism was transferred from the Department of Trade and Industry to the Department of Employment in 1985. This heightened political interest allowed the ETB to reintroduce growth points in their modern form of Tourism Development Action Plans (TDAPs). This time TDAPs were based on areas of significant tourism potential. But during the last part of 1988 and throughout 1989, the UK balance of payments reached unprecedented deficit levels, while at the same time unemployment declined – particularly youth unemployment, due to the fall in the number of young people coming on to the labour market as a result of population changes. Thus 1988/89 once more saw tourism being extolled for its foreign exchange benefits and the British people being encouraged to take holidays at home to help the balance of payments.

A further shift in emphasis was the Fowler Review of 1988/89, which altered the structure of the BTA and ETB. Section 4 assistance schemes were suspended for England, and devolution

from the centre became the order of the day. The BTA was required to devolve more of its authority and activities to its overseas offices, and the ETB likewise had to transfer many of its responsibilities and its funds to the twelve Regional Tourist Boards. The ETB was left with a role which was more of a 'think-tank', but the downside was the loss of its co-ordinating powers to influence tourism programmes at ground level. The process of devolution saw the transfer of some overseas marketing powers to the STB and the WTB. In 1992 responsibility for tourism was given to the Department of National Heritage.

There is little doubt that the frequent alterations in direction have been more of a handicap than a benefit to the development of public-sector tourist organizations in Britain. There have been continual changes in tourism ministers followed by one tourism review after another. In 1985 the Trade and Industry Committee of the House of Commons summed up the government's tourism policy thus:

> The truth is that the Government cannot quite decide what its own role is. Along with general policy on industry, the present Government does not want to interfere with the development of the tourism industry in the private sector. Indeed, we were told that 'the Government see their own main role in relation to tourism as promoting a general economic climate favourable to the industry's development'. Given that the Government cannot control the most important climatic factor in this context – the weather – more specific strategies are needed. The Government minimises the appearance of involvement by reducing policy aims to statements of the obvious but maintains the fact of involvement in the tourist boards and the grants provided through them. The trouble is that this actual financial commitment is then left without there being any clear specific strategy to guide its use. (Vol. 1, para. 73)

On the question of financial commitment, the WTO has long used the rule that the minimum of 1 per cent of a country's tourist receipts should be devoted to the NTO. In Britain, this has never been the case.

The UK experience of tourism policy is not uncommon in other countries. For political reasons there is always the temptation for governments to switch policy directions. This gives the impression of the dynamics of change, but can, in practice, generate chaos through conflicting objectives. It takes a long time to create tourist destinations and build up market positions. It is therefore somewhat simplistic to behave as if the factors influencing such developments can be turned on and off like a tap.

One of the principal difficulties is that tourism is a diverse and fragmented industry with many different economic agents acting in their own interests (often on the basis of imperfect information), which may not be to the long-term benefit of tourism as a whole. Unco-ordinated market competition can, in these circumstances, produce cyclical growth patterns, with a consequent waste of resources. This places a premium on an overall planning body, such as an NTO, which is able to give a sense of direction by marketing the destination and acting as a distribution channel, drawing the attention of potential tourists and the travel trade to the products that the numerous suppliers in a country have to offer.

ADMINISTRATIVE FRAMEWORK

There are considerable variations in the structure of public administration of tourism, which in turn depend on the size of the tourist industry and the importance the government attaches to the various reasons advanced for public-sector involvement in tourism. A list of some of the most common arguments put forward for government participation is shown in Table 14.1.

In most cases where tourism is a significant element of economic activity, so that a good deal of weight is attached to the factors presented in Table 14.1, it is common practice to have a Ministry of Tourism. This is particularly true of island economies, which often form some of the world's most attractive tourist destinations. The

Table 14.1 Reasons for government involvement in tourism

- Foreign exchange earnings and their importance for the balance of payments.
- Employment creation and the need to provide education and training.
- Large and fragmented industry requiring careful co-ordination of development and marketing.
- Maximize the net benefits to the host community.
- Spread the benefits and costs equitably.
- Building the image of the country as a tourist destination.
- Market regulation to protect consumers and prevent unfair competition.
- Provision of public goods and infrastructure as part of the tourist product.
- Protect tourism resources and the environment.
- Regulate aspects of social behaviour, e.g. gambling.
- Monitor the level of tourism activity through statistical surveys.

position of the NTO within this framework may be inside or outside of the ministry. In the latter case, the NTO becomes a government agency or semi-governmental body. It usually has a separate constitution, enacted by law, and a board of directors appointed from outside government, which in theory gives it independence from the political system. However, the link is maintained through the NTO being the executive arm of government policy as agreed by the ministry and public money providing the major source of funds for most NTOs. The reality is that few governments can resist giving specific policy directions for developments which are likely to influence election results in marginal areas.

Some NTOs, normally termed visitor and convention bureaux, are simply private associations whose constitution is determined by their membership, which may include government representation. Income is thus raised from a variety of sources, and, like other business, the existence of these bureaux is dependent on the demand for their services in the market place. In times of recession, such associations often have difficulty raising funds from the private sector to maintain their activities, and they need to have injections of public funds to continue with long-term projects.

During the 1980s, the upsurge in market economics saw more and more governments urging their NTOs to generate matching funds from the tourist industry. Methods to achieve this objective have included joint-marketing initiatives and charging for a range of services: for example, market research reports and brokerage fees from arranging finance. However, the main obstacle to raising private-sector revenue has always been the long-term and non-commercial nature of many of the tasks undertaken by NTOs. Added to this is the fact that when NTOs do embark on commercial activities they may be criticized by the private sector for unfair competition, because they are largely funded from taxation. Some countries – for example, many of the island tourist destinations – have recognized these difficulties and have levied specific tourist taxes on the private sector to pay for the work of the NTO, although where such

taxes are not separately set aside for tourism, it can also be argued that the tourist industry is just another source of tax revenue.

The structure of a national tourism organization

A stylized layout for an NTO, illustrating its principal divisions, is presented in Figure 14.2. This type of NTO is at 'arm's length' from the Ministry of Tourism by virtue of having its own chairman and board of directors. Where an NTO is a division of a ministry, which may have a wider portfolio of activities than just tourism, it is usual for the director of tourism to report to the senior civil servant in the ministry rather than to a board. Some NTOs only have marketing responsibilities, in which case Figure 14.2 would not have a development division, and research activity would probably be included under the marketing division.

Clearly, the exact structure of an NTO will depend upon the objectives laid down for it by government and the tasks the organization has to

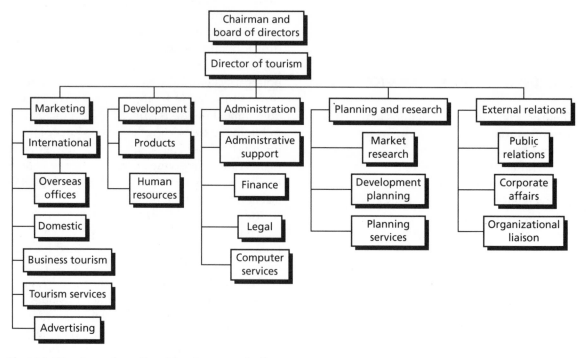

Fig 14.2 Structure of a national tourism organization

Table 14.2 Policy objectives of the Wales Tourist Board (WTB)

The Board seeks to develop and market tourism in ways which yield the optimum economic and social benefit to the people of Wales. Implicit in this is the need:

- To sustain and promote the culture of Wales and the Welsh language.
- To safeguard the natural and built environment.

To meet this, the Board has the following specific policy objectives:

- To encourage the development of tourism facilities and amenities in Wales, with a view to enhancing the quality, market appeal and competitiveness of the product.
- To conduct a cost-effective and targeted programme of strategic marketing aimed at presenting Wales as an alternative destination for holiday and day visits through the year.
- To encourage the provision of tourist information, quality controls and other means of securing visitor satisfaction within Wales.
- To encourage education and training facilities for employees in tourism, and to promote the industry as an effective and proper source of employment.
- To inspire and work with all other organizations whose activities can help to develop and market tourism in Wales.
- To assist developers and operators within the tourism industry in Wales through advisory services.
- To encourage greater community involvement and indigenous enterprise in tourism, and to seek to integrate tourism development more closely with other forms of economic, community and social development.
- To undertake research and provide policy advice, with a view to assisting decision making within the industry and helping to monitor the performance of the industry and the Board.

Source: WTB.

undertake in order to meet those same objectives. A specific example is shown in Table 14.2, which lists the objectives of the Wales Tourist Board. To meet these objectives the WTB is organized into four functional areas: marketing; development; research and corporate planning; and finance

and administration. It will be noticed that the word 'optimum' rather than 'maximum' is used as a description of the economic and social benefit. This is deliberate in the sense that trying to maximize the economic gain, particularly in the short term, may not be in the long-run interests of the host community and could be at variance with the objective of protecting the natural and built environment.

It is important that governments do not set NTOs objectives that may seriously conflict with each other. Too often governments talk of tourism quality yet measure the performance of the NTO in terms of tourist numbers. Examples of policy objectives which are most likely to be at variance with each other are as follows:

- Maximizing foreign exchange earnings versus actions to encourage the regional dispersion of overseas visitors.
- Attracting the high-spend tourist market versus policies to expand visitor numbers continually.
- Maximizing job creation through generating volume tourist flows versus conservation of the environment and heritage.
- Community tourism development versus mass tourism.

Marketing is the principal responsibility of an NTO and therefore usually forms the largest functional area, especially when overseas offices are included. The marketing division formulates the NTO's marketing strategy and is given the task of producing advertising and publicity materials, and promoting sales through the media and the travel trade. Many governments do not actively promote domestic tourism, so their NTOs have this section absent from their structure.

Business tourism often merits its own section within an NTO because of its importance in terms of tourist expenditure and the different servicing requirements of meetings, exhibitions and incentive travel groups when compared to leisure tourism. Likewise, advertising is such a key activity that it may command its own specialist group to plan campaigns and deal with outside advertising agencies. Tourism services include a multitude of tasks:

- Operating a reservation system.
- Handling tourist complaints.
- Licensing and grading accommodation and other suppliers (which may include price controls).
- Programming festivals, events and tours.
- Managing tourist facilities provided either solely or jointly by the NTO: for example, tourist information centres (TICs) or tourist beaches as in Cyprus.

The *development* division can have truly operational involvement only if it is given funding to engage in projects with the private sector and to implement training programmes and activities. If this is not the case then it can only take on a co-ordinating and strategic role. The former is achieved by acting as a 'one-stop shop' for prospective developers through intermediation to obtain planning permission, licences and any financial assistance or incentives from the relevant authorities.

In a strategic role the development division will acquire the planning functions that have been allocated to the *planning and research* division in Figure 14.2. The reason for the separation in Figure 14.2 is that an operational development division is likely to be too heavily involved in day-to-day project management to be able to incorporate long-term development planning. The latter is a research activity and therefore is best located in the unit equipped for this task. The planning services section is an important addendum to the role of an NTO in that it seeks to capitalize on the expertise of the organization to provide advice and even to undertake studies for the private sector and other public bodies: for example, drawing up tourism plans for local communities.

The remaining divisions shown in Figure 14.2 are to a large extent self-explanatory. *Administration* is responsible for the internal smooth running of the NTO and will normally adjudicate on legal matters in respect of tourism legislation, including, in some countries, carrying out prosecutions. *External relations* is a functional area of considerable significance because the NTO is frequently the representative of the government, both at home and overseas, and has to deal with a mass of enquiries from the public, the media and commercial operators, as well as taking an active stance in public relations to support the advertising and sales promotion activities administered by the marketing division. It is for the latter reason that the external relations division may be allocated to marketing, although the tasks given to the division are usually much broader than those required by marketing, as is the case in liaison activities with a variety of public bodies and voluntary associations which have an interest in tourism.

THE IMPACT OF THE PUBLIC SECTOR

In the light of public-sector involvement with tourism, either directly through a ministry with responsibility for tourism and the NTO, or indirectly through, say, foreign policy, legal controls or the provision of infrastructure, the government has at its disposal a series of instruments which can be used to manage tourism flows to meet its policy objectives. The manner in which actions by governments influence tourism may be classified in two ways:

- Demand and revenue management.
- Supply and cost management.

Demand and revenue management

We can identify four primary policy instruments used by governments to manage demand:

- Marketing and promotion.
- Information provision.
- Pricing.
- Controlling access.

Marketing and promotion

As we have already observed, marketing is the principal function of the NTO, and its specific techniques are discussed in Part 4 of this book. It is sufficient here to point out that the key requirements for effective marketing are clear objectives, a thorough knowledge of markets and products, and the allocation of adequate resources. Typically, with many other calls on the government's budget, treasury officials are naturally parsimonious with regard to expenditure on marketing because of difficulties in measuring effectiveness. As a rule, the amounts spent by governments and other public organizations on destination promotion are only a fraction of what is spent in total by the private sector.

Information provision

The ability of tourists to express their demands depends upon their awareness of the facilities available, particularly the attractions, which are a key component of leisure tourism. The evidence suggests that the creation of trails or tourist circuits will enhance the visitor experience as well as regulating tourist flows.

The establishment of a network of TICs and tourist information points (TIPs) at transport terminals and prominent tourist spots will both help the visitor and assist in dispersion. It is often not appreciated that it is the poorly informed visitor who is likely to contribute to crowding and traffic congestion due to lack of knowledge about where to go and what to see at the destination.

Normally, visitors will first look for the main attractions and then 'spill over' into lesser attractions as their length of stay increases. Giving prominence to the variety of attractions available, restricting advertising and informing excursion operators of times when congestion can be avoided are examples of the way in which information management can be used to try and relieve pressure on sensitive tourist areas.

In some countries, NTOs use the provision of information to influence tourists' behaviour. This may come about through editing the information in the tour operator's brochure so that it does not generate unrealistic expectations about a destination, but rather presents the tourist with an informed view of the culture of the host community. An alternative approach is a poster and leaflet campaign aimed directly at the tourist to explain the do's and don'ts of acceptable behaviour. For example, several island resorts offering beach holidays produce leaflets on standards of dress and the unacceptability of wearing only swimsuits in shops, banks and so on.

Pricing

There are several ways in which the public sector may affect the price the tourist pays for staying at a destination. The direct influence arises out of state ownership, notably in the case of attractions. Many of the most important attractions at a destination fall within the public domain, an issue that is examined in some detail in Chapter 18, which is specifically about attractions. The trend in market-orientated economies is for governments to introduce charges for publicly owned attractions. The majority of the world's airlines are owned by governments, and it is not uncommon in less developed countries to find state ownership of hotels and souvenir shops. Thus, in some countries, the key elements making up holiday expenditure are directly affected by the public sector, to the point of reaching total control in the situation that existed in the former centrally planned economies of eastern Europe.

Indirect influences come from economic directives such as foreign exchange restrictions, differential rates of sales tax, special duty-free shops for tourists, and price controls. Exchange restrictions are commonly employed in countries where foreign exchange is scarce, and the tourist is usually compelled to change money at an overvalued exchange rate which serves to increase the real cost of the trip. Tourists are discouraged from changing money on the black market by threats of legal prosecution and severe penalties if caught. The case for price controls is advanced in terms of promoting the long-term growth of the tourist industry and preventing monopolistic exploitation of tourists through overcharging, a practice which can be damaging to the reputation of the destination.

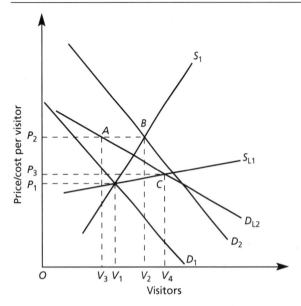

Fig 14.3 Price controls

The argument for price regulation is illustrated in Figure 14.3. Initially the destination is receiving V_1 visitors, paying an average package price of P_1 for their stay, with equilibrium being determined at the intersection of the demand schedule D_1 and the short-run supply curve S_1. Demand expands to D_2 which gives the opportunity for suppliers to raise prices to P_2, at the market equilibrium point B. This approach, characterized as 'making money while you can', can be counterproductive, because demand in the longer term is more sensitive (elastic) to price than in the short run, as illustrated by the slope of D_{L2}. The reasons for this are the number of competing destinations and the holiday price consciousness of travellers. By keeping price at P_2, existing suppliers will make excess profits at the expense of the destination's market share. Market equilibrium is achieved at A and visitor numbers fall back from V_2 to V_3. The country is perceived as 'pricing itself out of the market'.

There is no doubt that destinations are aware of their price competitiveness, and some NTOs compile a tourist price index for their own country as well as others, in order to assess their relative market position. Where governments regulate prices, the objective is to set them at a level, say P_3, which is sufficient to encourage the long-run growth in supply as shown by S_{L1} and commensurate with market expansion to an equilibrium point such as C, giving a growth in visitor numbers to V_4. Producers, on the other hand, are prevented from making short-run excess profits.

Where price controls are enforced, they are normally another stage in an overall market regulation package which commences with the registration and licensing of establishments. In the case of hotels this will include classification and possibly a quality grading system. Price regulation can be found in almost all instances where the government manages capacity and therefore restricts competition. Worldwide, the most common example is the licensing and metering of taxis. Where competition exists, the argument put forward in Figure 14.3 hinges upon whether supply adjusts more quickly than demand. There are many examples of Mediterranean resorts where the growth of bed capacity has outstripped demand, so the problem for the authorities has been controlling standards rather than prices, as well as trying to prevent ruinous competition among hoteliers.

In market economics there is a basic ideology which is against regulating prices. Where opportunities for suppliers to make excess profits in the short term do arise, control is often exercised informally through exhortation that it will not be in the long-term best interests of the destination. It is reasonable to assume that firms themselves will be aware of competition from other countries, though often they are under considerable short-term pressure to increase profitability.

Controlling access

Controlling access is a means of limiting visitor numbers or channelling visitor flows. At an international level, the easiest way for a country to limit demand is by restricting the number of visas issued. Prohibiting charter flights is a means by which several countries have conveyed an image of exclusiveness to the market and, in some instances, have protected the national air carrier. At the destination, controlling access is usually concerned with protecting popular cultural sites and natural resources. Thus visitor management techniques may be used to relieve congestion at peak times, and planning legislation may be invoked to prohibit or control the development of tourist infrastructure (particularly accommodation) near or around natural sites.

Supply and cost management

Government activity on the supply side is concerned with influencing the providers of tourist facilities and services, as opposed to demand management policies aimed at guiding the tourist's choice, controlling the costs of stay or stimulating/regulating visitor numbers.

In the majority of countries, the development of tourism is regarded as a partnership between the private and public sectors. The extent of government involvement in this partnership depends upon the prevailing economic, political and social policies of a country.

Where the government envisages a particular direction for tourism growth or wishes to speed up the process, it may intervene extensively in the market place by setting up a Tourist Development Corporation (TDC) and assigning it the responsibility for building resorts. A well-known example of this process was the building of new resorts in Languedoc–Roussillon, France, but many countries have instituted TDCs at one time or another: for example, Egypt, India, Malaysia, New Zealand and a number of African countries. In theory, once the resort has been built, the development corporation's function ceases and the assets are transferred to the private sector (at a price) and the local authority. This is the general trend in market-orientated economies, but in countries where there is a strong degree of central planning, the TDC often maintains an operational role in running hotels and tours.

The methods that are frequently used by governments to influence the supply side of the tourism industry are as follows:

- Land use planning and control.
- Building regulations.
- Market regulation.
- Market research and planning.
- Taxation.
- Ownership.
- Investment incentives.

Land use planning and control

Control over land use is the most basic technique, and arguably the one that has the greatest influence on the supply of tourist structures. All governments have a form of town and country planning legislation whereby permission is required to develop, extend or change the use of almost every piece of land. As a rule, the controls are designed to protect areas of high landscape and amenity value. Zoning of land and compulsory purchase are commonly used as a means of promoting tourism development. One of the key aspects of land control is that, before any detailed site plans and future land requirements for tourism are published, the appropriate administrative organization and legislation are in place in order to prevent speculation, land division or parcelling. Dealings or speculation in land prior to legislative control have been a common cause of failure in tourism master plans.

Building regulations

Building regulations are used to supplement land use control and typically cover the size of buildings, their height, shape and colour, and car parking arrangements. The latter do not always receive the attention they deserve in some resorts. To private-sector operators, car parks are often considered unproductive space, so there is a tendency to avoid having to provide them, leaving visitors little alternative but to park their cars in nearby streets. This may only serve to add to traffic congestion and the annoyance of local residents. In addition to structural regulations, many countries also have protective legislation governing cultural resources such as historic buildings, archeological remains, religious monuments, conservation areas and even whole towns.

Market regulation

Governments pass legislation to regulate the market conduct of firms in matters of competitive practices and also to limit the degree of ownership in particular sectors of the industry to prevent the abuse of monopoly power. Governments may also regulate markets by imposing on suppliers a number of obligations to consumers. This does not have to be legislation; it could take the form of industry-enforced codes of conduct of the kind laid down as conditions for membership of national travel trade associations.

One of the economic criteria dictating the optimal workings of markets is that consumers should have complete knowledge of the choices open to them. If consumers do not have the right to safety, to be informed, to choose and of redress, and if firms are not behaving according to the accepted rules of conduct, then resources will be wasted, which may be considered inefficient.

The economic aspects of a consumer policy are shown in Figure 14.4. As the level of protection increases, so wastage or compensation payments decline, while at the same time the costs of protection increase. The optimum amount of protection is where the two schedules intersect at point *A*, which defines level *L* on the axis below. This is the economic rationale: on social or political grounds, the state may legislate to ensure nearly 100 per cent protection. But the economic consequences of such an action could be to raise the supply price of the good or service to the point where the market is substantially diminished. In 1988 the EC issued a directive to member states concerning the protection of tourists buying package tours. This was opposed (and subsequently amended) on the grounds that its compliance would significantly raise holiday prices.

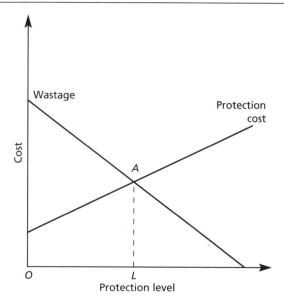

Fig 14.4 Economics of consumer protection

Market Research and Planning

The tourist industry usually expects the public sector to collect statistical information and carry out market surveys. For their own part, governments are interested in monitoring changes in the industry and carry out research to identify the social benefits and costs of tourism.

Taxation

There are two main reasons why governments levy specific taxes on the tourism sector. The first is the classic argument for a tourist tax: namely, to allocate to the supply price the external costs imposed on the host community through providing public amenities for tourists. The second is for purposes of raising revenue: tourists are seen as part of the overall tax base. The most common methods of raising public income from tourism are airport or ticket taxes and taxes on hotel occupancy. When it comes to raising revenue, casinos can be a very profitable source: governments have been known to take as much as 50 per cent of the 'handle', which is the net amount of money taken in from the tables.

Although a tourist tax may be paid by the guest at the hotel and collected from the hotelier, the matter of who bears the tax will depend on the responsiveness of demand and supply to a price change. In Figure 14.5, the imposition of a tax raises the supply price by moving the supply curve from S_1 to S_2, which in turn reduces the quantity of, say, room sales demanded from Q_1 to Q_2. However, the amount of tax income raised, P_2ACD does not all fall on the tourists in the form of a higher price. Price rises from P_1 to P_2 only, and the larger share of the incidence of the tax, P_1BCD, falls on the supplier in the form of reduced profits. Tourists contribute P_2ABP_1 of the tax revenue. The less sensitive tourists are to price, something that can be reflected in a much steeper demand schedule D, the greater is the ability of suppliers to pass on the tax in the form of a higher price, and therefore the larger will be the share of the tax burden falling on the tourists.

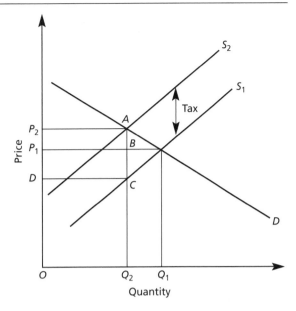

Fig 14.5 Distributive effects of a tourist tax

Ownership

Mention has already been made of state ownership of attractions, natural amenities and some key revenue-earning activities such as hotels, modes of transport (especially airlines) and souvenir shops. It is possible to add to this list conference centres, exhibition halls, sports and leisure complexes (including casinos), and the provision of general infrastructure. The latter may include banks, hospitals, public utilities (water and energy supplies), telecommunications, road networks, transport terminals, and education and training establishments.

The arguments for public ownership of these facilities rest on their importance as essential services for any economic development; outside investors would expect such provision and the resulting economies of scale in production. Traditionally, public infrastructure and transport networks have been regarded as natural monopolies: that is, the minimum scale of production is such as to make it impossible for more than one firm to enjoy all the economies in the market, so

that even if they were not publicly owned, these organizations would need to be publicly regulated.

Investment incentives

Governments around the world offer a wide range of investment incentives to developers. They may be grouped under three broad headings:

- *Reduction of capital costs.* This includes capital grants or loans at preferential rates, interest rate relief, a moratorium on loan repayments for x years, provision of infrastructure, provision of land on concessional terms, tariff exemption on construction materials and equity participation.
- *Reduction of operating costs.* In order to improve operating viability, governments may grant tax 'holidays' (5–10 years), give a labour or training subsidy, offer tariff exemption on imported materials and supplies, provide special depreciation allowances and ensure that there is double taxation or unilateral relief. Tax reliefs involve government-to-government agreements which prevent an investor being taxed twice on the same profits.

- *Investment security.* The object here is to win investors' confidence in an industry which is very sensitive to the political environment and economic climate. Action here would include guarantees against nationalization, free availability of foreign exchange, repatriation of invested capital, profits, dividends and interest, loan guarantees, provision of work permits for 'key' personnel and the availability of technical advice.

The administration of grants or loans may be given to the NTO, a government-sponsored investment bank or the TDC. Tax matters will usually remain the responsibility of the treasury or the ministry in charge of finance. Less developed countries are often able to attract low-cost investment funds from multinational aid agencies, which they can use to augment their existing resources for the provision of development finance.

It may be taken that policies to ensure investment security are primary requirements for attracting tourism developers. The objective of financial incentives is to improve returns to capital so as to attract developers and investors. Where there is obvious market potential the government may only have to demonstrate its commitment to tourism by providing the necessary climate for investment security. Such a situation occurred in Bermuda during the early 1970s, and so, in order to prevent overexploitation of the tourism resources, the Bermuda government imposed a moratorium on large hotel building.

The impact of financial incentives on the amount of investment is illustrated in Figure 14.6. The schedule *SS* represents the supply of investible funds, while D_1D is the schedule of returns to capital employed. D_1D slopes downwards from left to right as more and more investment opportunities are taken up – the declining marginal efficiency of investment. In the initial situation, equilibrium is at *A* with the amount of investment being I_1 and the rate of return i_1.

The government now implements a range of financial incentives which have the effect of raising the rate of return per unit of capital to i_2,

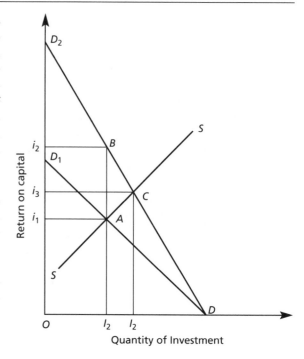

Fig 14.6 Impact of financial incentives

moving the marginal efficiency of investment schedule to D_2D. The new return i_2 equals $(1+s)i_1$, where *s* is the effective rate of subsidy. If the amount of investible funds available for tourism is limited at I_1, then the impact of incentives serves merely to raise the return to investors by raising the equilibrium point to *B*. The loss to the government treasury is the area $i_1AB i_2$ which equals the gain to private investors.

There is no doubt that many countries have been forced by competitive pressures for foreign investment into situations that are similar to those above. Countries can become trapped in a bidding process to secure clients, and as a result the variety of financial incentives multiplies together with an escalation of the rates of benefit, without their necessity or their true cost to the economy being evaluated. Given that the supply of investment funds is responsive or elastic, the net effect of an incentives policy is to expand the amount of tourism projects to I_2 and the rate of return settles at i_3, the equilibrium point being *C*.

It is important to note that there are frequent instances where it is gross uncertainty, as in times of recession, rather than limited potential that prevents the private sector investing. In such situations the principal role of government intervention is to act as a catalyst to give confidence to investors. Thus public funds are able to lever in private money by nature of the government's commitment to tourism, and enable the market potential of an area to be realized.

In implementing a tourism investment policy the government has to decide to what extent incentives should be legislated as automatic entitlements, as against being discretionary awards. It has already been noted that automatic incentives may give too much money away, when what is required to ensure that the treasury receives maximum benefit from its funds is the application of the concept of 'additionality'. This seeks to provide financial support or the equivalent benefits in kind to the point where the developer will just proceed with the project.

The implication of additionality is an ideal situation where all incentives are discretionary and therefore offered selectively. The legislation would be fairly general, empowering the ministry responsible for tourism to offer loans, grants, tax exemptions and equity investment as it sees fit. Such legislation is embodied in the UK Development of Tourism Act 1969. The granting of incentives to prospective developers is in accordance with ministerial guidelines, which are regularly reviewed in response to the level of tourism activity. To have only discretionary incentives, however, is a counsel of perfection. Competition for tourism investment frequently requires countries to legislate for automatic financial help in order to attract investors in the first instance. Some countries may legislate for all the incentives discussed here; others for a subset of them. Several countries have been guilty of copying the incentive legislation of their neighbours without any real grasp of the meaning of this legislation.

Ensuring the appropriateness of the various financial incentives available depends on understanding the nature of the business risk and the likely returns to the tourist industry, as well as the ability of the country to afford them. Thus developing countries may find themselves in no position to offer grants or cheap loans, which highlights the importance of contributions from aid agencies. One of the main sources of business risk in tourist enterprises is the tendency to have a high ratio of capital charges in relation to operating expenses. It is for this reason that incentives to reduce capital costs are the preferred form of assistance when the viability of the business is being considered.

INTERVENTION POLICY

The range of policy instruments available to governments is considerable and enables the public sector to exercise varying degrees of influence over the direction of tourism development. Around the globe governments have intervened to assist and regulate the private sector; this is because the complex nature of the tourist product makes it unlikely that private markets will satisfy all the tourism policy objectives of a country. As noted previously, the extent of public involvement depends on the economic philosophy of the government. The trend towards pure market-led economics in the 1980s led to a clawback of state involvement and the questioning of intervention as more likely to lead to market distortions than market corrections. This is in total contrast to the concept of sustainable development, which challenges the ability of private markets to improve the distribution of income and protect the environment.

The baseline scenario for sustainable development is the alleviation of absolute poverty and the replenishment of the resource stock so that at a minimum no one generation is worse off than any other. The spillover benefits of tourism are well known, and, more than any other industry, tourism deals with the use of natural and cultural resources. The lessons of the past indicate that it is unwise for governments to abandon their ability to influence the direction of tourism development.

References and further reading

Barnard, C. (1989) 'Taxing international tourism', in Witt, S., and Moutinho, L. (eds), *Tourism Marketing and Management Handbook*, Hemel Hempstead: Prentice Hall.

Bodlender, J.A., and Davies, E.J.G. (1985) *A Profile of Government Financial Grant Aid to Tourism*, London: WTO, Horwath and Horwath.

Burkart, A., and Medlik, S. (1981) *Tourism: Past, Present and Future*, London: Heinemann.

Heely, J. (1989) 'Role of national tourism organisations in the United Kingdom', in Witt, S., and Moutinho, L. (eds), *Tourism Marketing and Management Handbook*, Hemel Hempstead: Prentice Hall.

Holloway, J.C. (1989) *The Business of Tourism*, London: Pitman Publishing.

Joppe, M. (1989) 'State tourism policy', in Witt, S., and Moutinho, L. (eds), *Tourism Marketing and Management Handbook*, Hemel Hempstead: Prentice Hall.

Lavery, P., and Van Doren, C. (1990) *Travel and Tourism: A North American/European Perspective*, Huntingdon: Elm Publications.

Middleton, V.T.C. (1988) *Marketing in Travel and Tourism*, Oxford: Heinemann.

Mill, R.C., and Morrison, A.M. (1985) *The Tourism System*, Englewood Cliffs, NJ: Prentice Hall.

Pearce, D. (1992) *Tourist Organisations*, Harlow: Longman.

Trade and Industry Committee (1985) *Tourism in the UK*, Vol. 1, Session 1985–1986, London: HMSO.

Wanhill, S.R.C. (1989) 'Development and investment policy in tourism', in Witt, S., and Moutinho, L. (eds), *Tourism Marketing and Management Handbook*, Hemel Hempstead: Prentice Hall.

CHAPTER 15

Accommodation

OVERVIEW

In this chapter we outline the key operating characteristics and trends in the accommodation industry. Accommodation is an essential component of tourism, given that any definition of tourism involves a stay away from home. We demonstrate the fact that accommodation becomes the psychological base for the tourist during his or her stay away, and that different markets then make differing demands upon the accommodation. We also outline the various types of accommodation and identify the common characteristics of all accommodation units. These include seasonality and cost structures which display a high ratio of fixed to variable costs. Clearly, this has implications for the operation of accommodation units. Finally, we examine the trends which will affect the accommodation industry in the future.

ACCOMMODATION AND TOURISM

The feature that distinguishes the WTO definition of a tourist from that of an excursionist is that the tourist must spend at least one night in the destination visited. Assuming that few people will sleep on the streets or park benches, this definition indicates a core role for the provision of accommodation of all types and descriptions.

Figure 15.1 illustrates the central role that accommodation plays in tourism. Tourists arrive from their previous destination, which may or may not be their home, via some means of transport. The accommodation provision then becomes the core of their activities as they proceed to inter-

act with other services in the area. Visiting local attractions or using local shops or restaurants may be the chosen pursuit of the leisure tourist. The business tourist may be more involved with local business transactions and the public sector. At all stages, the tourist will have to take their place in the local environment and may also be involved with travel agents and tour operators for booking accommodation and other services.

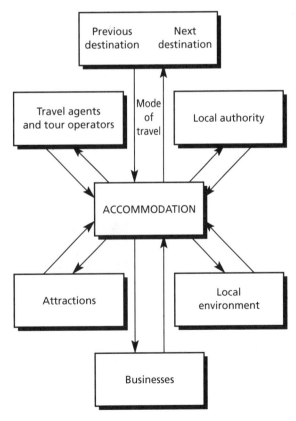

Fig 15.1 Role of accommodation in the tourist product

If the visit is for longer than one night, then it is the accommodation that will become the 'home' base for other pursuits and the demands made upon the accommodation will depend upon the purpose of visit. For example, business tourists may demand business facilities such as secretarial services. In all cases, the accommodation provides a base of operation and becomes regarded as the tourist's own territory.

The central role of the accommodation provision is not restricted to providing a psychological base for the tourist, it also takes a large part of the total revenue from the tourist. 1990 figures for the UK (shown in Figure 15.2), illustrate this clearly, with accommodation alone accounting for around one third of all spending for domestic and overseas tourists (excluding the amount overseas tourists spend on travel to the UK). The second and third areas are eating out and shopping.

THE RANGE OF ACCOMMODATION PROVISION

There is a very wide range of accommodation types. The side headings in Table 15.1 illustrate the names used to describe accommodation types in the UK and a number of distinctions between accommodation types can be seen by examining this Table.

Paying/non-paying

The commercial provision of accommodation for payment accounts for just half of all the nights spent away from home. The other half is spent mainly with friends and relatives but also extends to owned caravans and second homes.

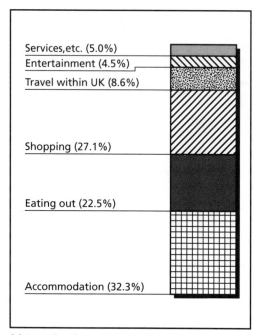

Services,etc. (5.0%)
Entertainment (4.5%)
Travel within UK (8.6%)

Shopping (27.1%)

Eating out (22.5%)

Accommodation (32.3%)

(a) Spending by overseas tourists

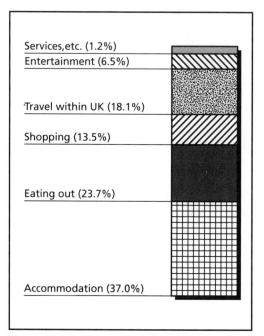

Services,etc. (1.2%)
Entertainment (6.5%)

Travel within UK (18.1%)

Shopping (13.5%)

Eating out (23.7%)

Accommodation (37.0%)

(b) Spending by domestic tourists

Fig 15.2 Distribution of spending by overseas and domestic tourists in the UK, 1990

Table 15.1 Accommodation in the UK, 1991

Accommodation used	Trips (2) millions	Nights (3) millions	Spend (4) millions	Conversion Trips→Nights (5) units	Conversion Trips→Spend (6) units	Conversion Nights→Spend (7) units
1991	94.4	395.6	10 470	4.19	110.91	26.47
Hotel/motel/guest house	22	18	36	0.82	1.64	2.00
Paying guest in:						
Farmhouse		1	1			1.00
Other private house/B&B	2	2	2	1.00	1.00	1.00
Self-catering in rented:						
Flat/apartment	2	4	5	2.00	2.50	1.25
House/villa/bungalow	4	7	8	1.75	2.00	1.14
Hostel/university/school	2	2	2	1.00	1.00	1.00
Friends'/relatives' home	45	39	22	0.87	0.49	0.56
Second home/time-share	1	1	1	1.00	1.00	1.00
Holiday camp/village:						
Self-catering	2	3	3	1.50	1.50	1.00
Serviced	1	1	1	1.00	1.00	1.00
Camping	4	4	3	1.00	0.75	0.75
Caravan:						
Towed	4	6	4	1.50	1.00	0.67
Static owned	4	4	3	1.00	0.75	0.75
Static not owned	4	6	6	1.50	1.50	1.00
Boat	1	1	1	1.00	1.00	1.00
Sleeper cab of lorry/truck	1		1	0.00	1.00	
Other/transit	2	1	1	0.50	0.50	1.00
Total commercial accommodation	46	51	69	1.11	1.50	1.35
Of which serviced	25	21	40	0.84	1.60	1.90
Of which self-catering	21	30	29	1.43	1.38	0.97
Total non-commercial accommodation	54	49	31	0.91	0.57	0.63
Total all accommodation	100	100	100	1.00	1.00	1.00
Purpose of visit						
Holiday	62	75	74	1.21	1.19	0.99
VFR	22	14	8	0.64	0.36	0.57
Business	11	7	14	0.64	1.27	2.00
Other	5	4	4	0.80	0.80	1.00
Total	100	100	100	1.00	1.00	1.00

Source: Adapted from ETB/BTA *The UK Tourist: Statistics: 1991*.

Serviced/non-serviced

Staying in serviced accommodation the customer would expect things to be done for them. In a hotel for example, linen will be changed and the room cleaned and tidied daily. In some hotels, the bed would also be 'turned down' in the evening. However, nobody would expect this service to be provided on a camp site or self-catering flatlets, which are examples of non-serviced accommodation. Even within a non-serviced style of accommodation such as the villas at Center Parcs, some elements of service – such as cleaning – may be available on request at an extra charge.

Owned/rented

Most accommodation occupied by tourists is provided on a rental basis. The growth of second homes and timeshare does, however, constitute a growing sector of owned accommodation to add to the large numbers of owned caravans.

Primary purpose/secondary occupation

Some accommodation is provided in units that were designed specifically for that purpose and whose primary role is the provision of accommodation. This would include hotels, guest houses, holiday villages and so on. Other tourist accommodation is provided in establishments whose main purpose is not accommodation. This distinction would extend to rooms in farmhouses, universities and schools or the rental of rooms in private houses (which has seen such a growth in Eastern Europe).

Static/mobile

Whereas most accommodation types are firmly rooted to the ground, others are either temporary or can be moved freely. For example, caravan parks tend to use static vans but these can be moved more easily than a traditionally built property. A camp site may provide tents already erected but again these can easily be moved should the pattern of demand change. Towing caravans, camper vans and boats provide examples of freely mobile accommodation provision.

Purpose of visit

Some accommodation types are designed with a particular purpose of visit in mind, where others are open to a variety of uses. Holiday camps, as the name suggests, are designed for the holiday tourist and are not suitable for business tourism. Hotels, on the other hand, may have a mixture of guests staying all at the same time and this can lead to some conflict of interest.

ACCOMMODATION TYPES IN EUROPE

The types of accommodation provided vary from country to country. If we just look across Europe, it is possible to identify many different accommodation names and types.

France

As the world's major tourist destination, France provides a wide range of accommodation types that can be split into three main sectors.

1. Firstly, hotels which are graded from one to four star luxury. In addition to the hotel groups, there are collections of private hotels such as the Logis de France or the Relais Chateaux.
2. Secondly, camping and caravanning sites with four grades from one to four star.
3. The third accommodation type is the *Gîtes de France*. These provide reasonably priced self-catering accommodation in or near small country villages. The gîte itself may be a small cottage, village house, flat in the owner's house or part of a farm.

Switzerland

With its long tradition of commercial hospitality, Switzerland provides accommodation in hotels (the Swiss Hotels Association lists around 2 600 hotels and pensions that are members of the association), chalets and apartments, 450 camping and caravanning sites, and youth hostels primarily for the under 25 year olds. In addition, Switzerland is able to offer a wide range of health spas, clinics, climatic health resorts and convalescent homes and hotels.

Holland

All Dutch hotels are classified according to the Benelux Hotel Classification which, besides awarding one to five stars for facilities, consists of the following types:

- Hotel–cafe–restaurant (HCR) – an establishment built and fitted out to provide accommodation and in which a cafe and a restaurant or a cafe-restaurant are also operated.
- Motel (M) – a hotel–cafe–restaurant integrated with a motorway or trunk road and adapted to the special needs of road users.
- Hotel–restaurant (HR) – an establishment fitted out to provide accommodation in which a restaurant is also operated.
- Hotel-garni (HG) – an establishment providing accommodation in which only bed and breakfast are provided.
- Apartment-hotel (AH) – an establishment providing accommodation in flats, studio flats or the like, let out by the day.

The relative importance of different types of accommodation is difficult to assess but the figures given in Table 15.1 provide some interesting insights into this problem.

Nights per trip

According to *The UK Tourist: Statistics 1991* quoted in Table 15.1, the average trip in the UK lasted just over four nights. Column (5) of Table 15.1 shows the conversion ratio of trips into nights calculated as the percentage of nights spent in a particular type of accommodation divided by the percentage of trips this represents. A figure of less than 1 represents a shorter than average stay while a figure over 1 represents a longer than average stay. Excluding tourists in transit, the lowest conversion ratio is shown for the hotel, motel and guest house sector at 0.82 or just over 3 nights per trip. The highest figure is for self-catering flats and apartments at 2.0 – or over 8 nights per trip. As a whole, the commercial accommodation sector shows a longer stay than non-commercial accommodation. However, within the commercial sector, a stay in serviced accommodation will be much shorter than in non-serviced or self catering accommodation.

Spend per trip

Using a similar calculation, column (6) shows the conversion ratio for the amount of money spent per trip. Not surprisingly, the lowest spends per trip were shown for staying with friends and relatives, where no charge will be made for the accommodation itself, camping and static owned caravans. The highest spends per trip were recorded for self-catering flats and apartments where people were staying for long visits, and hotels, motels and guest houses where the short duration of stay was compensated for by the cost per night.

Spend per night

Column (7) shows the conversion ratio for spend per night. The hotel sector, as previously indicated, has the highest spend per night, while the lowest costs are incurred when staying with friends and relatives, camping or sleeping in your own caravan.

Purpose of visit

Breaking down the figures by purpose of visit is also revealing. Holiday trips are of a longer than average duration and cost more per trip than the average, but they cost slightly less than the average

---

CASE STUDY 15.1

UK hotels: an historical perspective

The development of the hotel industry can be traced back as far as the Druids and the Romans, who represent the earliest recorded examples of the hospitality industry. The history of the industry can be traced through the ages with the emergence of the inn, the tavern and the ale house to the first appearance of the 'hotel garni' in the early 1760s. It was not, however, until the early 1800s that hotels as we know them today began to appear, and even then development was slow until the 1860s.

There are three major influences that have historically affected the development of the industry: transport, social patterns and habits, and the economic climate.

Transport has probably been the most important influence on hotel development. In particular, it has affected their location because staying away from home inevitably involves some degree of travel and the mode of transport will influence where one may want to stay. The posting points on the main stage coach routes provided the locations for the growth of the inns between the sixteenth and nineteenth centuries. The terminal points of those routes saw the growth of inns accommodating over 100 guests.

As transport moved to the railways, so the railway companies built hotels at their terminal stations to offer competitive advantage over their rivals and to house guests whose trains were late. The railways were also responsible to a large extent for the development of seaside resorts like Blackpool and Bournemouth, which only became accessible to the masses when the railways arrived.

Airport hotels have similarly provided accommodation for travellers as a stopping point before or after travel. The dynamic growth in air transport has mirrored a similar growth in hotel capacity at airports. The success of the Post House chain has shown the continued importance of transport. Forte chose locations for these hotels to catch the motorist – on business or pleasure.

Social patterns and habits have also played their part in shaping the industry. In the Middle Ages, travel was very dangerous. The nobility travelled the most and they tended to stay *en route* either with their fellow noblemen or in the monasteries. As travel became easier, some private houses grew in reputation as good places to stay. The dissolution of the monasteries saw the growth of these houses into inns. The large hotel capacity at the coast owes it origins to the eighteenth century passion for health associated with sea bathing and its development into the 'fashionable thing to do'. Similarly, the post-war phenomenon of mass national and international tourism has strongly influenced hotel developments worldwide.

The economic climate has always influenced hotel development, although two Acts of Parliament brought about some more specific changes. The Limited Liabilities Act 1862 saw the risk of investment in hotels reduced dramatically. Many hotel companies were floated in the tide of investment from the wealth generated by Britain's industrial leadership at that time. One of the first off the mark was the Langham Hotel Company, which opened its hotel in Regent Street. This hotel closed in the 1940s and the BBC bought it for offices. Ladbrokes have recently renovated it, and it has opened as a luxury hotel once more. The Development of Tourism act 1969 created the Hotel Development Incentive Scheme. This scheme encouraged the building of many new hotels in London between 1969 and 1976 to cope with the shortfall of accommodation in the capital. Report reports from Horwath and Horwath suggested that a similar shortfall would occur in the early 1990s.

The success of the industry in servicing business needs and the provision of tourist accommodation must be influenced by the general economic climate of the country and the world. Demand patterns are dramatically influenced by world events, as shown by the decrease in American tourists to the UK in the summer of 1986 following the Chernobyl disaster and the bombing of Libya.

per night. Visiting friends and relatives has a short duration of stay and an even lower cost per trip based on a very low spend per night. Business travel, while having the same short duration as visiting friends and relatives, has the highest spend per trip because of a very high cost per night. It is easy to see how this pattern has affected the figures already discussed for the individual accommodation types based on the amount of their trade coming from any of these three sources.

CHARACTERISTICS OF ACCOMMODATION OPERATIONS

Table 15.1 illustrates the important influence that the type of customer has on the characteristics of operation for any accommodation type. It is,

however, possible to identify certain characteristics that are common to all types of accommodation from a basic camp site to a luxury hotel. In addition, some features are only found in one accommodation type and have no influence upon others.

Demand for accommodation

Figure 15.3 shows, in simplified form, the possible sources of demand for any type of accommodation.

First, it is possible to distinguish between business demand and holiday demand. Some units will cater almost exclusively for one source of business, while others will have a balance of sources that may vary according to the time of year. For example, it is difficult to see many business travellers using a camp site, but a large hotel will cater

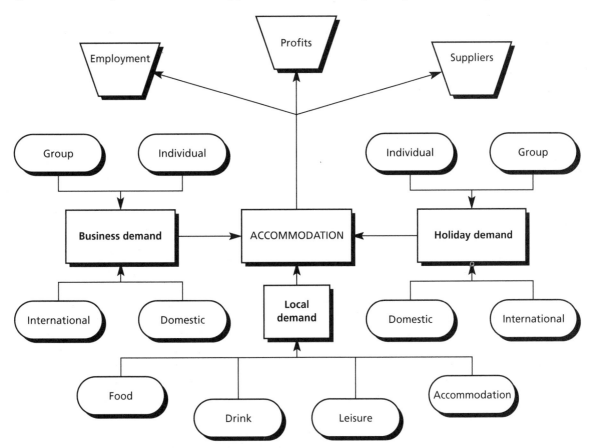

Fig 15.3 Sources of accommodation demand

for both business and holiday guests – business guests usually on Monday to Thursday, and short-break holiday guests from Friday to Sunday.

Second, we can split both these sources of demand into group travel and individual travel. Again different types of accommodation will have a different balance of demand and this will vary according to the time of year. At the beginning of the summer holiday season, a holiday village may cater mainly for large groups from a particular area of the country or a social organization. In the middle of the season most of the bookings will be for individuals. On the other hand, a hotel in York, for example, may cater mainly for group tour bookings during the peak summer season and individuals for the rest of the year. Group bookings also occur for business travel, but would usually be in the form of meetings, conferences or conventions.

A further distinction can be made between domestic demand and international demand. Some areas of the country will see very few international tourists, whereas others, on the main tourist routes or in the key destinations, will be inundated at certain times of the year.

In addition, an accommodation unit will receive a certain amount of its demand from the local community. This may be in the form of meals in the restaurant or use of the public bars, but could also occasionally extend to the accommodation side.

Common characteristics

Importance of location

The history of the development of the hotel industry shows how important location is to the success of an accommodation unit. Being in the most prominent or best location for a particular type of customer is one of the key influences on the success of any accommodation unit. The desirability of a particular location may well change over time. A popular hotel catering for passing motorists may well have its demand drastically reduced if a local motorway or bypass is built.

The issue of location has to be balanced with the subject of construction costs. Such costs could include the land itself, planning permissions, construction periods and building costs. One recent report quoted a French hotelier as saying 'land prices in Paris and London are comparable but provincial land in France is 50% of that in the UK' (NEDCa, 1992).

Land prices are also linked to planning permission. The time taken to get planning permission for the most part is shorter in continental Europe than in the UK.

Fixity of premises

Unfortunately, although the circumstances of demand may change, it is very difficult to change the accommodation unit. Once built it is almost impossible to move a hotel to another location – although modern prefabricated building techniques may make that more of a possibility in the future. Even changing the use of an existing unit can be very difficult or very expensive.

Cost structures

The heavy reliance on space and buildings needed for most accommodation types means that the cost structure is heavily biased toward high fixed costs and low variable costs. In order to break even, an accommodation unit must achieve a relatively high level of occupancy. Any room, flat or placement unlet means a loss of potential revenue. On the other hand, once the fixed costs are covered, profits rise quite quickly.

In order to help to cover fixed costs at times of low demand, many units will sell their accommodation at reduced rates that will allow them to cover their variable cost and make a contribution to their fixed overheads. The impact of recession in recent years has seen a 'discount culture prevail amongst consumers and published tariffs ... with significant disparities when compared with average achieved room rates' (Horwath Consulting, 1992, p. 4).

Demand dependence

These first three factors combine to make all accommodation units highly dependent on customer demand. Unless the right type of demand for the product provided at the right price is available in that location, the business will not be able to survive. Indeed, when carrying out a feasibility study to look at the viability of developing accommodation in an area, the first area for study should always be an assessment of the demand.

Contact dependence

Another consequence of the fixity of premises is 'inseparability': that is, all customers must be brought to the accommodation. This stresses the importance of raising customer awareness of the availability of the product and making it as easy as possible for customers to find the premises. Few customers will struggle down dark twisting country lanes pulling their caravans toward a distant, badly signposted site. This also raises the issues of accessibility and transport networks.

Core service/territory/ownership

As we mentioned earlier, the accommodation forms the focal point of a tourist's visit and becomes, for the duration of stay, that visitor's personal territory. Any infringement of these rights of territory or ownership will raise strong feelings.

Variable characteristics

Range of services and facilities

Food and beverage provision grew rapidly in hotels over the 1980s. In addition, most accommodation units now provide a range of extra services that can vary from television and video in the room, to a resident disco or entertainer, or more frequently these days a swimming pool and fitness centre.

The importance of these extra facilities will vary depending on the particular market the unit wishes to attract. Their importance will, for example, vary with the gender of the customer

---

CASE STUDY 15.2

Systems of grading

There is no compulsory registration and grading system for accommodation in operation in the UK, although these do exist in many other European countries. In the UK, the Regional Tourist Boards (excluding N. Ireland) operate a system of voluntary registration, classification and grading.

The English Tourist Board offers a National Classification and Grading scheme for three types of accommodation operation: hotels, motels, guest houses, inns, B & Bs and farmhouses are classified as one to five crowns depending on the range of facilities and services offered; holiday homes including cottages, bungalows, flats, houses, apartments, chalets and house boats are similarly classified as one to five keys; caravan holiday homes and holiday parks are classified in the British Graded Holiday Parks Scheme as qualifying for one to five √s.

In addition, the owners of the accommodation can ask to be graded following an inspection visit by English Tourist Board inspectors. This grading assesses the quality standards of what is provided, taking into account those intangible but very important aspects such as warmth of welcome, efficiency of service and appearance, as well as the quality of the furnishings and fittings. There are three levels of commendation: approved, commended and highly commended. The prime purpose of the commendations is to help potential customers identify places providing the quality standards they seek at a price they are prepared to pay.

---

and his or her age group. Not surprisingly, videos are most likely to appeal to those under 35 years while television is important to all age groups. Discos and dancing tend to appeal to those under 25 years, while sports and fitness facilities appeal to all age groups. The older the age group is, the more likely it is that the interest in sports facilities will be directed to swimming or tennis or golf.

The importance of these extra services can also

be considered by type of travel – business or leisure. Business travellers tend to stay in hotels on their own and so tend to prefer activities that can be done on their own. These may include television, swimming and visiting the gym/fitness centre.

Business mix

The international accommodation industry derives its demand primarily from the two main activities of business and leisure travel. Guests come geographically from the domestic or foreign market, and from a distribution point of view either direct or through intermediaries in the travel industry.

Domestic and foreign markets each account for about half of the accommodation business worldwide. In North America the domestic traveller provides more than 80 per cent of business; in contrast, in Africa and the Middle East foreign travellers are the most significant, providing two-thirds of hotel occupancy.

Ownership

In Europe the accommodation industry is highly fragmented both in total and by individual country. The two largest groups (ranked by rooms in western Europe) are the French companies Accor and Club Mediterranean. Accor is the only European hotel company that can boast a pan-European presence with representation in almost every western European country (except Denmark, southern Ireland and Luxembourg). In addition, it is the only company represented in the full range of product segments. Accor is the largest operator in France, where it has 55 per cent of its worldwide room supply and a 9 per cent share of total rooms. It is also the largest operator in Belgium and Germany.

Club Mediterranean leans towards the leisure market, with most of its room supply in holiday villages, villas and time-share apartments. It is concentrated in holiday destination countries. Club Mediterranean's room supply in Europe represents three-quarters of its worldwide room supply.

Excluding the reservation groupings of Best Western, these two groups are twice the size of the nearest competitors – the Sol Group, based almost exclusively in Spanish resort hotels, and Forte, with most of its room supply in the UK. The remaining hotel groups are heavily concentrated in their home country. However, the main international chains, Hilton International, Intercontinental, Holiday Inn and Sheraton, are represented broadly throughout the continent.

Seasonality

The seasonality of demand for accommodation depends upon two factors: location and the nature of demand. Business demand tends to be restricted to the working week and the hotels – generally in major cities. Such demand tends to peak in the spring and autumn of each year. Business demand at holiday resorts tends to be restricted to the conference markets.

In contrast, leisure demand tends to peak at the weekends for the short-break market, and during the summer months. It is concentrated in coastal resorts and in major cities, with a high level of heritage attractions such as London or Paris.

TRENDS AND DEVELOPMENTS

Reservations

The growth of the computerized reservation systems designed and developed by the airlines has had some profound effects on the hotel industry. These systems allow customers to book, through a single computer terminal, their complete package of tourist requirements, from airline tickets through car hire to accommodation. The terminals can be situated anywhere in the world and can be accessed through the airlines, travel agents or directly by large corporate customers.

Hotel companies must pay to join a CRS and it is not surprising, therefore, that it is the major chains who have elected to join the system,

---

CASE STUDY 15.3

Hotel industry concentration

The concentration of an industry is an important variable in the market structure of that industry and will affect an individual firm's behaviour and performance. Seller concentration refers to the size distribution of firms that sells a particular product or range of related products and services. The larger the average size of firms, the greater the concentration is said to be. Normally, the greater the concentration and therefore the smaller the number of competitors, the more aware a firm will be of the behaviour of its rivals.

Akehurst (1984) suggests a number of different ways of measuring the concentration of an industry. The simplest of these is the concentration ratio. This is calculated as the share of the market taken by the largest firms in that industry. The choice of size parameter is quite wide, but in the accommodation market, concentration ratios are normally based on the number of beds, bedrooms or units. This, of course, measures potential output and not actual output, for which sales value would be a better indicator.

Kleinwort Benson (1991) use a concentration ratio based on the number of rooms owned by publicly quoted companies and have calculated the following comparison of the hotel industry in the USA and Europe.

Country	Number of quoted companies	Average number of rooms	Hotel room concentration (%)
USA	19	44 198	30.0
UK	59	1 995	23.5
Netherlands	14	731	20.4
France	14	6 688	18.1
Belgium	14	603	14.1
Portugal	7	566	13.0
Eire	5	505	12.2
Luxembourg	4	289	11.6
Germany	11	3 043	10.0
Spain	14	832	3.2
Denmark	2	416	2.3
Italy	11	1 459	1.7
Greece	5	382	1.0

Source: Kleinwort Benson (1991).

---

although some independent operators are also involved. At the same time, it must be recognized that only certain types of customer will make reservations in this way. The main users will tend to be business tourists and those booking international travel through their travel agent. It is unlikely that the small independent operator specializing in the domestic holiday market would see much benefit in joining.

However, the technology that is now available makes it possible to organize, cost effectively, databases and reservation systems on a much smaller and more local basis. One example might be the service offered by Cottage Holiday Organizers to represent, market and handle bookings for a large number of individual cottages and self-catering apartments or flats at a destination. This provides the independent operator with a much wider target market. Similar facilities can easily be offered by consortia of independent operators or local, regional or national associations and tourist boards.

Branding

A significant recent development in the accommodation market has been the development of branding strategies by the major chains. By building a strong brand image for their products, companies are able to position their product for a specific target market and to appeal directly to the needs and requirements of these customers. At the same time they are able to build brand loyalty, which is particularly important in the international market place.

A prime example of this branding strategy is offered by the French group, Accor. Each of Accor's brands across the accommodation, restaurant, tourism and catering services fields is developed as an independent concept targeted directly at a specific set of customers. For example:

- Hotelia is a concept combining the comfort and hospitality of a hotel with the high-quality care and medical attention required by senior citizens either for short stays or for permanent residence.
- Atria's mission is to combine quality lodging with state-of-the-art business centres located in downtown business districts. These units provide a conference centre, temporary office suites, data processing and office automation, telecommunications and secretarial assistance as well as complete hotel facilities.
- In addition, Accor runs the following accommodation brands: Hotels Pullman, Sofitel, hotel Mercure, Altea, Ibis, Urbis, Formule 1, Motel 6 and Parthenon.

Other hotel chains, such as Forte and Holiday Inn, are also developing their branding strategy to allow them to compete for different sectors or levels of the market. There is limited evidence that other sectors of accommodation provision are following this lead, largely due to the predominance of smaller independent operators in these sectors.

Environmental issues

The environmental problems that are likely to arise from the accommodation industry are well documented, and the requirement for the 1990s is to identify the specific policy options to deal with them. Consumers travel to the places they visit for the products they buy, and it is an inevitable consequence that the greater the pressure of visitor numbers, the more comprehensive environmental management influences must be. However, it appears that, with few general exceptions, most corporate attitudes to the environment date from the early 1990s.

The policies for the accommodation industry should cover eight key points:

- Energy conservation.
- Environmental protection.
- Waste reduction.
- Recycling of waste.
- Reduction of emission.
- Protection of employees' public health and safety.
- Reduction of chemical usage.
- Education of employees about the environment.

Environmental commitment should start with the full support of the chief executive and be an integral part of management practice, communicated to all personnel. Once they have been agreed, corporate policies can only be implemented through management techniques such as environmental audits. Environmental problems can only be identified effectively through a formal monitoring system such as auditing.

Quality

The accommodation market is highly competitive, and like any industry that markets a product in a highly competitive market, competing for the consumer's disposable income, it has to be aware of the quality issues. This is especially important to the accommodation sector, where competition often centres on issues of facilities, image, service and the quality of that provision. Hotels, for example, have been quick to use quality as a marketing strategy and have themselves fuelled higher expectations of the accommodation product.

There has also been a recent growth in 'consumerism' generally, which has resulted in customers expecting to receive products and services of a higher minimum acceptable level. British customers have also travelled more widely than ever before, due to package holidays and cheaper transportation, returning with new ideas and new standards regarding accommodation provision.

CASE STUDY 15.4

IHA hotel 2000 study

In the summer of 1987, the International Hotel Association, which represents, directly or indirectly, over 300 000 hotels in 142 countries, commissioned Horwarth and Horwarth (now Horwath Consulting) to prepare a report on the challenges facing its members over the following 20–5 years. After an extensive round of discussions, postal questionnaires, personal interviews, seminars, contributions from selected hotel schools and desk research, the report was published in September 1988 (Horwath and Horwath, 1988).

The report made recommendations of the action to be taken by hoteliers in the following areas:

- *General* – improving the image of the industry with governments, the public and financial institutions; improving the co-ordination between resort accommodation suppliers and other tourism sectors, particularly air transport; becoming more environmentally conscious and involved with the local community.
- *Product* – carrying out periodic assessment of the hotel product to identify changing customer needs, e.g. in-room office facilities, ventilation systems, lighting; periodically reviewing the hotel's catering concepts for design and theme, branding and marketing; assessing the need for in-house sports and leisure facilities; providing improved facilities for the handicapped.
- *Conference facilities* – improving the working conditions for delegates, especially ventilation, lighting and ergonomics; employing meeting specialists; installing new technology as appropriate.

- *Segmentation* – defining their product philosophy regarding physical and service standards; considering the possibility of offering different product lines within the same hotel.
- *Marketing* – keeping abreast of demographic and social trends and tailoring marketing to match these changes; assessing the value of marketing approaches such as joining consortia, yield management and computerized reservation systems.
- *Seasonality* – continuing existing low-season initiatives; examining the potential of different markets, such as the senior citizen or youth tourism markets.
- *Technology* – monitoring developments in technology in the areas of computerized reservations systems, property management, hotel security and life safety.
- *Management structure* – ensuring that responsibility and accountability are aligned; assessing the possibility for eliminating junior management/heads of department categories.
- *Human resources* – improving the performance and image of the industry as an employer; ensuring adequate training at all levels, including improving language tuition; introducing multifunction staffing; exploring new labour markets, such as the newly retired; assessing the benefit of productivity control systems.
- *Industry structure and finance* – establishing a framework for performance clauses; improving the priority ranking of the industry in relation to government grant aid; developing innovative financing arrangements, particularly in developing countries.

The accommodation market depends on high levels of repeat business through regular clientele at both the individual and the institutional level. This reliance on repeat business and the effects of word-of-mouth recommendation make quality and the resulting guest satisfaction of paramount importance in maintaining high occupancy levels.

Many establishments have also found that

improving the quality image of their operation has resulted in increased staff commitment and improved levels of performance. It must be recognized that any marketing effort aimed at customers will also influence employee perceptions.

The accommodation sector in general, however, has been slow to respond to changes in customer expectations. For example, few hotels have attempted to work for national recognition of their quality management systems through British Standard BS5750. This reluctance to make changes to improve quality has several causes, ranging from the substantial capital investment required, through the time involved in renovation and the limitations of an existing physical structure, to a lack of awareness of customers' needs. There is obviously much scope for operators which do respond to the call for quality to make substantial improvements in their market share.

It is a widely held belief that improving the quality of the product or service delivered to the customer must involve increased cost and therefore a reduction in overall profitability. However, experience across a wide range of industries has demonstrated that an increased emphasis on quality can in fact lead to substantial cost savings as internal and external failure costs are reduced. Nevertheless, achieving an appropriate standard of quality is a complex task.

References and further reading

Akehurst, G.P. (1984) 'The measurement of concentration in the hospitality industry', *International Journal of Hospitality Management*, vol. 3, no. 1, pp. 25–33.

Euromonitor (1992) *The European Hotel and Catering Marketing Directory*, London: Euromonitor.

Horwath and Horwath (1988) *Hotels of the Future: Strategies and Action Plans*, London: Horwath and Horwath.

Horwath Consulting (1992) *United Kingdom Hotel Industry 1992*, London: Horwath Consulting.

IHA (1987) *Hotel 2000 Study*.

Jeffrey, D., and Hubbard, N.J. (1988) 'Temporal dimensions and regional patterns of hotel occupancy performance in England: a time series analysis of midweek and weekend occupancy rates in 266 hotels in 1984 and 1985', *International Journal of Hospitality Management*, vol. 7, no. 1, pp. 63–8.

Kleinwort Benson Securities (1991) *Quoted Hotel Companies: The World Markets – 5th Annual Review*, Slattery, P., and Johnson, S.M., London.

Kleinwort Benson Securities (1992) *Quoted Hotel Companies: the European Markets – 6th Annual Review*, Slattery, P., and Johnson, S.M., London.

Lockwood, A. (1993) 'Quality management in hotels', in Witt, S., and Moutinho, L. (eds), *The Tourism Marketing and Management Handbook*, 2nd edn., Hemel Hempstead: Prentice Hall.

Lockwood, A., and Brunner, S. (1991) 'BS 5750: Quality system guidelines', *HCIMA Technical Brief*, No. 20, July, London: HCIMA.

McGuffie, J. (1990) 'CRS development and the hotel sector', *Travel and Tourism Analyst*, no. 1, pp. 29–41.

Mintel (1992) *Hotels Special Report, 1992*, London: Mintel International Group.

NEDC (1992a) *UK Tourism: Competing for Growth*, London: NEDO.

NEDC (1992b) *Costs and Manpower Productivity in UK Hotels*, London: NEDO in association with the Tourism Society.

Salomon Brothers (1991) *The European Hotel Industry: The Race is On*, London: Salomon Brothers.

Swiss National Tourist Office (1992) *Travel Tips: 1992*, Zurich: SNTO.

CHAPTER 16

Transportation

OVERVIEW

Tourism involves the movement of people, and, in consequence, the relationship between transportation and tourism development is a vital aspect of tourism studies. Adequate transportation infrastructure and access to generating markets is one of the most important prerequisites for the development of any destination. In most cases tourism has been developed in areas where extensive transportation networks were in place and the potential for further development was available. The fact that in most destinations worldwide the traveller can find adequate hospitality and leisure facilities close to transportation terminals demonstrates this point.

On the other hand, tourism demand has stimulated the rapid development of transportation. As millions of tourists expect to be transported safely, quickly and comfortably to their destinations at a reasonable cost, the transportation industry has had to adjust in order to accommodate to this increased, and also sophisticated, demand. In response, technology has allowed new forms of fleet to be produced rapidly, while there are also examples of a radical improvement in the quality of transport services for tourism in the last two decades.

In this chapter we provide a framework for the analysis of passenger transportation operations for tourism. We explore the modes and elements of transportation, examine issues such as the regulation of transport and perform a competitive analysis for the major modes of transportation. Finally, the chapter illustrates the major future political and economic trends which are expected to influence tourist transportation as it enters the third millennium.

TRANSPORT AS A COMPONENT OF THE TOURIST PRODUCT

We can define transportation as 'the means to reach the destination and also the means of movement at the destination' (Burkart and Medlik, 1981, p. 47). This broad definition allows us to distinguish between the numerous types of transportation service. It also emphasizes the functional element of transportation services: that is, passenger movement from point A to point B. Increasingly, as transport is viewed as part of leisure, the quality of the journey is at least as important as act of movement itself. For some categories of visitor, the trip is therefore seen as an attraction in its own right and certainly as part of the tourist experience. The view from the coach or the excitement of flying are both examples of the utility of travel.

If we interpret the tourist product, in its widest sense, as everything that the visitor consumes not only at the destination but also *en route* to the destination, transport provides some key elements of the product. For example, as part of an air inclusive tour, transport provides a variable proportion of the total cost to the tour operator; for short-haul destinations, transport may represent up to 55 per cent of the total cost, but for long-haul locations, the proportion may exceed this. Once at the destination, independent visitors make use of taxis, domestic air, rail, ferries and possibly scheduled coach services, whereas both packaged and independent visitors may purchase local tours which are often based on the coach. We can use visitor expenditure figures to illustrate the importance of transport as an element of the product – transport at the destination can represent as much as 15 per cent of international visitor expenditure within a country such as Indonesia.

Increasingly, there are instances of transport, both within and between countries, becoming an attractive tourist product in its own right. Examples include the following:

- Railway products – the Palace on Wheels (India), the Blue Train (South Africa) and the Orient Express.
- Air products – short trips on Concorde, nostalgic flights in vintage aircraft.
- Sea products – cruising, particularly themed cruising such as the Carnival Cruise Line products.

MODE OF TRANSPORTATION

The most obvious way of analysing transport is by mode to denote the manner in which transport takes place. There are four major modes of travelling:

- Road.
- Rail.
- Water.
- Air.

Some of these modes may be further distinguished by transport *to* the destination as opposed to transport *at* the destination.

To a substantial extent, the choice of mode of transport by the visitor is related to the purpose of travel. Table 16.1 provides a structure for the consideration of these relationships.

Table 16.1 Mode of transport and visitor type with examples of product types

| Visitor type | Mode of transportation | | | | | | |
| | Road | | Air | | Sea/water | | Railways |
	Car	Coach	Scheduled	Charter	Ferry	Cruise	
Holiday Inclusive tour (IT)	Car hire Fly-drive	Coach tour	Long-haul city break packages	Medium/ short-haul packages	Ferry package	World cruise	Orient Express
Independent	Touring Private car	Scheduled coach	Backpackers individual	Seat only to Villa Time-share	Private car	Runabout fare	
Business and conference	Company car	Executive coach	Fully flexible fare		Hovercraft		TGV
Visiting friends and relatives (VFR)	Private car	Scheduled service	Cheapest fare		Private car		Excursion fare
Other special and common interest, e.g. religion	Car hire Private car	Coach charter	Cheap or flexible fare	Group travel			Group fare
Same-day visitors (excursion)	Private car	Scheduled – excursion fare	Scheduled – excursion fare	Special flights	Coach/car excursion	Local 1-day cruise	Day excursion fare

In general, the visitor's choice of mode of transport is affected by the following:

- Distance and time factors.
- Status and comfort.
- Safety and utility.
- Comparative price of services offered.
- Geographical position and isolation.
- Range of services offered.
- Level of competition between services.

The relative importance of these major influences upon modal choice will vary from one visitor type to another. However, visitor types are no longer as homogeneous as previously assumed; some inclusive tour passengers will elect to travel business class by air rather than by charter, for example.

Increasingly, transport operators are attempting to identify segments of demand to whom specific categories of service will appeal. In Europe coaches now offer degrees of comfort and service unheard of 15 years ago, while UK ferry companies have become expert in organizing a range of centred or varied itineraries for motorists holidaying overseas with their own car.

Road transport

Road transport is dominated by the motor car and coaches. Indeed, the car is almost the perfect tool for providing door-to-door flexibility, giving views of the landscape and a means of transporting recreational equipment. It even offers residential accommodation in the case of recreational vehicles (RVs) and caravans or trailer tents. Hire cars almost exclusively serve visitors, but it is difficult to estimate the proportion of total car miles on the roads of any one country which are tourist and excursionist related. Coaches that are chartered are, by definition, almost exclusively for visitor purposes, but again scheduled services provide for commuters and shoppers as well as visitors.

Rail transport

The extent of provision of a mode of transport, and the use of it by visitors as opposed to other users, depend on a variety of factors such as history, government involvement and financing, topography and geography. Nowhere is this more relevant than with rail transport. In Europe, for example, an international network, often strongly supported by governments, offers specific services to visitors as well as commuters – Inter Rail, car transportation and special tariffs for holiday runabouts are examples here.

Railways provide examples of the specific development of business visitor products, such as the TGV (Train de Grande Vitesse, cf. bullet train) in France. For rail the main competition between modes is often based upon the time and distance, city centre to city centre, compared to air. Beyond a certain distance, some visitors see rail as being too cumbersome and tiring, and it is then that notions of adventurism and sightseeing take over as the attractions of the rail mode.

Air transport

The majority of travellers by air are by definition visitors; diplomats, crew and the other categories which are excluded for the purposes of tourist statistics make up the remainder. Air travel is attractive because of its speed and range, and because increasingly for business visitors it offers status as well as saving valuable work time when travelling on a long-haul basis. Where geographical isolation exists, such as with island communities, air is the dominant and often the only reasonably fast means of travel. Air transport comprises both scheduled and chartered categories and, in some parts of the world, air taxis. Charter transport by air emerged in the 1950s in Europe and North America, transporting holiday visitors from the colder northern climates to the southern sun destinations of the Mediterranean and Florida/the Caribbean respectively.

Sea transport

In broad terms, we can divide water-borne transport between short sea ferry transport and ocean-going cruises. Other categories exist, such as inland waterway craft and small pleasure craft, but these assume less significance as a means of transport as they are more destination products in their own right. Cruising should also be thought of as a holiday product as much as a mode of transport. Ferry services, which include or exclude vehicles, can provide lifeline services to islands as well as a focus for visitors, who are normally packaged holiday-makers, independent or same-day visitors. Hydrofoil and hovercraft tend to be faster than conventional forms of ship technology, but in general (unless for short sea commuting, such as between Hong Kong and Macau) business visitors tend to choose other modes of transport. Due to the vagaries of the sea, visitors either like, accept or dislike this means of transport. Geographical factors tend to determine the provision of ferry transport, leaving some destinations heavily dependent upon such links. Examples include the following:

- Aegean island hopping or travel to and from the Greek mainland.
- Channel crossings such as the English Channel, Irish Sea or the Cook Strait between the North and South Islands of New Zealand.

ELEMENTS OF TRANSPORTATION

We can identify four basic elements in any transportation system:

- The way.
- The terminal.
- The carrying unit.
- The motive power.

These elements vary for each transportation mode and vehicle.

The way

The way is the medium of travel used by a transport mode. It may be purely artificial, such as roads and railways; or natural, such as air or water. Roads, railways and inland waterways restrict vehicles to movement to a specific pattern, while air and sea allow flexibility. However, international regulations delineate both sea and air corridors and routes such that standard operating procedures are applied worldwide to limit the freedom of these ways. In considering transport modes, the availability of the way is very important in the case of roads, railways and inland waterways, where substantial investment would be needed to provide them. In the case of water and air, this is not an issue except for air traffic control procedures.

The terminal

The terminal represents the second important element of a transport mode, giving access to the way for the users, or acting as an interchange between different types of way. It is the furthest point to which the transport system extends – literally the end of the line. Probably the simplest terminal is parking for a private car, while the most complex one is an airport. In fact, most terminals are becoming integrated transportation points as they can act as interchanges where travellers can transfer between vehicles or modes. Airports, for example, can be used as transfer points between two aircraft, or between other modes of travelling, such as the car or train.

The design of terminals and the amenities they offer depend heavily upon the type of journey and transportation involved. Although we can observe a general tendency towards the development of integrated terminals which cater for all the potential needs of the traveller, not all modes need to have sophisticated points as terminals; coaches, for instance, can and do operate from roadside locations.

The carrying unit

The carrying unit is the actual transportation media: the vehicle which facilitates the movement. Each 'way' demands a distinctive form of carrying unit: aircraft for the sky, ships for the sea, vehicles for roads, and train or tram for rails. The nature of carrying units has been influenced by numerous factors which include travel demand and the technology employed, as well as the other elements of the mode (such as motive power). In the last few decades, developments have occurred in the carrying units which are designed towards greater efficiency and consumer orientation. Flexibility is also important – vehicles increasingly need to be altered easily and quickly, in order to accommodate changing tourism demand. Executive-style coaches with on-board services are an example.

The motive power

Motive power is perhaps the key element in transportation development. The natural power of horse-drawn carriages and sailing vessels provided the initial energy for transportation. The exploration of steam power provided the opportunity for the radical introduction of steam ships and railways, while the internal combustion engine stimulated the development of road and air transportation. Finally, jet propulsion enabled air transportation to be competitively priced and gave aircraft both speed and range. However, even in the 1990s a number of activity holidays such as cycling, pony trekking and sailing involve human-generated motive power as part of the recreational activity. Motive power is closely related to a number of issues, such as the capacity and type of the carrying unit, demand, and the desired speed and range of the vehicle. As costs of operation have been modified, the engine has had to become more fuel efficient and, for safety reasons, more reliable.

The changing roles of the transportation elements

The easiest way in which to demonstrate the role of the four basic elements is to consider the historical changes which have occurred over time. Except for being quieter due to continuous welded tracks, railways are little different from when first designed, although like airways they have become much busier and more congested. Roadways have become more continuous, and the autostrada or motorway now universally provides the functional means of movement; however, the view from the road is less interesting.

Terminals, especially airports, have become not only design pieces in themselves, but in some instances the centre of hub and spoke traffic. In some cases they have grown to the size of a small town to deal with transit traffic (as at Changi airport, Singapore). Also the shopping mall concept has been merged with the terminal as, for instance, at London Gatwick's North Terminal. However, the concept of complete inter-modal transfer for baggage and people is not yet a reality at all airport terminals.

The carrying unit in some instances differs little from previous decades, but in the case of coaches and trains comfort has been built into the design and operation. The last two decades have seen quieter but not necessarily faster aircraft being built; the latest Boeing 747–400 series has a longer range, but takes about as many passengers as previous models. Efficiency of motive power may have changed for all modes of transport, but speed of travel and size of fleet have stabilized in the last decade. The major changes are illustrated in Table 16.2.

The recent history of transport for tourism is characterized by changes in technology involving not only the jet age, but also more powerful and fuel-efficient engines for aircraft and automobiles.

The trend towards more universal access to travel has led to a wider but increasingly varied market; operators have responded with more

Table 16.2 The historical development of tourism: recent changes in transport

Mode of transport	1930s	1940s	1960s	1980s
Air	• Civil aviation established • Travel is expensive and limited	• Propeller technology • Travel still limited • Basic terminals • 400–480 kph	• Jet aircraft • Boeing 707 • Cheap fuel • 800–950 kph • Charters take off	• Wide-bodied jet 747 • Extended range • Fuel efficiency • No increases in speed except Concorde
Sea	• Ocean liners and cruises • Short sea ferry speed less than 40 kph	• Little competition from air • No increase in speed	• Air overtakes sea on North Atlantic • Hovercraft and faster craft being developed	• Fly-cruise established • Larger and more comfortable ferries • Fast catamarans developed
Road	• Cars 55 kph • Coaches develop	• Cars 100 kph • Roads improve	• Cars used for domestic tourism • Speed 115 kph	• Speed limits in USA • Rise in car ownership rates • Urban congestion • Green fuel • Improved coaches
Rail	• Steam era • Speed exceeds cars	• Railways at peak	• Electrification • Cuts in rail systems • Some resorts isolated	• High-speed networks develop in Europe • Business products offered – memorabilia and steam

differentiated products reflecting comfort of service for customers. Business-class products by air, plus executive-style rail services are examples. The history of competition has been one where, after the Second World War, an undifferentiated product was offered, whereas now speed, comfort and value for money are seen as bases for gaining or maintaining market share.

However, in recent decades the speed of travel has either stabilized or increased only in certain respects, such as with fast sea craft or high-speed rail services. The rising cost of fuel allied to the Arab–Israeli War of 1973–4, the Iranian crisis of 1978–9 and the Gulf War of 1991 has led to the development of fuel-efficient technology; air charter operators now need to use new fleet rather than the secondhand, older equipment operated in the 1970s. Airline operation illustrates the changing cost structure over time, and this can be seen by considering fuel as a percentage of operating costs. In 1973, for international scheduled services, fuel accounted for 12 per cent of total costs; by 1980 this had risen beyond 25 per cent. With the introduction of fuel-efficient aircraft during the ensuing decade, this item of variable cost was reduced: in 1989 fuel accounted for 14 per cent of all costs.

POLITICAL INFLUENCES ON TRANSPORT FOR TOURISM

International tourist movements have always been affected by the activities of governments, and transport for tourism has also been influenced by such factors. The barriers to communication, apart from distance, have been border controls, the need for visas or transit visas, and customs control. For rail and road, the boundary between nations is the point of control; for sea transport it is the land/sea interface or the port; and for air transport it is the airport terminal, wherever located.

The concept of the sovereignty of airspace as compared to the freedom of the high seas has always been a factor limiting and influencing provision of transport for tourism by air. Rail transport across and between nations, apart from gauge differences, has always been relatively smooth compared with the quota regulations for coaches in transit or entering other countries. The motorist has been affected by the insurance requirements for a Green Card and international driving licences, but in Europe with the introduction of the single market in 1993 such barriers and restraints will disappear.

Because of its very nature, transport for tourism by air has developed as a complex political issue and the key factors need to be highlighted. Airlines are important within the national economy for foreign exchange and for fare payments from foreign travellers. Generally, airlines have been owned by the state, have been subsidized by governments and have been seen to be symbols of prestige, flying the colours of the national flag. The Scandinavian Airline System (SAS) and Air Afrique are exceptions to the rule that most countries possess their own national airline. Equally, the size of an airline is not necessarily related to the size of traffic potential of that country; the examples of KLM and Swissair illustrate this point.

The notion of the territory held by a nation or the sovereignty that it exercises over its colonies has been important for air transport. The concept of cabotage is the carriage on routes within the national territory of any country or its overseas territories and has influenced routes and fares. Countries which had colonies in the past not only developed route structures to service these points, but also applied favourable pricing structures to benefit their own residents and those of the colonies.

Transport for tourism operates within a competitive political and economic environment, especially in the international context, because it represents the means to transfer across borders and to cross other territories to reach the intended destination. This competitive environment is illustrated by the extent to which transport for tourism has been regulated and controlled by governments.

REGULATION OF COMPETITION

Since their inception, transport media have been subject to regulation by governments for safety and technical reasons. In addition, legal and economic forms of regulation have applied to specific transport modes. In many countries transport operation has been subject to legislation to protect so-called 'pioneer operators' which incur costs and set up routes and pick-up points, but which are then vulnerable to another operator moving in without those costs to recoup. This was the basis of coaching legislation in the UK in 1930, which was modified as recently as 1980 by the deregulation of coaching. Railways tend to be national monopolies and to be state owned and subsidized, although in Britain the concept of privatization is being applied to the railway system in the 1990s. Sea transport has tended to be less regulated than other modes of transport, and the basis for this lies in the relative freedom of movement over water given to all vessels. However, in the 1970s the British government was concerned about the apparent collusion over fares between rival ferry operators on the North Sea and the English Channel routes.

Policies on regulation have tended to focus on air transport to a greater degree than other modes; international air law is a factor which controls the extent to which national airlines may operate. In the United States the so-called anti-trust provisions have always existed to prevent the development of price fixing, cartels and collusion between competitors. In Europe, under the Treaty of Rome, transport has been deemed to be subject to competition rules and the European Commission has outlawed agreements between pairs of national carriers which pool their capacity and revenues.

The need for regulation of transport has hinged on the fact that the barriers to entry are relatively low compared to other industries. Given that the evils of cut-throat competition can lead to the demise of a regular, reliable schedule and to social costs to travellers, regulation policies have specified procedures for entry into and exit from operation. The arguments for and against regulation are many – basically, in the short run customers benefit from increased competition and efficiency through lower fares, but in the long run they may suffer costs from the lack of an organized and reliable schedule of services as operators go out of business.

The Airline Deregulation Act 1978 was introduced in the Carter era in the United States and led to the development of an 'open skies' policy. This Act is often cited as the extreme of what deregulation can do in practice. The Civil Aeronautics Board was phased out; its role had been to devise regulations on conditions of service, such as frequency and capacity, on exit and entry into operation, and on fares and prices. Such matters then became the subject of free competition within the US domestic environment. Until the late 1970s, the International Air Transport Association (IATA) was the *de facto* controlling body worldwide, being a trade association for airlines, though in reality it represented governments as well. Ever since the famous Show Cause Order (1978), where IATA had to show good cause why it should be exempt from the provisions of US anti-trust provisions, this body has lost its strength to implement fare structures to protect its high-cost airline members. IATA's influence varies from continent to continent, however, and some would argue that it is still strong in parts of Europe, Africa and Latin America.

Following the Chicago Convention of 1944, where a truly multilateral agreement between countries was not reached, a series of bilateral arrangements between governments emerged. National governments approve and licence carriers to fly between the home country and an overseas destination; fares are fixed by reference to IATA conference machinery or between respective governments. Even in a truly deregulated environment, fares are fixed by mutual agreement between partners or merely filed. The so-called five freedoms of movement, giving technical and traffic rights to airlines, are still important for international movements. These are outlined in Case Study 16.1. Subsequent to the Chicago Convention, sixth and seventh freedoms have been formulated.

The extent to which US domestic policies have been translated to overseas situations has been limited. Within the USA a great number of air carriers entered the market and fares reached their lowest levels. However, in the following years only a few carriers could survive and most of the small or weak airlines were absorbed or merged with the stronger ones. Unfortunately, fares have increased while choice has been reduced.

European skies have been quite reluctant to open up to complete deregulation. This is partly because of the public sector's role in the airline industry, and partly because of the social role that the carriers perform, maintaining uneconomic routes in the peripheral areas purely for national and social reasons. Even after three directives from the European Commission, the development of true cabotage arrangements for Europe where it will be seen as one domestic territory will not happen until later in the 1990s.

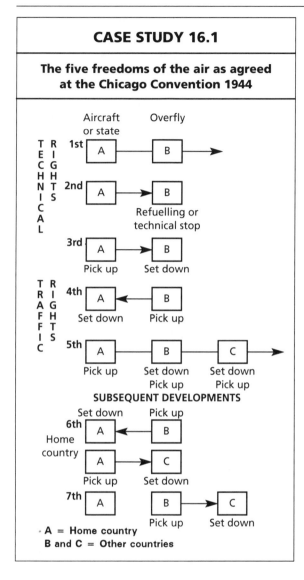

CASE STUDY 16.1

The five freedoms of the air as agreed at the Chicago Convention 1944

Aircraft or state / Overfly

TECHNICAL — RIGHTS
1st — A → B →
2nd — A → B — Refuelling or technical stop
3rd — A → B — Pick up / Set down

TRAFFIC — RIGHTS
4th — A ← B — Set down / Pick up
5th — A → B → C → — Pick up / Set down Pick up / Set down Pick up

SUBSEQUENT DEVELOPMENTS

6th — Home country
Set down / Pick up
A ← B
A → C
Pick up / Set down

7th — A — B → C — Pick up / Set down

- A = Home country
B and C = Other countries

- safety
- price/cost
- time/speed
- distance
- convenience
- departure and arrival times
- reliability
- availability
- frequency
- flexibility
- service quality
- comfort/luxury
- incentives
- ground services
- terminal facilities and locations
- status and prestige
- enjoyment of trip

Road Transport

Road transport has a number of attractions for tourists:

- The control of the route and the stops *en route*.
- The control of departure times.
- The ability to carry baggage and equipment easily.
- The ability to use the vehicle for accommodation.
- Privacy.
- Freedom to use the automobile once the destination is reached.
- The low perceived out-of-pocket expenses.

Some nations tend to utilize a car much more than others for recreation and tourism, depending upon the transportation facilities and climate. Trips by car account for 90 per cent of the pleasure/personal and business trips taken by Canadian and US residents and for almost 83 per cent of the total passenger kilometres in Europe. Furthermore, travellers in continental countries, such as Germany, Italy, Austria, Switzerland and France, tend to use the motor car for holidaying in the southern Mediterranean and at home.

The hired coach has traditionally been employed by groups for transfers from and to terminals. In addition, sightseeing trips and tours are normally conducted by coaches. This mode is particularly useful for short- and medium-distance journeys. It has traditionally attracted the elderly and inexpensive markets, and the stereotype is of

A COMPETITIVE ANALYSIS

We can see that modern passenger transportation is a very complex and competitive industry. This competition is expressed between the various modes and vehicles of transportation, between different companies and even between countries.

In this section we provide a competitive analysis of transportation modes, based on consumer behaviour variables. These variables have been identified as follows:

the lower occupational or social groups and the over-50s market.

Public coaches operate regular scheduled services and may transfer passengers to remote areas where there is inadequate infrastructure for alternative transportation (the Mountain Goat minibus service in the English Lake District National Park is an example). Beyond a certain threshold distance, lack of comfort and the relatively slow speed compared to other modes has to be traded off against cheaper and more attractive pricing structures.

Railway Transport

Trains are perceived to be safe and inexpensive, and to offer the convenience of movement within the carrying unit. They may also travel through attractive scenery and are a relatively 'green' form of travel. The fact that railway terminals are often in the centre of the destination is an asset in comparison with, say, airports which are often located 20 or 30 kilometres away from the centre.

Not all trains are fast, and trains do depend on the 'way' (track), which makes them inflexible in routing and overloads them with a very high fixed cost. Normally this cost is borne by the public sector. Although train operators try to emphasize the rest and relaxation of travel by train, rarely do they offer high-quality services throughout the network of a country. The luxury and comfort attributes are therefore limited to journeys of between 200 and 500 kilometres between major cities; current projections in Europe suggest that the greater speed of modern trains will increase this range to 1000 kilometres.

The most important reasons for travelling by train appear to be as follows:

- Safety.
- The ability to look out of the train and see *en route*.
- The ability to move around the coach.
- Arriving at the destination rested and relaxed.
- Personal comfort.
- Decongested routeways.

The traditional market for the train has been regarded as the independent holiday visitor, probably in the visiting friends and relatives (VFR) category; trains may also attract a significant 'fear of flying' market. Although in the USA trains are considered a second-rate means of passenger transportation, in western Europe trains hold a valuable market share of passenger traffic, primarily because of policies of protectionism and subsidy by the respective governments. However, the introduction of high-speed and intercity services such as the TGV in France has improved the level of service and comfort offered. Many new trains have good sleeping facilities and they are also able to carry automobiles. Moreover, the opening of the Channel Tunnel in 1993 will boost rail demand from London to Paris and Brussels initially, and also to other European cities later.

In addition, there has been a tendency to change the image and function of trains towards an environmentally friendly, traditional, stylish, relaxed, reliable and consumer-orientated form of transport. Consumers with entirely different lifestyles from the previous rail clientele have been identified; in Europe railway systems are likely to offer substantial competition for other modes of transport in the future.

Sea transport

For the transportation of vehicles and merchandise on short sea crossings, ferries offer inexpensive, reliable and safe services. Ferry transportation is the only option in the case of remote and small islands which have no airport. This situation can be found in Greece, where there are only 15 airports to serve 95 inhabited islands. In this case, large ferries provide coastal shipping services linking the mainland ports to the islands as well as the islands to each other. Furthermore, smaller regional ferries undertake transportation between the islands, especially during the summer peak period.

However, in many cases air can be a viable alternative to sea transportation between larger islands and the mainland. The main advantage of ferry operators when compared with air transportation is price, combined with the fact that passengers can carry their own vehicles and use them at the destination. Recent research undertaken on the routes Portsmouth–Cherbourg and Portsmouth–Le Havre identified that 80 per cent of the passengers were travelling in conjunction with a self-drive holiday, using their own vehicle. The popularity of motoring holidays and self-drive packages as well as the introduction of roll on–roll off facilities, which enable the ports to handle a much greater volume of vehicles, are indicative of the increase in passenger demand for ferry services.

In Europe, the gradual liberalization of air transportation, the decrease in air fares, the construction of the Channel Tunnel and the development of alternative modes of travel have forced the ferry companies to improve the luxury of their vessels, increase their cruising speed, install leisure facilities – casinos, swimming pools, sports and shopping – and offer a more consumer-orientated service.

Modern vessels such as the wave-piercing catamaran, the hydrofoil and the hovercraft have been introduced on some routes in recent decades. Their aim is mainly to offer a passenger-only service in a shorter crossing time than the traditional ferry service. Their speed is up to three times that of a conventional ferry, while they have great manoeuvrability, can turn around quickly in port and need minimum dock facilities. They therefore attract up-market tourists who appreciate the importance of their time and desire to reach the destination as soon as possible. However, these vessels are much more expensive than the ferries, they are vulnerable in rough seas and strong winds, and they are quite noisy. As they offer coach-type accommodation, they are uncomfortable for long-distance trips because they prevent free movement on the decks.

Cruising is more a leisure product than a mode of sea transportation. In this case the sea voyage, the entertainment and leisure facilities offered within the ship and the excursions at the ports are more important trip elements than the places visited. Thus, the cruise ship is the destination itself.

The decline in ocean liner shipping since the 1950s signified the development of the cruise industry as most shipping lines diversified into cruising. Increasingly, with the development of themed, special interest or hobby-type cruises, the trip can be as short as one day or as long as several months.

The typical cruise passenger used to be older, wealthy and predominantly North American. However, the cruise market now caters for all types of needs, ages and purchasing abilities. Fly-cruises are increasingly offered as holiday products, combining the speed and efficiency of air transportation and the relaxing, romantic attributes of cruise ships.

Air transport

Travelling by air is probably the most important transportation innovation of the twentieth century. It has enabled the transportation of passengers in the shortest time and has boosted the demand for long-haul trips. In fact no part of the world is now more than 24 hours' flying time from any other part.

Air transportation has managed in the last few decades to gain a very significant share of the transportation market, especially for movements over 500 kilometres. As new aircraft such as the Boeing 747–400 series extend their range up to 15 000 kilometres on non-stop flights, there are plans to extend their capacity to 800 passengers.

Scheduled airlines offer a safe, convenient, reliable, frequent and relatively consumer-orientated product; airlines attract business travellers, who appreciate its speed and flexibility between the various flights, especially on popular routes, as well as the leisure passengers who enjoy the ability to arrive at the destination quickly, and without spending time and money *en route*. Normally, ground services and the terminal facilities are much more advanced and sophisticated than for any other mode, and therefore the travelling experience is enhanced. The quality of services and the comforts offered on board have introduced new industry standards for the other modes of transport. Finally, airlines offer a number of incentives for their loyal customers through various 'frequent flyer' programmes. However, air transportation is the most expensive mode of transportation, especially for the short-haul routes, say in Europe, where the economic cruising speed cannot be achieved.

Promotional fares try to offer cheaper prices by minimizing the opportunities for alterations to the travel arrangements and by securing the passenger as early as possible. These fares include Advanced Purchase Excursion Fares (APEX); previously, standby and other forms of Instant Purchase Excursion Fares (IPEX) were experimented with. Yield management enables the airlines to alter their fares in order to achieve maximum yield by taking account of potential demand and supply factors, historical data, time lost before the flight and current load factors. Thus appropriate prices are suggested for the current market environment in order to maximize the airline yield.

Charter flights are utilized widely to facilitate the movement of holidaymakers on package tours or even on so-called seat-only arrangements. Sometimes charter airlines belong to tour operators which attempt to integrate their operations vertically, such as Britannia Airways and Thomson Holidays in the UK. Charter airlines offer *ad hoc* transportation services; they normally fly directly to the final destination and therefore passengers do not need to change aircraft at a hub. This can be achieved by a number of means:

- Minimizing the flexibility in altering flights.
- Flying at inconvenient and therefore not busy hours.
- Reducing the space within the aircraft.
- Offering elementary luxuries and services.

The higher load factor achieved on charter services

(90 per cent or more) compared with scheduled services (which can be as low as 20 per cent) is the final factor explaining the substantial difference in the unit cost of production and the price at which the product can be sold.

The bulk of air travel is orientated towards either business or leisure travellers. In the first case, people travel for their economic activities and their fares are paid by their employers. Maximum flexibility is required in order to be able to alter their travelling arrangements at short notice; as a result business travellers use only scheduled airlines. Services, terminals and aircraft have to be designed to facilitate the function of the busy business traveller. The fares are not an extremely important element of the product, especially in periods of economic growth. It is estimated that business travellers account for about 30 per cent of all international air traffic.

Leisure travellers' share in air transportation has increased rapidly during recent decades. Leisure travellers have much more time and they do not necessarily require very high-quality services. They are free to make their holiday arrangements well in advance, and thus they do not need a lot of flexibility. However, unlike the business traveller, they do pay their own fares and therefore they are price conscious. The development of specific leisure fares by scheduled airlines as well as the charter airlines in Europe has catered adequately for the needs of this market. Overall it is estimated that around 15 per cent of international tourism uses air transportation, while 86 per cent of the Europeans use planes for trips outside Europe. Growth in air travel is forecast to average 5.5 per cent per year from 1990 to 2000 and 5 per cent per year from 2000 to 2010.

EXTERNAL ENVIRONMENT AND FUTURE TRENDS

Currently passenger transportation is probably at its most competitive since it began; alternative forms and modes of travelling have developed strong competitive advantages and they compete to attract the bulk of the passengers. Of course, each mode has distinctive characteristics and attributes as well as strengths and weaknesses for each market segment. In this section we provide an analysis of the external environment and the future trends of passenger transportation.

Efficiency

Great pressure has been placed upon all transportation media to reduce their prices and offer a better quality of service. This has forced all companies to identify new methods of increasing their efficiency, especially in the airline world, where modern techniques such as yield management, hub and spoke operations and modern distribution channels like CRS have changed the way that the business is operated.

Yield management maximizes the airline's yield by suggesting the maximum prices which can be achieved for every available seat. It has been defined as the maximization of revenue through optimum seat mix, competitive buy-up pricing strategies, accurate overbooking, high yield spill and spoilage controls, and demand forecasting.

Following the deregulation of air transportation in the USA, *computer reservation systems* (CRS) undertook the mission to control the scheduled seats and fares in order to distribute their products effectively and maximise their profits. CRS enabled other efficiencies and competitive techniques (such as yield management and frequent flyer programs) to be developed, while becoming a source of strong competitive advantage and changing the balance of the airline world.

Development of *hub and spoke* systems increased the rationalization of air transportation by using major airports as transit points. Short-haul flights (spokes) connect through a limited number of airports (hubs), and passengers are transferred to long-haul trips. This enables the airlines to achieve higher load factors and keep prices down.

Air congestion is an emerging problem which will influence the airlines severely as the lack of terminal and air-corridor capacity becomes apparent. Almost 24 per cent of European flights were delayed on departures by more than 15 minutes in 1989. It is estimated that the intra-Europe traffic will double from 1990 to 2005, and that by the year 2000 all major airports will reach their capacity. The result may damage air transportation and stimulate people to switch to alternative modes.

A number of improvements are therefore required at airports and, more specifically, in control procedures, the design and construction of terminals and the inter-connectivity of airlines with other modes of travel. Furthermore, the efficiency of airlines should increase by extending hub operations, reorganizing the schedule, utilizing larger aircraft and achieving higher load factors. Major aircraft manufacturers are attempting to produce a mega aircraft with a maximum capacity of 800 passengers in a double deck craft, with extended range and able to fly at 850 kilometres per hour.

Globalization and integration

Globalization is one of the major trends in the international tourism industry. Leontiades defines it as 'a convergence in world tastes and product preferences' (1986, p. 96). The global firm, then, is one which capitalizes on this trend and produces standardised products contributing to the homogenization of the world tourism market. Essentially this means an increase in worldwide business between multinational corporations irrespective of the geographical location. As a result, a great concentration can be observed in tourism and transportation; some suggest that by the mid-1990s there will be 12 major global carriers dominating air transport with three or four flourishing in Europe.

As they expand their services on a global basis, airlines are forging strategic alliances for a number of reasons:

- The maturity of domestic traffic.
- The competition for terminal space and slots.
- The need for extensive networks worldwide.
- The necessity for economies of scale in airline operation.

- The control of the new distribution channels (CRS).
- The gradual deregulation in world transportation.

Many examples can be used to illustrate the globalization of airlines, but perhaps the best is British Airways, which in 1992 took over the British independent Dan Air, fought to buy a 44 per cent stake in America's fourth largest airline USAir, bought a controlling interest in France's regional carrier TAT, and was successful in purchasing a stake in Qantas.

As far as vertical integration is concerned, the transportation industry has always acknowledged that travellers need to use a combination of the various modes in order to complete their trip. Therefore, transportation companies are moving towards alternative modes which can be combined to offer integrated services. As a result, chauffeur services are offered by various airlines for their loyal and full-fare customers, while fly-drive programmes are very successful. Finally, the ambition of airlines such as Lufthansa to penetrate into rail transport, by offering private services primarily for their airline clients, demonstrates the point.

Railways also illustrate the trend to globalization as companies co-operate on the improvement and development of both the track and the units. The construction of new fast trains and the harmonization of tracks are also stimulated by major developments such as the Channel Tunnel. In the near future, intercity services are expected to connect most European capitals and major cities in order to transfer passengers as well as to reduce air and road congestion.

References and further reading

Burkart, A., and Medlik, S. (1981) *Tourism: Past, Present and Future*, 2nd edn, London: Heinemann.

Collison, F., and Boberg, K. (1987) 'Marketing of airline services in a deregulated environment', *Tourism Management*, vol. 8, no. 3, pp. 195–204.

Doganis, R. (1985) *Flying Off Course:The Economics of International Airlines*, London: George Allen and Unwin.

Doganis, R. (1992) *The Airport Business*, London: Routledge.

Gialoreto, L. (1988) *Strategic Airline Management*, London: Pitman Publishing.

Hanlon, J. (1989) 'Hub operation and airline competition', *Tourism Management*, vol. 10, no. 2, pp.111–24.

Holloway, C. (1989) *The Business of Tourism*, 3rd edn, London: Pitman Publishing.

Kosters, M. (1992) 'Tourism by train: its role in alternative tourism', in Smith, V., and Eadington, W. (eds), *Tourism Alternatives*, Philadelphia, Pa.: University of Pennsylvania Press.

Leontiades, J. (1986) 'Going global: global strategies versus national strategies', *Long Range Planning*, vol. 19, no. 6, pp. 96–104.

Middleton, V.TC. (1988) *Marketing in Travel and Tourism*, Oxford: Heinemann.

Mill, R. and Morrison, A. (1985) *The Tourism System: An Introductory Text*, Englewood Cliffs, NJ: Prentice Hall.

Pattison, T. (1992) *The Future for the Coach Industry*, Insights No. 5, 1991/92, London: English Tourist Board.

Peisley, T. (1992) *World Cruise Ship Industry in the 1990s*. Economist Publications Special Report No. 2104. London: Economist Publications.

Shaw, S. (1982) 'Airline deregulation and the tourist industry', *Tourism Management*, vol. 31, no. 1, pp. 40–51.

Shaw, S. (1990) *Airline Marketing and Management*, 3rd edn, London: Pitman Publishing.

Wheatcroft, S. (1982) 'The changing economics of international air transport', *Tourism Management*, vol. 3, no. 2, pp. 71–92.

Wheatcroft, S. (1988) 'European air transport in the 1990s', *Tourism Management*, vol. 9, no. 3, pp. 187–98.

Wheatcroft, S., (1989) 'Present and future demand for transport', in Witt, C., and Moutinho, L. (eds), *Tourism Marketing and Management Handbook*, Hemel Hempstead: Prentice Hall.

Wheatcroft, S. (1991) 'Airlines, tourism and the environment', *Tourism Management*, vol. 12, no. 2, pp.119–24.

Wheatcroft, S., and Lipman, G. (1990) *European Liberalisation and World Air Transport: Towards a Transnational Industry*, Economist Publications, Special Report No. 2015, London: Economist Publications.

CHAPTER 17

Intermediaries

OVERVIEW

In this chapter we show that the principal role of intermediaries is to bring buyers and sellers together, either to create markets where they previously did not exist, or to make existing markets work more efficiently and thereby to expand market size. For travel and tourism, intermediation comes about through tour operators or wholesalers assembling the components of the tourist trip into a package and retailing the latter through travel agents, which deal directly with the public. However, as this chapter shows, this is not the only way by which the tourist product reaches the customer, and we discuss several other distribution channels. Furthermore, the structure of intermediation is complicated by the fact that some retail agents and some of the principal suppliers, such as airlines, also act as tour wholesalers.

We examine the roles played by the travel agent and the tour operator consecutively, together with their respective economics of operation. We point out the differences between the North American and European travel trade systems, although our main emphasis is on the commonality of the underlying principles governing their activity. The conceptual aspects of tour operation are relatively straightforward, but the implementation requires considerable organization and planning, particularly in view of the time lags involved. We therefore discuss the main stages of tour operation in some detail. Finally, the factors making for market dominance are analysed.

THE NATURE OF INTERMEDIATION

In all industries the task of intermediaries is to transform goods and services from a form which consumers do not want, to a product that they do want. For everyday household requirements, this is performed mainly through holding bulk supplies and breaking these down into amounts required by individuals, as well as bringing the goods to the market place. In tourism the situation is somewhat different, for it is quite possible to buy the components of the tourism trip (accommodation, transport, excursions and entertainment) directly from producers. This dispenses with the need for a middleman. The fact that this does not happen in many cases is because the linkages (known as *distribution channels*) between the suppliers of tourism products and their potential customers are imperfect.

Given the above situation, we can see that it is possible for intermediaries to improve distribution channels and so to make markets by bringing buyers and sellers together. The bulk of this work falls upon the tour operator or wholesaler, who packages the main components of the tourist trip into a single product and sells this at one price through retail travel agents or, particularly in North America, airline sales offices. By and large, the role of the retail travel agent has been to provide an outlet for the actual sales of tours, tickets and travel services, such as insurance or foreign exchange, to the public.

Benefits

By making markets, travel intermediaries bestow a number of benefits on producers, consumers and the destination:

- Producers are able to sell in bulk and so transfer risk to the tour operator, although wholesalers do attempt to cover themselves by including release clauses in agreements. These may vary from four or more weeks to seven days.
- Suppliers can reduce promotion costs by focusing on the travel trade, rather than on consumer promotion which is much more expensive.
- By being able to purchase an inclusive tour, the traveller can avoid search and transaction costs in both time and money.
- Consumers gain from the specialist knowledge of the tour operator and the fact that the uncertainties of travel are minimized. For example, cruising and coach tours are attractive to senior citizens because the holiday starts the moment they board the ship or coach.
- The most significant gain for tourists is in lower prices, notably in the case of resorts dealing with large numbers of visitors as in the Mediterranean, Mexico and Hawaii. In such destinations, wholesalers are able through their buying power to negotiate discounts of up to 60 per cent off the normal tariff.
- Destinations, especially in developing countries where budgets are limited, may benefit considerably from the international marketing network of tour operators. However, it is naive to expect, as some countries do, that this should be a responsibility of these companies.

Structure

A schematic diagram of the structure of distribution channels is shown in Figure 17.1. Independent travellers put their own itinerary together. This they can do by purchasing the key components of accommodation and transport directly from

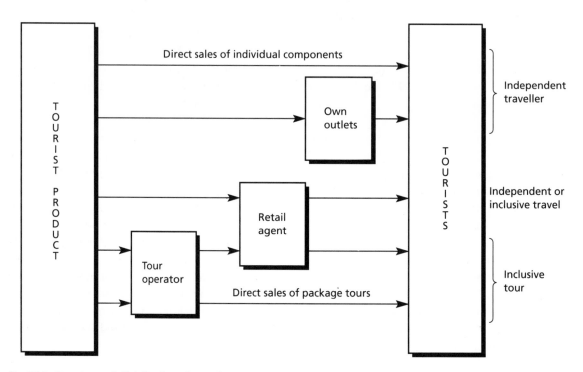

Fig 17.1 Structure of distribution channels

suppliers, or from their own outlets, or via the retail travel agent. It is common in domestic tourism for consumers to purchase their trip requirements directly because they usually have good product knowledge and ready access to a telephone to make reservations. However, in order to boost the market for the domestic product in Britain, the national and regional tourist boards do produce commissionable brochures which they distribute in a number of ways: directly through the mail in response to inquiries or from a mailing list, through Tourist Information Centres (TICs), or by persuading the travel trade to give the boards' brochures rack space in their shops.

It is not uncommon for airlines, bus operators and shipping companies to have their own outlets in large cities from which the public may purchase travel products directly. Airlines are particularly keen to secure their presence in the market by locating offices on flagship sites in capital cities. These serve both the trade and the public, and are especially important in cities such as Paris, London or New York, where there are not only large numbers of business travellers, but also many overseas holidaymakers travelling independently. International hotel chains also use their own establishments as retail shops for selling rooms in other properties belonging to the group. This has become increasingly easy with the continual development of more sophisticated computer reservation systems.

The founding companies of today's travel trade, Thomas Cook and American Express, are both travel agents and wholesalers, and so history is on the side of the retail agent which buys directly from producers. Through agency agreements, retailers sell the individual components of the trip, such as transport tickets, accommodation and excursions, but they may also put together their own brand of tours. The latter practice is much more common in North America than in Europe, as is the use of travel counsellors to assemble specially tailored packages for clients.

As a rule, travel agents make the bulk of their money from selling inclusive tours and airline tickets. In Europe most inclusive tours are associated with foreign travel, whereas in North America domestic trips are the dominant source of inclusive tour sales. A relatively recent trend has been the growth of agencies, usually belonging to a chain, dealing solely with business travel, to the extent of providing 'implants' in major corporations solely for the purpose of covering their travel needs.

The most common way of distributing foreign holiday travel in Europe is through inclusive tours packaged by tour operators and sold by travel agents. Some holiday packages are marketed directly to the public by wholesalers, and at one stage it was thought that the electronic revolution would lead more and more tours to be sold in this way, especially when there could be cost savings of 10 per cent or more. However, this method of selling has failed to capture the public's attention, and the percentage share of the market held by direct-sell holidays is still small.

Integration

Integration is a concept used in economics to describe formal linking arrangements between one organization and another. *Vertical integration* is where the linking occurs along the production process: for example, when an airline establishes its own tour operating company, as in the case of British Airways or Lufthansa. The latter are examples of vertical integration forwards into the market place, of which the most common form in terms of intermediaries is where a tour wholesaler acquires through merger or purchase a retail travel chain. The German experience is for wholesalers to own not only travel agents dealing exclusively in their products, but also direct mail systems. In Britain, the largest tour operator, Thomson Holidays, is part of Thomson Travel Group. The latter not only has a chain of retail outlets, Lunn Poly, but also has its own airline, Britannia Airways. The latter is an example of vertical integration backwards, and this is quite common among scheduled airlines which form links with (and even own) multinational hotel chains to secure trading advantages over their rivals.

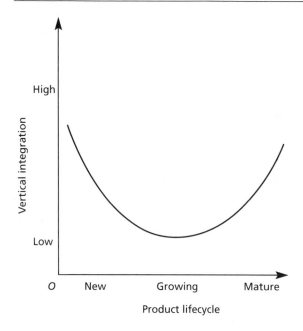

Fig 17.2 Extent of activity forward vertical integration

Looking at developments over time, it appears that the degree of vertical integration varies with the product lifecycle (see Figure 17.2). At the early stage of development, as in the case of Thomas Cook, there is a high degree of vertical integration as there are few suppliers. But as demand expands, specialists develop to increase the efficiency of the distribution channel. Operators are bound together by their mutual interest in helping the market to grow. As the market matures, competitive pressures for market share force companies to seek the benefits of forming vertical links. These include the following:

● Economies of scale through the linking of complementary activities, investing in new technologies, and improved management expertise in, say, foreign exchange transactions, forecasting and marketing.
● Cutting out the middleman by being able to control costs and quality standards under the umbrella of one organization.

● Securing supplies and increasing buying power.
● Protecting market position by guaranteeing retail outlets on prime high street sites.

It is important to note that vertical integration forwards does not necessarily have to come about through ownership. Control may be exercised by franchising. This is a licensing agreement whereby the parent company grants another, usually smaller, firm the right to sell its products and use its brand name, but in return the firm is not allowed to sell the products of its competitors.

Another organizational aspect of the travel trade sector that should be considered is *horizontal integration*. This occurs when two tour operators or two travel agents amalgamate, either through merger or takeover. This strategy was very prevalent among retail travel chains in Britain during the 1980s and became known as the 'march of the multiples'. The reasons for this are similar to those for vertical integration, but also include the spatial dimension of extending the geographical spread of outlets to ensure representation in all regions. Thomas Cook and Lunn Poly in Britain, and American Express and Ask Mr Foster in the USA, are examples of major chains that have increased their geographical representation.

For the retailers, horizontal integration strengthens their buying power with regard to wholesalers. They support this by developing their own corporate identity in the design and style of operation of their branch outlets, so as to raise the public's awareness of the company. Naturally, the march of the multiples has drawn criticism from independent travel agents due to the loss of their market share. In Britain, as in North America, many small travel agencies have formed themselves into consortia to give themselves the same negotiating power as the multiples. Large tour operators have also grown by amalgamation, but instead of enforcing a uniform brand image, as in the case of multiple retailers, they usually maintain a range of products, including acquired brands, to meet the consumer's need for choice.

Criticism of major tour operators usually comes from destinations, particularly less developed countries. The latter have expressed concern over the strength of the economic buying power of large wholesalers, which allows them to obtain prices below those that would occur in markets where competition prevailed. It is further argued that their specialist knowledge allows them to influence consumer choice in tourism-generating countries, and so gives them the opportunity to switch sales to destinations which are more profitable to the company.

THE ROLE OF THE RETAIL AGENT

The primary task of travel agents is to supply the public with travel services. This they do on behalf of their suppliers or 'principals', the latter being a trade term. A principal may be a tour operator, an hotel or a transport company. An agent may also offer travel-related services such as insurance or foreign exchange. For providing these services, the agent is rewarded by commission from the principals. Typically, commission amounts to 10 per cent of the selling price, but this is normally 1 or 2 per cent less for airline tickets, hotel bookings and rail travel. Insurance will usually generate commission of around 30 per cent, and car hire can, on occasions, make considerably more than the basic 10 per cent. Sales of traveller's cheques and currency will yield no more than about 2 per cent. However, by dealing with preferred suppliers and achieving specified sales targets, agents can achieve 'overrides', which are extra commission amounting to about 2.5 per cent of sales.

How a retail travel agency should set about discharging its primary function is a matter for discussion. Where an agent has no wholesaling function and therefore does not share in the risk of tour production by holding stock, it is suggested that the agent's main concern should be the choice of location to ensure ready availability of the principal's products in the market place. The agent has access to a principal's stock through the reservation system and here effi-

ciency is important. The customer expects instant confirmation, and staff at the agency do not want to waste time with repeated telephone calls. Instant availability on a VDU permits the staff to share the booking process with the customer to reinforce the buying decision. This approach to the role of the retailer likens the agent to a 'filling station' for travel. Creating demand is the responsibility of the principals. If demand is given, controlling costs is the best way for the agent to maintain profitability.

An alternative view argues that the acquisition of product knowledge and the assumption of the risks involved in assessing the extent and nature of demand is the job of the agent. The agent should thus take on the role of a travel counsellor to give the public impartial advice, and should seek to generate business in the local market area. The code of conduct of the Association of British Travel Agents (the US equivalent is the American Society of Travel Agents (ASTA)) requires agents to take an active promotional role.

It has already been noted that the counselling role has been far more prevalent in North America than in Europe. It appears that in Europe the tour operator's brochure, together with advertising and promotion, has held greater sway in destination choice. Thus, although there are many local exceptions, travel agents in Europe have tended to conform to the filling station model. The concept of impartial advice is also questionable in that, while agents want to meet their clients' needs, they are also mindful of the different rates of commission on offer and any bonuses. However, the expansion of corporate chains has involved not only the purchase of prime retail sites, but also the effort to improve staff competencies. They are aiming to provide specialists, as well as better career prospects in a sector which is well known for relatively low pay.

Retail agency economics

Traditionally, the retail travel trade has been characterized by ease of entry. This is because the retailer carries no stock and so capitalization is relatively low. All that is required is a suitable shop front and the acquisition of agency agreements from tour operators to sell their products. It is then up to the marketing skill of the agent to establish the business within the locality. If the agent wishes to offer air transport services worldwide, which is essential for dealing with business travel, then it is necessary that the agent holds a licence from the International Air Transport Association (IATA). This requires a thorough investigation of the agency by IATA, particularly the qualifications and experience of the staff.

In the USA virtually all retailers are members of both IATA and the Airlines Reporting Corporation (ARC), which allows them to sell both international and domestic air tickets. This is because the major part of an agent's income in the USA is obtained from the sales of airline tickets. An ARC appointment is essential for retail agents in the USA and normally enables an agent to obtain other licences without difficulty. In Britain the extra cost of obtaining IATA membership tends to deter smaller agencies and leads them to specialize in selling inclusive package holidays, which avoids the need for an IATA licence.

Many countries have national associations for travel agents which also act as regulating bodies. The Association of British Travel Agents (ABTA), which was established in 1950, has a continually evolving set of rules and regulations for membership. The most important milestones have been the implementation of financial bonding for new members (a financial guarantee from, say, a bank in the event of failure), laying down in its code of conduct the procedures for members to follow in their dealings with the public, and the agreement that no ABTA tour operator will sell foreign inclusive holidays through non-ABTA agents and conversely. The latter (termed 'Operation Stabilizer') has been the most contentious because it amounts to a restrictive practice. Nearly all British tour operators are members of ABTA, so it is extremely difficult for a retailer to trade without being a member of ABTA. This ruling has survived legal scrutiny in respect of unfair trading on the grounds that it operates in the public

Table 17.1 Travel agency operating accounts

Item	Currency Units
Sales	
Inclusive tours	530 000
Air tickets	330 000
Other transport tickets	49 000
Insurance	10 000
Car hire	3 000
Miscellaneous	78 000
TOTAL	1 000 000
Revenue	
Commission	96 000
Other income	5 000
Total	101 000
Costs	
Payroll expenses	46 500
Communications	12 000
Advertising	3 000
Energy	1 500
Administration	6 500
Repairs and maintenance	500
Accommodation expenses	12 500
Depreciation	2 500
TOTAL	85 000
Net Income	16 000

Source: Trade information.

interest by giving assurance on quality for a product that is bought unseen.

A representative breakdown of the operating accounts of a medium to large travel agent is shown in Table 17.1. The example is drawn from European experience and is standardized to one million currency units of turnover. Table 17.1 gives an indication of the items that enter the operating account and shows that inclusive tours and air tickets are by far the most important sales items. The item for other transport tickets includes sales arising from acting as an agent for rail, shipping and coach companies. Miscellaneous includes independent bookings of hotels, theatres, etc., foreign exchange transactions and the sale of travel goods such as luggage, sports items, first aid kits and travel clothes.

The most important item of income to the agent is commission, and since basic rates have not changed for decades, it will be appreciated that the ability of the agent to generate turnover is crucial, particularly for the independent retailer. The latter has been doubly squeezed: first, by fierce competition from the multiples; and second, by the fact that the relative cost of holidays has fallen in real terms while overheads have been generally increasing. Other income in the revenue statement includes interest earned on clients' deposit money. For accounting purposes this is a profit item which is only indirectly sales related. It could be excluded here and added into the net income statement afterwards.

The largest item of cost is remuneration to staff (including payments to directors or owners). The difficulty that independent agents have experienced in trying to expand turnover has tended to make them cost orientated in the operation of their businesses. Controlling costs, especially for the smaller agent, has been the short-term recipe for survival, and this in turn has served to keep staff salaries low, which creates difficulties in both attracting experienced staff and retaining existing staff. The problem is often compounded by cutting advertising, training and investment in new technology. Administration costs include printing, stationery, insurance, bonding levy, legal and professional fees, bank charges, accounting and record keeping, and any travel that may be incurred. Accommodation expenses refer to charges arising from occupation of the premises.

Although the independent retailer can compete with the multiple on the basis of the level of personal service, the argument put forward for raising commission rates appears to be a strong one. Ideally, the retailer is looking to wholesalers to provide a wide range of products which are regularly being upgraded, and which are capable of generating volume sales at high margins. The difficulty is that in a competitive environment higher commission rates may simply be countered by the multiples offering larger discounts.

THE ROLE OF THE TOUR OPERATOR

Since the dominant international leisure tourism flows are North–South to sun resorts, it is not surprising that much of the work of tour operators is bound up in providing single-destination inclusive or package holidays. Multicentred holidays are more common on long-haul travel, where the period of stay may extend to three weeks, and there is still a buoyant market for coach tours, which were the main form of package holiday before the arrival of low-priced air travel in the 1950s.

At its most fundamental, tour operating is a process of combining aircraft seats and beds in hotels (or other forms of accommodation) in a manner which will make the purchase price attractive to potential holidaymakers. As we noted earlier, tour wholesalers achieve this through bulk buying, which generates economies of scale that can be passed on to the customer. The most essential link in this process is the tour operator's brochure, which communicates the holiday product to the customer. The brochure must include the following:

- Illustrations which provide a visual description of the destination and the holiday.
- Copy, which is a written description of the holiday to help the customer match the type of product to his or her lifestyle.
- Price and departure panels, which give the specifications of the holiday for different times of the season, duration of stay and variety of departure points.

Large tour operators normally sell a wide portfolio of tours and therefore have a range of brochures. For instance, there will be separate brochures for summer sun and winter sun holidays, ski holidays, long-haul travel and short breaks. Popular destinations may have tour operators' brochures dealing solely with holidays to that country or region: for example, Greece, Florida or Turkey. Research has shown that the place to visit is often the first holiday decision made by some travellers. The brochure is designed to encourage customers to buy and is often the only information they have concerning the resort until they arrive there. However, it cannot be a comprehensive travel guide. The number of pages is limited by considerations of cost and size, and operators try to put as much detail about accommodation and resorts as they can in the space available. Clearly, this must be consistent with the brand image they are trying to convey, as they will each be competing for the customer's attention on travel agents' brochure racks.

Principal stages of tour operating

Although the conceptual principles of tour operating are easy to follow – linking transport and accommodation to produce a package that can be offered in a brochure – the practicalities of the tour operating cycle require careful planning, preparation and co-ordination. For example, media advertising in support of the brochure must be booked well in advance, particularly if television is to be used. The process of brochure production is initiated early on in the cycle to ensure that printing deadlines are met. There are a myriad of tasks to be performed, not only by separate divisions within the tour company, but also by outside contractors. The task of co-ordinating all these activities usually falls upon the marketing department.

Because of the complexity of organizing package trips, there are tour operators who do not put together their own programme. They simply contract the work out to a wholesaler and pass on the bookings as they come in. Examples of this are

ACTIVITY	Aug	S	O	N	D	Jan	F	M	A	M	J	J	A	S	O	N	D	Jan	F	M	A	M	J	J	A	S	O
Research																											
• Review market performance	X																										
• Forecast market trends	X	X																									
• Select and compare new and existing destinations			X	X	X																						
• Determine market strategy					X	X																					
Capacity planning																											
• Tour specifications							X	X																			
• Negotiate with and contract suppliers								X	X	X	X	X															
Financial evaluation																											
• Determine exchange rates											X																
• Estimate future selling prices											X																
• Finalize tour prices												X															
Marketing																											
• Brochure planning and production								X	X	X	X	X	X	X	X												
• Brochure distribution and launch													X	X													
• Media advertising and sales promotion													X	X		X	X	X									
• Market stimulation																			X	X	X	X	X	X			
Administration																											
• Recruit reservation staff											X																
• Establish reservation system												X															
• Receive reservations by telephone and viewdata																X	X	X	X	X	X	X	X	X	X	X	X
• Tour accounting and documentation																X	X	X	X	X	X	X	X	X	X	X	X
• Recruit resort staff																		X	X	X							
Tour management																											
• Customer care at resort																						X	X	X	X	X	X
• Customer correspondence																						X	X	X	X	X	X
• Payment of suppliers																						X	X	X	X	X	X

Fig 17.3 Tour operating cycle for an abroad summer programme

organizations known as 'affinity groups'. They range from travel clubs, whose members may have ethnic ties with particular countries, to professional associations which may arrange to have their meetings in different parts of the world.

Figure 17.3 presents a stylized layout of an operating cycle for a large-scale summer programme selling one million or more holidays. From initial research to the commencement of sales, the period spans some 14 months; and to first departures, 21 months. For winter programmes and short breaks, which are normally smaller in volume, the corresponding preparation periods are somewhat less. The example shown should not be taken as definitive since, by nature of the very many activities that are being performed and the differing objectives of tour companies, there will always be variances on timings. For example, the season may be spread into April or curtailed at the end of September or in mid-October.

Research

Key outcomes of research are the forecasts of overall market size and the changing patterns of holiday taking. These will assist in the selection of destinations, which in turn will be constrained by conditions of access, the extent of the tourist infrastructure and the political climate of the host country. In terms of destination choice, a specialist tour operator is able to respond far more quickly to changing market conditions than the volume or mass tour operator. The latter usually has long-term commitments to existing destinations, which may include capital tied up in resorts. From destination choice, the research process will enable the operator to derive a market strategy, giving answers to the kind of decision model shown in Figure 17.4.

Capacity planning

The market forecasts can be used to plan total capacity, which, together with the market strategy, will set tour specifications by type, destination and volume. Once the tour programme has

MARKETS	PRODUCTS	
	Existing	New
Existing	Market penetration	Product development
New	Market development	Diversification

Source: After Ansoff H.I., *Corporate Strategy*, Penguin, 1968.

Fig 17.4 Market strategy

been planned, negotiations for beds and aircraft or coach seats may take place. Bed contracts may take two forms: an allocation or a guarantee. An allocation operates on a sale-or-return basis with an appropriate release date. This type of contract is usually negotiated with medium-grade hotels and above, where opportunities for resale are generally easier. The risk is thus transferred from the tour operator to the hotelier. In turn the hotelier covers this risk by making contracts with several operators and quoting variable rates. With a guarantee, the wholesaler agrees to pay for the beds whether they are sold or not. Such a commitment naturally brings with it a cheaper rate than an allotment and is commonly applied to self-catering properties for the purpose of obtaining exclusive contracts.

Aircraft seats may be contracted in a variety of ways. The largest tour operators are likely to have their own airline, and some airlines, particularly in the USA, also have tour wholesaling divisions or companies. In other circumstances, the tour operator may contract an aircraft for the whole season (a 'time charter') or for specified flights (a 'whole plane charter'), or may purchase a block of seats on a scheduled service or a chartered airline (a 'part charter'). The use of scheduled services tends to be for specialist tours (which are often escorted) or tailor-made packages for customers. As scheduled flights are likely to work on a break-even 'load factor' of 60 per cent or less, airlines are prepared to give good discounts for inclusive tour excursion fares.

Where an operator has contracted for a time charter, it is important to maximize the utilization of the aircraft. The underlying principle is that charters should be operated back-to-back; namely, that the plane should fly out with a new tour group and return with the previous group. Empty flights (known as 'empty legs') will arise at the beginning and end of the season, and these must be allowed for in the costing of seats. In summer the aircraft is likely to be used for three return trips or 'rotations' per day (two in winter) following the flight patterns shown in Figure 17.5. Aircraft may be used to rotate from one point of departure to a range of destinations, or from a variety of departure points to one destination, or a combination of the two.

However, in the interests of protecting scheduled airlines from unfair competition from charters taking their normal traffic at peak times, aviation authorities have usually imposed operating restrictions on charter airlines. These may include the following:

- The trip must be an inclusive tour, which implies the provision of accommodation as well as an airline seat.
- Airport terminals used by passengers must be the same on both the outward and the return journeys.
- The air ticket must be for a round trip and is neither transferable nor part usable in the sense that the holder may use the return portion without having first travelled on the outbound flight.

Within the European Community, competition policy dictates that such restrictions are no longer valid, for they are not appropriate to a policy of transport liberalization or deregulation.

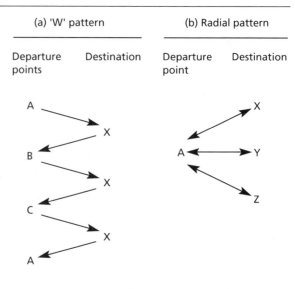

Fig 17.5 Time charter aircraft flight patterns

Financial evaluation

We can see from Figure 17.3 that tour operators have to finalise prices some eight months or more before the first tour departs. Apart from the usual hazards of forecasting so far in advance, there are three inherent risks that must be accounted for:

- Contracts with local suppliers are commonly made in the currency of the destination country.
- The currency for payment of airlines is usually US dollars.
- Airlines maintain the right to raise prices in response to increases in aviation fuel costs.

Many tour operators cover these risks (termed *hedging*) by buying forward the foreign exchange required at an agreed rate in order to meet contractual obligations and building this rate into their prices, and by bringing in surcharges at the point of final billing of customers. Because the latter have proved unpopular, operators have tried to avoid their negative impact by offering no surcharge guarantees, limiting the amount of surcharge liability, or offering cancellation options. In this context, it is worth noting that surcharges are often regulated by consumer protection legislation.

Marketing

Brochure production starts several months prior to the publication date with initial agreements about printing arrangements. It is usual for the layout of the brochure to be undertaken by a specialist design studio following the guidelines laid down by the tour operator's own staff. A variety of styles may be considered before the final choice is made. Particular attention is paid to the front cover to make sure that it conveys the right message to the target market segment and to ensure that it is likely to stand out on the travel agent's brochure racks. The draft final document is scrutinized for errors and corrected, with the pricing panels being left to the last possible moment before full production, to allow for any unforeseen economic changes.

It is important for the brochure to be launched well before the summer seasons starts because there is a section of the market that likes to book early in order to guarantee the destination and to take advantage of any promotional prices. The pattern of brochure distribution depends on the nature of the tours being offered, and also on a trade-off between the costs of sending to all agents in order to maximize brochure exposure and limiting the number of outlets in the knowledge that the majority of the business will come from a minority of agents. Specialist wholesalers offering high-priced trips will restrict the number of retailers and in so doing convey the message of product exclusiveness to the customer. In any event, they are unlikely to be in a position to support a large network of travel agents. For cost reasons even mass tour operators limit the number of agents they appoint, and, as indicated previously, very large wholesalers often have their own retail travel chain to distribute their products.

Monitoring the progress of advertising and sales campaigns is achieved through booking patterns. Typically, operators are looking for capacity utilization factors of 85 to 90 per cent in order to break even. Past experience enables wholesalers to establish reference booking patterns so as to compare actual against predicted bookings. Tour operators reserve the right to cancel or 'consolidate' holidays – for example, merging flights or combining itineraries and switching accommodation – if the demand take-up is insufficient. This makes it relatively easy for operators to test-market new products in their brochures.

However, on the supply side, merging charter flights is not normally feasible for a summer programme after January because of the cost of airline cancellation charges. Large operators benefit here by having their own airline. On the demand side, consolidation is a common source of annoyance to customers and leaves the travel agent with the unenviable task of advising his or her clients of the changes. Tour operators defend this practice on the grounds that, if they were unable to use cancellation or consolidation to reduce overcapacity, then the average price of a holiday would rise. Underestimating demand is less of a problem because there is usually some flexibility in the system for procuring extra flights and accommodation.

Due to the negative effects of consolidation on customers, and the wider impacts this may have on public relations, tour operators prefer to use market stimulation techniques to boost sluggish booking patterns. Such tactical marketing (as opposed to strategic) methods will depend upon the time available and may vary from increasing advertising expenditure, through special discounts for booking by a certain time, to substantial price cuts some six to four weeks before departure. Critical to obtaining last-minute sales is a network of retailers linked by viewdata into the operator's own computer reservation system, so that price promotions may be quickly communicated to the travelling public. Consumers, in turn, have recognized the bargains on offer and these have, over the years, encouraged later booking.

Administration

Due to the seasonal nature of tour operation, the extra staff required to run the reservation system and represent the operator overseas are recruited and trained when needed, with only a core being employed all year. Frequently, the same staff come and work for the same operator every year, which reduces the need for training.

The reservation system holds the tour operator's stock of holidays, and careful attention is paid to matching the information held by the system to that contained in the brochure. Increasingly, travel agents make direct bookings through viewdata terminals in their own offices, but many agents still make telephone bookings, either because the electronic systems are not in place or because there is a need for clarification of the product on offer.

Tour management

Specialist tour operators are most likely to offer escorted tours whereby a tour manager accompanies holidaymakers throughout the whole of their journey in order to oversee arrangements. For the volume package tour market, the function of the operator's resort representative is to host the tour. This involves meeting the tourists when they arrive and ensuring that the transfer procedures to the places of accommodation go smoothly. The representative will be expected to spend some time at the resort before the start of the season checking facilities, noting any variations from the brochure and, with the authority of the company, requesting discrepancies to be put right. During the holiday, the representative is required to be available to guests at the various hotels to give advice and deal with the many problems that may arise, as well as supervising (and sometimes organizing) social activities and excursions.

After the holiday the operator will receive customer correspondence that will include compliments, suggestions and complaints. Most correspondence can be dealt with by a standard letter, and justified complaints may receive a small refund. For serious complaints, national associations, such as ABTA, may offer arbitration services which can reconcile disputes before steps are taken to instigate legal proceedings.

Tour operator economics

We have already considered many of the economic aspects of tour operation in our discussion of the benefits of intermediation and the way in which a tour programme is put together. Essentially, the mass tour operator relies on the economies of scale generated by bulk purchase, and this in turn allows individual packages to be competitively priced to the consumer on the basis of a high take-up rate of offers made.

Once the tour operator is committed to a programme, the financial risks are substantial, irrespective of tactical risk avoidance strategies such as late release clauses, surcharges and consolidation. This is because most of the costs of running the programme, if it is to run at all, are unavoidable and therefore fixed. The marginal or variable costs of selling an extra holiday are very small, which accounts for the large discounts on offer for 'late availability' trips that give the customer only a short period of notice (sometimes just a few days) before departure.

Leverage

The financial structure of tour operation is illustrated in Figure 17.6. R is the revenue line, which increases with the level of capacity utilization, and C_1 is the total cost line attributable to running the tour programme. It may be seen that C_1 cuts the revenue and costs axis some way above the origin. This is caused by the high level of fixed costs in relation to the variable costs of tour operation. The financial term for this is *high operating leverage*. By way of contrast, C_2 is a total cost line which has a low operating leverage: fixed costs are relatively small when compared to the steeply rising variable costs.

Consider a tour operator with a high operating leverage which is planning a break-even capacity utilization level of O_2, but demand is such that O_3 holidays are sold. Clearly, O_3 is well above the break-even point (BEP) and so the operator makes substantial profits, as shown by the difference between R and C_1. A firm which has a low oper-

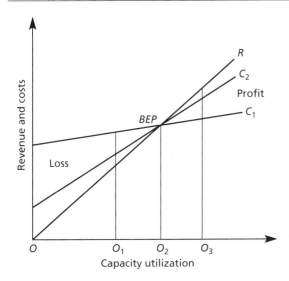

Fig 17.6 **Financial structure of tour operation**

ating leverage would not do so well, as can be seen from the difference between R and C_2. Conversely, if the tour operator does not manage to achieve targeted break-even sales and the realised utilization is some way below the required level, say O_1, the losses can be severe and may result in the collapse of the operator. We show in Figure 17.6 that a firm with a low operating leverage would not be so badly affected.

There is thus considerable financial risk associated with tour operation, and this acts as a deterrent to entry. Specialist operators cover this risk by dealing with niche markets, and by using scheduled airline services and high-grade hotels for which reservations may be readily cancelled if the minimum number of confirmed bookings for the tour is not met. The major tour operators address the risk by securing their market position through vertically integrating their operation both forwards and backwards.

It is in the middle ground, among wholesalers which have neither their own chartered aircraft (and so must purchase a part charter) nor their own retail network, where the financial risk tends to be at its highest. These are the tour operators that are most likely to go out of business when

demand falters. To safeguard the public from lost holidays or being stranded abroad when a tour operator collapses, most governments have legislation dealing with bonding arrangements, although the fund is not always sufficient to meet the losses or extra expenses incurred.

Sales mix

During the 1950s holiday tourism was largely centred around the traditional summer break at a coastal resort, but rising affluence, longer holiday periods and an increasing desire to travel have led to an increase in the degree of market segmentation. Tour operators have responded to changing consumer preferences by diversifying their portfolio of products. This in turn has helped to spread risk and generate all-year business. Thus most major tour operators now have a winter and summer programme.

Table 17.2 **Sales structure of a large tour operator**

Sales	Percentages
Summer inclusive tours	60
Winter inclusive tours	25
Minimum-rated packages	10
Excursions and insurance	4
Interest on deposits	1
TOTAL	100

Source: Trade information.

Table 17.2 presents the sales mix that would be appropriate for a large European operator offering summer sun holidays to Mediterranean resorts. Most holiday movements in Europe are still towards beach destinations in summertime, although winter holidays have increased their market share in response to more frequent holiday taking. Minimum-rated packages are effectively the transport cost only, with nominal accommodation provision so as to comply with the legal definitions of an inclusive tour.

Pricing

The price of an inclusive holiday in a wholesaler's brochure will be bounded above by what the market will bear and below by the cost of providing the holiday. Customers expect exclusive holidays to be relatively expensive, so price is used as an indicator of quality, which in turn gives the tour operator the opportunity of securing higher margins. The volume market for inclusive tours is sold competitively on price. Hence operators will consider a range of offers, taking account of a number of factors:

- Seasonal effects – the range of variation between low- and peak-season prices is usually around 20 to 30 per cent.
- Exchange rate movements.
- Competitors' prices and the degree of product differentiation.
- Promotional pricing to encourage early booking and late availability discounts.
- Market segmentation pricing, with special offers for senior citizens, young people and families with children below a certain age.
- Discounts for affinity group travel.

Table 17.3 Price structure of a 14-night inclusive tour

Item	Percentages
Price	100
Direct costs	
Accommodation	41
Air seat (including taxes)	35
Transfers, excursions, etc.	2
Agent's commission	10
TOTAL	88
Gross Margin	12
Indirect costs	
Payroll expenses	4
Marketing	3
Office expenses	2
TOTAL	9
Net income	
Trading profit	3
Interest on deposits	1
TOTAL	4

Source: Trade information.

The price structure for a typical mass-market inclusive tour undertaken within Europe is shown in Table 17.3. Competition keeps profit margins low, so the emphasis is on volume sales and cost control to sustain net income. In these circumstances, the importance of hedging on foreign exchange is readily appreciated, because uncovered fluctuations in exchange rates may easily erode slender profit margins. This does not entirely remove the risk, for the tour operator still has to predict the amount of business going to each destination.

Air seats

For wholesalers who operate their own airlines or secure whole plane or time charters, an important element in determining the tour price is the costing of an air seat. This is calculated from the following formula:

$$s = \frac{d.RO}{(d-1).L.N} + t$$

where

s = unit seat cost per round trip
d = number of aircraft departures
RO = aircraft cost per rotation
L = load factor
N = number of seats per flight
t = airport tax.

As an example, consider an aircraft of 150 seats contracted on a time charter for 30 departures. The rotation cost is calculated at 40 000 currency units and the load factor at 90 per cent, and airport tax is ascertained to be 4 currency units. By substitution into the above formula, the unit seat cost per return flight is:

$$s = \frac{30 \times 40\,000}{29 \times 0.90 \times 150} + 4$$

$$s = 310.51$$

Note that the number of departures in the denominator of the equation is reduced by one to allow for empty legs.

Strategic positioning

History has shown that, while there are no major constraints on entry into travel wholesaling, the mass holiday market in any country tends to be dominated by only a handful of companies. The tour operator has no monopoly over airline seats or hotel beds, and product standards are easy to emulate. This being the case, the lessons of success indicate strategic market positions secured by a combination of the following factors:

- Economies of scale through bulk purchase and volume distribution.
- Low-cost distribution network together with national coverage.
- Developing new products and markets, and adopting new technologies.
- Competitive pricing.
- Multibranding to attract different market segments.
- Product differentiation to avoid competing on price alone.

As with major retail stores and supermarket chains, volume throughput and national presence are critical to the success of a mass tour operator. This being the case, in a European context it is unlikely that any wholesaler can compete effectively, particularly on price, in the mass-market segment with sales of under a million holidays. When account is taken of the organization structure needed and bonding requirements of around 10 per cent of turnover, it will be appreciated that the costs of entry act as a considerable deterrent.

The factors giving rise to a winning strategy are also the cause of a high degree of sales concentration in the tour operation industry, leaving small operators to create their own distinctive market share through specialized holidays. The economics of the industry are such that this situation is bound to continue, for the large operators are prepared to defend their market position by diversifying their products even into specialist areas, by multibranding to reach economic sales levels quickly in particular markets, by undertaking price wars and generally by enforcing the success criteria outlined above.

References and further reading

Beaver, A. (1980) *Mind Your Own Travel Business*, Edgware, Middlesex: Beaver Travel.

Burkart, A., and Medlik, S. (1981) *Tourism: Past, Present and Future*, London: Heinemann.

Holloway, J.C. (1989) *The Business of Tourism*, London: Pitman Publishing.

Lavery, P., and Van Doren, C. (1990) *Travel and Tourism: A North American/European Perspective*, Huntingdon: Elm Publications.

Middleton, V.T.C. (1988) *Marketing in Travel and Tourism*, Oxford: Heinemann.

Mill, R.C., and Morrison, A.M. (1985) *The Tourism System*, Englewood Cliffs, NJ: Prentice Hall.

Renshaw, M. (1989) 'Tour operations', in Callaghan, P. (ed.), *Travel and Tourism*, Durham: Business Education Publishers.

Sheldon, P.J. (1989) 'Tour wholesaling', in Witt, S., and Moutinho, L. (eds), *Tourism Marketing and Management Handbook*, Hemel Hempstead: Prentice Hall.

CHAPTER 18

Attractions

OVERVIEW

We can group tourist attractions into those which are natural and those which are man-made. The former include landscapes, climate, vegetation, forests and wildlife. The latter are principally the products of history and culture, but also include artificially created entertainment complexes such as theme parks. Attractions may be further sub-divided into those which are site specific, because of the location of facilities, and events which are periodic. Events may be used to complement site-specific attractions.

Many attractions, both natural and man-made, come within the domain of the public sector, while others are owned by voluntary organizations and the private commercial sector. In this chapter we look at some of the reasons for these different ownership patterns and examine the business consequences. We also consider problems of cost structure, pricing and seasonality to demonstrate the economic aspects of operating attractions.

We discuss resource and visitor management techniques from the standpoint of alleviating the crowding brought about by the continual rise in tourist numbers. This leads on to the issue of sustainable tourism development, in which the object is to manage tourism growth in a manner which ensures that tourists do not destroy by pressure of numbers the very attractions they come to see. A related matter is the authenticity of the visitor experience. Countries frequently stage events and aspects of site-specific attractions as a means of serving the tourist efficiently. This results in a loss of authenticity from the travel experience.

CHARACTERISTICS OF ATTRACTIONS

We know that attractions provide the single most important reason for leisure tourism to a destination. Many of the components of the tourist trip – for example, transport and accommodation – are demands derived from the consumer's desire to enjoy what a destination has to offer in terms of 'things to see and do'. Thus a tourist attraction is a focus for recreational and, in part, educational activity undertaken by both day and stay visitors.

We also noted earlier that it is a common feature of tourist attractions that they are shared with the host community. This in turn may give rise to conflict in popular destinations where tourism is perceived to cause problems of crowding, traffic congestion, environmental damage and litter.

CLASSIFICATION

There are many different types of attractions, and a number of attempts have been made to classify them. Classification is possible along a number of dimensions:

- Ownership.
- Capacity.
- Catchment area.
- Permanency.
- Type.

An early attempt at classification was made by Peters in 1969, classifying attractions by type, and distinguishing between natural and man-made features. Man-made features were as follows:

- *cultural* – religion, modern culture, museums, art galleries, buildings, archeological sites.
- *traditions* – folklore, animated culture, festivals.
- *events* – sports (Olympic Games, World Cup), cultural events (Royal Weddings).

Natural features included national parks, wildlife, viewpoints and individual features such as Niagara Falls or the Grand Canyon.

Although straightforward and simple to use, Peters' approach does not add to the understanding of the nature of attractions, or assist in their planning, management or marketing.

Perhaps a more useful approach is the slightly earlier one of Clawson, who links the classification of attractions with proximity to the market and to their uniqueness (Figure 18.1). Clawson's approach is helpful because it is infinitely flexible and is best utilized as a way of thinking about attractions. For example, a major historic building is clearly a resource-based attraction, but it can extend its market by adding a 'user-based' element, such as a small theme park as at Beaulieu,

or a wildlife park as at Longleat, both in the UK. Parks Canada have used a variant of Clawson's ideas to zone their parks (Case Study 18.1).

We can also adopt a similar approach and consider attractions as 'reproducible' or 'non-reproducible'. Reproducible attractions are man-made and of no historic or cultural significance, in that they can be reproduced at any time or in any place. The original Walt Disney theme park in California, for example, is now reproduced in similar form in Florida, Japan and France. Non-reproducible attractions are elements of the natural or cultural heritage – historic houses, wildlife reserves, etc. – which cannot be reproduced, and therefore deserve greater protection and levels of management input. The approach also goes some way towards distinguishing between attractions which are public goods, owned and subsidized by government – (landscapes, beaches, historic monuments) and those which are not (such as theme parks). Again it is often the case that the public goods demand greater management inputs and protection from overuse by the private sector.

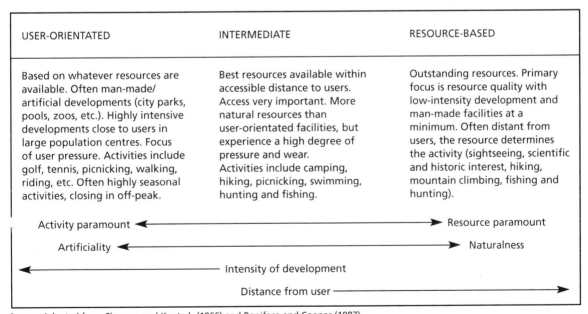

Source: Adapted from Clawson and Knetsch (1966) and Boniface and Cooper (1987)

Fig 18.1 Clawson's classification of recreation resources

CASE STUDY 18.1

Functional zoning applied by Parks Canada

Parks Canada has developed a classification of its park resources based heavily upon Clawson's ideas. In effect, the zones range from Zone I, a pure 'resource-based' zone, through to Zone V, a 'user-based' zone. Between the two extremes a continuum of zones is maintained through appropriate planning and management strategies.

ZONE I Special preservation areas: small and specific areas designated for a particular reason, such as the presence of endangered species. Entry is strictly controlled and access is by permit.

ZONE II Wilderness: areas with specific natural history and/or environmental value. Activities include dispersed hiking and some camping.

ZONE III Natural environments: access is compatible with the environment and this is the first zone where motorized access is allowed. However, this access is to the edge of the zone; entry is then via strategically located trails.

ZONE IV Recreation areas: includes camp sites, boating, skiing and motorized access. Interpretative services are designed to explain and protect the environment.

ZONE V Park services: includes centralized visitor support services, park administration offices, etc. all located and designed to blend in with the surroundings. In some parks this zone is located outside the park boundary.

Source: Adapted from Murphy (1985).

An excellent example of the practical utility of these approaches is Stonehenge. A classic 'resource-based' or 'non-reproducible' feature, Stonehenge has long suffered from over-visitation and very poor visitor facilities. Plans to solve these problems hinge on a new visitor facility some distance from the 'stones', with an artificial 'foamhenge' which visitors can approach, climb upon, etc. It is this 'user-based', 'reproducible' attraction which will take the pressure from the more vulnerable real monument.

We have adopted a straightforward classification in this chapter (Figure 18.2). Here attractions are divided between natural resources – for example, country parks in Britain, lakes in Canada, mountains in Switzerland and the coast in Spain – and man-made products. The latter are most commonly the results of the history and culture of a country, which leave a legacy of historic monuments and buildings, but they also include artificially created entertainment complexes such as theme parks, of which the most well known are the Disney parks.

Going further, it will be appreciated that the basic classification may be subdivided again into attractions which are site specific (because of the physical location of facilities) and therefore act as a destination, and attractions which are intangible and ephemeral because they are events. For events, it is what is happening at the time that

	SITE	EVENT
NATURAL RESOURCES	Country parks	Festival of the countryside
MAN-MADE	Historic monuments and buildings	Theatrical performance

Fig 18.2 Classification of attractions

takes priority rather than the location. Thus some of the most spectacular events in the form of parades or carnivals take place in large cities – for example, the Lord Mayor's Show in London or the Calgary Stampede in Alberta – because cities provide access to a large market and have the economic base to support them.

We can see that site and event attractions can be complementary activities, as illustrated in Figure 18.2. Staging a festival of the countryside can enhance the appeal of a country park, and the same applies to the performance of a Shakespeare tragedy in the courtyard of a historic castle. Events are frequently used to raise the image of a destination, a factor which lies behind the very competitive bidding for mega-events such as the Olympic Games. They are also used to give animation to object-oriented attractions, such as museums, to encourage new and repeat visitors, particularly in the off-season.

The division between natural resources and man-made attractions is not always clear cut. Many natural attractions require considerable inputs of infrastructure and management in order to use them for tourism purposes. This is the case with water parks, ski resorts, safari parks, aquaria and many other attractions based on nature. This infrastructure may also be put in place to protect the resource from environmental damage. In Britain, for example, it is no longer possible to have open public access to many forests. Specific sites are designated for cars, caravans and camping, and colour-coded trails are provided for walkers.

NATURAL RESOURCES

In the instance of natural features it is often the quality of the resource that provides the attraction, and location therefore becomes secondary. The appeal of such features is both national and international. Thus tourists come from all over the globe to enjoy the Himalayas in Nepal, the Grand Canyon in Colorado, the Blue Ridge Mountains of Virginia, the Lake District in Britain or the Ring of Kerry in Eire. Traditionally, water-based

resources, either coastlines or lakes, have always been the most important tourism resource and still are, but with more frequent holiday taking, the countryside and panoramic scenery have witnessed increasing usage. However, natural amenities are not confined to the landscape but also include, for example, climate (which accounts for the dominant tourist flows being North–South to sun resorts), vegetation, forests and wildlife.

The most common aspect of natural resources is that they are generally fixed in supply and are able to provide only a limited amount of services in any given time period. But in many cases, the services provided by this fixed stock of natural amenities can be put to several alternative uses. Thus, if it is proposed to increase the land available for tourism and recreation purposes, this may often be at the expense of other land users, say industry. Therefore a trade-off must take place to ensure that the resource is used to the best advantage of society.

This is demonstrated in Figure 18.3. The vertical axis represents the social net benefits (social benefits less social costs) of using a given area of land for tourism or industrial purposes. The schedule T illustrates how these net benefits decline as more land is made available for tourism. The same applies to the schedule I which represents industrial use. At Q_1 the social net benefit from the last portion of land devoted to

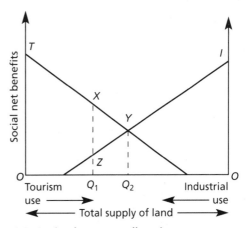

Fig 18.3 Optimal resource allocation

industry is measured by the distance ZQ_1, while that for tourism use is given by XQ_1. Clearly, the net benefits obtainable from tourism use are much greater than those that can be gained from industrial use, so it will pay society to switch land from industrial designation to tourist use. The optimal point will be at Q_2 where the net social benefits from each use are equalized. By undertaking such a move, society increases social net benefits by the amount XYZ, for the total gain from tourism use is XQ_1Q_2Y but this must be offset by a loss to industry of ZQ_1Q_2Y.

The essence of land use planning and the legislation that enforces it is to determine some optimal allocation in the manner shown by Figure 18.3. In this way land is zoned for a variety of uses, from tourism and recreation through to urban development, and when disputes occur as to use, it is customary to hold some form of public enquiry in which the benefits and costs of alternative choices are evaluated to reach an appropriate decision. Most governments maintain strict planning controls on alternative uses of land, whether it is publicly or privately owned. Thus social considerations via the political process are the main driving force behind land allocation. In the case of privately owned land, social choice may be enforced through compulsory purchase by the state.

In some cases the stark choice presented in Figure 18.3 is nullified in practice because multiple land use is possible. National parks in Britain, for example, include residential, farming, forestry and recreational activities and small-scale production within their boundaries.

Market failure and public provision

One of the problems concerning the provision of outdoor areas for leisure purposes on a large scale is that they are rarely commercially viable in terms of the investment costs and operating expenditure necessary to establish and maintain them. The reasons for this lie in their periodic use (weekends and holidays) and the political and administrative difficulties of establishing private markets in what

are perceived by the public as gifts of nature. This suggests that if it is left to market forces there is more likely to be underprovision of natural resources for leisure purposes than overprovision. Yet there are considerable social benefits to be enjoyed by the population from the availability of recreational amenities and from the control of land use to prevent unsightly development spoiling the beauty of the landscape.

Economists ascribe the term *market failure* to situations of the kind outlined above, and in such circumstances it is common for the state to make the necessary provision. Thus some 85 per cent of outdoor recreation areas in the USA are owned by the federal government, with the object of encouraging consumption and protecting the resource for the enjoyment of future generations. Public facilities made available for the purpose of encouraging consumption are termed *merit goods*, to indicate that the facilities are socially needed even if the willingness to pay for them in the market place is somewhat limited. The recognition of this principle in the USA goes back to 1872 with the enactment of the Yellowstone National Park. In Britain, planning and development for tourism purposes is largely a post-war phenomenon, commencing with the National Parks and Access to the Countryside Act 1949, although it was not until the 1960s that positive action in the field of tourism and recreation provision really began.

Another aspect of state provision is the so-called *public or collective good*. The principal feature of such goods or services is that it is not realistically possible to exclude individuals from consumption once they have been made available. Private markets for these goods would quickly disintegrate because the optimal strategy for the individual consumer is to wait until someone else pays for the good and then to reap the benefits for nothing. Thus if the good or service is to be provided at all, it may be consumed by everyone without exception and normally without charge at the point of use.

The natural environment is a typical example of a public good, and the growing pressure of tourist development has created concern for the environment in a number of countries. The point at issue is that public goods form no part of the private costs facing the tourism developer and are therefore open to abuse through overuse. In response the state, in addition to enforcing collective provision out of taxation, regulates individual behaviour through legislation to preserve environmental amenity.

For example, in Bermuda tourists are not allowed to hire cars, but only mopeds. Mauritius has a planning law which restricts buildings to a height no greater than the palm trees. In practice, this means that hotels are limited to two storeys and thus permits adequate screening on the seaward side. Where legislation is considered impractical, the approach is to try and change behaviour through educational awareness campaigns. An example of this is shown in Table 18.1, which lists the requirements of a code of conduct provided to visitors by the Yorkshire Dales National Park.

Table 18.1 The Yorkshire Dales Visitor Code

- Enjoy the countryside, but respect its lifestyles, work and customs. Support local skills, services and produce.
- Wherever you go keep to public routes and access areas.
- Use gates and stiles to cross dry-stone walls, fences and hedges.
- Leave all gates as you find them, open or closed.
- Avoid trampling meadow grass by staying in single file through meadows in summer.
- Protect wild animals, trees and other plants. In particular, leave wild flowers for others to enjoy, and avoid disturbing birds and other animals.
- Keep your dog under close control, preferably on a lead.
- Leave livestock and farm machinery alone. Be aware of farmyard dangers.
- Take your litter home.
- Guard against risk of fire.
- Help to keep rivers, streams and lakes clean.
- Whenever possible use public transport.
- Take special care on narrow roads.
- Park thoughtfully. Where available use car parks.
- Respect other people's peace and quiet.
- Show consideration for those who use the countryside in other legitimate ways.

Source: Yorkshire Dales National Park.

Resource management

Given a fixed amount of natural resources for leisure purposes, it is possible to alter the supply only by adopting different use patterns. Critical to this is the generally accepted premise that tourists should not destroy through excessive use the natural features that they come to enjoy. This view is encapsulated in the concept of sustainable tourism development, which argues that economic growth is acceptable only if it can maintain intact, at a minimum, the stock of tourist assets from one generation to another.

Emphasis tends to be placed on the natural environment because it cannot be directly substituted for man-made facilities, and the danger of irreversible damage appears more likely. This danger is also present with man-made attractions such as historic artefacts, but here the concept is more subjective in that it has to do with authenticity. For example, at what point does repair and replacement of stone on a historic monument because of erosion and visitor damage mean that it is no longer authentic? This is further complicated by the fact that perception seems to vary according to the nature of the historic artefact under consideration – whether it is glassware, tapestry, a sculpture or features of a building.

It has already been noted that the application of capital, labour and management to the natural environment is often necessary to render it suit-

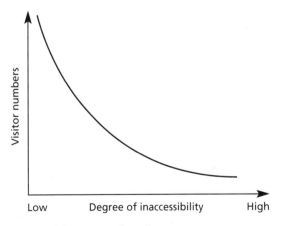

Fig 18.4 Visitor access function

able for tourist use, as in the case of a beach resource. This permits more intensive use of the beach, provided that the necessary safeguards are put in place to prevent over-exploitation of the free availability of the resource in its role as a public good. One way of achieving this is to restrict accommodation provision to match the desired density of the population on the beach. A high-quality resort might aim to allocate 20 square metres per person, compared to 10 square metres per person for a budget resort. In other situations, the degree of inaccessibility may be used to control visitor numbers.

This is illustrated in Figure 18.4, which demonstrates the inverse relationship between visitor numbers and difficulty of access. The latter may be due to time, distance or restrictions imposed by the managing authority. For example, with natural attractions which draw visitors both at the national and the international level, it is common for the authorities to implement 'park and ride' schemes so as to control the flow of cars in the area. Another popular strategy is the use of 'honey pots', whereby a variety of attractions, shops, restaurants and accommodation are clustered around one or two viewpoints to create a complex capable of absorbing a high visitor density.

The honey pot concept augments natural attractions with man-made, user-orientated attractions capable of drawing visitors away from the rest of the natural resource area. It is well known, for example, that the demand for domestic tourism and recreation facilities arises, in the main, from urban areas, but that pressures on attractions and rural areas generally decrease with distance from city centres. Hence greater opportunities for protection and management of natural sanctuaries for wildlife and vegetation can be found by locating them in areas remote from urban environments.

As the city centre is approached, so there is a need to provide purpose-built facilities to cope with day excursions and weekend trips. Depending on the climate and country these will include seaside or lakeside resorts, mountain resorts, health centres, spas, and theme and nature parks. Within the city boundary there will be a requirement for town parks, and sport and leisure complexes.

Thus, as the volume of leisure demand increases, so the need to augment natural attractions with man-made facilities arises. In this respect, capital cities such as London, Paris and New York have always been great magnets for tourists because of their historical and cultural resources. For these same reasons, cities everywhere are becoming tourist destinations in their own right rather than just places where people live and work.

MAN-MADE ATTRACTIONS

We know that a large number of man-made attractions are products of history and culture. The range of museums and art galleries in each of the world's top tourist destinations is usually extensive, and many focus on specific subjects: for example, the National Portrait Gallery in London or Chicago's Museum of Science and Industry. Added to this are numerous historic buildings, which include castles, palaces, churches, houses and even completely walled medieval towns such as Carcassonne in France, as well as a variety of early industrial sites which are capable of satisfying the public's interest in bygone times.

Where old industrial buildings, disused market halls, railway stations and docks are located close to urban centres, it has been quite common to convert them into tourist zones which serve both visitors and residents alike.

Since shopping is an important tourist activity, the focus has been on speciality shopping – as in Covent Garden, London – intermingled with hotels, leisure attractions and also business facilities – a convention centre, exhibition hall or trade centre. In this way, tourism has replaced the manufacturing and distribution industries, which have left the inner core for more spacious and cheaper locations on the outskirts of the city. Tourism has thus proved to be a feasible economic option for urban regeneration, as in the development of Baltimore's Inner Harbour or South Street Seaport, New York.

Over and above the man-made attractions left by historical legacy, there are numerous artificially engineered attractions whose principal role is one of entertainment. Such attractions are user-orientated and are capable of handling thousands of visitors per day: they include theme and leisure parks, sporting venues, theatres and all-weather holiday centres. Theme parks will also include an educational function – for example, EPCOT in Disney World – as well as providing exciting 'white knuckle' rides in the form of roller coasters, runaway trains, log flumes and oscillating 'pirate' ships.

One of the most famous theme parks (in the true sense), Colonial Williamsburg in USA, is a living museum. It was originated by establishing an old city within a new one, where the staff create a time capsule of the colonial period through role play and using the technology of the day. A similar re-creation has taken place at Beamish in the north of England. An open air museum has been positioned at a time just before the First World War and staff demonstrate the technology and converse with visitors in the way of life of that period. As far as possible the houses, shops, transport system, goods and artefacts are genuine articles of the time that have been brought to the site from all parts of the country.

In this manner, Beamish and Colonial Williamsburg have crossed the boundary between a theme park and a museum. In so doing they have captured the public's imagination by allowing participation. The public is now attuned to experiencing the sights and sounds of the era they are witnessing, which gives opportunities for the creative use of technology to enhance the visitor experience. We know that ultimately it is the visitor experience that is the marketed output of tourist attractions.

To this extent static attractions and object-orientated museums (unless they are national collections) no longer appeal to visitors as they once did. The quest for improving the attraction experience forces theme and leisure park operators to install more complicated rides and challenging entertainment as the public seek to increase the skill content of their consumption. Similarly, historic properties, museums and gardens need to change their displays and to feature special exhibitions and events in order to maintain interest and encourage repeat visitors. Some attractions are fortunate enough to be able to tie themselves to regular events aimed at an enthusiast market: for example, automobile rallies, for which demand is more or less continuous.

Economic aspects

As with natural resources, a great many man-made tourist attractions, because of their historical legacy, are not commercially owned. They are owned by one of the following:

- Central government (in the case of national collections).
- Quasi-public bodies, which are at 'arm's length' from the government.
- Local government.
- Voluntary bodies in the form of charitable trusts.

One of the most well-known examples of voluntary bodies in Britain is the National Trust, which maintains a wide range of historic properties, parks and woodlands. Acquisition has normally been via bequests from previous owners together with a substantial endowment. As in the case of many other non-profit organizations, the National Trust receives its income from admission charges, shops, catering, membership subscriptions, grants and donations, sponsorship, events and services rendered, eg. lecture programmes.

Public ownership

Publicly owned attractions may receive all or a substantial part of their funds from general taxation, either directly or via grant-in-aid for quasi-public bodies. They are thus provided in the manner of a merit good and in so doing impose a degree of coercion on everyone, as individuals are not free to adjust the amounts that are made available.

This is shown by Figure 18.5. The schedule S is the quantity of, say, museum services supplied to each person as a result of public provision. The distance $0t$ represents the amount of income forgone per person in terms of tax. A is the demand curve of individual A and B is the demand curve of individual B. At a tax cost $0t$, A demands only Q_A museum services while B demands Q_B. Clearly, the supply of services exceeds A's demand by XY, but falls below B's demand by YZ. It follows, therefore, that public provision is likely to generate political debate and lobbying as individuals try to alter the amounts produced to suit their own requirements.

In market-orientated economies the trend has been towards charging for national museums in order to cut public expenditure, although there is still considerable resistance among certain sections of the community, including museum managers, who feel that museums have a public obligation requirement. As a consequence, only voluntary admission donations have been introduced in some instances, with a recommended minimum contribution, while other museums have simply refused to charge for admission.

We can see from the above discussion that the classification of goods and services into public and private provision is by no means clear cut. It is up to society to decide upon the dividing line through the political process. Nevertheless, governments do have to make everyday decisions on which projects to develop and promote. This is particularly true of tourist attractions because they are frequently sponsored by local authorities and voluntary organizations which look to central government for grant assistance.

To aid decision making, economists have devised the analytical framework of cost–benefit analysis, which takes a wider and longer look at project decisions. The diversity of tourism expenditure is such that the most feasible method of assessing government support is to look at the impact that spending by visitors to the attraction has on local income and employment via the multiplier process. Implicit in this process is the requirement that the normal financial checks will be undertaken to ascertain whether the project is able to sustain itself operationally: if not, then it will need permanent subsidy if it is to proceed.

Voluntary organizations

Many museums and events have arisen out of the collections or interests of a group of enthusiasts who come together to provide for themselves and others collective goods and services which are unlikely to have any widespread commercial appeal (market failure) and which are equally unlikely to be of sufficient importance to attract central provision by the state. Mention has already been made of the National Trust in Britain; an events example is the Sealed Knot Society, which undertakes re-enactment battles of the English Civil War.

These organizations are in effect clubs, and because they normally have non-profit aims, they are entitled to claim the status of charities for tax purposes. However, in contrast to the public sector, they are not able to raise funds from taxation and so in the long run must cover their costs out of income. Yet, unlike the private commercial

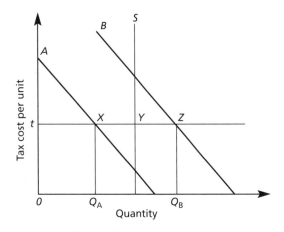

Fig 18.5 Public provision

sector, their income is not made up principally of admission charges and visitor spending inside the attraction. Membership fees, gifts and bequests often take on a far greater significance in their income statement. As a consequence, recruiting new members to share the collective visitor experience is a priority task for these organizations. On the cost side, voluntary societies benefit from the fact that much of the labour input and some of the materials are provided free of charge, although some operators have found that the use of voluntary labour can detract from the effectiveness of the attraction.

Commercial sector

For commercial attractions the rules of market economics apply. They are required to make profits so as to contribute a return on the capital invested. In theory this return, at a minimum, should be equal to the going cost of investment funds, and for new or 'venture' projects considerably more. In situations where attractions are owned by multiproduct firms or conglomerates, the ability of the facility to contribute to the cash flow of the overall business is often given a higher priority than return on capital. Production industries frequently have long lead times between incurring costs and receiving revenues. In these circumstances, the ownership of subsidiaries capable of generating ready cash inflows into the organization on a daily and weekly basis can contribute greatly to total financial stability.

The principal economic concerns of most commercial attractions are the same ones that face many other tourist enterprises: namely, their cost structure and the seasonal nature of demand. Furthermore, for user-orientated attractions, fashions and tastes also play a considerable part. As noted earlier, theme park owners have to add new rides and replace old ones long before they are physically worn out, simply to maintain attendances. Historic properties and museums can fall back on the intrinsic value of their buildings and collections, but even here presentation and interpretation have become more important.

Costs

Typically, the cost structure of tourist attractions is made up of a high level of fixed, and therefore unavoidable, costs in relation to the operational or variable costs of running the enterprise. The main component of the fixed costs is the capital investment required to establish the attractions in the first place and capital additions from new development. The economic consequence of having a high level of fixed costs is to raise the break-even point in terms of sales or visitor numbers, as shown in Figure 18.6.

The revenue line from sales to visitors over a given time period is represented by R. The lines C_1 and C_2 are total cost schedules according to different visitor numbers: the slope of these cost schedules is determined by the variable costs incurred per visitor (marginal costs), and where they cut the revenue and costs axis determines the level of fixed costs. It may easily be seen that with overall fixed costs of F_1 the break-even point (BEP$_1$), which is at the intersection of R and C_1, is achieved at V_1 level of visitors. If fixed costs are set at F_2, the number of visitors needed to break even rises substantially to V_2, which increases the amount of risk in the successful running of the operation.

This also has an impact on location, because for user-orientated attractions population catchment areas in terms of ease of access to the site are of

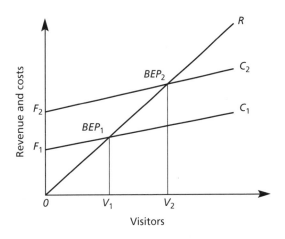

Fig 18.6 Fixed cost effects

prime importance. The greater the visitor numbers required in order for an attraction project to break even, the fewer are the number of acceptable locations. Hence EuroDisney, for example, undertook an enormous amount of research before deciding on a site close to Paris at Marne la Vallée (although the initial returns in visitor numbers have led people to question the decision). We can see from this that the success of government initiatives to stimulate the development of tourist attractions largely hinges on the amount of assistance that can be given to help with the capital costs of starting up the project. This assistance may take a number of forms:

- Cash grants.
- Subsidized ('soft') loans.
- Shared ownership.
- The provision of benefits-in-kind such as land, infrastructure and access routes.
- A combination of any of these.

As a rule, cash grants are perceived by the commercial sector as the most effective form of financial help.

Pricing policy

The effects of having high fixed costs also spill over into pricing policy. The difference between the price charged for admission to an attraction and the variable or marginal cost of providing the visitor experience for the customer is the contribution margin per customer towards paying the fixed costs and meeting targets on profitability.

We can see from Figure 18.7(a) (where the contribution margin desired is low because fixed costs are low) that the marginal cost of supplying an additional unit is relatively high and so provides a good guide to setting the price level. This is known as *cost-orientated* pricing. On the other hand, where there are high fixed costs, the admission charge has to be set considerably above the marginal cost of provision, in order to ensure a high contribution margin to meet the financial costs of servicing the investment that has been sunk into the attraction. In this instance, the

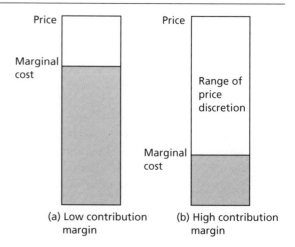

Fig 18.7 Market orientation

marginal cost of provision is no longer a good guide to pricing, and the enterprise is forced to take a *market-orientated* stance in its pricing policy.

The difference between the admission price and marginal cost is the range of price discretion that the organization has, for it must cover its operating costs in the short run, but may take a longer-term perspective in terms of how it might cover its fixed costs. By seeking out a range of different market segments with a variety of different prices, including discounts for volume sales and long-term contracts, the commercial attraction operator will try to optimize the yield on the site's assets. This is termed 'yield management' and the operator's ability to improve the yield will be constrained by the economic climate surrounding the firm. This will include the following aspects:

- The customers' perceptions of value for money ('what the market will bear').
- Personal income levels, particularly amounts for discretionary (non-essential) spending.
- The degree of competition.

Seasonality

Seasonality becomes an issue in tourist attractions because the product, the visitor experience, cannot be stored. This being the case, it is peak demand that determines capacity, and user-orientated attractions are frequently designed to a standard based on a fixed number of days per annum when capacity is likely to be reached or exceeded. This implies that at most times of the year the attraction has too much capacity. The level of investment is therefore more than what would be required if the product were storable. In turn, seasonality can affect pricing policy, as presented in Figure 18.8. S is the supply schedule representing the incremental cost of expanding visitor numbers. D_2 is the demand for the visitor experience in the main season, while D_1 is the off-season demand. Market clearing requires a policy of seasonal price differentiation, charging P_2 in the main season and P_1 in the off-season. However, in practice many attraction managers are opposed to seasonal pricing because, they argue, it simply reacts on customers' perceived value for money. They see satisfaction ratings falling at peak times because visitors are aware that at other times of the year they can have the same experience for much less money. To counter this perception problem, attraction operators tend to narrow seasonal price ranges and offer additional product benefits, in the form of free entrance to different parts of the site, to those visitors coming when the attraction is not busy.

Another method of smoothing the difference in prices is to charge a two-part tariff. Instead of the major contribution to fixed costs being borne by main season visitors, the admission price is made up of a fixed charge to meet the requirement to cover fixed costs in the long run, and a variable charge depending on the level of usage.

Visitor management

Price has often been used as a method of regulating demand and enforcing exclusivity, as in luxury resorts such as Malibu and Monaco, or in luxury hotels such as the Savoy and Dorchester in London. To be able to use price to limit the number of visitors requires that consumption should be excludable – only those who pay can benefit from the visitor experience. But this is often deemed undesirable in the case of natural resources or the historical and cultural artefacts of a country, either because they are public goods, so that it is not practical to exclude consumption, or because they are merit goods, whereby it is to the benefit of society that consumption should be encouraged.

Even commercial attractions would have difficulty in using price as the sole regulator of visitor numbers. In any one year such attractions have a variety of peaks and troughs which would therefore entail a whole range of different prices. In western economies, the public does not respond well to wildly fluctuating prices, so all attractions resort to some non-price methods to manage visitor flows.

Table 18.2 presents a list of possible actions to manage visitors at busy times, and thereby to avoid congestion and improve the visitor experience. These start with marketing and information provision and go through to techniques which can influence the visitor's behaviour on the site. Some attractions have adopted deliberate demarketing at peak times, but where they are nationally or internationally known this is only of limited effectiveness. For example, first-time visitors to London nearly always want to see the Tower of London, Buckingham Palace and Westminster Abbey.

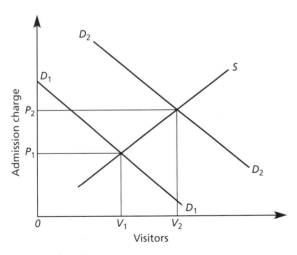

Figure 18.8 Seasonal demand

Table 18.2 Visitor management techniques

Marketing and information provision

- Withdrawing promotion at peak times and informing local radio stations and Tourist Information Centres when the attraction is nearing capacity.
- Encouraging visitors to come out of season.
- Promoting alternative attractions and ensuring that Tourist Information Centres make visitors aware of the full range of attractions available.
- Targeting specific market segments only.

Influencing on-site behaviour

- Visitor orientation centres.
- Signposts, information points and marked routes.
- Use of guides, actors in role play and audio cassette tours to channel visitor movements.
- Temporary closure, restricted access using rope barriers, one-way systems and dispersal to less sensitive areas.
- Timed ticketing and advanced booking systems.
- Queue management systems and queue entertainment.
- Zoning areas or time scheduling for different activities.
- Managing car parks to direct visitors to alternative locations on the site.
- Installing on-site transport systems.

The first task at the site is to deal with car and bus traffic, if only to prevent congestion building up and blocking main roads. Once on-site, visitors can be channelled using internal transport systems, such as land trains, where distances involve a considerable amount of walking. For theme parks, queue management is often necessary for popular attractions and rides, so that excessive waiting does not detract from the visitor's enjoyment. This may be achieved by ensuring that the queue line passes through a stimulating environment, with the ability to view the attraction as it is approached, by providing entertainers and by using markers to indicate the length of time people will have to wait at different stages of the queue.

Authenticity issues

It is the concern of social researchers that tourists should be given a genuine appreciation of the destination they are visiting. In too many cases, it is argued, tourists are given the impression that the destination is some idyllic fantasy world, and they are fooled into this by attractions, particularly events, which are staged and may have little relevance to the culture of the country. Thus the tourists do not see the real landscape and way of life of the host community. This implies a loss of authenticity in the visitor experience. Of course, some tourists do not want an authentic experience: the purpose of going to leisure or theme parks to participate on the rides is for entertainment and excitement.

The ideal situation is considered to be where both the host community and the visitor see the experience as authentic. However, given mass tourism flows, it is virtually impossible to meet the curiosity of visitors without staging events and certain aspects of historic attractions. Many historic properties in Britain stage period tableaux to give visitors an impression of what living was like in those times. The visitor knows that they are staged, yet at the same time every effort is made to give the most authentic representation possible – even including the reproduction of smells, as in the Jorvik Viking Centre in York, which places visitors in a 'time' car to travel around the recreation of a Viking village.

Authenticity becomes questionable when the destination tries to conceal the staging of an event by giving visitors the impression that what they are seeing is real, when in fact it may be an artificially created event or may belong to a time gone by and have no place in the current life of the community. But historic and cultural staging presents the visitor with the salient features of a community's heritage and reduces the need for encroaching on the private space of the host population. It may also generate pride and interest among the local community, which may previously have taken these aspects for granted.

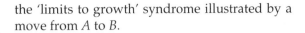

Environment

The concern for the tourism environment, be it natural or man-made, is linked with the notion of sustainable development. Rarely in history has any society willingly absorbed the imposition of a variety of outside cultures upon it, yet, in the interests of generating local economic activity and employment, this is precisely what host communities are expected to do with regard to the development of tourism. The situation is depicted in Figure 18.9.

Suppose the local economy is positioned at A and the desire is to increase employment. The adverse consequence arises where such a policy can be accomplished only by a move from A to B, which trades off employment against environmental quality. The concept of sustainable tourism development argues that economic growth and environmental quality are not mutually exclusive events. Through changes in technology to improve the use of resources, control waste and manage visitor flows to prevent damage to non-renewable tourism resources, it is possible to reach a position such as C in Figure 18.9. Going 'green' can build a platform for long-term growth by offering a better tourist product, saving resources and stimulating the public's perception of the tourism industry. Sustainable development thus offers a mechanism to escape the 'limits to growth' syndrome illustrated by a move from A to B.

Control or market solutions?

The question posed is: how should this mechanism work? In market-orientated economies, the policy preference is for solutions based on the principle that the 'polluter" should pay. Thus, prices should reflect not only the economic costs of provision but also the social costs.

The different approaches to the impact of visitors on the tourism environment are shown in Figure 18.10. D is the demand schedule, and at low rates of tourist consumption, say V_1, the social cost per unit (SC) is equal to the economic cost (EC) of usage. Thus, up to V_1 current consumption does not interfere with future consumption or damage the resource. If only current demand is considered then the resource will be used to a level V_2 with visitor expenditure settling at point B. This results in resource depletion to the extent that SC is as high as A. The market solution is to drive consumption back to V_3 by imposing a tourist tax CE on usage to compensate for the renewal cost of the resource.

As we have seen, the difficulty with market solutions is that many natural attractions have public good properties, whereby consumption is

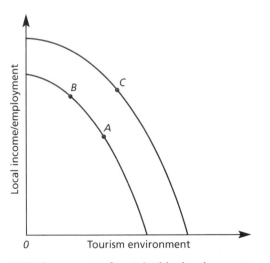

Fig 18.9 The concept of sustainable development

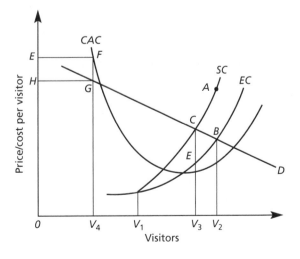

Fig 18.10 Control versus market solutions

non-excludable and there is public resistance to charging for a nation's heritage, which is presumed to belong to all (although some museums and galleries, such as the Prado in Madrid, do discriminate between domestic and foreign visitors). In such situations there is little choice other than to control visitor flows by influencing behaviour and/or to follow a programme of continual repair and maintenance. The British experience has been one where it is uncommon for visitors or tourist businesses to be charged directly for the social and environmental costs generated by their actions. The money is paid indirectly through general taxation, and most of the burden of coping with congestion, litter and visitor management falls on the public sector, particularly local authorities. To this extent the government tries to take account of the influx of visitors in its support grant for the local provision of public services.

The control or conservation solution requires that demand is driven back to V_1 by simply limiting the number of visitors. However, society cannot afford to be overzealous in its actions. CAC represents the combined average cost curve of the tourism plant in the community. If demand is forced back to V_4 it may be seen that this plant is no longer viable, for the average cost of supply (point F) is greater than the average visitor spend (point G). In order to survive in the longer term the tourism enterprises have to be subsidized by an amount $EFGH$. One of the paradoxes of tourism is that those who do not see their income as directly dependent on the tourism industry are frequently opposed to it. However, closing down the tourism plant reverses the multiplier process. Quite soon local businesses and employment are affected, and the economic rationale for the community may be impaired, which can affect the jobs of those very people who are opposed to tourism development.

Control and market solutions to managing the tourism environment are not necessarily mutually exclusive. A compromise is to assign quotas to tourist enterprises at the conservation level V_1, but at the same time to allow market forces to work by levying a graduated environmental charge on those businesses exceeding their quotas. The object here is to position society as near as possible to point C in Figure 18.10. To ensure that allocations are adjusted in an optimal manner, firms are allowed to buy and sell quotas so as to reach a level appropriate to their own businesses.

Clearly, the model depicted in Figure 18.10 is not static. In times of growth this is of benefit, for it is politically less painful to refuse planning permission for new projects than it is to regulate existing operators. Over time it is expected that new technologies for maintenance and repair, and improved visitor management techniques, will enable the SC schedule to be shifted to the right. This should allow a greater number of visitors to be handled at a lower cost to the environment, which is the essence of the sustainable tourism development argument depicted in Figure 18.9.

References and further reading

Beioley, S. (1981) *Tourism and Urban Regeneration*, London: English Tourist Board.

Boniface, B., and Cooper, C. (1987) *The Geography of Travel and Tourism*, Oxford, Heinemann.

Burkart, A., and Medlik, S. (1981) *Tourism: Past, Present and Future*, London: Heinemann.

Clawson, M., and Knetsch, J. (1966) *The Economics of Outdoor Recreation*, Baltimore, Md: Johns Hopkins University Press.

Corze, J.C. (1989) 'Theme and leisure parks', in Witt, S., and Moutinho, L. (eds), *Tourism Marketing and Management Handbook*, Hemel Hempstead: Prentice Hall.

Getz, D.E. (1991) *Festivals, Special Events and Tourism*, New York: Van Nostrand Reinhold.

Holloway, J.C. (1985) *The Business of Tourism*, Plymouth: Macdonald and Evans.

Hughes, H.L. (1989) 'Entertainment', in Witt, S., and Moutinho, L. (eds), *Tourism Marketing and Management Handbook*, Hemel Hempstead: Prentice Hall.

Middleton, V.T.C. (1988) *Marketing in Travel and Tourism*, Oxford: Butterworth-Heinemann.

Mill, R.C., and Morrison, A.M. (1985) *The Tourism System*, Englewood Cliffs, NJ: Prentice Hall.

Murphy, P.E. (1985) *Tourism: A Community Approach*, London: Methuen & Co.

Peters, M. (1969) *International Tourism*, London: Hutchinson.

Stevens, T.R. (1991) 'Visitor attractions: their management and contribution to tourism', in Cooper, C. (ed.), *Progress in Tourism, Recreation and Hospitality Management*, Vol. 3, London: Belhaven.

Wheeller, B. (1992) 'Is progressive tourism appropriate?', *Tourism Management*, vol. 13, no. 1, pp. 104–5.

PART 4

Marketing for tourism

CHAPTER 19

Introduction

As the tourism market matures, marketing will become a vital activity for all tourism enterprises. In this part of the book we consider in detail the management of tourism marketing and, in particular, strategies and techniques which can be applied to deliver the tourism product effectively and to satisfy the tourism consumer.

There are some who argue that tourism is sufficiently distinctive as to demand a different marketing approach, and indeed that one reason why tourism can be thought of as lagging behind other industries in its marketing is that this different approach is not yet fully developed. Others suggest that marketing in tourism lags behind other industries as a consequence of its immaturity as an industry; the practice of developing managers from the grass roots; and the late development of technology in the tourism industry (such as computer reservations systems).

While some of these criticisms are true, and reflect the issues raised in Chapter 13, we believe that tourism has firmly to embrace the concept of consumer marketing. Of course, the very nature of tourism as a service does need to be recognized by marketers, but there is now a body of knowledge and a battery of techniques and approaches for marketing in the service industries. Tourism can benefit from these, and in this part of the book we therefore outline an approach to the marketing management of tourism.

It is perhaps in this part of the book that the linkages within tourism become highlighted. For example, while we espouse in this section a professional and sophisticated approach to the marketing of tourism, the very fact that many enterprises in tourism are small and family owned does mean that they have neither the expertise nor the resources to devote to a fully fledged marketing management approach. This immediately creates an opportunity for the larger enterprises in tourism, which can take advantage of the approaches we outline here, and in so doing can increase their market share and prominence within the industry. The tourism industry does, however, create its own handicaps to effective marketing:

- Data relating to the market and to the actions of competitors are scarce.
- Short-term outlooks prevail, denying a structured planning approach.
- Managers tend to have come up through the ranks and to be 'jacks of all trades'. The organization of the industry thus works against the development of specialists in marketing, and indeed some managers do not respect this type of skill.

In addition, the industry is subject to government regulation of its activities, and consumer protection is well developed in tourism. These facts can act to restrict the marketing options of a tourism company.

Public-sector organizations in tourism are also somewhat handicapped in adopting a true marketing orientation. It is, for example, not uncommon to find visitor and convention bureaux with the following problems:

- Being hidebound by government personnel operating guidelines in terms of working hours and rewarding their staff.
- Having insufficient resources to build a presence in the market place (particularly in the international market place).

- Lacking marketing expertise.
- Having to be even-handed in their support of products and enterprises at their destination.
- Having no control over the quality of the product they are marketing.
- Being driven by 12-monthly budgeting cycles which preclude long-term planning.

The nature of tourism demand is inextricably linked to marketing. This is obvious in the case of seasonality, where pricing strategies can help, but also the decision-making process of the consumer has to be taken into account in tourism marketing.

Marketing is an important tool in an industry where loyalty both in the distribution chain and in the company is low; indeed, many companies have promotional campaigns targeted at other sectors of the tourism industry (such as retail agents) as well as the consumer. Similarly, government organizations often find it more cost effective to market to intermediaries and carriers rather than to the potential traveller. In the next four chapters we therefore provide a new way of thinking about tourism marketing and outline the approaches and techniques which should be adopted by tourism marketers.

CHAPTER 20

Marketing for tourism – the historical roots

OVERVIEW

In this chapter we introduce the evolution and concept of marketing as it applies to tourism. We demonstrate that tourism marketing has evolved due to the different business and social changes which have occurred throughout the twentieth century. The chapter stresses that marketing has developed as a reaction to the conditions which impinge on business operations. While we can identify different business philosophies, the marketing concept and the benefits of a marketing orientation, the real understanding of marketing lies in the way marketing management functions in attempting to create consumer satisfactions.

WHAT IS MARKETING?

Tourism can be traced back for centuries, but because the elements of the product and the conditions of the market place have changed, there has been a corresponding requirement for a change in business methods. This has led to the use of tourism marketing. Everyone has his or her own idea of what marketing is, as it affects us all in different ways. We are all involved in, or influenced by, marketing in one way or another. It will not have been long since you last saw a promotion for an airline, hotel group, holiday, leisure centre or overseas country. We are continuously bombarded with advertising and sales material, and all shops have numerous promotional messages. We are surrounded by invasive messages

and communications paid for out of marketing budgets. However, as we shall see, marketing is far more than the promotion of a product: this forms only one aspect of marketing.

If the statement is made that we live in an era of marketing, what does this mean? A possible method of understanding marketing is to treat it as the development of ideas. If this is the case, all we have to do is to trace what has been written of marketing in the past. Unfortunately, this is not possible because, while historical accounts show that trade has always existed, the term 'marketing' was first used as a noun only in the first part of this century. There is also no equivalent for this word that can be found in other languages. For example, in France the term *le marketing* is used, and in eastern European countries there is similarly no translation for the word 'marketing'. The use of the word in the early part of the twentieth century was associated with a number of factors which were loosely related to the activity of achieving a sale. Therefore marketing as we know it today must be a recent development.

One way of attempting to answer a question about the meaning of marketing is to look at a definition. It is in fact very easy to describe what is meant by marketing, but in reality it is far more difficult to describe the actual practice of marketing. This is because a central tenet of marketing is the body of underlying concepts which form the general guide for organizational and managerial thinking, planning and action. For a comprehensive understanding of marketing it is necessary to master the underlying concepts.

THE EVOLUTION OF MARKETING

Marketing has evolved against a background of economic and business pressures. These pressures have required an increased focus on the adoption of a series of managerial measures based upon satisfying consumer needs. The key to the importance of marketing within tourism has been the level of economic growth throughout the twentieth century, which has led to improvements in living standards, an enlargement of the population, and increases in discretionary time. Such changes led Disney management in 1955 to launch the Disneyland theme park concept and McDonald's to open their first fast-food restaurant. In a short period of time the tourism industry has become one of the most important industries in the world.

At the same time there has been a concentration of a major portion of the tourism business into fewer large companies. Many of the recent changes in the size of organizations have led to the creation of a widening gulf between managers of the business and the consumer. A consequence of the distance which has been created is the lack of first-hand knowledge of the consumer's tastes and needs.

Where marketing has been adopted, the emphasis is on developing a full understanding of the dynamics of consumer behaviour. We should be aware that organizations that use marketing are not limited to commercial companies. Marketing techniques are being used by tourist boards and museums, and by charities organizing free or subsidized holidays for the elderly or handicapped.

Within the market place the companies that have adapted most successfully to contemporary changes are those that have directed management resources to obtaining research on market and consumer trends and also to improving channels of distribution and communication campaigns. The nature of the tourism industry is one where custom and tradition have been particularly strong. The interpersonal service delivery aspects of the industry have created styles of interaction where the service provider remains distanced from the act of service provision. As with many other industries in the service sector, this has preserved the customary, well-established ways of doing business.

The need for change has been forced upon the industry by the changes which have occurred in relation to the consumer and market forces. Modern tourism marketing has emerged as a business reaction to changes in the social and economic environment, with the most successful companies or tourist bodies having demonstrated a keen sense of providing the right organization structure and product offer for the consumer or visitor. This relies as much upon an approach or attitude to business or the market, as it does upon specific management expertise. Marketing is therefore initially a philosophy which relies on the art and science of different management approaches.

The development of marketing is fashioned as the outcome of social and business pressures. The most widely accepted account of the development of marketing is that proposed by Keith (1981, p. 44) who discerned an evolution of production, to sales, to marketing, in the Pillsbury company in the USA. In 1960 Keith (in Enis and Cox (1981, p. 44)) argued that the growing recognition of consumer orientation 'will have far reaching implications for business, achieving a virtual revolution in economic thinking'. He inferred that, in the late 1950s, consumer orientation was only just beginning to be accepted as a business concept. A survey of the literature reveals that marketing and modern business practice developed in three distinct stages (Gilbert and Bailey, 1990).

(1) *The production era*. This occurred when there was a belief that, if products were priced cheaply enough, they would be bought. Therefore it was important to supply products to the market place with the emphasis on consistently reducing costs. The focus of management was on increasing efficiency of production, which involved an *inward, product-orientated* emphasis rather than an

outward, market-orientated emphasis. The overriding objective for management was the development of a standardized product which could be offered at the lowest price to the market.

(2) *The sales era*. This is an evolutionary phase where companies attempted *to sell the products they had formulated*. This led to a search for more effective means of selling. As competition increased, companies realized that they could not survive without knowing more about different markets and improving their sales techniques. Therefore they attempted to influence demand and tailor it to meet their supply.

(3) *The marketing era*. This is characterized by a reversal of the preceding philosophy. Companies started to provide the products they could sell *rather* than trying to sell what they had produced. Companies adopted a consumer-led approach and concentrated on improving the marketing mix. This meant that it was recognized that *customer needs and satisfaction were the most effective basis for planning* and that the company has to be outward looking to be successful.

There are continuing arguments as to the dates of the above eras, whether they can be treated as discrete periods, and indeed whether new eras are emerging – such as 'societal marketing' with a concern for the environment and broader issues. For our purposes, in the majority of texts the marketing era is considered to have been established from the 1950s onward. The important factors which ushered in the marketing era during the twentieth century are as follows.

(1) The increases in demand were at a lower rate than the rises in productivity. In tourism, this culminated in an oversupply of accommodation in specific locations, and of aircraft seats on important routes, and too many companies in the market place. The increase in competition and the risks associated with the tourism market place led to more reliance on the use of marketing. The business system can be viewed as an organism which is concerned with survival and proliferation. Following this argument, when a business system is

threatened it will take functional steps to improve the situation. As marketing can provide for tactical change and modification of the system, in times of risk where there is oversupply and market saturation marketing assumes a much more important role.

(2) The consumer was becoming more affluent, and therefore it was possible to develop products which could be sold using a range of non-price attributes. This required the development of methods of creating, and changing, consumer attitudes and beliefs.

(3) The distance between the tourism product provider and the tourist was continuously increasing. This led to a need for marketing research related to gathering information on market trends, evaluating levels of satisfaction and understanding consumer behaviour.

(4) As society developed, the mass market splintered into a number of submarkets, while at the same time the mass market became increasingly difficult to reach. This was due to the increase in specialist media and the potential for a whole range of alternative leisure pursuits. The changes required improved expertise in the segmentation of markets and the provision of different marketing mix strategies which would maximize demand for individual segments.

DEFINITIONS AND CONCEPTS OF MARKETING

No definition of marketing can ever disregard Philip Kotler, who has established himself as the most widely referenced proponent of general marketing theory. Kotler defines marketing as 'a social and managerial process by which individuals and groups obtain what they need and want through creating and exchanging products and value with others' (1988, p. 3). Kotler argues that this definition is built on the main concepts of wants, needs, demands, satisfactions and marketers, because they are central to the study of marketing.

In 1984 the British Chartered Institute of Marketing defined marketing as 'the management process responsible for identifying, anticipating and satisfying customers' requirements profitably'.

An examination of both definitions reveals significant core similarities. Both emphasize marketing as a management process. In addition, the British Chartered Institute clarifies the management responsibility as one of assessing consumer demand through the identification and anticipation of customer requirements. This denotes the importance of research and analysis as part of the process. One major difference is that Kotler's definition is more appropriate to non-profit organizations where there is free entrance or a subsidy towards the cost of a service. It is also more fitting when facilitators of tourism such as tourist boards are considered.

However, the most important aspect, and one that should be at the heart of any definition of marketing, is the emphasis placed on the consumer's needs as the origin of all of the company's effort. The marketing concept has been expressed in many succinct ways from the 'Have it your way', of Burger King to the 'You're the boss' of United Airlines. This is the basis of the modern marketing concept, which holds that success is based not only on identifying different consumer needs, but also on delivering a tourist product whose experiences provide sets of satisfactions which are preferable to those of the competitors. In addition, these satisfactions have to be delivered with attention to their cost effectiveness, since marketing has to be evaluated on the basis of its expenditure.

We have seen how the definition of marketing leads to the marketing concept, whereby the consumer is the driving force for all business activities. We now have to ensure that there is no confusion between the idea of marketing and sales, and we will then proceed to introduce the notion of marketing orientation.

THE DIFFERENCES BETWEEN MARKETING AND SELLING

By now it should be obvious to the reader that marketing and selling are not the same. Levitt describes the difference as follows:

> Selling focuses on the needs of the seller; marketing on the needs of the buyer. Selling is preoccupied with the seller's need to convert his product into cash; marketing with the idea of satisfying the needs of the customer by means of the product and the whole cluster of things associated with creating, delivering and finally consuming it. (1960, p. 45)

Drucker points out: 'selling and marketing are antithetical rather than synonymous or even complementary. There will always, one can assume, be a need for some selling, but the aim of marketing is to make selling superfluous' (1973, p. 64).

The contrast between the sales and marketing approaches highlights the importance of marketing planning and analysis related to customers and the market place. The sales concept focuses on products and uses selling and promotion to achieve profits through sales volume. The underlying weakness is that the sales concept does not necessarily satisfy the consumer and may only culminate in short-term, rather than long-term, company success. The marketing concept focuses on customer needs and utilizes integrated marketing to achieve profits through customer satisfaction (Figure 20.1).

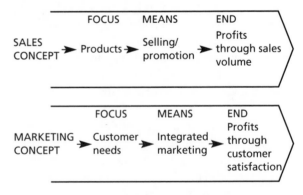

Fig 20.1 The sales and marketing concepts compared

DIFFERENT BUSINESS PHILOSOPHIES

As we have seen, marketing is a business philosophy which places the consumer and his or her needs at the forefront of all activities. For example, it is known that business travellers want frequent and reliable transport systems with sensible timings of departure and arrival. They favour priority check-in and check-out facilities, and efficient, good-quality staff. Business travellers need to feel that they can make their trips and have their meetings without any worry of delay or discomfort. A knowledge of business travellers' needs occurs only when someone takes care to identify those needs.

While it is important to recognize the importance of structuring any organization so that it focuses upon the customer, there are a number of alternative philosophies which can be recognized (Figure 20.2). Each of these philosophies acts as a guiding orientation and a system of approaching the market. And while a product-led company may be less effective, it is still possible to identify such companies within the tourism industry.

(1) PRODUCT–ORIENTATED COMPANY

Product creation ⟶ Promotion ⟶ Sales

(2) SYSTEMS/TECHNOLOGY-ORIENTATED COMPANY

Technology/ ⟶ Product ⟶ Product ⟶ Promotion ⟶ Sales
organization   formulation   creation

(3) MARKET-ORIENTATED COMPANY

Marketing ⟶ Product ⟶ Product ⟶ Promotion ⟶ Sales
research   formulation   creation

(4) INTEGRATED COMPANY

Marketing reasearch ⟵
            Product ⟶ Promotion ⟶ Sales
            creation

Product formulation
and company-wide marketing
principals incorporated

Fig 20.2 Four possible business philosophies

It is important to understand the initial starting place within the chains of the individual systems in Figure 20.2, as this is the first stage in a sequence of events which clearly demonstrates the locus of the company's approach to effecting exchange relationships.

Examples (1) and (2) in Figure 20.2 can be ineffective due to problems encountered in having the wrong product for the market, and therefore having to waste more resources on promotion and selling in order to achieve a sale. In these examples it is normal to find companies which believe that their products are acceptable, and that all that is required for sales to occur is the identification of prime markets and methods of selling.

Such an approach to the market place by a destination, hotel or airline marketing department is characterized by an emphasis on pictures of empty bedrooms, government buildings or the exterior of an aircraft. An emphasis on the product rather than on the benefits that the consumer is seeking is still at the heart of a great deal of today's tourism marketing. Quite often tourist promotional literature is devoid of scenes of tourists enjoying rest, enjoyment or good service. A product-focused philosophy is acceptable when there is a shortage or during boom times, which are characterized by little competition. However, both the first two philosophies provide for inward-looking management which concentrates on improvement within the company, rather than for outward-looking management which concentrates on the consumer and emerging tourist needs.

Examples (3) and (4) in Figure 20.2 offer the ideal approach to organizing business in the modern tourism market place. They are driven by research which creates an understanding of the consumer, the business and the market place. Research will be both secondary and primary. Information has to be collected from within and outside the company in order to establish a clear picture of the marketing environment. The integrated approach provides for a sequence of events which commences with an understanding of the consumer, the competitors and the types of product that the company is capable of providing, and a system which sensitizes the whole company to a marketing orientation. The integrated system helps to ensure that methods of improving the satisfaction levels of the consumer are incorporated into each department's objectives.

Within these two examples of company philosophy, it can be seen that the feedback process allows the marketing department to develop products as well as different forms of promotion which are right for the consumer. This establishes a more effective means of ensuring that products are successful and that marketing budgets are used efficiently.

The tourism industry is spending vast sums of money on developing new attractions, improving products, building hotels and investing in technology. The only way for the risk level to be kept to a minimum is through the adoption of a marketing philosophy which provides products related to the needs of consumers.

Marketing starts with the consumer and the market. The sovereignty of the consumer is clear. This has to be the correct strategy because it is the consumer who can dictate what he or she wants from tomorrow's tourism market place.

MARKETING ORIENTATION

The dynamic nature of business activity has led to many different sales and marketing opportunities in the tourism industry. The industry has thrown off many of its traditional attitudes towards the customer. This has come about through the realization of the importance of a marketing orientation. Five main areas can be identified.

(1) *It is a management orientation or philosophy.* The focus of company effort is placed on the consumer, and this then leads to an integrated structure and decision-making process within the company. There is a recognition that the conduct of the organization's business must revolve around the long-run interests of the customers it serves. This is an outward-looking orientation which requires responsive action in relation to external events.

(2) *It encourages exchange transactions.* These involve the attitudes and decisions of consumers in relation to their willingness to buy from producers or distributors. Marketers have to develop innovative methods to encourage exchange to take place. Creativity and the willingness to accept change are essential aspects of management thinking.

(3) *It involves long- and short-term planning.* This concerns strategic planning and tactical activity. The long-run success of a company requires the efficient use of resources and assets, while tactical action will be required to keep plans on course.

(4) *It requires efficient, cost-effective methods.* Marketing's principal concern within any company has to be the delivery of maximum satisfaction and value to the customer at acceptable or minimum cost to the company, so as to ensure long-term profit. However, in many companies the dilemma is that management are judged by short-run success in relation to sales and profit performance.

(5) *It requires the development of an integrated company environment.* The company's efforts and structure must be matched by the needs of the target customers. Everybody working for the company must participate in a total corporate, marketing environment with each division maximizing the satisfaction level of consumers. Integration is not just a smile or politeness. Barriers to serving the customer have to be destroyed. The onus is on the company to provide organizational structures which are responsive and will undergo change to suit customer needs.

References and further reading

Chartered Institute of Marketing (1984), Cookham, Berkshire.

Drucker, P. (1973) *Management Tasks, Responsibilities, Practices*, New York: Harper and Row.

Gilbert, D. C., and Bailey, N. (1990) 'The development of marketing: a compendium of historical approaches', *Quarterly Review of Marketing*, vol. 15, no. 2, pp. 6–13.

Keith, R.J. (1981) 'The marketing revolution', in Enis, B.M., and Cox, K.K. (eds), *Marketing Classics*, 4th edn, London: Allyn and Bacon.

Kotler, P. (1988) *Marketing Management: Analysis, Planning, Implementation and Control*, Englewood Cliffs, NJ: Prentice Hall.

Levitt, T. (1960) 'Marketing myopia', *Harvard Business Review*, July / August, pp. 45–56.

CHAPTER 21

Marketing management

OVERVIEW

In this chapter we show that the marketing management of tourism cannot ignore the primary characteristics which set tourism apart from other products. Tourism as a specialized service product creates a number of important considerations which need to be fully understood if a tourism enterprise or organization is to be successful. The management of tourism cannot be divorced from the management of service and quality. In addition, the need to undertake the tasks of research, analysis, product formulation, recommending price policies, promotion and distribution are of paramount significance for those involved in tourism marketing management.

We show that a great deal of management involves decisions based upon judgement, information and experience. All these areas rely on an understanding of the characteristics and issues which apply specifically to the market conditions for a product. When marketing any one of the different tourism products that we find in the market place, there are a number of tasks and characteristics which we need to be aware of. In this chapter we stress that the first factor which managers of tourism have to understand is the service management aspects related to the purchase of the tourism product.

THE SERVICE PRODUCT

With tourism, hospitality and leisure products we are dealing with a *service product* which has specific characteristics. These characteristics set the product apart from the more general goods sold in the market place. An understanding of the complexity of the service product concept is an essential prerequisite for successful marketing. The emphasis is more and more placed upon the service provider to develop a deeper understanding of the consumer benefits which are sought and the nature of the service delivery system itself. A starting point is an examination of the dimensions of the service product concept.

Products can be found to fall on a continuum between services and goods with most products being a combination of the two. A pure service would be consultancy or teaching, whereas a pure good would be a can of beans or clothing. Some products will have more of a service content than others, and if they are able to be placed on the left-hand side of the continuum shown in Figure 21.1, they may be termed service products.

Intangibility

This means that the product cannot be easily evaluated or demonstrated in advance of its purchase. For example, a travel agent cannot allow for the testing or sampling of the tourism product. On the other hand, an automobile or computer game can be tested prior to purchase, and clothing can be tried on. Greater difficulty is therefore faced by the marketers of tourism and hospitality products. Because of fixed time and space constraints they cannot easily demonstrate the benefits of the products they are selling. The problem for the tourism service marketer is overcome by the production of a range of printed literature, videos or other means of providing clues as to the type of product on offer.

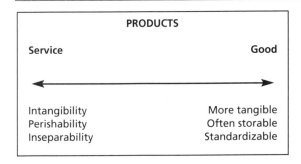

Fig 21.1 Services and goods continuum

Perishability

This means that, unlike goods, the service product cannot be stored for sale on a future occasion. For example, a hotel bed, an airline seat or a convention centre left empty represents revenue which can never be recouped. This indicates the high-risk nature of the tourism industry. Marketers in the tourism and hospitality industry have to devise complex pricing and promotion policies in an attempt to sell 'off-season' periods and create greater synchronization of staffing levels and supply with demand patterns. Weak demand is not the only problem because the industry is characterized by hotels, airlines, attractions, museums, galleries, etc., all of which have fixed capacity with a maximum upper demand constraint. In peak periods the industry often has difficulty in coping with demand and therefore charges premium prices or uses queuing, but in the low periods there is a need for greater marketing activity. The reaction to perishability is for marketers to try to smooth out demand curves by careful use of the marketing mix.

Inseparability

This means that the product is often consumed and produced simultaneously. Because there is less opportunity to precheck a tourism or hospitality product, it can vary in the standard of its service delivery. This is sometimes characterized by authors as *heterogeneity*. Variance occurs due to the inseparable nature of the product's delivery

when the customer is part of the production system. The simultaneous process of production and consumption can lead to situations where it is difficult to ensure the overall satisfaction of consumers. For example, peak loads of demand cannot always be forecast and may create dissatisfaction and secondary problems. There is also the ever-present danger of having one set of clients upset another. Whether on the aircraft, in the hotel or in the restaurant, it could be a clash of social values, noisiness, drunkenness, high spirits or a child crying. Staff may also have had personal problems or be feeling ill or tired, and this can affect their level of commitment to giving good service or resolving problems.

As the nature of the tourism service product is largely one of interpersonal relationships, where the performance level of staff is directly related to the satisfaction and experience of the consumer, there is a need for quality assurance programmes. Staff are emotional and changeable, and if a high content of the product is based upon interpersonal relationships between 'strangers', as guest and service provider, it is important to ensure that standardized service levels are adhered to. Quality is important as a basis of planning for competitive advantage.

TOURISM PRODUCTS AND RISK

Tourism products are important in relation to the type of marketing they require. Tourism has developed rapidly over the past few decades, led by a marketing thrust which has created diversity of supply, focused on important consumer segments and stimulated high levels of demand. Within this development marketing has often concentrated more on improving the product than on understanding the consumer and the complexity of his or her decision processes.

A major aspect of consumer behaviour, linked to the purchase of tourism products, is the notion of risk. Tourism products involve complex decision making because the purchase is of relatively high risk.

Economic risk

Economic risk involves the tourist in the problem of deciding whether or not the product offer is of good value. Consumers face economic or financial risk when they purchase tourism products which they are not sure will deliver desired benefits. Tourism involves the purchase of an expensive product which cannot easily be seen or sampled prior to consumption. This type of risk is heightened for those with low levels of disposable income, for whom the purchase represents a major expenditure.

Physical risk

Some overseas destinations can be perceived to be dangerous due to disease or crime, and some transport companies such as ferry or airline operators are thought to be safer than others. Some people have a fear of flying no matter what company they fly with.

Performance risk

The quality of different destinations or unknown hotel brands cannot be assessed in advance. This type of risk is associated with feelings that the product may not deliver the desired benefits. It is rarely possible for those who have had a bad holiday to make up for it by attempting to have another better holiday in the same year. Most consumers do not have the additional money or holiday entitlement to make good the holiday that went wrong. This heightens their awareness of the risk involved. One important performance risk for UK travellers is weather. The risk of poor weather in the UK is one reason why many people travel abroad.

Psychological risk

Status can be lost through visiting the wrong country or travelling with a company which has a poor image. This risk occurs when the potential customer feels that the purchase may not reflect the self-image he or she wishes to portray.

From a marketing point of view, these risks have to be minimized through product and promotion strategies. Creating and delivering information in brochures and leaflets which helps to convince the potential traveller of the reliability of the company will lessen the risk. By acquiring information the consumer builds up mental pictures and attitudes which create the expectation of positive benefits from the travel or destination experience.

It is also important for the quality of the product to be controlled, especially in relation to the process of service delivery.

PLANNING THE SERVICE ENCOUNTER

If we examine a systems perspective which identifies the linkage between the consumer's needs and the service delivery, we can be more aware of the management principles associated with service products. The linkage can be considered to fall within four levels (see Figure 21.2):

(1) Consumer wants/benefits sought.
(2) The service provision philosophy.
(3) The service product formulation.
(4) The service delivery system.

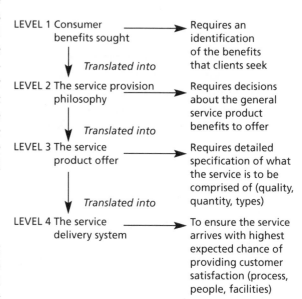

Fig 21.2 Planning the service encounter

QUALITY MANAGEMENT

We cannot adequately describe the management of tourism marketing without touching upon the growing emphasis on quality management. Quality has emerged as a major competitive component of service company strategies. There are three main reasons which may account for the increasing relevance of quality management:

- Companies need to find ways of creating differential advantage by having better service levels than their competitors.
- The increased level of consumerism and the greater media attention on quality have meant that companies have to be more responsive to quality issues.
- There has been a growing sophistication of consumer markets, with the non-price factors of image, product positioning and service delivery processes becoming more important.

We can classify the different approaches to quality management into two categories: the product attribute approach; and the consumer-orientated approach.

The product attribute approach is based upon trying to judge the product's conformance to standardized requirements which have been set by reference to what company managers think the failure point to be. Product attribute approaches rely on trying to control the company's products using an internal product perspective. This relies on an inward-looking, product-led approach.

It is therefore more appropriate to adopt a consumer-orientated approach, which recognizes that the holistic process of service delivery has to be controlled by taking into consideration the expectations and attitudes of tourism and hospitality clients. If the starting point for management is the understanding of how quality is judged by clients, then the perception processes of this judgement, as to whether a service is good or bad, can be managed. Gronroos is a leading author who has clarified this concept.

The Gronroos model

Gronroos (1982) has developed a model to explain what he calls the 'missing service quality concept'. The model shown in Figure 21.3 focuses mainly on the construct of image, which represents the point at which a gap can occur between expected service and perceived service. Gronroos makes us aware of the ways in which image is created from the aggregation of different aspects of technical and functional variables. By following his model of different inputs we are alerted to the fact that we should not reduce quality to a simplistic description, but should try to understand the full range of inputs. This is because to speak just of 'quality' gives the manager no indication what aspects of the product should be controlled.

Gronroos argues that the function and range of resources and activities include what customers are looking for, what they are evaluating, how service quality is perceived and in what way service quality is influenced. He defines the 'perceived quality' of the service as dependent upon two variables. These are 'experienced service' and 'perceived service', which collectively provide the outcome of the evaluation.

The analysis of Gronroos distinguishes between 'technical quality' and 'functional quality' as the components of the service image delivery:

- Technical quality refers to what the customer is actually receiving from the service. This is capable of objective measurement, as with tangible goods.
- Functional quality refers to how the technical elements of the service are transferred. We know that a customer in a restaurant will evaluate not only the quality of the food consumed, but also the way in which it was delivered (the style, manner and appearance of the staff or the ambience of the place itself). Figure 21.3 shows that the attitudes, behaviour and general service-mindedness of personnel can be influenced by management.

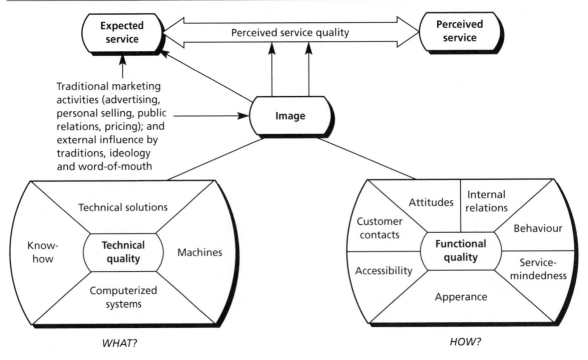

WHAT?   HOW?

Source: Gronroos (1982)

Fig 21.3 Managing the perceived service quality

The Parasuraman, Zeithaml and Berry model

Parasuraman, Zeithaml and Berry (1985) have also developed a model of service quality which claims that the consumer evaluates the quality of a service experience as the outcome of the difference (gap) between expected and perceived service (Figure 21.4). The model highlights the main requirements for a service provider delivering the expected service quality. From the model we can identify five gaps that may lead to unsuccessful service delivery. By understanding the flow of this model we believe it is possible to provide greater management control over tourist service relationships. This should lead to an improved realization of the key points at which the marketer can influence the satisfactions of the consumer.

(1) *Gap between consumer expectation and management perception.* This may result from a lack of understanding of what consumers expect in a service. An extensive study by Nightingale (1983) confirms this disparity, by revealing that what providers perceive as being important to consumers is often different from what consumers themselves actually expect.

(2) *Gap between management perception and service quality specifications.* This gap results when there is a discrepancy between what management perceives to be consumer expectations and the actual service quality specifications established. Management might not set quality standards or very clear ones, or they may be clear but unrealistic. Alternatively, the standards might be clear and realistic, but management might quite simply not be committed to enforcing them.

(3) *Gap between service quality specifications and service delivery.* Even where guidelines exist for performing a service well, service delivery may not be of the appropriate quality owing to poor employee performance. Indeed, the employee plays a pivotal role in determining the quality of a service.

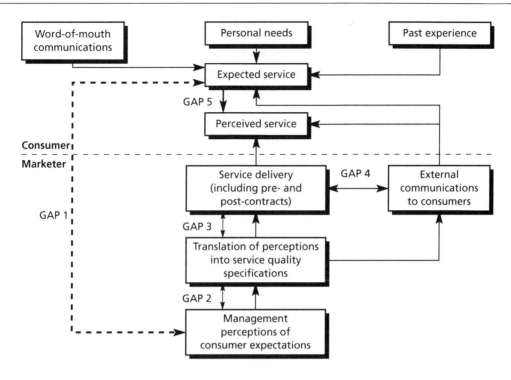

Source: Parasuraman *et al.* (1985)

Fig 21.4 Service quality model

(4) *Gap between service delivery and external communications.* Consumer expectations are affected by the promises made by the service provider's promotional message. Marketers must pay close attention to ensure consistency between the quality image portrayed in promotional activity and the actual quality offered.

(5) *Gap between perceived service and delivered service.* This gap results when one or more of the previous gaps occur.

The focus on perceptions and expectations provides a guideline for quality management intervention strategies. To this end, on examining the model proposed by Parasuraman, Zeithaml and Berry, we believe that it has two main strengths to recommend it:

● The model presents an entirely dyadic view of the marketing task of delivering service quality. The model alerts the marketer to consider the

perceptions of both parties (marketers and consumers) in the exchange process.

● Addressing the gaps in the model can serve as a logical basis for formulating strategies and tactics to ensure consistent experiences and expectations.

Providing promotional methods which lead staff to achieve high levels of customer care and service quality is becoming increasingly important. One poster targeted to staff read, 'Good enough is not good enough', which sets the standards and aims of the company personnel above the average. This type of inward marketing provides a means to change the general attitudes of staff towards quality.

MANAGEMENT TASKS

A marketing orientation relies on a series of management responsibilities. To clarify the situation,

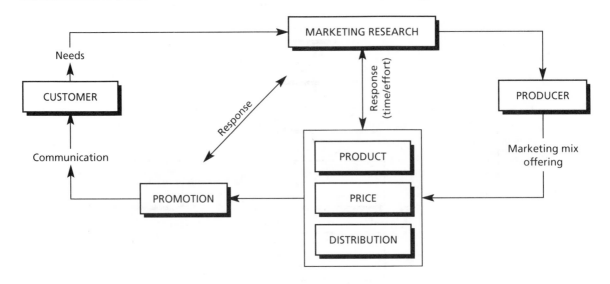

Fig 21.5 The marketing system

marketing can be seen to provide for a business-to-customer interface with responsibility for specific management tasks. These tasks are more clearly explained in Chapter 23 on the marketing mix. However, it should be quite clear that tourism companies without a proper commitment to a marketing orientation have little likelihood of effectively executing the marketing function.

The marketing function can therefore be treated as a system which is designed to be an interface with the customer. This system is outlined in Table 21.1 and Figure 21.5.

THE ADOPTION OF A MARKETING ORIENTATION

The tourist industry, due to the high service-based content of the product, has been characterized by custom and tradition. There has been a lack of vision in the industry, which has meant the demise of many companies in the last 20 years. The airline sector has probably been the most at risk. An acknowledgement of the degree of competition between airlines brought about

Table 21.1 The business-to-customer interface

Task	Marketing function
• Identifying the customers' needs for a service-based tourism product	• Marketing research
• Analysing marketing opportunities	• Analysis and selection of target markets (segments)
• Translating needs into products	• Product planning and formulation
• Determining the product's value to the customer at different seasonal periods	• Pricing policy
• Making the product available	• Distribution
• Informing and motivating the customer	• Promotion (selling and advertising)

CASE STUDY 21.1

The British Airways experience

British Airways (BA) offers a recent case study of success due to the adoption of a marketing orientation for the company. In the late 1970s BA suffered from considerable overmanning and a growth rate which was too slow. The management of the time adopted a price reduction strategy to achieve growth, but this did not achieve the desired results. The problems for BA were identified as poor management and structure. There were also external pressures as the company became caught up in the OPEC oil crisis, which culminated in a doubling of the price of kerosene and a damping of world trade. The growth that BA had expected was not realized.

The change at BA commenced with the key appointment of Colin Marshall, whose previous success at Avis had been built on an understanding of the importance of service and marketing. On one day in 1983, 60 of the senior managers were dispensed with and the company set about changing the workforce philosophy to one of believing in customer care. After one of the largest and fastest turnarounds from loss to profit by a large commercial concern, the company stated that its success was due to its marketing orientation. The company reported (*Marketing*, May 1985) that 'until reorganization British Airways had not been truly marketing led. Even though it had a marketing department, it had been operations led. The key change was to ensure operations delivered what the marketing department requested due to an identification of consumer needs.' It was explained that the overall success could be attributed to three main thrusts: satisfying customer requirements; becoming more people orientated; and creating overall long-term strategies.

This is not to say that BA always got it right. In 1983 the company lost a great deal of its share of the domestic market to British Midland. BA had identified that the business market was influenced by the technical aspects of punctuality, access to business centres and courtesy. However, because it did not serve an adequate meal, the consumer discriminated against the company. BA was forced to develop the super shuttle concept, which included a free breakfast.

CASE STUDY 21.2

The SAS experience

The Scandinavian Airline System (SAS) is another example of a company which recovered its position through properly planned, market-orientated leadership. SAS was losing money when, in 1980, Jan Carlzon took over as its new president. Carlzon introduced a consumer orientation into the company, which led to an emphasis on research, improvements of service and new values to provide the company with a new direction. The changes produced an improved reputation for SAS and contributed to its gradual recovery. Carlzon's vision and leadership, in redefining the focus of the company on to the satisfaction of the consumer, led to a series of changes which culminated in higher profits.

the tourism industry's earliest transformation to a marketing orientation (see Case Studies 21.1 and 21.2).

It might seem a simple change to listen to customers and provide what they say they want. But if we examine the marketing of the most important piece of leisure equipment today, this is not occurring. If you want to rent a television or have one repaired, suppliers are notoriously inflexible in working to their own delivery and work schedules. This leads to consumers having to take time off work, cancel social arrangements or reorganize the children's travel to or from school. In 1989 Radio Rentals finally recognized the advantage of offering to install or repair televisions and a range of other equipment at a time when it was convenient to the consumer, including various times at weekends or evenings. As installations only take minutes, and since repairs more often than not involve the replacement of a complete circuit board or part, the cost in time to the company was not excessive. On the other hand, the company was able to build customer loyalty and stabilize the number of accounts it held.

From the previous pages you should now be aware that tourism marketing involves a number of special characteristics:

- Marketing is a philosophy with the overriding value that the decision-making process of any company has to be led by the consumer's needs, the market place and the company's assets and resources.
- Successful marketing requires a special organization structure which believes in integrating the principles of consumer orientation throughout the company.
- It also requires innovative methods of thinking and planning so that new ideas are generated to take advantage of opportunities or to improve existing methods of marketing.

CRITICISMS OF THE MARKETING CONCEPT

As we move into the twenty-first century there is a growing concern for business policies which lead to sustainability of the earth's resources. The new values emerging are placing pressure on the underlying concepts of marketing. This is creating a major debate about the ethical standpoint of marketing. Some of the most significant criticisms are considered in this section.

Disregard of the environment and non-consumers

The marketing concept can lead to tunnel vision, focusing on the potential consumers of the product and not on the wider society. Other groups, such as the host population of a country, can be adversely affected by insensitive tourism marketing policies. In addition, pollution and damage as a by-product of tourism activities is an environmental and social cost carried by the whole of society and not simply by the company's consumers. Tour operators have continuously developed new areas, expanded successful resorts and created promotional campaigns without due regard to the cost of impacts on the area and local population.

Another type of marketing pollution is the overabundance of promotional material, which itself makes a home or overseas destination less attractive. There are roadside poster sites, advertisements on taxi cabs, messages painted on buildings, and leaflets which are given away and then discarded, all of which create invasive pollution. There is a trend to produce advertisements which aim to shock, and there are others which offend, such as those for sex-talk telephone numbers. The overall effect of these trends is to lead the general public to mistrust marketing.

Overemphasis on profitable products

The marketing concept dictates that products can only be offered to the market place when they are profitable. This has culminated in the axing of bus and train transport routes and the disregard of low-spending individuals. Where a want exists and the marketing opportunity cannot deliver the required profit return, the product is seldom developed. The market-based system is guided by self-interest and profit motivation, and consumer preferences are only accounted for if there is an ability to pay. These values are represented by a lack of concern for those who cannot afford a holiday, or for the supply of amenities to cater for those who are disadvantaged or handicapped. Facilities for blind, infirm and handicapped people are of low priority in resort and accommodation planning.

Invasion of privacy

The power of modern computers allows companies to capture a complete range of personal information for use in targeting direct mail campaigns. As companies begin to spend more on research, there is also the problem of a greater use of telephone and high street interviews. And research is not confined to the business world because there are an increasing number of projects carried out in schools and colleges. A consequence of the amount of interview requests is the growing refusal by many members of the public to take part in any form of research.

Waste of resources on tourism marketing

Marketing is seen as wasteful due to the large amounts of money spent on promoting products. The money given over to tourism promotion is often associated with convincing consumers to buy products which it is believed they do not want. It is believed that the most disadvantaged tourist consumers are the ones most likely to be influenced by high expenditure on tourism marketing.

The levels of marketing expenditure are quite often blamed for changing consumer attitudes and bringing about a materialistic society in which status is derived from the number and type of destinations we visit, or leisure activities we undertake, rather than from how good we are as members of society.

A SOCIETAL MARKETING APPROACH

It has been argued that the pressures affecting the image of marketing need to be considered. This has culminated in the movement towards a societal concept of marketing which stresses the enhancement of the needs of society as well as the consumer. We believe that this is an academic exercise, since definitions have to evolve out of business practice rather than from academic debate. Some companies such as brewers and distillers are creating campaigns to warn people of the excesses of drinking, but it is questionable whether they are worried as much about the health of the customer as about the legislation which could affect their operations.

While some companies may pay lip service to a societal concept for public relations purposes, in a competitive situation many of the problems related to tourism, and its marketing, will continue. It is also important to recognize that consumers are now better educated and might be considered competent enough to select products which are not creating undue problems for society. Moreover, if companies or their products do create problems, there are articulate pressure groups and government legislation available for consumer and environmental protection.

References and further reading

Dann, G.M.S. (1981) 'Tourist motivation: an appraisal', *Annals of Tourism Research*, vol. 8, no. 2, pp. 187–219.

Gilbert, D.C. (1989) 'Tourism marketing: its emergence and

establishment', in Cooper, C. (ed.), *Progress in Tourism, Recreation and Hospitality Management*, Vol. 1, London: Belhaven.

Gilbert, D.C. (1991) 'An examination of the consumer behaviour process related to tourism', in Cooper, C. (ed.), *Progress in Tourism, Recreation and Hospitality Management*, Vol. 3, London: Belhaven.

Gilbert, D.C., and Joshi, I. (1992) 'Quality management and the tourism and hospitality industry', in Cooper, C., and Lockwood, A. (eds), *Progress in Tourism, Recreation and Hospitality Management*, Vol. 4, London: Belhaven.

Gronroos, C. (1982) *Strategic Management and Marketing in the Service Sector*, Helsinki: Swedish School of Economics and Business Administration (in US published by Marketing Science Institute, Cambridge, Mass.)

Nightingale, M. (1983) 'Determination and control of quality standards in hospitality services', unpublished M.Phil. thesis, University of Surrey.

Parasuraman, A., Zeithaml, V.A., and Berry, L.L. (1985) 'A conceptual model of service quality and its implications for future research', *Journal of Marketing*, vol. 49, no. 4, pp. 41–50.

CHAPTER 22

Marketing planning

OVERVIEW

In this chapter we outline an approach to marketing planning in tourism. We suggest that the marketing plan is a structured guide to action. As such, it acts as a systematic method of data collection, objective setting and logical analysis of the most appropriate direction for the organization, destination or product. If a marketing plan is to be accepted by all concerned then the compilation of the plan has to involve all levels of personnel. This is because marketing plans require company-wide commitment if they are to be successful.

The plan has to reflect the dynamic nature of the market place, and as such the plan needs to be thought of as a loose-leaf binder rather than as a tablet of stone. This means that the plan acts as a working document which can be updated to take into account opportunities or problem situations.

WHAT IS MARKETING PLANNING?

We all have to plan if we are to make a success of our lives. Very few Olympic medallists could be successful without a planned programme of training and events leading up to their Olympic finals and achievements. Whether it is for examinations, sports events, going on holiday or organizing a party, the use of planning leads to a greater certainty that the event will be a success. Without the right approach, and a sensible plan, the alternative courses of action will seldom have been considered, and consequently there is the likelihood that an individual, company or organization will not function as well as it could.

Planning is the most important activity of marketing management. It should provide a common structure and focus for all of the company's management activities. It is therefore essential for us to understand planning in its context as the key function of management.

The tourism industry provides for a combination of different products and activities, which range from the small taxi firm and guest house to the largest airline or hotel group. The concepts of change and survival are as important to the small business as they are to a destination, major international hotel or airline company. The fact that change will occur and with increasing speed is the most predictable aspect of contemporary business life. It would therefore seem sensible to try to become familiar with the underlying trends and forces of change which impinge upon tourism business activities. This enables the management of change towards desired objectives rather than being driven blindly before the tide of market forces. This is particularly the case in tourism, where the rapidly changing market place sometimes deludes companies into taking a short-term, rather than a long-term view.

The long-term survival of any company is dependent upon how well the business relates to its environment. This relies on devising forward plans of where a company, destination or product would be best placed for the future.

- The plan therefore requires control over the changes that have to be made.
- It needs to allow for the exploitation of any short-term advantages.
- It has to promote the use of analysis and reason as part of planning procedure.

A range of problems can happen if marketing planning is ignored. For a destination this could involve any of the following:

- Failure to take advantage of potential growth markets and new marketing opportunities.
- Lack of maintenance of demand from a spread of markets, and erosion of market share due to the actions of competitors.
- Demand problems in low-season periods.
- Low level of awareness of the destination's product offering.
- Poor image of the destination.
- Lack of support for co-operative marketing initiatives.
- Poor or inadequate tourism information services.
- Decline in quality levels below acceptable limits.
- Difficulty in attracting intermediaries to market or package holidays.
- Disillusionment and lack of motivation of employees.

We can therefore see that there are many problems which face tourism organizations. While planning cannot guarantee success, it can make the organization less vulnerable to market forces. Perhaps the demise of Laker Airways, Braniff Airways, Courtline and the International Leisure Group could have been avoided if more attention had been given to their planning activities, especially in relation to their cash flow, fixed cost and expansion attributes. The early no-frills price advantage of Sir Freddie Laker's operation, the image of Braniff with Gucci-designed uniforms, and the cheap price policy of the International Leisure Group provided excellent market positions for the products, yet the weakness of financial planning played a major part in each company's downfall.

Companies or destinations which rely on *ad hoc* initiatives or fail to manage their future will find that their future has been managed for them. Each company will adopt a different approach to the task of planning based upon the way senior executives see the purpose of marketing plans. The values of any company fall somewhere along a continuum which begins at *wait and see*, moves through the next set of values to *prepare and predict*, and finally ends with companies who want to *make it happen*. A company will benefit more from a future that is made to happen by providing clear direction for the workforce and other company resources.

PURPOSES OF THE MARKETING PLAN

The marketing plan is normally a short-term plan which will direct the company for one to three years. Normally, a five-year plan will be a strategic plan, which is more general and less detailed than a marketing plan.

The strategic plan will concern itself more with external environmental influences and opportunities, and less with the detail of company marketing activities. Strategic plans are normally either medium or long term, and marketing plans are short or medium term.

The marketing plan and its compilation are able to provide a number of benefits for a company. The purposes of creating a marketing plan involve the achievement of a whole range of management benefits:

- To provide clear direction to the marketing operation based upon a systematic, written approach to planning and action. The planning system allows a written mission statement and set of objectives to be established, which can be transmitted to the workforce. This provides a sense of leadership and allows the workforce to feel that their own efforts are essential to the achievement of desired results.
- To co-ordinate the resources of the company. This eliminates confusion and misunderstanding in order to achieve maximum co-operation. Tasks and responsibilities can be set which clarify the direction and objectives of the company. To ensure there is a united effort, recommendations have to be presented in such a way that they can be fully understood at all

company levels. The plan then acts as a master guide which will underpin all endeavour and decision making. The plan should lead to greater employee cohesion and make everyone feel part of a team in which each individual believes he or she can make a valuable contribution.

- To set targets against which progress can be measured. Quantified targets for volume of clients or revenue provide the focus for individual, departmental or company performance. Some companies will set targets at achievable levels, whereas others will set targets at a higher than expected level in order to stretch the employees to gain better results.
- To minimize risk through analysis of the internal and external environment. The planning procedure allows managers to identify areas of strength and weakness so that the first can be exploited and the second surmounted. Additionally, threats and opportunities can be assessed.
- To examine the various ways of targeting to different market segments. This allows for different marketing mix strategies to be appraised prior to their implementation.
- To provide a record of the company's marketing policies and plans. This allows managers to check on what has been attempted in the past and to evaluate the effectiveness of previous programmes. It also provides continuity and a source of reference for new managers joining the company.
- To think about the long-term business objectives so that the company can be in the best position to achieve its future aims. This allows management to develop continuity of thought and action from one year to the next.

We know that company objectives should be based upon relevant market-centred opportunities. It is the responsibility of tourism marketers to identify these opportunities and to devise a system of planning which may lead to their exploitation.

SUCCESSFUL PLANNING

Most textbooks suggest that planning involves following a series of simple steps. However, the true art of planning is to understand both the human aspects and the procedural necessities involved. A poor planning experience may be a function of one or more of the following:

- A major problem, and one which is difficult to resolve, is if there is weak support for the plan from the chief executive and other senior people.
- The system of planning which is adopted may not suit the company. Within the company there is often the separation of different planning functions from each other, leading to a lack of integration. Therefore the system often has to be designed to match the company and to achieve harmony between groups.
- The planning system is often blamed when the weakness is actually poor planning and management. Sometimes there is confusion over data or planning terms. The requirement is for a plan to be compiled which clarifies times and responsibilities for different actions and meetings.
- Unexpected environmental changes may have adverse effects on the company's performance. Planning is then often blamed for not having incorporated such a scenario. In tourism, the 1990/1991 Gulf Crisis is a classic example.
- The values of the management team will imply different acceptance levels of the plan, and will ultimately determine its success or failure. There is often hostility towards plans because people feel they have not been involved in the planning process. This often occurs when the planning is left solely to a planner, or when it becomes an annual ritual.
- Problems occur when there is an overabundance of information which has to be filtered for its relevance. Too much detail in the early stages can produce 'paralysis analysis'.

It is distressing that travel companies which have recognized the need for a more structured approach to planning, and subsequently have adopted the formalized procedures found in the literature, seldom enjoy the advantages claimed for embarking on planning. In fact, it is often planning itself which is brought into disrepute when it fails to achieve the desired changes within a company.

The problems faced in marketing planning have led to a growing body of literature which indicates that companies should do what they are good at, rather than embarking upon higher-level planning exercises. We believe this is a retrograde step: companies should attempt to take the most logical direction and not be hampered by internal failings of the human resource aspects of implementation, lack of planning expertise or disregard of the involvement of others in the planning process.

An understanding of the social aspects of the company is a prerequisite for successful planning. It is necessary for those involved in planning to recognize the need for involvement of all departments in the company in the formulation of the plan. This means that personnel are more likely to be motivated towards its successful implementation. Moreover, key personnel bring valuable knowledge and expertise to marketing plan formulation. It is also important to understand that most accomplishments in tourism, and in service industries in general, are made through people. The control of schedules, budgets, monitoring performance or corrective decisions can take place only with people. Each employee who has responsibility requires clear objectives against which he or she can judge what tactical action needs to be carried out.

It is important to ensure that plans are not prepared within the vacuum of one department or by a marketing team which believes it is an élite. Structured management meetings can offer a setting where deliberation, responsibility and authority are shared by all. This precludes dogmatic assertions about the particular methods of preparing and organizing marketing planning.

The marketing planning system offers a structured approach to organizing and co-ordinating the efforts and activities of those involved in deciding the future of an organization. However, there is no one right system for any particular tourism company, since companies differ in size and diversity of operations, the values of the senior management and the expertise of those involved in the planning exercise.

STRUCTURE OF THE MARKETING PLAN

The construction of the marketing plan is characterized by a range of headings which have been developed by different theorists. Some authors offer a list of sections: the first headed 'SWOT issues' or 'situational analysis', the second headed 'statement of objectives and goals' or 'setting objectives', the third called 'strategy or marketing programming' and the last 'monitoring' or 'control'. We prefer to use different stages which are more easily understood by managers and students:

- What is it we want?
- Where are we now?
- Where do we want to go?
- How do we get there?
- Where did we get to?

These are represented in Figure 22.1.

In reading the model it is important to realize that the system is not always the linear progression it appears. Quite often the process needs to involve an interplay between the various stages with the flexibility to move backwards as well as forwards. We should also understand that refinement of the plan takes place as understanding of the interconnections improves. We should not presume that perfection will be achieved until a number of drafts have been completed.

The model of marketing planning can be described as involving six stages:

(1) Corporate mission and goals.
(2) External and internal audit.
(3) Business situation analysis.
(4) Creating the objectives.
(5) Providing an effective marketing mix strategy.
(6) Monitoring the plan.

Corporate mission and goals

It is important to understand what is expected of the plan from the long-term goals set at corporate level. The goals may be based upon the values and objectives of the key shareholders, board directors or senior managers. In some situations, goals are set only after the establishment and evaluation of marketing programmes. This is a parochial, programme-led method of planning, where management does not attempt to meet higher-level corporate goals within the planning process because managers are prepared to settle for what they believe will work. A company with this approach

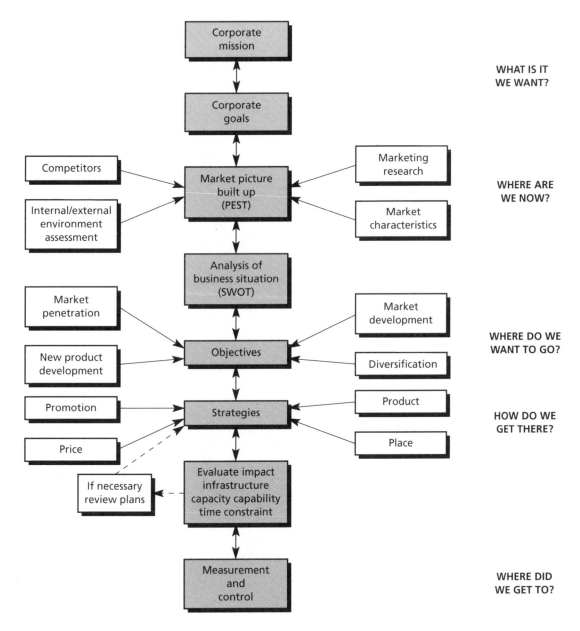

WHAT IS IT WE WANT?

WHERE ARE WE NOW?

WHERE DO WE WANT TO GO?

HOW DO WE GET THERE?

WHERE DID WE GET TO?

Fig 22.1 A model of marketing planning

will not investigate as broad a range of strategies as a company which is driven to ensure consistency with the overall corporate strategy and goals.

The most effective form of planning creates a balance between corporate direction and different levels of employee involvement (see Figure 22.1). If goals are dictated to employees, there is very little sense of ownership of the plan and a corresponding lack of motivation. Goals can be set in a functional, top-down approach or as a negotiation of goals through the combination of bottom-up and top-down processes.

The mission statement is a guide for employees to know what the purpose of the company is. The mission statement acts as a confirmation of what business the company is in from a consumer viewpoint. It then represents the overriding goal of the company or organization. In the 1991/92 British Tourist Authority marketing plan the mission statement is 'to strengthen the performance of Britain's tourist industry in international markets by encouraging the improvement and provision of tourist amenities and facilities in Britain'.

External and internal audit

It is necessary to gather enough relevant information about the external and internal company environment to be able to construct a business and market picture of current and future pressure and trends. One important part of marketing planning is knowing what to analyse. Executives have to be careful that they do not have too limited a view of the environment. Having checklists of necessary information is one way to prevent companies scanning the environment based upon what they intend to do, rather than in relation to what they could or should do.

The information collected should, at the very least, form the basis of a PEST investigation. PEST analysis is an examination of the political, economic, social and technological changes which may affect the company and the market. Information gathering is part of an internal and external audit which should collect a range of information, as detailed below.

Business/economic environment

- *Economic* – inflation, unemployment, fuel costs, exchange rates, average salaries.
- *Political* – taxation, duty, regulation, tourism policies, constraints on local authorities.
- *Social* – demographics, holiday/leisure-time entitlement, values (consumerism), lifestyle, male/female role changes, delay of first child, education, workforce changes.
- *Technology* – innovations, new systems (reservations, yield management), home technology, electronic fund transfer.
- *Companies* – level of investment, takeovers, promotion expenditures, redundancies, profits.

Market environment

- *Total market* – size, growth, trends, value, industry structure, barriers to entry, extent of under- or overcapacity of supply, marketing methods.
- *Product development* – trends, new product types, service enhancements.
- Price – levels, range, terms, practices.
- *Distribution* – patterns, trade structure, policies.
- *Promotion* – expenditure, types, communication messages.

The above information should be gathered on the basis of how it affects the company.

Business situation analysis

Once sufficient information has been collected, there is the need to carry out an analysis of the business situation, in particular the major strengths, weaknesses, opportunities and threats facing the company. This is the so-called SWOT analysis. There is also the need to check these against the information provided from PEST analysis.

The systematic analysis carried out at this stage provides for the formulation of a number of assumptions about past performance, future conditions, product opportunities, resources and service priorities, which all lead to a range of strategic options for an organization in the tourism industry.

At this stage of planning, it is possible to circulate the assumptions and forecasts to different company divisions. These should be offered as a range of alternatives. For example, if you have assumed the market will grow at X% and this will create £Y with a specific strategy, then it is also wise to create alternative scenarios. You should estimate sales at lower and higher rates than expected, so that the impact on profits can be assessed. For example, a rate of growth of $X + 2$% may create a profit of $1.3 \times £Y$, or alternatively $X - 2$% gives $0.5 \times £Y$.

Managers can then involve their team in discussions about the relevance of the material created from the foregoing environmental scanning stage. The involvement of different departments will help reduce resistance to future changes or tasks. Continuous concern about the human aspects of planning can increase the chances of the plan's success. The planner or planning team should be aware that they are only a technical service to a wider team. However, it is important not to make the system too open or the company will be in danger of creating anarchy. On the other hand, the system should not be too closed as this leads to bureaucracy.

One vital behavioural consideration in any plan which affects all aspects of the company is that it should not clash with the company culture. Such a clash can be overcome by ensuring that staff values are incorporated into various stages of the planning cycle. The involvement of the full range of staff leads to a situation where the company culture values of staff are reflected in the 'bottom-up' comments. This helps to ensure that the plan is created as part of a process which makes it compatible with the company culture.

It is clear that companies have to plan for the involvement level of staff as well as for the market. Figure 22.2 provides one approach to dealing with marketing planning involvement levels.

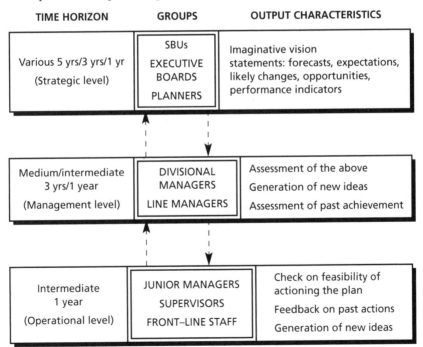

TIME HORIZON	GROUPS	OUTPUT CHARACTERISTICS
Various 5 yrs/3 yrs/1 yr (Strategic level)	SBUs EXECUTIVE BOARDS PLANNERS	Imaginative vision statements: forecasts, expectations, likely changes, opportunities, performance indicators
Medium/intermediate 3 yrs/1 year (Management level)	DIVISIONAL MANAGERS LINE MANAGERS	Assessment of the above Generation of new ideas Assessment of past achievement
Intermediate 1 year (Operational level)	JUNIOR MANAGERS SUPERVISORS FRONT–LINE STAFF	Check on feasibility of actioning the plan Feedback on past actions Generation of new ideas

Note: SBU refers to 'Strategic Business Unit'.

Fig 22.2 Involvement levels for marketing planning

One other important factor when including a cross-section of people in planning is their capability to hinder or help the plan. Within any company or organization, managers' competence to plan will be based upon how busy they are, their preoccupation with other business, their career goals, their experience and their ability to think analytically. These attributes are linked to other managers' values and the cultural climate within the company, which may be more or less responsive to change and adaptation through adherence to the planning system.

Creating the objectives

Objectives are a combination of what is expected of the company by its shareholders or directors, and an evaluation of the options emerging out of the first three stages of the planning process. The objectives should emerge as the most logical course of action that the company should embark upon given the analysis which has occurred in the preceding stages.

We also have to ensure that the objectives are not only volume related and financial but also concerned with marketing. One danger in planning is that large leisure groups or major hotel chains tend to set financial objectives stated in terms of growth rate in earnings per share, return on equity or investment and so on, and to ignore marketing objectives such as the selection of specific segments as target markets and the improvement of products, brand image or consumer awareness. Objectives should also include the expected market share achievements because this performance may only be realistic if certain budgets are made available.

The objective inputs of Figure 22.1 are based upon growth strategies whereby a company is attempting to expand. Companies will normally want to attack the market share of others by penetrating the market to increase their own share. Larger organizations or companies will try to develop markets by selling the benefits of, say, self-catering holidays to those who take hotel holidays. Companies may also develop their markets by expanding internationally, as the Ibis

hotel group has done. Objectives may also include new product development or diversification. Tourism companies often develop new destinations or new air routes, which need to be planned as new product development. Diversification has occurred where hotel companies have created contract catering operations and vice versa. There has also been the diversification of airline companies into hotel operations.

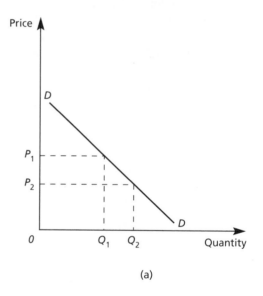

(a)

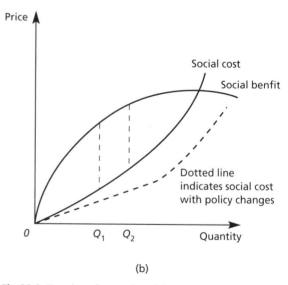

(b)

Fig 22.3 Tourism demand problems

Providing an effective marketing mix strategy

The success of the plan relies on creating the right marketing mix strategies for achieving the objectives (see Chapter 23 for a clear explanation of the different aspects of the marketing mix). The use of the marketing mix involves balancing the elements of the mix to achieve the highest expected probability of meeting the plan's objectives. However, mix strategies have to be checked to ensure they are acceptable. For example, if the strategy is for expansion of a destination, an impact or environmental analysis will have to be considered. Figure 22.3 shows a situation where there is no extra benefit in expanding tourist numbers, since the costs increase at the same rate as the benefits.

Figure 22.3(a) shows the demand for a tourism destination. If the price is reduced from P_1 to P_2 then the demand for the area increases from Q_1 to Q_2. Tourism destinations can reduce the average price of visits through government policies such as allowing more charter arrivals or reducing tourist taxes. If the positions of Figure 22.3(a) are examined against the social cost and benefit curves in Figure 22.3(b), it will be seen that position Q_2 is no better than position Q_1 as the social costs have increased at a rate which cancels out the increase in social benefits. The result is that the destination is no better off socially after an increase in arrivals, and may have to check other criteria before it agrees to expansion policies.

If it is found that there are no problems with the objectives, and the plan is to be adopted, there has to be some assessment of whether the objectives can be achieved within specific time constraints. Competitors may be able to develop more quickly, or the company may find it too difficult to change in a short period of time. The ability to change is often related to the availability of resources. It is necessary to question whether the resources available are sufficient to achieve the objectives (budgets, personnel, technology, existing hotels, aircraft or built facilities). If after evaluation it is decided that the strategy is unacceptable, there is a need to review and revise the plan's objectives.

Agreeing the marketing mix strategy has to be linked to laying down task-related programmes which will allocate budgets and create responsibilities and timings for the plan's implementation. There is always a need to link planning with budgeting, which will allow for the adoption and execution of an effective marketing mix strategy to achieve the objectives of the plan.

Monitoring the plan

There should be a means of monitoring the achievements of the plan so that tactical action can be taken either to get the plan back on course or to take advantage of new opportunities. There is therefore the need to provide assessment and measurement methods which will monitor progress towards the achievement of the plan's overall objectives. There is also the need to know what deviations from the initial objectives are either acceptable or unacceptable. This will allow for the review and amendment of the plan on a continuous basis.

The tourism and hospitality industry has invested in reservation systems which provide for a continuous flow of financial and booking pattern data. This has allowed for the modelling of different performance indicators. These can include forecasts of likely load factors or occupancy levels as well as assessment of the effectiveness of regional or national sales promotion, price changes and sales representative campaigns.

CHAPTER 23

Marketing mix

OVERVIEW

Anyone who buys a tourism product has probably been influenced by a promotion campaign, assessed the product offer, considered whether he or she is willing to pay the price, and finally thought about how easy it would be to buy it. Each of these aspects of purchase are carefully planned by tourism marketers in an attempt to convince you to buy their products. They are the basic ingredients of the marketing mix, which we will consider in this chapter.

In fact, a great deal of this book could have been written on the marketing mix, as it involves a whole range of different topic areas. Each of the areas which make up the marketing mix involves a complex set of management decisions which have to take into account both the individual mix strategy and the combined effect of the whole mix on the target market groups. At the same time, the distinctive nature of tourism as an activity has to be considered when making these decisions. This chapter will therefore provide the most important considerations for planning the tourism marketing mix.

In this chapter we will also show that, in the competitive tourism market place, a business can be successful only if its complete marketing mix offer matches what the consumer wants. To be truly successful the offer has to be as good as, but preferably better than, that of the competition. The marketing mix is planned and co-ordinated by marketers, so the onus is on them to control the inputs in such a way that the overall effect maximizes the demand and satisfaction of the consumer.

WHAT IS THE MARKETING MIX?

Kotler indicates that the marketing mix is one of the key concepts in modern marketing theory. He defines the marketing mix as 'the set of marketing tools that the firm uses to pursue its marketing objectives in the target market' (1988, p. 71).

It is customary to accept that the marketing mix is made up of the four Ps: product, price, promotion and place (distribution). However, there are alternative approaches where authors stress the need for an expansion of these four classic ingredients. This is an interesting development because the four Ps were provided by McCarthy (1978) as an abridged version of a much wider spectrum of what were termed 'marketing ingredients'. McCarthy based his four Ps upon a whole range of marketing ingredients offered much earlier by Borden (1965).

Target market

The fundamental starting point for the creation of a successful marketing mix strategy is to ensure that the target market is clearly defined. While the target market is not part of the mix, its role in dictating the different ways in which the mix is used makes it indistinguishable from the concept and of paramount importance.

The target market is the focus for all marketing mix activity. A market for a product is made up of actual and potential consumers. This total available group of consumers will be analysed and a decision will be made as to segments or subgroups who will be targeted. The segments will probably have been identified as part of the marketing planning process and will have been specified at the time when the objectives were set (see Case Study 23.1).

CASE STUDY 23.1

Benefits of targeting

- Fuller understanding of the unique characteristics and needs of the group to be satisfied. The target market acts as a reference point for marketing decisions, especially as to how the marketing mix should be planned. This should lead to greater effectiveness for the mix, which in turn provides for the success of the programme.
- Better understanding of who your competitors are, because it is possible to detect those who have made a similar selection of target markets. If a company does not clarify the markets it wishes to target, it may treat every other company in its sector as an equal competitor. If main competitors are identified, their marketing efforts can be more closely followed.
- Better understanding of changes and developments in the needs of the target market. Awareness is heightened by the focus upon the target group's actions and reactions to slightly different forms of the marketing mix.

For both the international and the domestic tourist, the holiday visitor and the recreationalist, target markets can be based upon a number of factors:

- Socioeconomic groups.
- Geographic location.
- Age.
- Gender.
- Income levels.
- Visitor type.
- Benefits sought.
- Purchase behaviour.
- Attitudes.

Fig 23.1 **The marketing mix**

The target market acts as the means of tailoring the mix so that targeted customers will judge it to be superior to that of the competition. Segmentation and target marketing are central to marketing because different customer groups should dictate the search for the correct marketing mix strategy.

Product

The effectiveness of planning the marketing mix depends as much on the ability to select the right target market as on devising a product which will generate high levels of satisfaction. The tourist has to believe that the product offers added value in order for it to be successful.

Decisions regarding the formulation of product involve the following factors.

Service

Service is concerned with creating the level of services to be offered. For a hotel, a tour operator, a restaurant or an airline, how much of the service should the client be expected to perform and how much should be provided by staff? For example, self-service of food and the carrying of hand luggage by the customer are now thought to be acceptable and at times desirable by clients. Tea- and coffee-making facilities in hotel rooms are important if the provision of room service is planned to commence at breakfast time. Service provision for air travellers now satisfies communication needs, with some airlines offering an improved business product with in-flight telephone, telex and access to a personal computer. These developments are indicative of the relentless quest for cost-effective improvements to the service content of the tourism product.

Quality

Quality involves deciding on quality standards and implementing a method of assurance on the performance level of staff and facilities. The management of quality is becoming an increasingly important management function. It is important to create a reputation for the good quality of the product and service offered as this provides a positive image for the company or organization. A reputation for good quality is a major advantage because the perception of risk for many tourism consumers is high. Tourism service providers are more likely to be successful if they can be depended upon to deliver higher-quality service levels than their competitors. With this in mind, Swissair aims for at least 96 per cent of its passengers to rate the quality of its service as good or superior, otherwise it will take remedial action.

Range

It is necessary to decide how different products will fit into the overall range of the company products offered to the market place. A tour operator has to decide whether to include five-star or two-star hotels in its range of offerings, or if it should operate to traditional or newly emerging destinations. The range of offers and how each product fits into the product mix are important considerations.

Brand name

A brand name which is well known and associated with high satisfaction levels provides an improved image and added value to the product. This can also lead to consumers insisting on the product by brand name and being less price sensitive. Brand names can be family brands where each of the company's products adopts the same brand name, such as the recent Forte Hotel branding exercise. Alternatively, they can be individual brand names where each product is branded differently. For example, British Airways has individual brand names within its tour operation businesses, with its long-haul and medium- and budget-priced offerings each having individual brand names.

The individual brand name approach allows the company to search for the most appropriate brand name. Its weakness is that the promotional budget for each brand has to be sufficiently large to support that brand. With family brands there is a spin-off effect for each of the brands from the expenditure on any one brand. Conversely, if one of the family brands obtains poor publicity, because of association, there will be damage to the other brands. For family branding, careful attention has to given to the quality control of the products. One other benefit of family branding is that each product brand performance (PBF) can be measured against the overall family brand performance (FBF). When FBF is divided by PBF and shows an increase over time, without good reason, it may mean that the product brand needs modification, revitalization or a detailed review.

With individual branding a company is able to position brands and products at the cheaper (bottom) end of the market without the brand damaging the image of the rest of the company's brands. In addition, if there is bad publicity for one of the company's brands, the other company brands do not necessarily suffer.

Features and benefits

We know that consumers buy products for the benefits they deliver. It therefore makes sense to include different features in the product which will help to differentiate it from competitors. Adding in the right features creates a higher probability that a purchase will occur.

Tourism is normally associated with the risk of delayed flights, exchange rate fluctuations or little snow for skiing holidays. The risk of flight delay or inadequate snow cover on ski slopes can be insured against by the operator, which passes on only a small premium to its clients in the price of

the trip. The early buying forward of currency or aircraft fuel will allow a company to offer the guarantee of no increase in a quoted price.

Arranging a contract with car parks near to airports in off-season periods can allow a company to offer the car-parking service free to its clients. The cost is passed on to each client as a fraction of the true cost of the service because the arrangement allows the car park to acquire business at a difficult time. Features such as free car hire, pick-up at the airport, fast checkouts, study bedrooms, and free tickets to tourism attractions or the theatre are all added benefits which can be planned into the product offer.

Price

The pricing policy selected for a tourism product is often directly related to the performance of its future demand. Setting the right price is also crucial to the profitability of the tourism enterprise. We believe that, of all the decisions in the marketing mix, pricing decisions are the hardest to make. This is because prices for tourism products have to take into account the complexity created by seasonality of demand and the inherent perishability of the product. Also within tourism there are major differences in segments such as business travellers and those taking a vacation. The relative elasticities of demand for these segments are dissimilar, and there are different factors which affect price sensitivity.

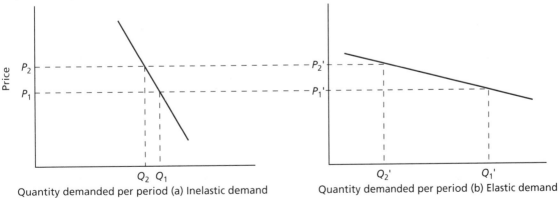

Quantity demanded per period (a) Inelastic demand   Quantity demanded per period (b) Elastic demand

Fig 23.2 Price elasticity of demand

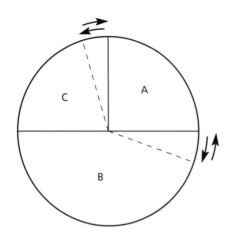

(a) Reactive price cutting, creating medium/long-term stabilization but with less total revenue

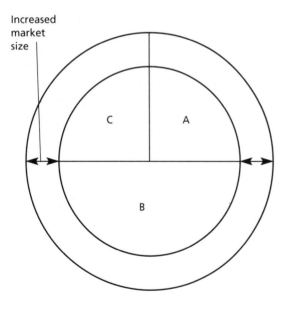

(b) Lower prices increasing market size, but not necessarily to total revenue levels before the price cut

Fig 23.3 Price cutting

Figure 23.2 shows demand curves which indicate different market reactions to price change. Tourism industry products related to vacations are associated with an elastic demand curve, where a small increase in price creates a large fall in demand. This happens for a number of reasons:

- The ratio of tourism prices to income is normally high. This is the case not only for overseas travel, but also for leisure centres, cinemas and attractions in times of recession.
- The consumer can choose a substitute or forgo the purchase if the overall value is considered unacceptable.
- It is relatively easy to judge the offer of alternative brands and products, and therefore easy to switch demand to cheaper alternatives. Although price may be an indicator of quality, the consumer is able to choose between several offers by referring, for example, to the type of aircraft, the star rating or the brand of accommodation.

The setting of price cannot be solely concerned with the consumer. Care and attention have to be given to appraising both the reaction of the consumer and the reaction of the competition. Due to the high-risk nature of the tourism industry, a price advantage which takes market share from a competitor will provoke a hostile repricing reaction.

In Figure 23.3(a), if company A attempts to increase its market share by price cutting, it will need to take share from companies B and C. This is a situation in which B and C will react by cutting their own prices. The outcome is that the market shares remain similar. The action can lead the market to grow in volume, as in Figure 23.3(b), although not necessarily in overall revenue. The long-term result is that the market remains extremely unstable due to smaller margins being applied. In this situation a company has to ensure that it has a high volume of business in order to exceed its break-even point. Price-cutting policies have been a feature of the tour operating business in the UK and have led to the collapse of a whole range of companies.

Influences on pricing in the tourism industry

- The perishable nature of the product, which is unable to be stored until a future occasion, leads to various forms of last-minute tactical pricing.
- The high price elasticity of demand exhibited by holiday and leisure markets places emphasis on setting prices at the right levels.
- The volatility of the market due to short-run fluctuations in international costs, exchange rates, oil prices and political events requires sophisticated forward planning.
- Many companies are reliant on high volumes to break even and will forgo short-run profit in order to create acceptable load factor or occupancy levels.
- Cost control is an important part of pricing policy. Many tourism enterprises have high fixed costs and price near to break-even positions. This can make them vulnerable to financial collapse or takeover if costs are not controlled.
- Some regions and countries have price controls for airline travel and hotel accommodation.
- Seasonal demand leads to peak and low-season periods, which require demand management pricing to cope with short-run capacity problems.
- Price is associated with the psychological aspects of both quality and status. It is therefore always important to gauge the way prices or their change will be perceived by the different target segments.
- Cash flow is high due to much of the payment for tourism products being made in advance of consumption. Many tourism companies make a profit on the investment of this money.

Pricing policy has to consider a variety of factors and therefore the scope of choice is remarkably wide. The choice will probably be one or a combination of the following.

Cost-orientated pricing

Cost-orientated pricing refers to setting prices on the basis of an understanding of their costs.

(1) *Cost-plus pricing* sets prices in relation to either marginal costs or total costs including overheads. A percentage mark-up is then normally applied to reach the final price. This form of pricing is often used for the retail outlets of tourist attractions. Its weakness as a method of pricing for tourism is that it does not take into consideration demand for the product or what prices the market place will bear, and it is not based upon the price levels of the competitors. Knowing the cost breakdown of the product is extremely important, however, since it allows the marketer to know what the effect of any tactical price reduction will be.

(2) *Rate of return pricing* provides the company with an agreed rate of return on its investment. Whereas the cost-plus method concentrates on the costs associated with the running of the business, the rate of return method concentrates on the profits generated in relation to the capital invested. This approach is not appropriate for tourism enterprises as it ignores the need to link the pricing policy to the creation of a sales volume which is large enough to cover overheads and which remains consistent over time. To use cost-plus or rate of return methods of pricing is generally not appropriate for tourism products, which have to survive in a highly competitive market place.

Demand-orientated pricing

Demand orientated pricing takes into consideration the factors of demand rather than the level of costs in order to set the price. A conference centre may charge one price for admission to a rock concert and only half that price for admission to a classical concert.

(1) *Discrimination pricing*, which is sometimes called flexible pricing, is often used in tourism where products are sold at two or more different prices. Quite often students and older people are charged lower prices at attractions, or events, than other segments. Discrimination pricing is often

time related, with cheaper drink charges in 'happy hour' periods or cheaper meal prices in the early evening prior to high-demand periods. For price discrimination to be successful it is necessary to be able to identify those segments which without the price differentials would not purchase the product.

To obtain a high flow of business a hotel will have to discount for customers who offer significant volume. This means that, while business travellers may benefit from corporate rates, those on vacation may be staying on tour operator rates. Discrimination can also be based upon increasing the price of products which have higher potential demand. For example, if rooms in a hotel are all the same but some have good scenic views of the countryside or sea, then those rooms could be given a higher price.

(2) *Backward pricing* is a market-based method of pricing which focuses on what the consumer is willing to pay. The price is worked backwards. First, an acceptable margin is agreed upon. Next the costs are closely monitored so that the price that is deemed to be acceptable can be matched. If necessary an adjustment is made to the quality of the product offer or service to meet the cost-led needs of this technique.

Tour operators selling on a price-led basis will often contract hotels one or two blocks back from the sea front, if this lowers the room rates making up the final price. Other methods include lowering the flight content of a holiday price by organizing cheaper night flights, which may also save on the first night's accommodation cost. To be successful with this method of pricing it is important to understand the psychological effects of creating products which may appeal to the price conscious, but may not give satisfaction if the holiday experience and company are considered to be of poor quality.

(3) *Market penetration pricing* is adopted when a company wants to establish itself quickly in a market. Prices are set below those of the competition in order to create high growth for the company's products. Tour operators, when setting up an operation to a new destination, will use market penetration pricing for that destination in

the first couple of years and then, when established, will slowly increase the prices.

(4) *Skimming pricing* is utilized when there is a shortage of supply of the product and where demand will not be dampened by charging a premium price. Luxury villas with pools and set in good locations are normally priced with higher margins than other accommodation products because of their shortage. Market skimming policies can occur only where there is a healthy demand for the tourism product on offer.

Whatever pricing policy is adopted, a company has to take into consideration the potential tourist's perceptual assessment. In deciding to buy a product a consumer has to be willing to give up something in order to enjoy the satisfactions that the product will deliver. This concept is more complex than it seems. The majority of tourists are looking for value when they buy a product. Value is a function of quality and price, i.e.

$$\text{Value} = \frac{\text{Quality}}{\text{Price}}$$

If a consumer believes the quality of a product is good, he or she will be willing to make greater sacrifices in order to purchase that product. That is how first-class travel can still continue to be successful on different forms of transport, such as trains, aircraft and cruise ships.

If prices change then this can affect the consumer's quality perception. A price reduction can be associated with a belief that the company is in financial trouble, that it will have to cut service and quality, or that the prices are falling and, if the customer waits, will come down even more. The value of the product will decrease if quality is seen to have fallen more than prices. The following shows the perception that the new value is at only half the level of its former position:

$$\text{Value} = \frac{\text{Quality}}{\text{Price}}$$

$$\text{If } V = \frac{Q \div 2}{P \div 1} \text{ then } 2V = \frac{Q}{P}$$

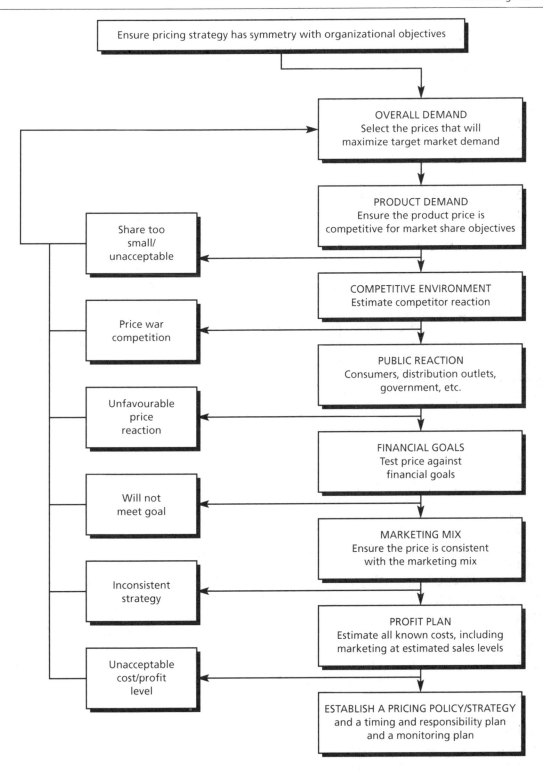

Fig 23.4 Pricing policy considerations

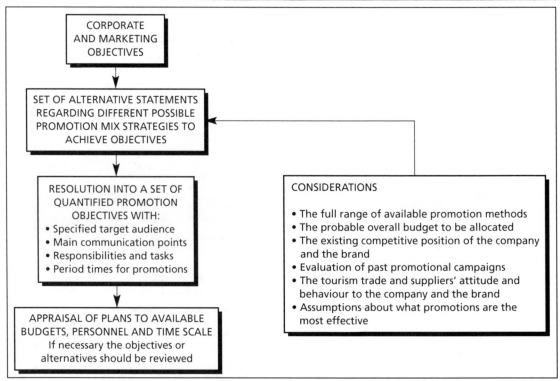

Fig 23.5 Development of promotional objectives

Alternatively, a price increase may be interpreted as the way in which the company is going pay to improve the quality and service of the product. However, some consumers may simply think that the company is being greedy and that quality has not improved. This also means that the consumer judges the value to have fallen.

To ensure the maximum chance of success for the pricing policy adopted, there is a need to check each stage of the procedure as in Figure 23.4. This figure identifies the important considerations in the successful evolution of a pricing policy.

Promotion

Promotion is the descriptive term for the mix of communication activities which tourism companies, or tourist boards, carry out in order to influence those publics on whom their sales depend. The important groups which need to be influenced are not simply the target market group of current and potential customers. There is the need also to influence trade contacts such as retail agents and suppliers, as well as opinion formers such as journalists and travel writers. Even local, national and international politicians and important professional groups may need to be influenced.

Setting objectives

A range of promotional methods can be employed by the tourism marketer, so it is important to define what the promotion has to achieve. It is necessary to define the marketing objectives clearly so that the most effective types of promotion can be utilized. Figure 23.5 explains how promotional objectives can be developed.

Communication effects

There is always the need to plan to achieve the most effective response from the target market.

An important part of the promotional effort is the *building of brand and product awareness*. Sometimes it will take a long time for the consumer to know about the brand and the types of product which will be on offer. A promotion campaign should aim to provide for knowledge of the product, to ensure the consumer will feel favourable towards the product, and to build up preference for it. Any campaign has to sell the benefits that a customer is seeking in a credible way so that the potential customer feels conviction and is more likely than not to make a purchase.

Figure 23.6 shows how a promotional campaign should aim to create awareness through information. It also shows that the development of a positive image for a product creates a more price inelastic demand curve, which means that the product is more resilient to price rises and does not have to rely on having low prices. In Figure 23.6 (a) P_1Q_1 is existing demand before a campaign has

been developed to create more awareness in the target audience. At P_1Q_2 demand has increased because more people are aware of the company, the product and the benefits it can deliver. At P_1Q_3 in Figure 23.6(b) the campaign has improved the image of the company or destination, so that more status is derived from travelling with the brand or to a destination. In these circumstances, the demand curve becomes more inelastic.

Advertising and sales promotion are the most widely used forms of promotion. Because of the intrusive nature of these forms of promotion, most consumers relate ideas of marketing to their use. Other forms of promotion include public relations and personal selling.

Advertising

Advertising is any paid form of non-personal communication through the media about a product that has an identified sponsor. The media may include travel guides, newspapers, magazines, radio, television, direct mail and billboards. Advertising is used to achieve a whole range of objectives which may include changing attitudes or building image as well as achieving sales. Advertising is often described as above-the-line promotion with all other forms of promotion being termed below-the-line.

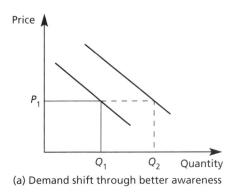

(a) Demand shift through better awareness

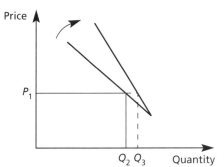

(b) Demand becomes more inelastic
due to image improvement

Fig 23.6 Promotional effect on demand

Sales promotion

Sales promotion involves any activity which offers an incentive to induce a desired result from potential customers, trade intermediaries or the sales force. Sales promotion campaigns will add value to the product because the incentives will ordinarily not accompany the product. For example, free wine or free accommodation offers are frequently used in sales promotion campaigns for hotel restaurants which need improved demand at certain periods. Most incentives are planned to be short term in nature.

As part of sales promotion there is the important area of merchandising. Merchandising involves materials used in travel agents or in-house to stimulate sales. For a hotel these would include tent cards which may attempt to sell cocktails or desserts, menus, in-room material, posters and displays. Merchandising is important as a means of creating impulse purchase or reminding the consumer of what is on offer.

Personal selling

Personal selling is an attempt to gain benefit through face-to-face or telephone contact between the seller's representative and those people with whom the seller wants to communicate. This sort of selling may be used by a non-profit-making museum as well as by the conference manager of a large hotel.

Public relations

Public relations (PR) is non-personal communication which changes opinion or achieves coverage in a mass medium, and which is not paid for by the source. The coverage could include space given to a press release or favourable editorial comment. PR is important not only in obtaining editorial coverage, but also in suppressing potential bad coverage. A company which has good links with the media is more likely to have the opportunity to stop or moderate news which could be damaging.

Other promotional activities

There is a growing use of *sponsorship* and *direct marketing*, which do not fit comfortably into the other four promotion categories. Sponsorship is the material or financial support of a specific activity, normally but not exclusively sport or the arts, which does not form part of the sponsor company's normal business. Direct marketing is used extensively by direct-sell tour operators such as Saga holidays and Portland. The main method is direct mail, which is postal communication by an identified sponsor.

In addition, because tourism is an intangible product, a great deal of promotion includes the production of *printed communications* such as

brochures or sales leaflets. The design, compilation and printing of tourism brochures is one of the most important promotion functions. Printed communications are often costly. In fact, the printing and distribution costs of brochures comprise the largest part of most marketing budgets within the tourism industry. This is a necessary expenditure as the brochure or leaflet is the major sales tool for tour operators and tourist organizations.

Characteristics of each promotion

Each of the above promotional elements has the capacity to achieve a different promotional objective. While personal selling has high potency for achieving communication objectives, only a relatively small number of people can be contacted. Therefore advertising is a better method of reaching a high number of people at low cost. Public relations is more credible than advertising, but there is more control over advertising messages and they can be repeated on a regular basis. When it is difficult to raise advertising budgets, public relations is a lower-cost alternative, but it is difficult to control the timing and consistency of PR coverage. Sales promotion, such as leaflet drops which offer price discounts, may produce an initial trial for a product, such as the purchase of a leisure break in a hotel, but this type of promotion can only be used over a short period.

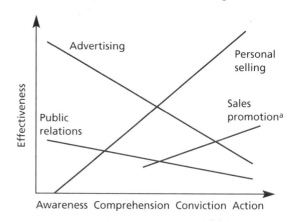

^a Effectiveness varies depending on the type of campaign.

Fig 23.7 Effectiveness of different promotion methods

Each part of the promotions mix has its own strengths and weaknesses. While these may include the factors of cost, ability to target different groups, and control, there are other important considerations. Figure 23.7 indicates the relative strengths of each of the four main forms of promotion. They are compared on the basis of the level of awareness of the communication and its comprehension, as well as on whether it can build conviction and succeed in creating action.

Place (distribution)

The special characteristics of the tourism product have led to specific forms of distribution. The tourism product is one where no transfer of ownership takes place and the service is simply rented or consumed. However, prior to consumption the tourism product has to be both available and accessible. This requires a distribution system. A distribution system may be defined as the channel used, or means by which a tourism supplier gains access to the potential buyers of the product.

The following aspects of tourism distribution should be noted:

- There is no actual product which is being distributed. There are only clues given through persuasive communication about the product.
- Tourism normally involves the purchase act, the consumer travelling to the product, and the consumer becoming part of the production and consumption process. Therefore the method of selling and the environment within which the purchase is made becomes part of the tourism experience.
- Major amounts of money are allocated by the industry to the production and printing of literature as well as to its delivery direct to the customer or to the retail travel agent. Brochures are produced in large quantities, and often the distribution cost involves an amount for warehousing and the planned despatch of packs of brochures through different modes of transport.

- Distribution of overseas holidays in the UK is dominated by travel agents which sell a homogeneous set of alternatives. These agents have a vast amount of power and control over the companies who supply the product (principals). Agents decide on the brochures to display on their racks and the companies they will recommend to consumers.

Different tourism distribution needs

There are some forms of tourism, such as museums, theme parks and physical attractions, where no form of prior booking is required. There is almost always excess supply available, and in peak periods queuing is the method of allocation. There are others forms where excess demand and more complex product packaging and financial risk create the need for sophisticated advance booking systems. The booking system enables the company to spread demand because the consumer can often be convinced to arrive or travel at a different time.

In order for a tourism company to sell in advance of consumption, and to have a record of the reservation, the company has to sell its available capacity through an inventory system. Whether it is a small guest house or large hotel, a farmhouse or cruise ship, some method of allocating capacity and creating reservations without creating overbooking is important. The timing of these bookings may range from minutes prior to departure for an aircraft or a reserved place on a train service to several years for a major conference. For these reasons, the use of computerized reservation systems (CRS) is increasingly common in tourism. These systems combine the memory capacity of computers (to update and store information constantly) with the communication facility of telecommunications, which rapidly inform travel agents of the current capacity remaining. Such systems can then be programmed to maximize the 'yield' of the capacity as it is sold to the customer.

The next consideration is related to the location of the business. A well-located hotel or retail agent will be able to pick up passing demand. In this case the consumers will find the product easily and there may be no need for a distribution channel. This will make the product easily available for purchase.

In an increasingly competitive world, however, it has been necessary for most companies to consider different forms of distribution. Companies are able to sell direct either from their place of location, or through direct marketing methods. Many hotels will organize weekend breaks to improve the weekend occupancy levels. These weekend packages are often promoted directly in newspapers and booked directly with the hotel.

In the UK there is also the opportunity to have access to a wide network of 7000 travel agency distribution outlets. These agents charge commission on the sales they make, and they need to hold a stock of the company's brochures or sales literature. The bookings made for travel abroad from the UK are mostly organized either through high street travel agents, for holidays, or through specialist business travel agents for business travel. The UK has a different distribution pattern from the rest of Europe, where most bookings are made direct rather than through agents. In many European countries it will be found that twice as many bookings as in the UK are made direct.

Consumers and distribution

The British holidaymaker has been slow to buy overseas holidays direct, although there is a tradition of booking domestic holidays direct. There is little doubt that for many the convenience of using an agent is an important element in the buying process. This is because a travel agent may offer greater opportunities for one-stop shopping, which allows the parallel purchase of insurance, car hire, rail travel to the airport, traveller's cheques and so on (see Case Study 23.2).

CASE STUDY 23.2

Reasons for the use of retail travel agents

Easy Accessibility
- To a range and choice of brochures.
- To product components such as visas, traveller's cheques and insurance.
- To booking points in every main town and city.
- To an alternative agent as well as products and brands.

Convenience
- For obtaining information and advice.
- For making the purchase and payment for the holiday.
- For making complaints and being represented if things go wrong.

Habit
- People can get into a pattern of behaviour which becomes habit forming. Only a major campaign by direct mail operators could change this habit.

Security/Risk
- Consumers feel more secure when dealing with a reputable operator or agent. Those who buy from members of the Association of British Travel Agents (ABTA) feel they obtain ABTA protection and that products which are offered have been vetted.

Environment/Atmosphere
- Travel agents offer an environment which is part of the holiday experience. The travel agency environment is the perfect setting for personal selling methods, which are a powerful means of generating bookings.

Economic
- Because travel agents compete on price or added value, and tour operators have the smallest of margins, there is little difference in the price between travel agents' products and those which are purchased through direct-sell channels.

Source: Based on Gilbert (1990).

PRODUCT	PRICE	PLACE	PROMOTION	PEOPLE	PHYSICAL EVIDENCE	PROCESS
Range	Level	Location	Advertising	Personnel:	Environment:	Policies
Quality	Discounts:	Accessibility	Personal selling	Training	Furnishings	Procedures
Level	Allowances	Distribution	Sales promotion	Discretion	Colour	Mechanization
Brand name	Commissions	channels	Publicity	Commitment	Layout	Employee
Service line	Payment terms	Distribution	Public relations	Incentives	Noise level	discretion
Warranty	Customer's	coverage		Appearance	Facilitating	Customer
After-sales	perceived			Interpersonal	goods	involvement
service	value			behaviour	Tangible clues	Customer
	Quality/price			Attitudes		direction
	Differentiation			Other customers:		Flow of
				Behaviour		activities
				Degree of		
				involvement		
				Customer/		
				customer		
				contact		

Source: Booms and Bitner (1981).

Fig 23.8 The marketing mix for services

THE MARKETING MIX REVISITED: ARE THE FOUR PS SUFFICIENT?

The adaptation of the marketing mix by authors such as Booms and Bitner (1981) has been based upon arguments stressing that the original marketing mix is more appropriate to manufacturing than to service companies. For example, Booms and Bitner add three extra Ps: people, physical evidence, and process (see Figure 23.8). Authors such as Booms and Bitner argue that the marketing mix of four Ps is not comprehensive enough for the tourism and hospitality industry. The major difference is said to be the intangible element of human behaviour, where quality and its control is of paramount importance.

We believe that there is a need for more research into the industry and its marketing before the four Ps require revision. For the present it is believed that the four Ps offer an adequate framework into which the differences can be incorporated. The main task of marketers in tourism and hospitality is to understand the characteristics of the products they plan, control and manage. This will ensure that managers will attempt to control the aspects of the marketing mix which have most bearing on

the satisfaction level of consumers. We provided the basis for this assessment in Chapter 21 on marketing management.

While it is obvious that there are differences between manufactured and service products, the framework of the four Ps is sufficient for planning purposes because physical evidence, people and process may be considered part of the category of *product* or its implementation. The four categories do not presuppose the relegation of service product considerations to secondary importance. On the contrary, the four categories should ensure that, within product formulation, greater emphasis will be placed on the integration of all the different service management considerations.

It should be apparent that marketing mix decisions must be geared to achieving the objectives of the company or organization, and should be linked to acceptability throughout the company. While marketing departments often lead in setting the marketing mix strategy, they should not ignore input from others and should not fail to check with others that the strategy will be workable from an operational standpoint.

The marketing mix offers the range and spread of alternative strategies by which a marketer can influence demand. However, while the available range is very similar for all tourism marketers, the choice is not. For example, a national tourism organization will not normally be involved in developing products or setting prices. The process of mix formulation and balancing is quite often unique to each organization.

For a company to be successful with its marketing mix it has to develop a differential advantage which will distinguish the company's offer from that of the competition. Only when a company has built an advantage will it find that customers seek it out, in which case it is easier to create higher profits. The advantage may be based upon quality, image or product concept. Centre Parcs in the UK has developed such an advantage, and the results can be seen in the high year-round demand for its product.

References and further reading

Booms, B.H., and Bitner, M.J. (1981) 'Marketing strategies and organization structures for service firms', in Donnelly, J., and George, W.R. (eds), *Marketing of Services*, Chiacago, Ill.: American Marketing Association.

Borden, N.H. (1965) 'The concept of the marketing mix', in Schwartz, G. (ed.), *Science in Marketing*, Chichester: Wiley.

Gilbert, D.C. (1990) 'European product purchase methods and systems', *Service Industries Journal*, vol. 10, no. 4, pp. 664–79.

McCarthy, E.J. (1978) *Basic Marketing: A Managerial Approach*, 6th edn, Homewood, Ill.: Irwin.

CHAPTER 24

The future of tourism

OVERVIEW

In this chapter we attempt to synthesize the trends and influences upon the future of tourism. Initially, we identify a number of factors which, although outside the control of tourism, will have an impact upon its development. We then closely examine some of the variables which are linked to the future development of the tourism system itself. In fact, most of these trends and variables are interlinked and are combining to accelerate the pace of change. For example, we show that, while there is no doubt that the social and economic trends that we identify will encourage the growth of tourism, the nature of the market will also change with consequent implications for the management of destinations and products. The 'new' consumer of tourism is becoming knowledgeable and discerning, and is seeking quality and participation. Moreover, in the developed world, he or she is increasingly drawn from an older age group. Motivations for travel are moving away from passive sunlust towards educational and curiosity motives. At the same time, travel will be facilitated by flexible working practices and early retirement.

The increasingly knowledgeable and sophisticated 'new' tourist can now be catered for by a tourism industry which is firmly embracing the marketing concept, facilitated by technological developments such as computer reservation systems (CRS) and database marketing. At the same time, shifts in the economic and political map of the world will be reflected in changing tourism flows as new generators of international tourists and new destinations emerge. There is no doubt that these new destinations will need to be better planned and managed, and to show more concern for their environment and host community, than did their earlier counterparts. The trend is clearly away from mass passive tourism and towards more tailor-made, individual consumption of active tourism. But none of this will be possible without a well-trained tourism workforce. We therefore conclude the chapter with an examination of future trends and issues in human resource management in the tourism industry.

A FRAMEWORK FOR CHANGE

A study of tourism trends to the year 2000 and beyond by the World Tourism Organization (1992) provides a useful starting point from which to consider the future of tourism. The study identifies two groups of factors which will 'shape' tourism in the future:

- *Exogenous variables*. These include demographic and social trends; economic and financial issues; political, legislative and regulatory trends; technology; transport; trade; and safety. Although not considered in the WTO study, other issues such as the environment and global warming cannot be ignored.
- *Market forces of demand*. These are the tourism-related trends which encompass the demand, supply and distribution of tourism and travel products and services.

In Chapter 1 we introduced Leiper's tourism system as a way of thinking about tourism. It is possible to recast this model to take into account the ideas and issues involved in the future of tourism, and to act as a framework for this chapter (Figure 24.1).

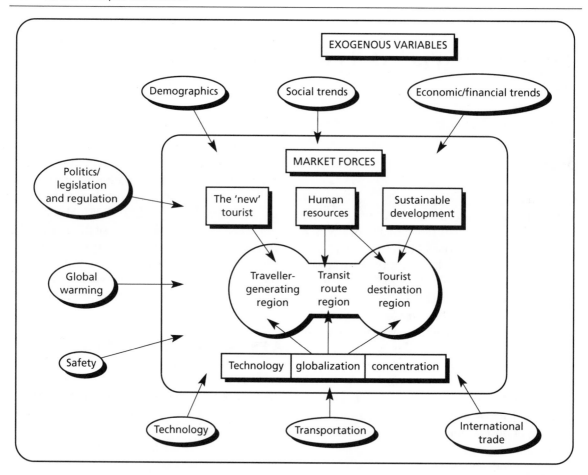

Fig 24.1 Forces of change in the tourism system

EXOGENOUS VARIABLES

Demographic and social trends

Future demographic and social trends will be critical in shaping tourism demand to the year 2000 and beyond. Demographic trends such as ageing populations in the major generating countries, allied to the declining numbers of young people as the post-war baby bulge works through the decades, are particularly important. Demographics are inextricably entangled with the social trends which are leading to later marriage, couples having children later in life and increased numbers of single and childless couple households. In the Third World a burgeoning workforce will lead to immigration to the developed world, and the growth of knowledge and interest in other countries will see a convergence of lifestyles worldwide. With increased media attention and levels of education, these trends will give people more time, resources and inclination to travel. This will be encouraged by the growth and spread of discretionary incomes and the liberalization of trade on an international scale.

Political developments

In late 1980s we saw a redrafting of the political map of the world, and this has a number of implications for tourism. The emergence of market economies in eastern Europe, and the opening of the borders symbolized by the demolition of the Berlin Wall, will pave the way for eastern European countries to participate more fully in travel movements, particularly to western countries. However, although many former eastern Europeans are already travelling, the fact that international travel is expensive and hard currency at a premium means that it is unlikely that eastern Europe will become a significant generator of international tourism until 1995 and beyond. Already Hungary has become a leading international destination for tourism, and other parts of eastern Europe will become important destinations (particularly for business and specialist leisure tourism) as travel restrictions are eased, as infrastructure improves and as attitudes to service change.

At the same time, the European Community is expanding to encompass the countries of the European Free Trade Area to form the European Economic Area. These countries are likely to be joined by other new entrants such as Turkey and the former eastern European countries before the year 2000. In the shorter term, the completion of the single European market in 1993 has implications for the future of European tourism. The prime initiative for European integration was to allow Europe to compete with the world economic powers of the USA and Japan. The single European market aims to create 'an area without internal frontiers in which free movement of goods, persons and services is ensured'. Tourism will be encouraged by initiatives such as the abolition of border controls, the harmonization of taxes and the deregulation of transport in the European Community.

The spread of democracy and the liberalization of trade are complemented by a contradictory trend – the rise of regionalism and the search for local identity. Of course, this may lead to conflict (as in the regions of the former Yugoslavia, or the damage to second homes in Wales), but elsewhere the trend is less sinister as 'city states' emerge as major tourist destinations whether it be as cultural centres or for hosting major events.

Transportation developments

We know that tourism is highly dependent upon transport technology and the consequent improvements in efficiency, range and safety of travel. However, tourism may also be constrained by transportation in the future as old systems fail to accommodate increased levels of demand. The European air traffic control system is a case in point here. However, there is no doubt that transport innovations and tourism development do go hand in hand. To quote Boniface and Cooper:

In the 1990s intercontinental airline operations will be characterised by the use of larger aircraft and more non-stop, very long flights – aided by the development of Concorde's hypersonic successor. The increased emphasis on hub and spoke operations, where airlines realign schedules at their hub and time schedules on the spokes so they connect at the hub, will also continue. This gives the hub airline a potentially strong competitive position and leads to a system of 'fortress' hubs keeping out newcomers. These airports will need well coordinated flights, a prime geographical location, and good terminal facilities.

Although it is generally accepted that total deregulation of the international airline industry is not practical, the trend towards deregulation will continue in the 1990s in Europe. In the US deregulation has led to domination by a small number of larger airlines – a trend which is emerging in other sectors of the tourism industry.

Forecasts of international transport over the next 10 years predict that technological developments, increased airline efficiency and labour productivity savings will offset any rises in aviation fuel prices and thus, in real terms, fares will continue to fall. This will support the continued trend towards long haul travel. However, if energy costs do rise significantly, then a shift towards surface transport and shorter journey lengths can be expected.

Despite the focus of much writing on air transport, most tourism journeys are by car. Whilst the use of the car for inter-city travel has declined in the USA there seems little prospect for use of the car to decline in Europe where the market is nowhere near reaching saturation. Continued developments of the European highway network; developments of car technology to make driving more comfortable and environmentally acceptable; and improved fuel efficiency will all make motoring cheaper and more attractive. (1987, p. 42)

At the same time, we believe that by the year 2000 there will be a gradual switch away from air to surface transport. This will be underpinned by improved rail services and rail-based tourism products; the realization of the environmental advantages of rail; and continued technological developments in the area of high-speed train networks. Similarly, wave-piercing catamarans will shorten journey times on sea crossings.

Other trends and influences

We can identify a range of other variables which also impinge upon the future of tourism. These include such intangibles as the changing value systems of the consumer as well as more long-term factors such as global warming. There is no doubt that the raising of the earth's temperature and the consequent rise in sea level will affect tourism. Much of tourism investment is found in locations fringing the coast, and vital tourism resources such as the flora and fauna of destinations will be altered by global warming.

Human behaviour too is a threat to tourism as the spread of AIDS may render some otherwise attractive destinations no-go areas; increasing incidence of skin cancer may reverse the fashion for a sun tan; and disease in some parts of the world and decreasing levels of safety will constrain the uninhibited expansion of tourism. As with all the considerations in this section, these are outside the control of tourism and its managers, but their consequences may be severe.

Finally, technological innovations such as 'virtual reality' may one day replace the authentic travel experience altogether. By simply strapping on a body suit and plugging into the virtual reality programme, you could be transported to the sights, sounds and sensations of the Caribbean – but without any risk of skin cancer, AIDS or other side-effects.

MARKET FORCES OF DEMAND

The 'new' tourist

Many commentators have suggested that the maturing of the tourism market is creating a 'new' tourist, who can be characterized as experienced, sophisticated and demanding. This means that the traditional annual family holiday mostly spent in a beach resort may be gradually superseded by multi-interest travel and a range of innovative travel experiences (such as activity, adventure and ecotourism). As a result, the relative importance of packaged tours will decline in favour of independently organized tourism, or at least a more 'bespoke' form of tourism.

To an extent the new sophisticated traveller has emerged as a result of experience. Tourists from the major generating regions of the world have become frequent travellers, are linguistically and technologically skilled and can function in multicultural and demanding environments overseas. Add to this media exposure of tourism destinations and the reduction of perceived distance to reach such places and the stage is set for a reappraisal of holiday formulae. Education too has played a part, together with enhanced communications, and has led to more sophisticated requirements from holidaymakers who are now looking not just for new experiences but also for rewarding activities to fill their leisure time and to satisfy their cultural, intellectual and sporting interests.

Of course, the sophistication of the customer will have an impact upon product development throughout the industry: not only will there be an increased requirement for high standards of product design, efficiency and safety, but also the tourist will be more critical of the product and have the experience to compare offerings. This will mean that customer convenience in all its forms will be demanded by the new travellers, a trend fuelled by consumer legislation in tourism (such as the European Community Package Travel Directive).

Every tourist is different, bringing a unique blend of experiences, motivations and desires. In the 1990s tourism is following the trend of other industries towards 'customizing'. Here technology enables products to be tailored to meet individual tastes. The 'old' tourism products did not adopt this approach. Instead they were general and unspecialized with very similar characteristics, and were traded under the mass tourism philosophy as commodities rather than services. This philosophy said that tourism products should appeal to all tastes and be sold at a low price in order to attract as wide a range of customers as possible.

Much of the discussion above points to the need for effective segmentation of the tourism market. Traditionally, tourism marketers have been using geographic and demographic criteria in order to describe their markets, but psychographics and behavioural criteria will be increasingly used in order to provide detailed customer profiles, to identify their motivations, needs and determinants, and to offer an appropriate marketing mix and service delivery strategy.

Technology, globalization and concentration

As the tourism market matures, heightened competition will force enterprises both to identify and to utilize modern methods of management which minimize operational costs and maximize output. This search for efficiency has spread throughout the tourism industry. Technology is a major facilitator here.

At the micro-level, technology will wire the entire enterprise and enable effective and quick management. Integrated property management systems in hotels, for example, can perform a range of functions:

- Streamlining the front office operation by supporting the reservation and billing functions.
- Facilitating food and beverage management by improving inventory control and transmitting orders and bills.
- Enhancing housekeeping by improving communication and checking procedures.

- Controlling energy and security systems.
- Improving the productivity of charging departments by using automatic points of sale, which will make all transactions and the charging of clients and departments easier.
- Supporting the marketing operation by distributing the product and providing database marketing packages.

At the macro-level an integrated system of information technologies will allow diagonal integration in the tourism industry by facilitating the production, distribution and delivery of an integrated tourist product and by wrapping the entire variety of tourism products within a single computer reservation system (CRS).

The widespread use of technology in the tourism industry will enable tourist enterprises to improve their profitability. Yield management is used by hotels and airlines to manipulate their demand in the most effective way. The most appropriate price for the product at a particular moment is identified by assessing the demand and supply for the requested period, and the timing of the request, as well as by taking into account the historical pattern of sales. The system suggests a price which maximizes the yield of an airline seat or bed for the sale in question.

In addition, technology enables tourism enterprises to have a closer relationship with their customers and to reward their loyalty. Database marketing allows personalized treatment and the launch of initiatives such as 'frequent flyer' schemes by airlines. Hotels can also create 'guest history' databases, where information is stored relating to guest requests and preferences.

The need for efficiency in the international tourism market has accelerated the emergence of multinational corporations which provide tourism services in various countries. Globalization is one of the major trends in the international tourism industry. It is based on convergence in world tastes and product preferences to produce globally standardized products. Of course, it is only the larger, international companies which can take advantage of these trends. Indeed, globalization goes hand in hand with increased concentration in the tourism industry as major companies gain market share and market influence. The pace of concentration being generated by both horizontal and vertical integration is such that for the small entrepreneur in tourism the days ahead may be difficult.

For a tourism enterprise operating in a multinational market there are many advantages to increased size:

- Economies of scale.
- Ability to resource high-profile promotional campaigns.
- Brand name benefits through standardization and quality control.
- Ability to spread the risk among various markets.
- Implementation of advanced marketing techniques on an international basis.
- Utilization of technology (especially CRS).
- Optimization of capacity/inventory usage and reduction of seasonality problems.
- Access to the international labour market.
- Advantages over other members of the distribution channel.
- Improved political influence.
- Managers who have more time to 'manage'.
- Market prominence and stronger branding.

A particular problem associated with the concentration of the tourism industry is that most of the larger corporations do not have a relationship with a specific destination. Some commentators feel that they will therefore be less sensitive to the impact of their operations on the host environments, economies and communities. In addition, small and medium tourism enterprises and local destinations fear the 'neo-colonial relationship' which can emerge from dealing with large companies, such as tour operators.

Computer reservation systems (CRS) are a good example of the convergence of these trends of technology, globalization, concentration and a focus on the 'new' tourist. CRS have already caused major structural changes within the tourism industry. In its simplest form a CRS is a database which enables tourism enterprises to manage their supply inventory. Airlines were the first sector to develop CRS, followed by hotel chains and tour operators.

Airline CRS were established in the late 1960s when American Airlines introduced SABRE to improve its productivity and efficiency. All major airlines followed and developed their own CRS, which eventually established valuable networks for exchanging information on availability and reservations. Airline deregulation in the USA boosted the demand for CRS in the airline industry so that airlines could continually alter their prices and schedules. As tour operators adopted the technology, the introduction of CRS terminals in travel agencies signified the start of a radical change in the distribution of the tourism product, and intermediaries were 'locked in' to particular suppliers.

For their vendors, the advantages of CRS are clear. They provide important financial benefits in organization and distribution; they allow the adoption of new techniques such as yield management; they increase revenue by offering reservation services to other companies; and they earn incremental revenues from increased sales to vendor companies due to bias and the 'halo effect' (that is, the ease of utilizing their system). At the same time CRS, combined with a more knowledgeable tourist market, will see the emergence of a growing number of independent travellers and the gradual bypassing of intermediaries – travel agents and tour operators – in the tourism distribution chain. Suppliers will therefore be able to target their products more closely to meet the desires of their customer segments.

Global distribution systems (GDS) have emerged from airline CRS. Since the late 1980s the major systems have started to expand their business geographically, while new trends to both horizontal and vertical integration have spread rapidly. Moreover, GDS attempt vertical integration by incorporating a wide range of tourist products such as accommodation, rent-a-car, non-airline transportation and entertainment. Thus, modern GDS provide a one-stop reservation facility for the entire range of tourist products. This trend is expected to dominate the development of GDS as they evolve to offer an organizational platform for the distribution of the integrated tourist product.

Sustainable tourism development

It is only recently that the negative effects of tourism have been set against the more tangible economic gains. This has become all the more potent with the rise of environmentalism and 'green' consciousness in the mid to late 1980s. In part, these trends are a reflection of the growing maturity of both the tourist as consumer and the tourism industry itself. Mass tourism began with short-term perspectives as the industry and public agencies attempted to handle growing demand. In the 1980s and 1990s growth rates have slowed and consumers are questioning some of the excesses of tourism development. In response, longer planning horizons are being considered and alternative forms of tourism advocated.

Sustainable tourism development is a concept which will be a watchword of the 1990s. Archer and Cooper speak of:

the belated discovery of the relevance of the sustainable development concept to tourism. As with many service industries, some of the most important ideas and innovations come from outside the industry or the subject area. The concept of sustainable development has a long pedigree in the field of resource management and, at last, is becoming an acceptable term in tourism. The Brundtland Report puts it simply as 'meeting the needs of the present without compromising the ability of future generations to meet their own needs' (World Commission on Environment and Development, 1987). The concept of sustainability is central to the reassessment of tourism's role in society. It demands a long-term view of economic activity, questions the imperative of continued economic growth, and ensures that consumption of tourism does not exceed the ability of a host destination to

provide for future tourists. In other words, it represents a trade-off between present and future needs. In the past, sustainability has been a low priority compared with the short-term drive for profitability and growth but, with pressure growing for a more responsible tourism industry, it is difficult to see how such short-term views on consumption can continue long into the 1990s. Indeed, destination 'regulations' are being developed in some areas and already, the bandwagon for sustainable development and responsible consumption is rolling. Public agencies are issuing guidelines for acceptable development; tourism consumer groups are growing in number and influence; and guides to responsible tourism are available. (forthcoming)

CASE STUDY 24.1

Center Parcs Environmental Policy Statement

Mission Statement

Center Parcs is the world leader in short break holidays. We strive to create a unique short break which meets the leisure needs of our guests by offering relaxation and sporting opportunities, and a natural environment which encourages a closeness to and an understanding of nature. Caring for nature and the landscape is thus a key objective of our business. We will develop our business activities by continuing to invest in those resources which are central to our success – our people and the environment.

Center Parcs and the environment

The original Center Parcs concept was based on creating a 'villa in the forest'. We aim to meet people's needs for leisure, sport and relaxation in surroundings which encourage a closeness to and understanding of nature.

Centre Parcs aims to implement the concept of sustainable tourism and thus define the way forward for the industry as a whole. To this end we endeavour to ensure that our use of the environment does not compromise its use by future generations.

(continued overleaf)

Our environmental objectives and policy strive to achieve a balance between use of the environment and its conservation and enhancement.

Care for the environment has always been central to our way of thinking. Our commitment to environmentally sustainable development is evident in our track record but, not content with the exceptionally high standards already achieved, we have set out our vision for the future as expressed through our environmental policy.

Principles for environmental action

The tourism industry as a whole needs a code of practice which involves continued environmental stewardship. The approach evolved by Center Parcs demonstrates an industry standard which ensures that every aspect of the environment is included in the provision of tourism and recreational facilities.

Our objectives of protecting, maintaining and improving the environment are visible in everything Center Parcs does. In developing systems of implementation and control Center Parcs not only complies with but also goes beyond the requirements of statutory regulation.

Statement of environmental objectives and policy

- To make a positive contribution to the global environment by our efforts at a local level.
- To accept responsibility for the environmental consequences of our activities and therefore to aim to minimise any adverse environmental impacts we may have.
- To conduct all our activities in the spirit of being custodians of the environment within and around our villages.
- To enable our guests and employees to experience the process of environmental care at first hand, so that they too will be encouraged to make a contribution in their daily lives.
- To be acknowledged as setting the standards for our industry by demonstrating that sustainable tourism is achievable and by offering to share our experience with others.

Implementation of our aims

The natural environment

At Center Parcs we aim to create and maintain the highest quality of landscapes and habitats. As part of this we seek to work with original landscape to give it a positive and natural future direction based upon its ecological history. We endeavour to maximise the diversity of habitats and species and to enrich the visual quality of the surroundings. We recognise that the natural, living dynamics of landscapes are attractive features in themselves. We prepare and work to a definitive management plan, which includes detailed specifications for all aspects of landscape and ecological management. Annual monitoring enables continual updating of the plan to take place, should potential improvements emerge.

The built environment

Center Parcs is continually reviewing the environmental performance and function of all the materials used in our villages. We aim to achieve further improvements in the sourcing of building and site materials to ensure, where possible, that they are derived from sustainable sources. This will entail undertaking supplier audits. Our maintenance programmes will also be reviewed regularly to ensure principles of good environmental practice are consistently achieved and improved upon.

Facilities

At Center Parcs we aim to ensure that the health, safety and comfort of our guests and employees are safeguarded at all times and that all statutory requirements are met in full if not exceeded.

Our waste policy is based upon the idea of 'reduce, reuse and recycle'. Guests are encouraged to use on-site recycling facilities, which are provided in every village for glass, paper and metal.

Water features are an important part of our villages and we have applied painstaking purification and recycling methods, so as to minimise the use of this valuable resource.

Energy conservation and efficiency is a design pre-requisite of our villages. Villas are comprehensively insulated and triple-glazed, and the use of heat exchangers means energy input is kept to the minimum that current technology and guest comfort allows.

Supplier policy

In the future Center Parcs will expect and require suppliers of services and products to apply similar environmental policies to our own. Center Parcs will make responsibility for the environment a criterion for choice of suppliers and will reserve the right to cease any business or contractual relationship where a supplier is shown to be having an unacceptable impact upon the environment.

Local and community involvement

Center Parcs aims to deliver a package of environmental benefits not only to the holiday villages themselves but to their neighbouring communities. By creating wildlife sanctuaries and managing the landscape within our villages, we are helping to improve the environmental conditions in surrounding areas.

In addition, works contracting and employment is deliberately local, wherever possible, as are bought-in services. The existence of our villages often means that the locality benefits from road schemes and other infrastructure improvements such as better sewerage treatment facilities.

Environmental education

Center Parcs incorporates environmental objectives and work programmes into routine induction, promotion and refresher training pro-

grammes for our employees. In each village we have nominated members of staff as contact points for environmental information who liaise with guests and run environmentally-based education activities.

We realise that one of the ways we can most influence the future of our environment is through contact with and education of our guests. At Center Parcs we are aware that our guests come from all over the country and that we have a responsibility to ensure they take back with them a better appreciation of the environment after their stay at Center Parcs.

Monitoring our policy

Management and employees are expected to be fully aware of and committed to the environmental policy and objectives. A team of expert, qualified consultants and selected Center Parcs management meets regularly to review the company's environmental objectives, targets and performance. The company management undertakes to allocate sufficient resources, both in terms of people and finances, for their implementation.

The external consultants in this team will continue to provide an objective and independent environmental auditing and reporting service and Center Parcs is committed to acting upon their advice in the pursuit of environmental excellence.

We can see that the central issue here is the gradual shift from short-term to longer-term thinking and planning in tourism. It is no longer acceptable for the industry to exploit and 'use up' destinations and then move on. Consumers will place pressure upon the industry and destination managers to behave in a responsible manner; if they do not then their destination may be shunned as environmentally 'unacceptable' to visit (Case Study 24.1). Destinations are responding to these demands in a variety of ways. Resource-based destinations are adopting sophisticated planning, management

and interpretive techniques to provide both a welcome and a rich experience for the tourist, while at the same time ensuring protection of the resource itself. It is felt that once tourists understand why a destination is significant they will want to protect it. Good planning and management of the destination lie at the heart of providing the consumer of the 1990s with a high-quality experience, and it may be that tourists will have to accept increasingly restricted viewing times at popular sites and even replicas of the real thing.

Careers, human resources and training

Many of you reading this book will be looking towards the tourism industry for a career. Indeed, the challenges facing the tourism industry will be met successfully only by a well-educated, well-trained, bright, energetic, multilingual and entrepreneurial workforce who understand the nature of tourism and have a professional training. The quality of human resources in tourism will allow enterprises to gain a competitive edge and deliver added value with their service. Tourism is a high-touch, high-tech, high-involvement industry where it is the people who make the difference.

There is no doubt that companies in the tourism industry are under pressure. Changing markets, industry restructuring and more competitive domestic and international markets are placing great burdens on their expertise. The ability to succeed, and the future performance of tourism and related activities, will depend largely upon the skills, qualities and knowledge that managers will be able to bring to their business.

In the past tourism has been characterized by a lack of sophistication in human resource policies and practices, imposed by outmoded styles of man-management and approaches to operational circumstances. This leaves tourism vulnerable to ideas, takeovers and domination by management practices found in other economic sectors. Indeed, practices which are commonplace in other service industries – comprehensive induction, regular appraisal, effective employee communications – are underdeveloped in many tourism and leisure businesses. Educators and trainers have a role to play here in facilitating innovation and, in partnership with industry, working to overcome the specific problems of tourism.

A high-quality tourism workforce can be achieved only through high standards of tourism education and training. Tourism education and training involve the communication of knowledge, concepts and techniques which are specific to the field of tourism. Traditionally, the domain of tourism education has been the encouragement of analytical thinking and the understanding of conceptual issues in order to contribute to the professional and intellectual development of a person. Tourism training, on the other hand, is concerned with delivering practical knowledge, skills and techniques.

Tourism training has a long pedigree and emerged as the tourism industry grew in both size and complexity. Initially, training was linked to the operations of intermediaries, particularly in areas such as ticketing, or in the various craft operations for hospitality. In the developing world much of tourism training is still confined to these areas, but in the developed world it has expanded to embrace many functions as the industry becomes more professional and demands higher standards of its practitioners. Tourism education is a much more recent activity. Aside from a handful of institutions, most tourism education courses are a product of the 1980s and 1990s. Indeed, the infrastructure of tourism education around the world is still being put into place. This is because it is only in recent years that governments have recognized the value of tourism to their economies, and in particular have linked manpower planning and education/training for tourism with competitiveness and productivity.

The benefits of both education and training for tourism should be clear:

- For the industry as a whole it adds value, raises the quality of personnel and infuses a sense of professionalism and ownership.
- It also helps to define the industry and points up the underlying similarities of the many different sectors (transport, hospitality, attractions, etc.).
- Those working in the industry also understand the interrelationships of the sectors and begin to perceive business opportunities.
- Training, in particular, delivers skills and practical knowledge which boost the performance and productivity of personnel across the industry, and the linking of education and training with manpower planning allows a closer gearing of the needs of the sector with the output of tourism schools.
- Education and training help to retain staff, provide a career path for employees and, overall, achieve a better use of human resources in the tourism industry.

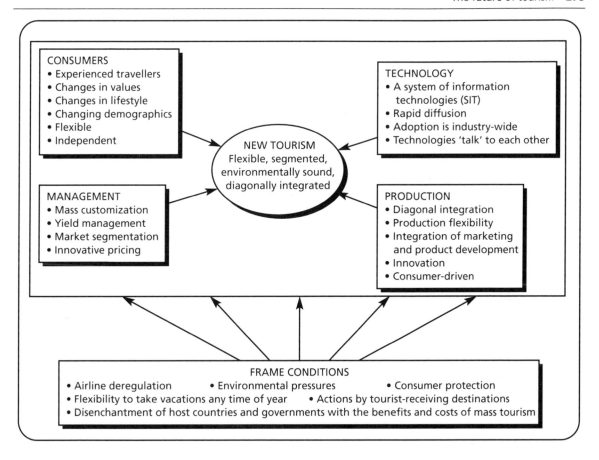

Source: Poon (1993).

Fig 24.2 Poon's new tourism

EMERGENT PATTERNS

Poon, a leading commentator on future trends in tourism, predicts the demise of the 'old' tourism and the emergence of a 'new' tourism (Figure 24.2). She sees the key trends leading to this new tourism as:

the diffusion of a system of new information technologies in the tourism industry; deregulation of the airline industry and financial services; the negative impact of mass tourism on host countries; the movement away from sun-lust to sun-plus tourism; environmental pressures; technology; competition; and changing consumer tastes . . . (Poon, 1989, p. 92)

In other words, the future of tourism will be one of flexible, segmented, customized and diagonally integrated tourism rather than the mass, rigid, standardized and packaged tourism of the 1970s.

Industry forecasts suggest that tourism will continue to grow to the year 2000 – on average at about 5 per cent annually, although slower than average rates of growth will be experienced in the first half of the 1990s and in the early years of the next century. Demand for domestic tourism will expand at a slower rate than international tourism, but even so, by the year 2000 around 650 million international arrivals will be experienced. Some countries will have reached ceilings of capacity and available leisure time which will constrain further growth, and on the supply side problems of terrorism and disease may also discourage tourism growth in some areas.

The distribution of tourism by the year 2000 will also differ in some respects from the position in the early 1990s. In particular, the countries of East Asia and Pacific (EAP) will become important both as generators of tourism and as major tourist destinations. In particular, the strong growth of the economies of Japan, Taiwan and Korea will allow these countries to become major generators of tourists not only within but also outside the region. By the year 2000 the EAP region will rival Europe and North America in its significance for tourism. In fact, the success of the EAP region will be at the expense of traditional regions such as Europe and the Americas.

SYNTHESIS

This chapter has attempted to draw together the many disparate trends which influence the future of tourism. It has also, in a sense, acted to draw together the threads of this book as a whole. The message is clear. Tourism will be an acceptable and successful industry in the future only if a well-trained and professional workforce is in place and able to implement the very best practices in managing tourism.

This book has brought together these practices and wrapped them around a state-of-the-art commentary on tourism, its principles and practice. Of course, any book written in the early 1990s will be tested in a number of ways because it faces the dynamic nature of the modern world. However, we have tried to provide general principles and practices rather than specifics which will date. We offer you the challenges of tourism management

and believe they will become clearer if you follow the frameworks and approaches that we have provided.

References and further reading

Archer, B.H., and Cooper, C. (forthcoming) 'The positive and negative impact of tourism', in Theobold, W. (ed.), *Critical Issues in Tourism*, Oxford: Butterworth-Heinemann.

Boniface, B., and Cooper, C. (1987) *The Geography of Travel and Tourism*, London: Heinemann.

Botterill, T.D. (1991) 'A new social movement: tourism concern – the first two years', *Leisure Studies*, vol. 10, no. 3, pp. 203–17.

Butler, R. (1990) 'Alternative tourism: pious hope or Trojan Horse?', *Journal of Travel Research*, Winter, pp. 40–5.

English Tourist Board (1991) *The Green Light: a Guide to Sustainable Tourism*, London: ETB.

Leiper, N. (1990) *Tourism Systems*, Massey University Department of Management Systems Occasional Paper 2, Auckland, New Zealand: Massey University.

McIntosh, R.W., and Goeldner, C.R. (1990) *Tourism: Principles, Practices, Philosophies*, New York: Wiley.

Medlik, S. (ed.) (1991) *Managing Tourism*, Oxford: Heinemann.

Poon, A. (1989) 'Competitive strategies for a new tourism', in Cooper, C. (ed.) *Progress in Tourism, Recreation and Hospitality Management*, Vol. 1, London: Belhaven.

Poon, A. (1993) *Tourism, Technology and Competitive Strategies*, Wallingford, Oxon, UK: Commonwealth Agricultural Bureau International.

Ritchie, J.R.B. (1992a) 'New horizons, new realities: perspectives of the tourism educator', in Ritchie, J.R.B., and Hawkins, D. (eds), *World Travel and Tourism Review*, Oxford: Commonwealth Agricultural Bureau.

Ritchie, J.R.B. (1992b) *New Realities, New Horizons*, New York: American Express.

Smith, V.L., and Eadington, W.R. (eds) (1992) *Tourism Alternatives*, Philadelphia, Pa.: University of Pennsylvania Press.

Wheeller, B. (1991a) 'Tourism's troubled times', *Tourism Management*, vol. 12, no. 2, pp. 91–6.

Wheeller, B. (1991b), 'Is progressive tourism appropriate?', *Tourism Management*, vol. 13, no. 1, pp. 104–5.

Witt, S., and Moutinho, L. (1989) *Tourism Marketing and Management Handbook*, Hemel Hempstead: Prentice Hall.

Wood, K., and House, S.L. (1991) *The Good Tourist*, London: Mandarin.

World Commission on Environment and Development (1987) *Our Common Future*, New York: Oxford University Press.

World Tourism Organization (1992) *Tourism Trends to the Year 2000 and Beyond*, Madrid: WTO.

COMPENDIUM OF TOURISM TEXTS AND JOURNALS

General texts

Ashworth, G. *Recreation and Tourism*, Bell and Hyman, London, 1984

Burkart, A.J., and Medlik, S. *Tourism, Past, Present and Future*, Heinemann, London, 1981

Chubb, M., and Chubb, H.R. *One Third of Our Time*, Wiley, New York, 1981

Foster, D. *Travel and Tourism Management*, Macmillan, London, 1985

Gee, C.Y., Choy, D.J.L., and Makens, J.C. *The Travel Industry*, AVI, Westport, 1984

Hodgson, A. (ed.) *The Travel and Tourism Industry*, Pergamon, Oxford, 1987

Holloway, J.C. *The Business of Tourism*, Pitman Publishing, London, 1989

Hurdman, L.E. *Tourism: A Shrinking World*, Wiley, New York, 1980

Lundberg, D.E. *The Tourist Business*, Van Nostrand Reinhold, New York, 1975

McIntosh, R.W., and Goeldner, C.R. *Tourism: Principles, Practices and Philosophies*, Wiley, New York, 1990

Medlik, S. (ed.) *Managing Tourism*, Butterworth Heinemann, Oxford, 1991

Mercer, D. *In Pursuit of Leisure*, Sorret, Melbourne, 1980

Mill, R.C. *Tourism. The International Business*, Prentice Hall, New Jersey, 1990

Mill, R.C., and Morrison, A. *The Tourism System*, Prentice Hall, New Jersey, 1985

Pigram, J. *Outdoor Recreation and Resource Management*, Croom Helm, London, 1993

Ryan, C. *Recreational Tourism*, Routledge, London, 1991

Wahab, S. *Tourism Management*, Tourism International Press, London, 1975

Witt, S., Brooke, M.Z., and Buckley, P. *The Management of International Tourism*, Unwin Hyman, London, 1991

Subject-based approaches

Boniface, B., and Cooper, C. *The Geography of Travel and Tourism*, Heinemann, London, 1987

Bull, A. *The Economics of Travel and Tourism*, Pitman Publishing, London, 1991

Burton, R. *Travel Geography*, Pitman Publishing, London, 1991

Edington, J.M., and Edington, M.A. *Ecology, Recreation and Tourism*, Cambridge University Press, Cambridge, 1986

Lavery, P. (ed.) *Recreational Geography*, David and Charles, Newton Abbot, 1971

Pearce, D. *Tourism Today*, Longman, Harlow, 1987

Pearce, P.L. *The Social Psychology of Tourist Behaviour*, Pergamon, Oxford, 1982

Smith, S.L.J. *Recreation Geography*, Longman, Harlow, 1983

Smith, S.L.J. *Tourism Analysis*, Longman, Harlow, 1989

Smith, V.L. (ed.) *Hosts and Guests: The Anthropology of Tourism*, Blackwell, Oxford, 1978

Urry, J. *The Tourist Gaze*, Sage, London, 1990

Tourism themes

Ashworth, G.J., and Goodall, B.C. (eds) *Marketing Tourism Places*, Routledge, London, 1990

Ashworth, G.J., and Goodall, B.C. (eds) *Marketing in the Tourism Industry*, Routledge, London, 1990

Ashworth, G.J., and Turbridge, J.E. *The Tourist-Historic City*, Belhaven, London, 1990

Butler, R.W., and Pearce, D.G. *Tourism Research*, Routledge, London 1993

Buttle, F. *Hotel and Food Service Marketing*, Holt, London, 1986

Inskeep, E. *Tourism Planning*, Van Nostrand Reinhold, New York, 1991

Lea, J. *Tourism and Development in the Third World*, Routledge, London, 1988

Lockwood, A.L., and Jones P. *Management of Hotel Operations*, Cassell, London, 1989

De Kadt, E. (ed.) *Tourism – Passport to Development?* Oxford University Press, Oxford 1979

Edgell, D.L. *International Tourism Policy*, Van Nostrand Reinhold, New York, 1990

Jefferson, A., and Lickorish, L. *Marketing Tourism*, Longman, Harlow, 1988

Johnson, P., and Thomas, B. (eds) *Choice and Demand in Tourism*, Mansell, London, 1992

Johnson, P., and Thomas, B. (eds) *Perspectives on Tourism Policy*, Mansell, London, 1992

Heath, E., and Wall, G. *Marketing Tourism Destinations*, Wiley, New York, 1992

Holloway, J.C., and Plant, R.V. *Marketing for Tourism*, Pitman, London, 1988

Jones, P., and Pizam, A. *The International Hospitality Industry: Organizational and Operational Issues*, Pitman Publishing, London, 1993

Krippendorf, J. *The Holiday Makers*, Heinemann, London, 1987

Mathieson, A., and Wall, G. *Tourism: Economic, Physical and Social Impacts*, Longman, Harlow, 1982

Middleton, V.T.C. *Marketing in Travel and Tourism*, Heinemann, Oxford, 1988

Morrison, A.M. *Hospitality and Travel Marketing*, Delmar, New York, 1989

Murphy, P.E. *Tourism. A Community Approach*, Methuen, London, 1985

Patmore, J.A. *Land and Leisure*, Penguin, Harmondsworth, 1972

Patmore, J.A. *Recreation and Resources*, Blackwell, Oxford, 1983

Pearce, D. *Tourist Development*, Longman, Harlow, 1989

Pearce, D. *Tourism Organisations*, Longman, Harlow, 1992

Ritchie, J.R.B., and Goeldner, C.R. *Travel, Tourism and Hospitality Research*, Wiley, New York, 1987

Smith, V.L., and Eadington, W.R. *Tourism Alternatives*, University of Pennsylvania Press, Philadelphia, 1992

Teare, R., and Boer, A. *Strategic Hospitality Management*, Cassell, London, 1991

Teare, R., and Olsen, M. *International Hospitality Management*, Pitman Publishing, London, 1992

Turner, L., and Ash, J. *The Golden Hordes. International Tourism and the Pleasure Periphery*, Constable, London, 1975

Wahab, S., Crampon, L.J., and Rothfield, L.M. *Tourism Marketing*, Tourism International Press, London, 1976

Witt, S., and Witt, C., *Modelling and Forecasting Demand in Tourism*, Academic Press, London, 1991

Regional tourism approaches

Hall, D. (ed) *Tourism and Economic Development in Eastern Europe and the Soviet Union*, Belhaven, London, 1991

Harrison, D. (ed) *Tourism and the Less Developed Countries*, Belhaven, London, 1992

Williams, A.M., and Shaw, G. (eds) *Tourism and Economic Development*, Belhaven, London, 1988

Yearbooks and encyclopaedias

Cooper, C.P. (ed) *Progress in Tourism, Recreation and Hospitality Management*, Belhaven, London (annual)

Ritchie, J.R.B., and Hawkins, D. (eds) *World Travel and Tourism Review*, CAB, Oxford (annual)

Witt, S., and Moutinho, L., (eds) *Tourism Marketing and Management Handbook*, Prentice Hall, Hemel Hempstead, 1989

Statistical sources

Organization for Economic Co-operation and Development, *Tourism Policy and International Tourism in OECD Member Countries*, OECD, Paris (annual)

World Tourism Organization, *Compendium of Tourist Statistics*, WTO, Madrid (annual)

Abstracts

Articles in Hospitality and Tourism (monthly), Universities of Surrey; Oxford Brookes; and Bournemouth

Leisure Recreation and Tourism Abstracts (quarterly), CAB, Oxford

Journals

Annals of Tourism Research
Cornell Hotel and Restaurant Administration Quarterly
Hospitality Research Journal
International Journal of Contemporary Hospitality Management
International Journal of Hospitality Management
International Tourism Reports
Journal of Leisure Research
Journal of Tourism Studies
Journal of Travel and Tourism Marketing
Journal of Travel Research
Leisure Studies
Tourism Management
Tourism Recreation Research
Tourist Review
Travel and Tourism Analyst

INDEX